KB264172

TEPS 달인이 되는 법 Final 독해

저자 | 황혜선
초판 1쇄 발행 | 2008년 3월 19일
초판 6쇄 발행 | 2010년 1월 10일

발행인 | 박효상
편집책임 | 김상호
편집 | 조승주
영업책임 | 이종선
영업 | 이태호
출판등록 | 제 10-1835호
발행처 | 사람in
주소 | 121-839 서울시 마포구 서교동 378-16 4F
전화 | 02) 338-3555(代)
팩스 | 02) 338-3545
e-mail | esaramin@nate.com
Homepage | www.saramin.com

만든 사람들
표지 디자인 | 장선숙
내지 디자인 | 한현식
Native Consultant | Vince Cheng, Tracy Hong

● 책값은 표지 뒷면에 있습니다.
● 파본은 바꾸어 드립니다.

ⓒ황혜선 2008

ISBN 978-89-6049-073-4 13740
ISBN 978-89-6049-041-3 (세트)

teps 달인이 되는 법 final 독해

황 혜 선

사람 in
saramin.com

머리말

〈TEPS 달인이 되는 법 - 기본종합〉 교재를 냈을 때가 엊그제 같은데 벌써 해가 바뀌고 〈TEPS 달인이 되는 법 - Final〉의 출간을 앞두고 있습니다.
제게 있어 2007년은 커피를 여물 삼아 소처럼 열심히 일만 했던 한 해였고, 그 결실로 2008년을 열며 새로운 교재를 출간하게 되어 너무나 뿌듯합니다.
TEPS를 공부하시는 분들이 이 교재를 통해 TEPS라는 괴팍한 시험을 이겨내고, 궁극적인 목표에 한 걸음 더 가까이 다가서게 되시길 진심으로 바랍니다.

중고등학교 시절 불만 많은 학생이었던 저는, 과학과 가사가 너무나도 싫었고 왜 이렇게 싫은 과목도 공부를 하고 시험을 봐야 하는지 늘 고뇌했습니다. 다행히 가장 좋아하고 가장 잘하는 영어를 가르치는 일을 직업으로 갖게 되어 지금은 집필의 고통이 아무리 저를 짓눌러도 행복한 비명을 지르고 있지만요.
중고등학교 때 그렇게도 싫어했던 과목이 과학과 가사였던 것처럼 여러분에게는 그것이 영어일수도 있다는 생각을 합니다. 저의 사명은 그토록 싫고 어려운 영어를 조금이라도 쉽고 효율적으로 공부하시도록, 그래서 빨리 TEPS 시험이라는 과정을 힘을 덜 들이고 지나가도록 여러분을 돕는 것이라는 생각을 하며 이 교재를 집필했습니다.

〈TEPS 달인이 되는 법 - 기본종합〉이 수학의 정석과 같이, TEPS를 공부하는 분들이라면 누구나 보아야 할 지침서의 역할을 하는 교재라면, 〈TEPS 달인이 되는 법 - Final〉은 기본기가 다져진 상태에서 점수 향상을 바라는 분들을 위한 교재입니다.
설명을 들으면 다 알 것 같은데 시험 점수는 제자리걸음인 분들이나 고득점을 위해 실전 난이도의 문제를 많이 풀어보고 싶으신 분들은 〈TEPS 달인이 되는 법 - Final〉을 통해 원하는 점수에 도달할 수 있으실 거라고 확신합니다.

마지막으로 항상 걱정해주시는 부모님, 하나뿐인 언니, 많은 도움을 준 친구 지윤이, 집필 중에 잠수를 타곤 해도 이해해준 친구들과 윤석환 선생님, 전병기 팀장님께 감사드립니다.

황혜선

Contents

독해 Reading Comprehension

1st Week

2nd Week

3rd Week

4th Week

청해 Listening Comprehension

1st Week

2nd Week

3rd Week

4th Week

Contents

문법 Grammer

1st Week

2nd Week

3rd Week

4th Week

어휘 Vocabulary

1st Week

Day 1	중요 어휘 1
Day 2	중요 어휘 2
Day 3	혼동 어휘 1
Day 4	혼동 어휘 2
Day 5	혼동 어휘 3

2nd Week

Day 6	중요 어휘 3
Day 7	중요 어휘 4
Day 8	동사구 1
Day 9	동사구 2
Day 10	Idiom 1

3rd Week

Day 11	Idiom 2
Day 12	중요 어휘 5
Day 13	중요 어휘 6
Day 14	다의어 1
Day 15	다의어 2

4th Week

Day 16	중요 어휘 7
Day 17	중요 어휘 8
Day 18	Collocation 1
Day 19	Collocation 2
Day 20	Collocation 3

이 책의 특징

이 책은 TEPS 독해의 완벽한 마무리를 위한 최종 실전서이다. 어휘 출제 유형을 20개로 정리해서 출제 포인트를 확인할 수 있으며, 실전에 가장 가까운 기출 문제와 예상 문제로 충분한 연습을 하고 1회분 모의고사로 최종 점검을 할 수 있도록 구성했다.

1. 20일로 TEPS를 마무리할 수 있다

20개의 유형정리로 TEPS 독해를 유형별로 완벽하게 정리했다. 실전 시험을 앞두고 모든 파트를 매일 골고루 풀어 봄으로써 실전에 대한 감을 키우도록 한다. 마지막에 실전 모의고사 1회분을 풀어봄으로써 실전을 단기간에 대비한다. 이론적 기반은 있으나 TEPS 유형에 아직 익숙하지 않아, 실전에서 실력 발휘를 제대로 못하는 학습자는 독해 유형을 빠르게 파악할 수 있고 문제를 풀면서 충분하게 유형 연습을 할 수 있다.

2. 실전에 가장 가까운 문제를 풀 수 있다

최근 3년간의 기출 문제를 완벽하게 분석해서 각 파트별 비율에 맞게 문제를 구성했다. 독해의 5회분 200문제는 TEPS 고득점을 위해 엄선된 문제이다. 학습자는 기출 변형 Catch Up, 예상 문제 Build Up, 1회분 모의고사 Final Check 문제를 풀면서 정기 시험과 유사한 문제 유형을 익힐 수 있다.

3. 전문 TEPS 강사의 노하우를 배울 수 있다

매월 TEPS 정기 시험을 보는 전문 강사가 TEPS의 특징과 TEPS에서 요구하는 공부 방식을 담았다. 학습자는 TEPS의 특징과 TEPS에서 요구하는 공부 방식을 배울 수 있다.

4. 독해 Handy Book을 통해 TEPS 실전 독해를 정리할 수 있다

정확한 구문 분석을 위해 본문의 Final Check에서 중요 지문을 뽑았다. Handy Book을 통해서 정답이 왜 정답이 되는지 오답은 왜 오답이 되는지를 파악한다면 실전에서 정답률을 높일 수 있다.

이 책의 구성 및 활용

TEPS 독해를 20일에 끝낼 수 있게 다음 구성에 따라 학습한다.

1. 핵심 정리 20

시험에 자주 출제되는 TEPS 독해를 유형별로 정리했다. 20개의 독해 정리를 Catch Up과 Build Up 문제를 통해 확인한다면 시험 전에 TEPS 중요 독해를 빠르게 정리할 수 있을 것이다.

2. 기출로 감을 익히는 Catch Up

기출 변형 문제로 실제 시험 문제와 가장 가까운 지문들을 다뤄볼 수 있다. TEPS 독해 영역을 각 파트별로 정리하여 실전감각을 익히도록 하였다.

3. 예상 문제로 실전 감각을 익히는 Build Up

TEPS 독해 영역 3개 파트의 다양한 문제를 다뤘다. 실전에 대비할 수 있는 연습이 충분히 되도록 하였다.

4. 최종 실전 점검 Final Check

독해 1회분 모의고사를 실었다. 난이도는 정기시험과 동일하다. 실전 난이도와 유형의 문제를 통하여 실전에 대비할 수 있고, 자기 실력을 정확히 파악할 수 있다.

5. 한 눈에 보는 정답 및 해설

본문의 내용과 함께 지문과 해석, 해설을 〈정답 및 해설〉에 모두 실어 문제 풀이와 보충 학습을 〈정답 및 해설〉 한 권만으로도 가능하게 했다.

TEPS 독해 유형 및 형식

TEPS의 구성

TEPS는 청해, 문법, 어휘, 독해 4개 영역에 걸쳐 총 200문항으로 구성되어 있으며 시험 시간은 140분이다. 만점은 문항 반응 이론(IRT)에 따라 채점하기 때문에 전부 맞아도 990점이고 모두 틀려도 10점은 나온다.

영역	PART별 내용	문항 수	시간/배점
청 취 Listening Comprehension	Part Ⅰ : 문장 하나를 듣고 이어질 대화 고르기	15	55분/396점
	Part Ⅱ : 3 문장의 대화를 듣고 이어질 대화 고르기	15	
	Part Ⅲ : 6-8 문장의 대화를 듣고 이어질 대화 고르기	15	
	Part Ⅳ : 단문의 내용을 듣고 질문에 해당하는 답 고르기	15	
문 법 Grammar	Part Ⅰ : 대화문의 빈칸에 적절한 표현 고르기	20	25분/99점
	Part Ⅱ : 문장의 빈칸에 적절한 표현 고르기	20	
	Part Ⅲ : 대화에서 어법상 틀리거나 어색한 부분 고르기	5	
	Part Ⅳ : 대화에서 어법상 틀리거나 어색한 부분 고르기	5	
어 휘 Vocabulary	Part Ⅰ : 대화문의 빈칸에 적절한 단어 고르기	25	15분/99점
	Part Ⅱ : 단문의 빈칸에 적절한 단어 고르기	25	
독 해 Reading Comprehension	Part Ⅰ : 지문을 읽고 질문의 빈칸에 들어갈 내용 고르기	16	45분/396점
	Part Ⅱ : 지문을 읽고 질문에 가장 적절한 내용 고르기	21	
	Part Ⅲ : 지문을 읽고 문맥상 어색한 내용 고르기	3	
총계	13개 PARTS	200	140분/990점

독해(Reading Comprehension) 50문항

교양 있는 수준의 글(신문, 잡지, 대학 교양과목 개론 등)과 실용적인 글(서신, 광고, 홍보, 지시문, 설명문, 도표, 양식 등)을 이해하는 데 요구되는 총체적인 독해력을 측정하기 위해서 실용문 및 비전문적 학술문과 같은 독해 지문의 소재를 균형 있게 다루었다.

<table><tr><td>**PART 1**</td><td>16문항</td></tr></table>

Read the passage. Then choose the option that completes the passage.

In late eighteenth and early nineteenth centuries so many people were attracted by the simplicity of banking and high profits that many mushroom banks sprang up and bankruptcies were frequent. Every bankruptcy meant not only the failure of the banker but brought __________ to the depositors and borrowers. Commercial life became very unstable so that the government in1844 passed the Bank Charter Act to regularize banking.

(a) prosperity
(b) hardship
(c) peace
(d) opportunity

Part 1은 빈칸 넣기 유형이다. 한 단락의 글을 주고 그 안에 빈칸을 넣어 알맞은 표현을 고르는 16문항으로 이루어져 있다. 글 전체의 흐름을 파악하여 문맥상 빈칸에 들어갈 내용을 찾는 문제이다.

<table><tr><td>**PART 2**</td><td>21문항</td></tr></table>

Read the option that correctly answers the question.

With the popularization of the concept of calorie counting, physical features-such as shape and body weight-were considered things under conscious control. The idea of controlling weight through the restriction of calories implied that being overweight resulted solely from lack of control. In other words, to be fat constituted a failure of personal morality.

Q. What is the main idea of this passage?

(a) Physical features have a lot to do with the mind.
(b) Dieting is as simple as reducing calories.
(c) People do not have to reduce their body weight.
(d) Appetite control is an issue of personal morality.

Part 2는 글의 내용 이해를 측정하는 문제로 21문항으로 구성되어 있다. 주제나 대의 혹은 전반적 논조 파악, 세부내용 파악, 논리적 추론 등이 있다.

Identfy the sentence that least fits the context of the passage.

There will be a reception this coming Saturday to greet the new vice Principal Ms. Lara Rumsfeld. (a) West Bloomfield High School has no custodian. (b) She was vice Principal at Andover for 3 years before this. (c) She was Depuly Principal for 2 years and Associate Principal for one year. (d) When Ms. Rumsfeld came to West Bloomfield High, she was very nervous but extremely excited to be here.

Part 3는 한 문단의 글에서 내용의 흐름상 어색한 곳을 고르는 문제로 3문항으로 이루어져 있다. 전체 흐름을 파악하여 흐름상 필요 없는 내용을 고르는 문제이다. 이런 유형의 문제는 응집력 있는 영작문 실력을 간접적으로 측정할 수도 있다.

TEPS, TOEIC, TOEFL 점수 비교

TEPS	TOEIC	TOEFL(CBT)	TOEFL(iBT)
951 ~	980 ~	287 ~	117 ~
901 ~ 950	950 ~ 975	273 ~ 287	111 ~ 117
851 ~ 900	910 ~ 945	253 ~ 273	101 ~ 111
801 ~ 850	875 ~ 905	247 ~ 253	98 ~ 101
751 ~ 800	835 ~ 870	237 ~ 247	92 ~ 98
701 ~ 750	790 ~ 830	223 ~ 237	84 ~ 92
651 ~ 700	750 ~ 785	213 ~ 223	79 ~ 84
601 ~ 650	705 ~ 745	204 ~ 213	76 ~ 79
551 ~ 600	650 ~ 700	193 ~ 207	69 ~ 76
501 ~ 550	600 ~ 645	177 ~ 193	62 ~ 69
451 ~ 500	545 ~ 595	167 ~ 177	58 ~ 62
400 ~ 450	490 ~ 540	163 ~ 167	57 ~ 58

※CBT와 iBT 점수 비교는 ETS 발표를 참고했습니다.

READING
COMPREHENSION
Week 1

Day 1　▶▶ 비전문적 학술문

유형정리 – 〈TEPS RC 지문 흐름 파악〉 비전문적 학술문의 특징

Catch Up – Part 1 빈칸 채우기

Day 2　▶▶ 비평문

유형정리 – 〈TEPS RC 지문 흐름 파악〉 비평문

Catch Up – Part 1 빈칸 채우기

Day 3　▶▶ 설명문

유형정리 – 〈TEPS RC 지문 흐름 파악〉 설명문

Catch Up – Part 2 주제 찾기

Day 4　▶▶ 편지글

유형정리 – 〈TEPS RC 지문 흐름 파악〉 편지글

Catch Up – Part 2 세부사항 확인

Day 5　▶▶ 광고/공지

유형정리 – 〈TEPS RC 지문 흐름 파악〉 광고/공지

Catch Up – Part 3

Day 1

비전문적 학술문

TEPS 독해 영역에서 다수를 차지하는 지문이 비전문적 학술문이다.

실용문에 편지글, 광고글 등이 포함된다면, 비전문적 학술문에는 신문이나 뉴스, 저널 등의 유형이 포함된다고 생각하면 된다. 비전문적 학술문은 사회, 문화, 경제, 과학, 의학 등 여러 분야에 걸쳐 유명한 사건이나 인물에 대한 정보를 다루거나, 요즘 이슈가 되고 있는 사안이나 새로운 발견 등을 다루는 글이다. 따라서 비교적 가볍지 않은 주제를 다루지만, '비전문적' 학술문이므로 사전 지식이 없이도 문제를 풀 수 있도록 출제된다. 즉, 수험자들은 친숙하지 않은 주제의 지문을 대하게 되어도 지문의 내용만 충실히 파악하면 문제를 맞출 수 있으므로 당황하지 말고 거부감 없이 지문을 읽고 정답을 고르면 된다.

Example

The National Sleep Foundation says sleeping habits are a key factor in weight loss. People who get a recommended 7-9 hours of sleep daily weigh less on average than those who do not. The majority of obese people falls into the category of sleep deprived. It is estimated that only 25% of Americans currently get enough sleep, causing the majority to suffer at least some endocrine system problems leading to fluctuations in insulin production. This causes a breakdown of the body's ability to metabolize sugar and can lead to diabetes. Sleep apnea is another condition caused largely by obesity, and although most sufferers show lighter symptoms such as interrupted breathing patterns, it can be fatal.

Q. What can be inferred from the passage?

(a) Getting enough sleep daily is the key to becoming obese.
(b) Diabetes is caused directly by sleep deprivation.
(c) A link between obesity and sleeping habits is unproven.
(d) Getting 7-9 hours of sleep each day can control weight.

위의 지문은 수면과 체중의 상관관계를 다루고 있는 과학–의학의 범주에 포함되는 지문이다. 글의 논지는 충분한 수면을 취하지 못하면 비만과 비만에 관련된 다른 질병에 취약할 수 있다는 것이다. 첫 문장에서 이 글의 주제를 파악할 수 있으며, 하이라이트된 두 번째 문장은 정답을 고르는 직접적인 단서가 된다.

위의 지문과 같이 차분히 읽으면 상식적인 선에서 이해할 수 있는 정도의 수준으로 출제되므로 사전지식이 없는 분야의 지문이 출제되어도 당황하지 말자.

해설: 231p

Catch Up

Part I Read the passage and choose the option that best fits the blank.

1. A study conducted between lonely and non-lonely people indicated perceived observational differences between these different types of people. Lonely people were viewed to possess undesirable traits _____________________ than these that are non-lonely. They appeared to be less adjusted, less successful, less sociable, more passive, less sincere and weaker than non-lonely people. Hence, not only can loneliness lead to consequences that are detrimental to one's emotional, physical and spiritual well being, but it also affects the social perception of those that are lonely.

   (a) such as heightened self esteem and confidence
   (b) that are common to the only child with single parent
   (c) such as low psychological attributes and interpersonal attractions
   (d) which develop psychological problems to the extent that needs medical treatment

2. The ISO 9000 Series documents are focused on continual improvement towards customer satisfaction through the use of an effective and efficient business management system – a group of interrelated processes and activities that together serve to meet defined goals and objectives. The challenge facing most companies just starting this journey is to understand that the term "quality" is nebulous, defined only by the customer. The ultimate intent of the ISO 9000 Series Standards and Guidelines is to _____________________________.

   (a) assist customers in serving their company
   (b) group interrelated processes and activities together
   (c) challenge competing companies
   (d) assist companies in serving their customers

# Answers 

TEPS 독해 영역에 출제되었던 실전 문제를 자세한 설명과 함께 완전히 이해하도록 하자.

1

A study conducted between lonely and non-lonely people indicated perceived observational differences between these two types of people. Lonely people were viewed to possess undesirable traits ________________________ than those that are non-lonely. They appeared to be less adjusted, less successful, less sociable, more passive, less sincere and weaker than non-lonely people. Hence, not only can loneliness lead to consequences that are detrimental to one's emotional, physical and spiritual well being, but it also affects the social perception of those that are lonely.

(a) such as heightened self esteem and confidence
(b) that are common to the only child with single parent
(c) such as low psychological attributes and interpersonal attractions
(d) which develop psychological problems to the extent that needs medical treatment

해석 외로운 사람과 외롭지 않은 사람 사이에서 행해진 연구는 이 다른 유형의 사람들 사이에서 인식된 관찰상의 다른 점들을 제시했다. 외로운 사람은 외롭지 않은 사람보다 낮은 정신적 특성들과 대인관계에서의 낮은 매력 등 바람직하지 않은 특징들을 가진 것으로 보였다. 그들은 외롭지 않은 사람보다 적응을 잘 못하고, 덜 성공적이고, 덜 사회적이고, 더 많이 수동적이며, 덜 성실하고 심약함을 나타낸다. 그러므로 외로움은 한 사람의 감정적, 육체적 영혼적 행복에 불리한 결과를 가져올 뿐만 아니라, 외로운 사람들에 대한 사회적 인식에도 영향을 준다.

해설 빈칸 앞의 undesirable traits에서 첫 번째 단서를, 뒷문장에서 두 번째 단서를 찾아 쉽게 정답 "(c) 낮은 정신적 특성과 대인관계에서의 낮은 매력과 같은"을 찾을 수 있다.

오답 분석 (a) 높아진 자존심과 자신감과 같은 – 빈칸에 들어갈 말과 반대의 내용이다.
(b) 형제가 없이 편부모 하에 있는 아이들에게 흔한 – 이 지문의 소재에서 벗어났다.
(d) 의학적 치료가 필요한 심리학적 문제들을 발전시키는 – 의학적 치료에 대한 내용은 이 지문에서 언급되지 않았으므로 너무 나아간 추론으로 볼 수 있다.

어휘 **attribute** 특질, 특성, 속성
undesirable 탐탁지 않은, 바람직하지 못한
sincere 성실한, 참된, 진실의
detrimental 해로운, 불리한
perception 지각, 견해

The ISO 9000 Series documents are focused on continual improvement towards customer satisfaction through the use of an effective and efficient business management system – a group of interrelated processes and activities that together serve to meet defined goals and objectives. The challenge facing most companies just starting this journey is to understand that the term "quality" is nebulous, defined only by the customer. The ultimate intent of the ISO 9000 Series Standards and Guidelines is to _______________________________.

(a) assist customers in serving their company
(b) group interrelated processes and activities together
(c) challenge competing companies
(d) assist companies in serving their customers

해석 ISO 9000 시리즈 문서들은 효과적이고 효율적인 관리 시스템의 사용을 통한 고객 만족의 계속적인 향상에 중점을 두고 있습니다. 이것은 모두 정해진 목표와 목적을 충족시키는 역할을 하기 위해 서로 밀접한 관계가 있는 과정들과 활동들입니다. 이제 막 이러한 일들을 시작하는 대부분의 회사들이 직면하고 있는 도전 요소는 '품질'이라는 용어가 애매모호하며 고객들에 의해서만 정의된다는 것을 이해하는 것입니다. 'ISO 9000 시리즈의 표준과 지침서'의 궁극적 목적은 회사들이 고객들에게 서비스하는 것에 있어 도움을 주려는 것입니다.

해설 '품질'이라는 애매한 용어 때문에 어려움을 겪을 수 있으므로 ISO 9000 시리즈의 관리 시스템에서 표준과 지침서를 내놓았다는 내용이므로 정답이 (d)가 된다.

오답 분석
(a) 고객들이 자신의 회사에서 일하는 것을 도우려는 것 – 빈칸 앞 문장에서 볼 수 있듯이 'ISO 9000 시리즈의 표준과 지침서'는 회사들이 겪는 어려움을 해소하기 위한 것이다.
(b) 상호 관련된 과정과 활동을 함께 묶으려는 것 – 과정과 활동을 하나로 묶는다는 내용은 언급되지 않았다.
(c) 경쟁 회사들에게 어려움을 주기 위한 것 – 다른 회사들과의 경쟁에 도움을 주기 위한 것이 아니라 고객 서비스와 품질에 대한 어려움에 도움을 주기 위한 것이다.

어휘 nebulous 애매한, 흐린
satisfaction 만족, 만족감
interrelated 서로 관계가 있는

Answers:

1. (c) 2. (d)

▶▶ Part I Read the passage and choose the option that best fits the blank.

1. An overlooked yet essential aspect of human life is the intrinsic desire to create works of art. Arguably, a basic understanding and appreciation for art can help develop one's character and broaden the intellect. Many artists suggest that they engage in creating art not only to satisfy their creative dive but also as a means to learn about themselves. Thus, not only do these individuals create marvelous artwork for others to enjoy and marvel at, but they also ___________________________.

   (a) gain material wealth and a comfortable senior life free from any financial worry
   (b) develop an aesthetic sense to make them more mature
   (c) make many friends across borders through works of art
   (d) experience the euphoria of getting in touch with their inner selves

2. Economies of scale occur when long term ___________________________ through specialization. Specialized inputs occurring during an increase in the scale of production of a company may allow it to utilize specialized labor and machines resulting in greater efficiency. This is because workers would be better qualified for a specific job; for example someone who only makes French fries, would not waste extra time training for tasks exterior to his specialization, such as tossing salads. Plant items, such as single-use deep fryers, would also enjoy a slower rate of depreciation because they would not be overused or used for a secondary purpose.

   (a) average costs are increasing as output is falling
   (b) average business costs fall whilst output increases
   (c) costs remain static contrary to market fluctuations
   (d) conditions and outlooks for the market sector deteriorate

3. The use of some words in the English language is highly regrettable, but a dictionary still has a duty to report and describe their existence. If we were to pretend that offensive words didn't exist, and then didn't include them, we'd be charged with dishonesty. Even if we did ignore such words they wouldn't stop being used and, in fact, may be used more without a proper conveyance of their exact meaning. People need accurate information about words in day to day use, including offensive words, and that is what we strive to provide.

Q. What is the main idea of the passage?

(a) Offensive words are a part and parcel of the English language.
(b) Offensive words have no place in the English language.
(c) English books are meant to include offensive words.
(d) If we don't use offensive words, they will eventually disappear from English.

4. It is wrong to assume that all university students are capable of self-directed learning. Self directed learning is a lifelong endeavor because it requires not only high levels of thinking, but also motivation and persistence. But those who can identify their own strengths and weaknesses are able to make decisions about how to develop their skills through a devised program. In other words, people like this can select and carry out their own learning goals, objectives and methods, while also assessing their own progress to ensure that these goals are met.

Q. What can be inferred about self-directed learning?

(a) Its practice leads student to success in university.
(b) Its success depends on one's level of self discipline.
(c) It is mainly accomplished by those who seek higher level education.
(d) It should be pursued upon assessing one's own life goals.

▶▶ **Part III** Identify the sentence that least fits the context of the passage.

5. With the onset of Modernism, people began to look at the world with a different view. (a) They wished to reject tradition and convention by stressing freedom of expression, experimentation, and radicalism. (b) Along with culture and politics, art was greatly affected by modernism. (c) However, radical designers are often viewed with the negative stereotype that they were actually more interested in commerciality than art itself. (d) Radical artists sought to support modernism by applying new materials and technologies to their artwork.

정답: 200p

READING
COMPREHENSION
Week 1

Day 1	 ▶▶ 비전문적 학술문
	유형정리 – 〈TEPS RC 지문 흐름 파악〉 비전문적 학술문의 특징
	Catch Up – Part 1 빈칸 채우기

Day 2	▶▶ 비평문
	유형정리 – 〈TEPS RC 지문 흐름 파악〉 비평문
	Catch Up – Part 1 빈칸 채우기

Day 3	▶▶ 설명문
	유형정리 – 〈TEPS RC 지문 흐름 파악〉 설명문
	Catch Up – Part 2 주제 찾기

Day 4	▶▶ 편지글
	유형정리 – 〈TEPS RC 지문 흐름 파악〉 편지글
	Catch Up – Part 2 세부사항 확인

Day 5	▶▶ 광고/공지
	유형정리 – 〈TEPS RC 지문 흐름 파악〉 광고/공지
	Catch Up – Part 3

Day 2

비평문

TEPS 독해 지문의 비전문적 학술문에서 자주 출제되는 것이 바로 비평문이다. 예술작품이나 영화, 소설 등 대중예술, 유명한 인물에 대한 비평문이 주로 출제되는데, 우리가 알 수 있는 Rodin(로댕), Van Gogh(반 고흐), Leonardo Da Vinci(레오나르도 다 빈치) 등의 미술가나 Che Guevara(체 게바라), Rosa Parks(로 자 파크스), Martin Luther King Jr.(마틴 루터 킹 주니어) 등 근현대사에서 중요한 인물들, 또는 Marx(마르 크스)나 Freud(프로이드) 등의 사상가들이 최근 2년간 출제되었던 인물들이다. 이들은 다시 소재로 다루 어질 가능성이 많은 인물들이므로 각각 어떤 업적이 있는지를 간략하게라도 알아두면 지문을 파악하는 데 도움이 될 것이다.

비평문은 어떤 인물이나 작품 등에 대해 긍정적이거나 부정적인 시각을 가지고 논하거나, 두 가지 관점 모 두를 다루기도 한다. 따라서 화자의 논지가 어떤 쪽인지를 파악하는 것이 중요하며, 어떤 점을 긍정적이거 나 부정적으로 보고 있는지를 파악하는 것 또한 중요하다.

Example

Lara Croft: Tomb Raider is a film highly recommended by many who consider it a great achievement to make a live action film look like a video game. However, I don't see anything remarkable in this, nor as any reason to celebrate. Live action that is indistinguishable from animation, does not make films more real for us; rather, it makes it hyper illusive. Furthermore, director Simon West's overuse of visual effects in *Lara Croft: Tomb Raider* diverts the viewers' attention from the storyline. What many of us should realize is that what he gives us is an over-fantasized world of violence to improve the heroine's aggression skills.

Q. Which best summarizes the writer's opinion of the film *Lara Croft: Tomb Raider*?

(a) It distorts the legend of the video game for the purpose of film making.
(b) It fails in using live action in a contemporary setting.
(c) It misrepresents the main character with underlying sarcasm.
(d) It compounds live action film inaccuracies with excessive visual effects.

위의 예시는 '툼 레이더'라는 유명한 영화에 대한 비평문이다. 하이라이트로 표시된 부분에서 알 수 있듯이, 이 글의 화자 는 이 영화가 시각 효과가 풍부하긴 하지만 그것이 비디오 게임과 같은 효과를 낼 뿐, 영화로서 훌륭한 점은 아니라고 비 판하고 있다.

문제에서 화자의 의견을 묻고 있으므로 정답은 '(d) 이 영화는 액션 영화의 오류들과 과도한 시각 효과를 혼합한 것이 다.'가 된다.

해설: 240p

Catch Up

TEPS 독해 영역에 출제되었던 문제를 풀어봄으로써 실전 문제 유형
을 확실하게 파악해두자.

Part I **Read the passage and choose the option that best fits the blank.**

1. The immediate family of Peter Riley, who was killed in an industrial accident at Energy Brix, launched an appeal trying to increase their court ordered compensation payouts. Six years ago Peter Riley was fatally engulfed by hot slag at Energy Brix. The company was initially ordered by the court to pay his family $35,000, comprising $20,000 to his daughter and $15,000 to his son. The attorney representing the family described the awards as "a gross insult" to the heirs and "manifestly inadequate." The case is currently before the Court of Appeals, where they are arguing for enhanced payouts ____________ ____________________________ .

   (a) to provide the extended family with a sense of joy and elation
   (b) with regard to the children's need for relief and relaxation
   (c) because their higher education costs are extremely high
   (d) to compensate the children for their pain and suffering

2. Antioxidants are molecules which can safely interact with free radicals and terminate the chain reaction before vital molecules are damaged. Although there are several enzyme systems within the body that scavenge free radicals, the principle micronutrient antioxidants are vitamin E, beta-carotene, and vitamin C. Additionally, selenium, a trace metal that is required for proper function of one of the body's antioxidant enzyme systems, is sometimes included in this category. The body ____________________________ ____________________ so they must be supplied in the diet.

   (a) is required to make the correct choice
   (b) responds the same way to them as to other nutrients
   (c) evaluates its own needs for nutrition
   (d) cannot manufacture these micronutrients

Answers

TEPS 독해 영역에 출제되었던 기출 문제를 자세한 설명과 함께 완전히 이해하도록 하자.

1

> The immediate family of Peter Riley, who was killed in an industrial accident at Energy Brix, launched an appeal trying to increase their court ordered compensation payouts. Six years ago Peter Riley was fatally engulfed by hot slag at Energy Brix. The company was initially ordered by the court to pay his family $35,000, comprising $20,000 to his daughter and $15,000 to his son. The attorney representing the family described the awards as "a gross insult" to the heirs and "manifestly inadequate." The case is currently before the Court of Appeals, where they are arguing for enhanced payouts ___________________________________.
>
> (a) to provide the extended family with a sense of joy and elation
> (b) with regard to the children's need for relief and relaxation
> (c) because their higher education costs are extremely high
> (d) to compensate the children for their pain and suffering

해석 에너지 브릭스에서 산업 사고로 죽은 피터 리일리의 직계가족은, 법정에서 명령한 보상금을 늘리기 위한 상소를 시작했다. 6년 전, 피터 라일리는 에너지 브릭스에서 뜨거워진 재에 뒤덮여 죽었다. 처음에 법원은 회사가 딸에게 2만 달러, 아들에게 1만 5천 달러로, 그의 가족에게 총 3만 5천 달러를 지급하도록 했다. 이 가족을 대변하는 변호사는 이 판정 금액이 상속인들에게는 '완전한 모욕'이며 '명백히 부적절하다'라고 말했다. 이 사건은 현재 항소 법원에 있는데, 이곳에서 아이들의 고통과 아픔을 보상하기 위해 더 많은 보상금이 주어져야 한다고 주장될 것으로 보인다.

해설 산업 사고로 죽은 직원의 가족에 대한 보상금을 다룬 지문이다. 변호사의 말에 정답 (d)에 대한 단서를 정확히 찾을 수 있다.

오답 분석
(a) 이 대가족에게 즐거움과 기분 좋은 감정을 제공하기 위해 – 이 가족이 대가족이라는 언급도 없을 뿐 아니라, 아버지를 잃은 아이들에게 즐거움의 감정은 알맞지 않다.
(b) 고통을 덜고 긴장을 풀기를 원하는 아이들에 대해서 – 지문에 나온 아이들의 상황에 '긴장 이완(relaxation)'이라는 표현은 알맞지 않다.
(c) 더 높은 수준의 교육에 대한 비용이 매우 높기 때문에 – 교육 비용에 대한 내용은 지문에 언급되지 않았다.

어휘
award 판정, 재정액
heir 상속인
manifest 명백한
inadequate 부적절한
elation 의기양양, 기분 좋음
with regard to ~에 관해서

2

Antioxidants are molecules which can safely interact with free radicals and terminate the chain reaction before vital molecules are damaged. Although there are several enzyme systems within the body that scavenge free radicals, the principle micronutrient antioxidants are vitamin E, beta-carotene, and vitamin C. Additionally, selenium, a trace metal that is required for proper function of one of the body's antioxidant enzyme systems, is sometimes included in this category. The body ______________________________________ so they must be supplied in the diet.

(a) is required to make the correct choice
(b) responds the same way to them as to other nutrients
(c) evaluates its own needs for nutrition
(d) cannot manufacture these micronutrients

해석 노화 방지제는 활성 산소와 안전하게 상호작용하여 중요한 분자가 해를 입기 전에 연쇄 반응을 끊는 미립자이다. 체내에 활성 산소를 찾아 모으는 몇 가지 효소 시스템이 있기는 하지만, 주요 미량 원소 노화 방지제는 비타민 E, 베타 카로틴, 비타민 C이다. 그리고 신체의 산화 방지 효소 시스템 중 하나의 적절한 기능에 필요한 자취 금속인 셀레늄이 때때로 이 범주에 속한다. 신체는 이러한 미립 원소들을 만들어 낼 수가 없기 때문에 식사에서 공급되어야 한다.

해설 지문이 다소 전문적인 화학 분야의 내용을 담고 있으므로 여러 생소한 어휘들 때문에 읽기가 수월하지 않을 수 있는 지문이다. 그러나 정답은 의외로 쉽게 찾아지는 문제이기도 하다. 빈칸 뒤에 이어지는 내용이 '식사에서 공급되어야 한다'이므로 정답 (d)를 쉽게 고를 수 있다.

오답 (a) 올바른 선택을 하기 위해 필요하다 – 지문과 관련 없는 보기이다.
분석 (b) 다른 영양소들에게 반응하는 것과 같은 식으로 반응한다 – 지문에 다른 영양소의 반응 방식에 대한 언급이 없다.
　　 (c) 영양소가 필요한가를 평가한다 – 지문에서 신체에 필요한 영양소가 무엇인지를 다루고 있는 것이 아니므로 오답이다.

어휘 **antioxidant** 산화 방지제, 노화 방지제
free radical 활성 산소
enzyme 효소
scavenge 청소하다; 아직 쓸 만한 물건을 모으다
micronutrient 미량 영양소, 미량 원소의
trace metal 자취 금속

Answers:

1. (d) 2. (d)

Build Up

TEPS 독해 영역의 실전 문제와 가장 가까운 유형과 난이도의 예상 문제를 통해 실력을 쌓자.

▶▶ **Part I** Read the passage and choose the option that best fits the blank.

1. Dear Valued Customer,

   We are writing to inform that our new CompuServe branch has moved and is now located at 1452 Bur Oak Avenue. Our brand new location not only offers the standard sections and services but also boasts an additional second level service for computer hardware and spare parts. To make your shopping experience more efficient and enjoyable, customers are now also able to browse through our catalogues and order online. ____________________________, all you have to do is contact us and we guarantee it will be available the next day. Hopefully our new location and shopping features will better meet your computing needs.

   (a) In the event that certain items are marked down
   (b) If there is a particular product that is not available
   (c) To ensure maximum efficiency in processing refunds
   (d) Whenever you have any questions regarding computers

▶▶ **Part II** Choose the option that correctly answers the question.

2. In today's competitive market, advertisers will resort to any means in convincing consumers to buy certain products. One of the most effective, yet ruthless methods is to take advantage of people's insecurities by pointing out their shortcomings. In fact, many advertisements and commercials often place an onus on people's imperfections and the ideal that they should strive for. An example is the many different advertisements for toothpaste. Many of them depict people whose teeth are not very white or attractive thus they are not satisfied with their lives. However, once those individuals use the particular brand that is being advertised, the individuals not only have better looking teeth, but their lives instantly become perfect.

   Q. Which of the following best summarizes the passage?

   (a) Toothpaste commercials are very silly and unrealistic
   (b) Advertisements achieve their goals by making people feel insecure.
   (c) Advertisers help consumers feel good about themselves.
   (d) We should keep our teeth healthy and attractive using toothpaste.

3. A sedentary lifestyle, where people get little or no physical exercise, contributes directly to a deleterious effect on the physical construction of our bodies, hence an acceleration of the aging process. Everyday activities such as taking out the trash, washing the car or even tying our shoelaces do not necessarily have to be accompanied by aches and pains as we grow older. It is up to the individual to decide how best to employ steps to slow the aging process. By making wise choices you can make your perceived age more closely resemble your chronological age. Father Time can indeed be turned back.

Q. Which of the following best summarizes the passage?

(a) The ability to tie our shoelaces is essential to the aging process.
(b) As people get older their need for physical activity diminishes.
(c) Aches and pains are a direct result of a sedentary lifestyle.
(d) Aging should not necessarily prevent normal activities.

4. In the rush to find those responsible for the September 11th destruction of the Twin Towers in New York and to determine the level of future vulnerability to such attacks, federal, state and local law enforcement officials began to target suspects of Middle Eastern appearance. This profiling exercise by the authorities led to an accusation that the detention and investigation of individuals were arbitrary and that it was based solely on their ethnicity. It has subsequently been proven that the foreign nationals of Middle Eastern origin who were of interest to the authorities often lacked any factors besides their appearance in warranting suspicion.

Q. Which of the following is correct about the passage?

(a) Post 9-11 racial profiling carried out by the federal authorities was somewhat absurd.
(b) Before 9-11 the FBI wasn't interested in people from the Middle East.
(c) The crime was carried out by American citizens whose cultural nationality was Middle Eastern.
(d) Federal, state and local law enforcement officials worked feverishly.

▶▶ **Part III** Identify the sentence that least fits the context of the passage.

5. The book *A Million Little Pieces* by James Frey has come under a considerable amount of criticism for stretching the truth in a memoir. (a) The book sold millions of copies worldwide, and was translated into over 20 different languages. (b) James Frey initially tried to publish his story as fiction, but was encouraged to present it as a true story instead. (c) So, *A Million Little Pieces* was sold as a memoir, as James Frey's personal account of overcoming addiction. (d) Many readers empathized with Frey's narrative, but were enraged at the later disclosure that some incidents were more fiction than fact.

정답: 202p

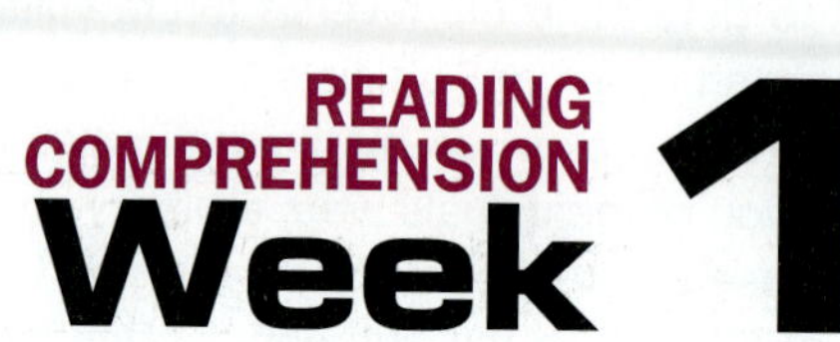
READING
COMPREHENSION
Week 1

Day 3
설명문

비전문적 학술문 중에서도 주장을 펴거나 입장의 차이를 보여주는 것이 아니라, 정보를 전달하기 위해 사실만을 언급하는 설명문들이 있다. 주장이 들어 있는 지문들과 달리, 설명문은 한 가지 소재에 대한 사실들을 나열하고 있을 뿐이므로 논지를 파악하고 내용을 이해하기 쉽다. 단, Part 2의 Which is correct ~? 문제 유형에서는 지문에 나열된 사실들을 기억하여 정답을 골라야 하기 때문에, 정보가 많이 들어 있는 지문의 경우 지문을 여러 번 읽지 않고 한 번에 문제를 풀 수 있도록 표시하며 읽는 습관을 들여야 한다.

Example

In today's modern society, leisure is defined as free time that is used for recreational purposes and fun. However, that was not always the case, **as perceptions of this word have had different meanings and interpretations over time.** This often depended on specific groups of people from particular periods in time. One notable example is that of the ancient Greek philosophers who considered leisure to be a form of mental work. In fact, they believed that this notion encompassed studying and focusing on academia in order to develop their intellect through an exertion of the mind. As a result, philosophy and the concept of debates originated from the Greek's use of leisurely time.

Q. What is the main idea of this passage?

(a) Many people today regard the main goal of leisure as educating themselves.
(b) The body as well as the mind was emphasized by many Greek philosophers.
(c) The concept and interpretation of leisure has varied depending on different time periods.
(d) Leisure is more important in the present day than it was during Ancient Greece.

위의 지문은 '레저'라는 단어가 시간의 흐름에 따라 여러 의미를 가져왔음을 구체적 예시를 들어 설명하는 글이다. 지문의 구조가 간단하고 주제를 명확하게 알 수 있으므로 상대적으로 어렵지 않게 풀 수 있다.

해설: 242p

Catch Up

TEPS 독해 영역에 출제되었던 문제를 풀어봄으로써 실전 문제 유형
을 확실하게 파악해두자.

Part II Choose the option that correctly answers the question.

1. The Neoclassical style of painting is one that arose from the anti-romantic movement in the mid 18th through mid 19th century. Jean Ingres's paintings present the common characteristics that the Neoclassical school of painting portray; such as precise outlining. Ingres continued to develop his artistic style even when other artists embraced the Romantic Movement's emotional and subjected approach to art. Romanticism was against everything Ingres stood for. So, it is not surprising that he developed a lifelong loathing for it, as he continued his success as a Neoclassical style artist.

   Q. What is the main topic of this passage?

   (a) Ingres's success as a Neoclassical artist and the abhorrence to Romantic art
   (b) The influence of Romantic artists on Ingres's style
   (c) Ingres's influence on the romantic school of painting
   (d) The Romanticism that brought about Ingres's descent

2. Democratic tactics such as disingenuous video campaigns and advertisements are nothing new to the Democratic process. While great attention has been paid to make sure thst such media manipulation is not very pervasive in character, it's been a part of politics since photography began and it will continue to play a large part of politics. So, political science students should never forget the fact that in political campaigns, images are routinely altered to advance a point of view. Even Lincoln published a now iconic campaign photograph of himself, featuring his head on the counterpart, Southern politician, John Calhoon's body.

   Q. What is the main idea of this passage?

   (a) Media manipulation has long been used as a tool for politicians.
   (b) Media manipulation is becoming increasingly insulting.
   (c) Political science students should be critical about current affairs.
   (d) Lincoln's reputation for being honest will continue to be well deserved.

Answers 

TEPS 독해 영역에 출제되었던 기출 문제를 자세한 설명과 함께 완전
히 이해하도록 하자.

1

The Neoclassical style of painting is one that arose from the anti-romantic movement in the mid 18th through mid 19th century. Jean Ingres's paintings present the common characteristics that the Neoclassical school of painting portray; such as precise outlining. Ingres continued to develop his artistic style even when other artists embraced the Romantic Movement's emotional and subjected approach to art. Romanticism was against everything Ingres stood for. So, it is not surprising that he developed a lifelong loathing for it, as he continued his success as a Neoclassical style artist.

Q. What is the main idea of this passage?

(a) Ingres's success as a Neoclassical artist and the abhorrence to Romantic art
(b) The influence of Romantic artists on Ingres's style
(c) Ingres's influence on the romantic school of painting
(d) The Romanticism that brought about Ingres's descent

해석 신고전주의 스타일의 그림은 18세기 중반부터 19세기 중반의 반 낭만주의운동으로부터 비롯되었다. 장 앵그르의 그림은 정확한 테두리와 같은 신고전주의 학파의 그림이 묘사하는 공통된 특징을 보여준다. 앵그르는 다른 화가들이 낭만주의 운동의 감정적이고 종속적인 미술에 대한 접근을 채택했을 때에도, 끊임없이 그의 예술적인 스타일을 발전시켜 나아갔다. 낭만주의는 앵그르가 나타낸 모든 것의 반대였다. 그래서 그가 신고전주의 화가로서 계속적인 성공을 거두며 낭만주의에 대해 일생동안 강한 혐오를 발전시켰던 것은 놀라운 일이 아니다.

해설 앵그르의 신고전주의 스타일에 대한 내용의 글로, 낭만주의에 반대하는 특징을 지녔으며 낭만주의를 매우 싫어하였다고 설명하고 있다. 따라서 정답은 '(a) 신고전주의 화가로서 앵그르의 성공과 낭만주의 양식에 대한 혐오'가 된다.

오답 (b) 앵그르의 스타일에 있어서 낭만주의 화가들의 영향 – 앵그르가 낭만주의의 영향을 받았다는 내용은 언급되지 않았다.
분석 (c) 낭만주의파 그림에 대한 앵그르의 영향 – 낭만주의가 앵그르의 영향을 받았다는 것도 언급되지 않았다.
(d) 앵그르의 몰락을 가져온 낭만주의 – 앵그르의 몰락은 지문에 나타나지 않았다.

어휘 **characteristic** 특성, 특징
precise 정밀한, 정확한
embrace 껴안다, 받아들이다, 채택하다
subjected 종속적인
loathing 몹시 싫어함, 혐오
abhorrence 혐오

2

Democratic tactics such as disingenuous video campaigns and advertisements are nothing new to the Democratic process. While great attention has been paid to make sure that such media manipulation is not very pervasive in character, it's been a part of politics since photography began and it will continue to play a large part of politics. So, political science students should never forget the fact that in political campaigns, images are routinely altered to advance a point of view. Even Lincoln published a now iconic campaign photograph of himself, featuring his head on the counterpart, Southern politician, John Calhoon's body.

Q. What is the main idea of the passage?

(a) Media manipulation has long been used as a tool for politicians.
(b) Media manipulation is becoming increasingly insulting.
(c) Political science students should be critical about current affairs.
(d) Lincoln's reputation for being honest will continue to be well deserved.

해석 부정직한 비디오 캠페인이나 광고와 같은 민주주의의 전략은 민주주의의 진보에 있어 새로운 것이 아니다. 미디어 조작이 그 성격에 있어 그리 널리 퍼지는 것이 아님을 확실히 하기 위해 많은 주의가 기울여지고 있음에도 불구하고, 이것은 사진이 시작된 이래로 정치의 일부분이었으며 앞으로도 계속해서 정치에서 큰 역할을 할 것이다. 그러므로, 정치학과 학생들은 정치 캠페인에서 관점을 내세우기 위해 이미지들은 늘 바뀌어지게 마련이라는 것을 잊지 말아야 한다. 링컨조차도 지금은 아이콘이 된 자신의 캠페인 사진을 발행했는데, 그것은 반대편에 있는, 즉 남부의 정치가 John Calhoon의 몸에 자신의 머리를 붙인 것이었다.

해설 미디어 조작이 민주주의의 캠페인 전략으로 많이 쓰여왔다는 내용의 지문이다. 따라서 정답은 '(a) 미디어 조작은 정치인들에게 오랫동안 도구로 사용되어 왔다.'가 된다.

오답 분석 (b) 미디어 조작은 점점 더 모욕적이 되고 있다. – 모욕적이라는 내용은 언급되지 않았다.
(c) 정치학과 학생들은 시사 문제에 대해 비판적이어야 한다. – 이 글의 소재는 정치학과 학생들이 아니다.
(d) 정직에 대한 링컨의 명성은 계속해서 가치를 인정받을 것이다. – 링컨은 예시로 등장했을 뿐이므로 주제가 될 수 없다.

어휘 **disingenuous** 부정직한, 불성실한
tactic 전략, 작전
manipulation 조작, 속임
pervasive 퍼지는, 널리 미치는, 스며드는
counterpart 상대자, 반대편에 있는 사람
current affairs 시사

Answers:

1. (a) 2. (a)

Build Up

▶▶ Part I Read the passage and choose the option that best fits the blank.

1. Besides sunglasses serving the traditional purpose of providing protection for your eyes from harmful ultraviolet (UV) rays, _______________________________________. The shape of your face, the lens color, and the amount of UV protection you want are a few items you must consider when buying a pair to make you look good. You should check yourself out in a full-length mirror when you try them on because it is important to match your sunglasses with the look you wish to achieve. A critical point is to also match the pair you have chosen to the proportions of your body - not only your face.

   (a) they can provide an aesthetic and style
   (b) they offset harsh colored room decor
   (c) they also control the ratio of direct sunlight
   (d) they come with complete manufacturer's specifications

2. Anti-quota petitioners before the Supreme Court in New Delhi argued that a law providing for 27 percent quota in Central Educational Institutions cannot last indefinitely and further demanded such special provisions be officially sanctioned. The Delhi Court was told by a group of private schools that an allocation of five more points to scheduled caste students for nursery classes would not be implemented at any time. The schools said it was an indirect way of introducing a discriminatory system for socially backward communities to gain access to private institutions. They added that _______________ _______________, saying that they would not be put in place in the schools during the student admissions process.

   (a) the decision has been made to recommend a scholastic cost waiver
   (b) they will not implement a quota system
   (c) it is unconstitutional to implement the quota system
   (d) previously enrolled students will no longer be fully eligible

3. Tired of your old, boring look? Do you ever wonder if you should give yourself a make-over and inject some life into your dull sense of fashion? If you have ever wished that you could simply reinvent yourself and transform into a stylish and bold goddess, look no further for *Beauty Magazine* is the answer for you! This new magazine offers everything an outgoing, independent woman yearning for the freedom to experiment with her sense of fashion needs. From tips for avoiding fashion blunders to suggestions on what the latest trends in clothing are, *Beauty Magazine* is the ultimate source for the modern, style conscious woman. Don't wait any longer, pick it up at your local newsstands!

Q. What is the purpose of the passage?

    (a) To advertise a magazine
    (b) To help avoid fashion blunders
    (c) To make a recruitment offer
    (d) To offer a fashion design course

4. The skeleton of Ron the dinosaur is the largest and most complete Velociraptor, or just simply, Raptor ever found. It has provided scientists with evidence that the smart, fast-running, bipedal dinosaur is more closely related to the group Theropods than Sauropodomorpha. Theropods had a hip structure similar to that of today's lizards – the pubis bone pointed downwards and forwards that allowed dinosaurs like the Raptors to have long back legs for speed. Ron's recent discovery also provides support for the much debated theory that birds evolved from meat eating dinosaurs.

Q. What can be inferred from the passage?

    (a) Raptors used to feed on various kinds of birds.
    (b) Pubis bones were common in dinosaur species.
    (c) Theropods were speedy carnivores.
    (d) Ron's bones prove an evolutionary link to birds.

▶▶ **Part III** Identify the sentence that least fits the context of the passage.

5. Monopoly, one of the most popular board games around the world, is somewhat ironic in that the game's initial purpose was to tell us about the terribleness of monopoly. (a) The origin of Monopoly, 'The Landlord's game' was invented by Lizzie Maggie in 1904. (b) He created the game to explain the vicious cycle that the working poor cannot but remain in poverty as industrialization progressed. (c) Finally, Charles Darrow revised it to make Monopoly during the Great Depression, and now it immediately monopolized the board game market. (d) Monopoly became so popular that most of the game's trademarks such as the community chest and the railroads are now copyrighted and legally protected.

정답: 205p

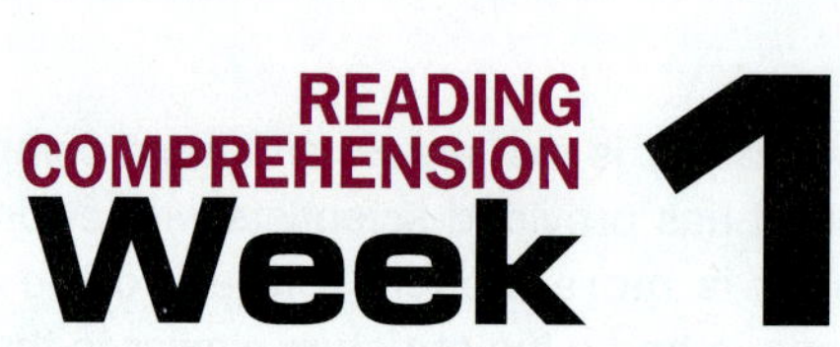

READING
COMPREHENSION
Week 1

Day 1

▶▶ 비전문적 학술문

유형정리 - 〈TEPS RC 지문 흐름 파악〉 비전문적 학술문의 특징

Catch Up - Part 1 빈칸 채우기

Day 2

▶▶ 비평문

유형정리 - 〈TEPS RC 지문 흐름 파악〉 비평문

Catch Up - Part 1 빈칸 채우기

Day 3

▶▶ 설명문

유형정리 - 〈TEPS RC 지문 흐름 파악〉 설명문

Catch Up - Part 2 주제 찾기

Day 4

▶▶ 편지글

유형정리 - 〈TEPS RC 지문 흐름 파악〉 편지글

Catch Up - Part 2 세부사항 확인

Day 5

▶▶ 광고/공지

유형정리 - 〈TEPS RC 지문 흐름 파악〉 광고/공지

Catch Up - Part 3

Day 4

편지

편지글은 보통 개인적인 편지와 업무적인 편지, 두 가지로 나눌 수 있는데, 개인적인 편지는 내용과 목적이 다양할 수 있어, 전체적인 맥락을 잡지 못하면 뉘앙스를 완전히 다르게 이해하게 되는 경우도 있다. 업무적인 편지가 더 자주 출제되며 주로 상식적으로 이해될 수 있는 내용이므로 그리 어렵지 않게 맞출 수 있다.

Example

Dear Valued Customer,

We are writing to inform that our new CompuServe branch has moved and is now located at 1452 Bur Oak Avenue. Our brand new location not only offers the standard sections and services but also boasts an additional second level service for computer hardware and spare parts. To make your shopping experience more efficient and enjoyable, customers are now also able to browse through our catalogues and order online. _______________________________, all you have to do is contact us and we guarantee it will be available the next day. Hopefully our new location and shopping features will better meet your computing needs.

(a) In the event that certain items are marked down
(b) If there is a particular product that is not available
(c) To ensure maximum efficiency in processing refunds
(d) Whenever you have any questions regarding computers

위의 예시는 업무상의 편지글로, 회사에서 고객에게 회사의 위치를 옮겼으며, 그에 따라 부가적인 서비스도 제공할 것임을 알리기 위한 편지이다. 첫 문장에서 We are writing to inform that ~으로 시작하고 있으므로 고객들에게 새로운 정보를 주기 위해 보내는 편지임을 쉽게 알 수 있다.
빈칸 바로 아래쪽에 하이라이트 표시된 부분에서 '필요한 것이 있으면 즉시 준비해 주겠다' 는 세부적인 내용을 파악할 수 있으므로 정답도 어렵지 않게 고를 수 있다.

해설: 202p

Catch Up

TEPS 독해 영역에 출제되었던 문제를 풀어봄으로써 실전 문제 유형
을 확실하게 파악해두자.

Part II Choose the option that correctly answers the question.

1. Playgrounds traditionally have been found in both schools and parks in America. Each year, Parent-Teacher Associations and school administrations, as well as park and recreation departments, spend millions of dollars to provide playground structures. However, since 1981, professionals and the public have become increasingly aware that these structures can also lead to injuries in children and pose a liability to the owner and operator of the play equipment. More than 200,000 children are injured annually in playground-related incidents that are serious enough for them to seek medical attention.

    Q. Which of the following is correct?

    (a) Millions of dollars are spent treating playground injuries.
    (b) No children were injured in playgrounds prior to 1981.
    (c) Park and recreation departments pose a liability to playground owners.
    (d) You can usually find playgrounds in parks and schools in the US.

2. Nathaniel Maurice is a well known British slave trader. He was probably the most successful and one of the most despicable individuals engaged in the trade. Maurice had been engaged in the slave trade business for many years but had always eluded justice. The particular voyage that proved fatal to him was in 1801 when he left Africa for Jamaica with as many as 700 slaves, most of whom were children and women. Maurice disguised himself as a countryman and tactfully evaded the British government officials searching for him, but finally got caught 21 years later.

    Q. Which is correct about the Nathaniel Maurice?

    (a) He offloaded slaves in Florida.
    (b) He sank with 700 captive slaves on board.
    (c) He fell ill during his voyage to Jamaica in 1801.
    (d) His last voyage was from Africa to Jamaica.

TEPS 독해 영역에 출제되었던 기출 문제를 자세한 설명과 함께 완전
히 이해하도록 하자.

1

Playgrounds traditionally have been found in both schools and parks in America. Each year, Parent-Teacher Associations and school administrations, as well as park and recreation departments, spend millions of dollars to provide playground structures. However, since 1981, professionals and the public have become increasingly aware that these structures can also lead to injuries in children and pose a liability to the owner and operator of the play equipment. More than 200,000 children are injured annually in playground-related incidents that are serious enough for them to seek medical attention.

Q. Which of the following is correct?

(a) Millions of dollars are spent treating playground injuries.
(b) No children were injured in playgrounds prior to 1981.
(c) Park and recreation departments pose a liability to playground owners.
(d) You can usually find playgrounds in parks and schools in the US.

해석 놀이터는 전통적으로 미국의 학교와 공원에서 찾아볼 수 있었다. 매년 공원과 레크리에이션 부서들은 물론, 육성회와 학교 행정부는 놀이터 시설을 제공하기 위해 몇 백만 달러씩 소비한다. 그러나, 1981년부터 전문가들과 대중은 이러한 시설이 아이들에게 상해를 입히거나, 놀이터 시설물의 운전사나 소유자에게 책임을 제시한다는 것을 점점 더 깨닫게 되었다. 한 해에 이십만 명이 넘는 아이들이 놀이터에 관련된 사고에서 의료 치료를 받을 만큼 충분히 심각한 상해를 입는다.

해설 지문의 첫 문장에서 정답이 '(d) 보통은 미국의 놀이터나 공원이나 학교에서 놀이터를 찾아볼 수 있다.' 라는 것을 알 수 있다.

오답 (a) 놀이터에서의 사고를 치료하는 데 몇 백만 달러가 쓰이고 있다. – 놀이터 사고의 치료 비용은 지문에서 언급되지 않았다.
분석 (b) 1981년 이전에는 놀이터에서 어떤 어린이들도 다치지 않았다.– 지문은 다치지 않았다는 내용이 아니라, 1981년 이후에 놀이터의 위험성이 인지되었다는 내용이다.
  (c) 공원과 레크리에이션 부서들은 놀이터 소유주들에게 책임을 제시한다. – 이 보기에 언급된 사람들은 놀이터 사고에 대해 모두 책임이 제시되는 사람들이다.

어휘 **association** 협회, 조합, 공동 단체
  administration 경영진, 집행부
  liability 책임, 책무, 의무
  equipment 설비, 장비
  a Parent-Teacher Association 육성회, 사친회

2

Nathaniel Maurice is a well known British slave trader. He was probably the most successful and one of the most despicable individuals engaged in the trade. Maurice had been engaged in the slave trade business for many years but had always eluded justice. The particular voyage that proved fatal to him was in 1801 when he left Africa for Jamaica with as many as 700 slaves, most of whom were children and women. Maurice disguised himself as a countryman and tactfully evaded the British government officials searching for him, but finally got caught 21 years later.

Q. Which is correct about the Nathaniel Maurice?

(a) He offloaded slaves in Florida.
(b) He sank with 700 captive slaves on board.
(c) He fell ill during his voyage to Jamaica in 1801.
(d) His last voyage was from Africa to Jamaica.

해석 Nathaniel Maurice는 잘 알려진 영국 노예 상인이다. 그는 아마도 가장 성공을 거두었으면서도 무역에 종사한 사람들 중 가장 악질적인 사람이었을 것이다. Maurice는 많은 세월 동안 노예 무역 사업에 종사했지만, 항상 처벌을 교묘하게 피했다. 그에게 치명적이었다고 입증된 항해는 1801년 대부분 어린이와 여성들이었던 700명의 노예를 데리고 아프리카를 떠나 자메이카로 향했을 때였다. 그러나 21년 후에 마침내 잡히고 나서야 Maurice는 영국 정부와 공무원들에 의해 처벌되었다.

해설 지문에서 아프리카에서 자메이카로 향했던 항해가 그에게 치명적인 것이었다고 하였고 처벌 받았다고 하였다. 따라서 그 항해가 마지막 항해라는 것을 알 수 있으므로 정답은 '(d) 그의 마지막 항해는 아프리카에서 자메이카로 가는 것이었다.'가 된다.

오답 (a) 그는 플로리다에 노예들을 내려놓았다. – 지문에 언급되지 않았다.
분석 (b) 그는 배 위에서 사로잡힌 700명의 노예와 함께 가라앉았다. – 지문에 언급되지 않았다.
　　 (c) 그는 1801년 자메이카로 가는 항해 중에 병에 걸렸다. – 지문에 언급되지 않았다.

어휘 **elude** 교묘히 피하다, 벗어나다
　　 fatal 치명적인

Build Up

TEPS 독해 영역의 실전 문제와 가장 가까운 유형과 난이도의 예상 문
제를 통해 실력을 쌓자.

▶▶ **Part I** Read the passage and choose the option that best fits the blank.

1. Far from being in a state of crisis and with its current standard of living among the world's highest, Japan is one of the wealthiest countries in the world. For example, the sales of luxurious brands on the high-end spectrum such as Burberry, Louis Vuitton and Gucci continue to remain very high. At one point in the late 20th Century, the economy of this Asian country was recorded as possessing the highest annual growth rate out of all the developed countries. __________, the speculation of this economic miracle has been tho chief subject matter of many debates around the world.

   (a) Nevertheless
   (b) Instead
   (c) After all
   (d) Hence

▶▶ **Part II** Choose the option that correctly answers the question.

2. Many consider businesses to be the biggest contributors to environmental degradation. While businesses are known to play a significant role, we also need to understand that individual homeowners should play their part as well in reducing their impact on Earth. In order for them to take part in energy reduction on a larger scale, local governments should give more incentives, such as easing the current restrictions on integrated solar panels and wind turbines to encourage homeowners to generate their own power.

   Q. What is the main idea of this passage?

   (a) It is the local government's responsibility to reduce energy waste.
   (b) Minimizing climate change requires help from businesses.
   (c) Businesses should be encouraged to generate their own alternative energy resources.
   (d) The Government should promote energy reduction in homes as well as in businesses.

3. Married life seems to have more benefits than we might have thought. The National Center for Health Research released a new study that proved the co-relationship between married life and longevity. The report, based on health examinations of 132,000 single and married adults, shows married people are less likely to smoke, drink heavily, or be physically inactive. They're also more likely than single adults to keep mentally and physically fit and to have less stress symptoms.

Q. Which is correct about married people?

(a) They tend to take up smoking after marriage.
(b) They are more likely to stress out over work.
(c) They are more motivated to stay fit than single people.
(d) They have fewer opportunities to drink than singles.

4. A new study suggests that liposuction may also help to treat chronic depression. The study is still undergoing final stages of scientific tests, but researchers believe they have good reasons to be confident. So far, the research has found that 9 out of 10 participants of liposuction treatment for reducing body fat experienced a lift in mood after the therapy. Conversely, skeptics disagree, stating that liposuction may temporarily trigger positive self image but it does not account for the overall happiness of the patient.

Q. What can be inferred about Liposuction from the passage?

(a) It blurs one's body image and level of self confidence.
(b) It contains a chemical that triggers brain activity.
(c) Its ability to cure depression makes it popular.
(d) Its influence on emotions has not been fully validated.

▶▶ **Part III** Identify the sentence that least fits the context of the passage.

5. Stephen William Hawking was born on January 8th, 1942 in Oxford, England. (a) He possessed one of the brightest minds in his time and his principal fields of research were theoretical cosmology and quantum gravity. (b) He was able to greatly contribute to the world of science through his research despite being diagnosed with Lou Gehrig's disease at the age of 21. (c) There is no particular medication or remedy for Lou Gehrig's disease, which became well-known to the public as the disease Hawking is suffering. (d) Stephen Hawking's works include *A Brief History of Time*; *The Universe of a Nutshell*, and *Black Holes and Baby Universes: and Other Essays*.

정답: 207p

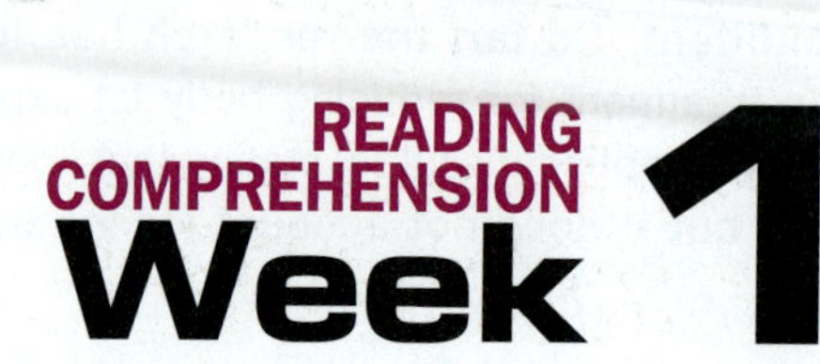
READING
COMPREHENSION
Week 1

Day 5

광고 / 공지

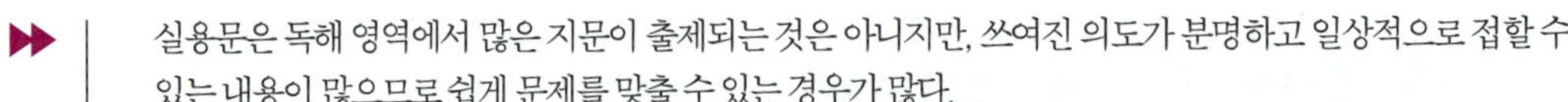

실용문은 독해 영역에서 많은 지문이 출제되는 것은 아니지만, 쓰여진 의도가 분명하고 일상적으로 접할 수 있는 내용이 많으므로 쉽게 문제를 맞출 수 있는 경우가 많다.

실용문 중에서도 특히 광고와 공지글은 의도와 내용이 명료하며, 광고와 공지의 특성상 어려운 단어가 출제되거나 복잡하고 긴 문장이 포함되는 경우가 별로 없으므로 빨리 정답을 맞출 수 있는 문제이다.

Example

Tired of your old, boring look? Do you ever wonder if you should give yourself a make-over and inject some life into your dull sense of fashion? If you have ever wished that you could simply reinvent yourself and transform into a stylish and bold goddess, look no further for *Beauty Magazine* is the answer for you! This new magazine offers everything an outgoing, independent woman yearning for the freedom to experiment with her sense of fashion needs. From tips to avoiding fashion blunders to suggestions on what the latest trends in clothing are, *Beauty Magazine* is the ultimate source for the modern, style conscious woman. Don't wait any longer, pick it up at your local newsstands!

Q. What is the purpose of the passage?

(a) To advertise a magazine
(b) To help avoid fashion blunders
(c) To make a recruitment offer
(d) To offer a fashion design course

위의 지문은 패션 잡지를 광고하는 글이다. 첫 문장부터 전형적인 광고글의 형태를 취하고 있으며, 하이라이트 표시가 된 부분들은 전형적인 광고문의 문구들이다. 마지막 문장에서 '더 이상 기다리지 말고 가까운 신문 가판대에서 하나 사십시오!'라고 끝맺고 있으므로 확실히 광고문임을 알 수 있다.

해설: 206p

Catch Up

Part III Identify the sentence that least fits the context of the passage.

1. Research conducted on human-animal bonds indicated that living with a pet has a positive effect on children. (a) Children may learn how to empathize with others as well as achieve an enhanced self esteem through their pets. (b) On the other hand, children may get bored of their pets and eventually abandon them. (c) Despite the benefits, the possibility of potential harm exists between animal and children if they behave inappropriately towards each other or if either one is neglected by the other. (d) Strong relationships between children and their pets are fostered and don't just happen overnight.

2. When land surveyors first began measuring the peninsula, they were unable to collect accurate measurements during winter. (a) This was discovered when measurements taken during winter differed greatly from those collected during summer. (b) The measurement is much more accurate these days because the average temperature has risen due to global warming. (c) The surveyors used long metal chain like a ruler that stretched across forests and swamps. (d) After some time, they realized the source of the inaccurate measurements, the long metal chain because metals contract under severely cold temperatures.

Answers 

TEPS 독해 영역에 출제되었던 기출 문제를 자세한 설명과 함께 완전
히 이해하도록 하자.

1

Research conducted on human-animal bonds indicated that living with a pet has a positive effect on children. (a) Children may learn how to empathize with others as well as achieve an enhanced self esteem through their pets. (b) On the other hand, children may get bored of their pets and eventually abandon them. (c) Despite the benefits, the possibility of potential harm exists between animal and children if they behave inappropriately towards each other or if either one is neglected by the other. (d) Strong relationships between children and their pets are fostered and don't just happen overnight.

해석 연구자들은 인간과 동물 간의 연대에 대한 연구에서, 애완동물과 사는 것이 어린이에게 긍정적인 영향을 끼친다는 것을 밝혀냈다. (a) 아이들은 애완동물을 통해 더 높은 자부심을 성취할 수 있을 뿐 아니라 어떻게 다른 사람들과 마음을 공감하는지 배울 수 있다. (b) 반면에 아이들은 그들의 애완동물이 지루해져서 마침내는 애완동물을 버릴 수도 있다. (c) 이런 장점에도 불구하고 만약 서로에게 부적당하게 행동하거나, 둘 중의 한쪽이 다른 한쪽에 의해 무시당하는 경우, 아이들과 애완동물 사이의 잠재적 유해성의 가능성이 존재한다. (d) 아이들과 그들의 애완동물 사이의 강한 유대관계는 점차 육성되는 것이며 단 하룻밤 사이에 생겨나지 않는다.

해설 문맥상 어린이가 애완동물을 가지는 것에 대한 장점이 언급되다가 유해성도 있을 수 있음을 나타내고 있다. (c)에서 '이러한 장점에도 불구하고'라고 하였으므로 그 앞 문장에서는 장점에 대해 언급되어야 한다. (b)는 단점에 대한 내용이므로 어색한 문장이 된다.

오답 분석 (d)문장이 이 지문에서 하는 역할은 마무리이다. 어린이와 애완동물 사이의 유해성이 존재하므로, 짧은 시간에 생겨나지 않는 유대관계가 육성되어야 함을 언급하고 있다. 따라서 (d)는 (c)와 유기적으로 연결되고 있음을 알 수 있다. 정답은 (b)이다.

어휘 **empathize** 감정 이입하다, 마음으로부터 공감하다
enhance 높이다, 강화시키다
self-esteem 자존, 자부심
inappropriately 부적당하게, 타당하지 않게
neglect 무시하다; 게을리 하다
overnight 밤새는, 하룻밤 사이의, 갑작스러운

2

When land surveyors first began measuring the peninsula, they were unable to collect accurate measurements during winter. (a) This was discovered when measurements taken during winter differed greatly from those collected during summer. (b) The measurement is much more accurate these days because the average temperature has risen due to global warming. (c) The surveyors used long metal chain like a ruler that stretched across forests and swamps. (d) After some time, they realized the source of the inaccurate measurements, the long metal chain,because metals contract under severely cold temperatures.

해석 토지 측량기사들이 처음으로 반도 측량을 시작했을 때, 그들은 겨울에 정확한 측량 수집을 할 수가 없었다. (a) 겨울에 측정된 수치가 여름에 수집된 수치와 크게 차이가 났을 때 이것이 발견되었다. (b) 지구 온난화 때문에 평균 기온이 높아져서 요즘의 측정은 훨씬 더 정확하다. (c) 측량기사들은 숲과 늪지대를 가로질러 뻗어 놓는 자와 같은 긴 금속 체인을 사용했다. (d) 시간이 흐른 후, 그들은 부정확한 측정의 원인을 깨달았다. 원인은 긴 금속 체인이었는데, 왜냐하면 금속은 격심하게 추운 온도에서는 수축하기 때문이다.

해설 과거의 토지 측정이 부정확했던 이유가 긴 금속 체인 때문이었음을 나타내는 글이다. (b)는 요즈음의 측정에 대한 내용이므로 이 지문의 흐름에서 벗어나는 문장이다.

오답 분석 (a)는 첫 문장과 이어지는 내용이며, (c)에서 언급된 금속 체인이 (d)에서 부정확한 측정의 원인임을 밝히고 있으므로 유기적으로 연결되고 있다.

어휘 **surveyor** 측량기사, 조사관
peninsula 반도
measurement 측정, 측량
swamp 늪, 늪지대
inaccurate 부정확한
severely 심하게, 엄격하게, 격심하게

Answers:

1. (b) 2. (b)

Build Up

▶▶ Part I Read the passage and choose the option that best fits the blank.

1. The International Dyslexia Association (IDA) is a non-profit organization dedicated to helping individuals with dyslexia and their families. IDA was founded in 1949 in memory of Dr. Samuel T. Orton. Its goal has been the sharing of knowledge, methods and experience, and providing the most comprehensive forum on the issue. Thanks to IDA's endeavor to let the public know about Dyslexia, many of us now understand the nature of this disorder; it is characterized by _______________________. Commonly sufferers may read and understand a given topic; however, upon transcribing details they will display a transposition of letters or words.

   (a) brutality and mercilessness toward foreigners
   (b) repetitive loss of memory related to everyday life
   (c) a speech impediment under some particular conditions
   (d) interference in the acquisition and processing of language

▶▶ Part II Choose the option that correctly answers the question.

2. "Urban sprawl" is a relatively new phenomenon in which it describes the process of cities spreading out and rural land being developed to sustain further expansion. From an urban planner's standpoint, the growth factor is very important. However, there are also those that are concerned about the effects of urban sprawl on the natural environment and agricultural resources, that don't regard development as a factor of importance. For them, what matters is the amount of land being used for development. Both sides have equally valid goals, although not necessarily mutually exclusive.

   Q. What is the main topic of the passage?

   (a) Urban sprawl is often the result of poor city planning.
   (b) Plans for sustainable development are accelerating urban sprawl.
   (c) Urban sprawl is bad for agriculture and the natural environment.
   (d) There are two different perspectives on urban sprawl.

3. In examining your daily life, perhaps you have a job that is no longer interesting and you work just for the money. Yet, your bills are difficult to pay and you spend your leisure time stressed about your finances. Or, perhaps you are at home every day, and bored with nothing to look forward to except cooking the next dinner and redecorating the spare room. The number of stressful scenarios can be endless for all of us, whether we are blue collar workers, high-powered executives, housewives or the unemployed. We should use some of our time to enjoy more stress-free hobbies and pastimes as we're all vulnerable to the lock-ins that stress our mental and physical health.

    Q. Which of the following is correct according to the passage?

    (a) Many people now regard the main goal of relaxation to be self-taught.
    (b) The body and the mind are to be emphasized over our life situation.
    (c) People should consider relaxation as integral to their lifestyle.
    (d) Relaxation is deemed to be more important in modern times than in times past.

4. Social mobility is the degree to which, in a given society, an individual or a family or a group's social status can change throughout their life within a system of social hierarchy. There are two types of social mobility: structural mobility and exchange mobility. Structural mobility is the movement up or down the social scale from a change in distribution of statuses in a society, as when an individual from a blue-collar background becomes a professional. Exchange mobility is when someone else must step up or down when a position is dropped. Although social mobility is common in places where achievement is the basis for one's position in society, most people remain close to the social level from which they started from.

    Q. What can be inferred from the passage?

    (a) Higher education is a prerequisite for a person's social mobility.
    (b) Structural mobility occurs more often in white collar professions.
    (c) Structural mobility and exchange mobility are rare these days.
    (d) Social mobility occurs when there is a demand of a particular occupation.

▶▶ **Part III** Identify the sentence that least fits the context of the passage.

5. The first adult figured toy available to children in the United States was the Barbie doll. (a) It was created by Ruth Handler, the wife of a co-founder of the Mattel toy company, inspired by their daughter Barbara. (b) For the age of 3 to 7, playing role games with dolls is very helpful for kids to develop sociability. (c) As we all know, the Barbie doll became a great success; however, it always has been the source of a series of controversies. (d) For example, many people blame that the shape of the doll created an unrealistic body image that young adolescent girls have tried to emulate by losing weight.

정답: 210p

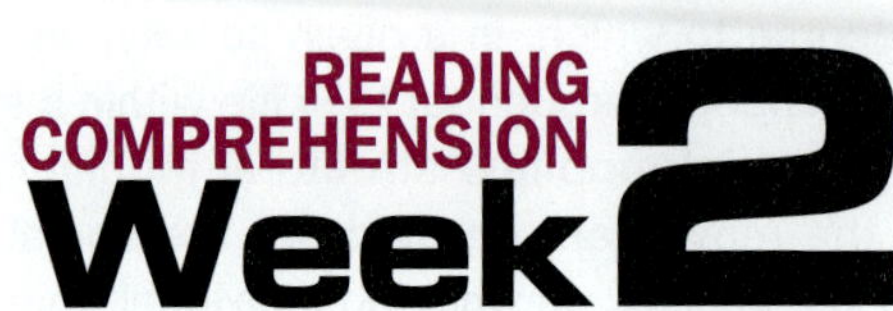

READING
COMPREHENSION
Week 2

Day 6 ▶▶ 역접

유형정리 – 〈TEPS RC 지문 흐름 파악〉 역접

Catch Up – Part 1 빈칸 채우기

Day 7 ▶▶ 예시

유형정리 – 〈TEPS RC 지문 흐름 파악〉 예시

Catch Up – Part 1 빈칸 채우기

Day 8 ▶▶ Part 1 주제 관련 빈칸 채우기

유형정리 – 〈TEPS RC 지문 파트별 패턴 파악〉 Part 1 주제 관련
빈칸 채우기

Catch Up – Part 2 추론

Day 9 ▶▶ Part 1 세부사항으로 빈칸 채우기

유형정리 – 〈TEPS RC 지문 파트별 패턴 파악〉 Part 1 세부사항으로
빈칸 채우기

Catch Up – Part 2 그 밖의 질문 유형

Day 10 ▶▶ Part 1 추론이 필요한 빈칸 채우기

유형정리 – 〈TEPS RC 지문 파트별 패턴 파악〉 Part 1 추론이 필요한
빈칸 채우기

Catch Up – Part 3

Day 6
역접

글의 흐름상 역접이 일어나는 경우, 역접의 접속사 however, yet, but, nevertheless 등의 뒤에는 그 앞쪽에 나온 내용과 정 반대의 내용이 이어지게 된다. 따라서, Part 1의 빈칸 채우기 문제에서 역접의 접속사 뒤에 빈칸이 있으면 그 앞의 내용과 반대가 되는 내용을 고르면 정답이 된다. 또, 처음 한두 문장이 전개된 뒤에 역접의 내용이 이어지면, 바로 그 역접이 일어난 부분이 그 지문에서 정말 중요한 부분이 된다. 즉, 역접을 이용하여 정말로 주목해야 할 부분을 더욱 강조하는 효과가 있는 것이다. 다음의 예시가 바로 이러한 경우를 볼 수 있는 지문이다.

Example

For many who lead today's busy lifestyle, breakfast may only be a luxury item on their grocery list. For others, cereal is the healthiest option in the morning. **However, while some breakfast cereals claim to be healthy from the outside, not all of them are.** Most breakfast cereals are made with processed sugars and refined white flour. Even with reduced sugar content, they are still high in simple carbohydrates. Therefore, they are not what they seem! That is why it is very important to check the ingredient contents. If it is not labeled as containing low sugar or made with whole grain, then it is probably not healthy for you.

Q. What is the main point of the passage?

(a) Most breakfast cereals are good for your health.
(b) Healthy people prefer processed sugars and refined white flour.
(c) Simple carbohydrates are healthier for you in the long run
(d) You should check carefully before you decide on a cereal.

첫 문장과 다음 문장에서, 아침식사를 하지 못하는 사람들에게 있어서는 씨리얼이 최선의 선택이라고 말하고 있는데, 이 부분은 글의 도입부일 뿐이다. 그 뒤의 However 뒤의 문장들에서는 그러나 사실상 씨리얼이 건강에 좋지 않을 수 있다는 내용이 이어지고 있다. 바로 이 부분이 이 지문의 논지이므로 우리가 주목하여 보아야 할 부분이다.

따라서 이 지문의 주제를 지문의 후반부에서 알 수 있으며, 이 문제의 정답은 '(d) 우리는 씨리얼을 선택하기 전에 잘 살펴보아야 한다.'가 되는 것이다.

역접의 접속사의 기능과 종류, 역접이 일어난 지문에서 어떤 부분을 주목하여야 하는지를 기억해두면 지문의 흐름을 논리적으로 파악하여 빠르고 정확하게 정답을 고르는 데 큰 도움이 된다.

해설: 116p

Catch Up

Part I Read the passage and choose the option that best fits the blank.

1. Thanks to the World Wide Web, _______________________________. In fact, the idiom "at one's fingertips" is very vivid in illustrating how so much knowledge is shared and available to anyone that is interested. The advantage of having such data and tools in an electronic format over the Internet is the fact that it is easily accessible and convenient. Individuals can access such websites and information from any part of the world provided they have a computer and an Internet connection.

   (a) it is possible to instantly send electronic mail anywhere
   (b) instant messaging has become a cultural phenomenon
   (c) the access to news and information has become readily available
   (d) people can stay in touch with one another regardless of distance

2. Anorexia is characterized by significant weight loss resulting from excessive dieting. Most women and an increasing number of men are motivated by the strong desire to be thin and a fear of becoming obese. Anorexics consider themselves to be fat, no matter what their actual weight is. Often anorexics do not recognize they are underweight and may still "feel fat" at 80 lbs. Anorexics close to death will show you on their bodies where they feel they need to lose weight. In their attempts to become even thinner, the anorexic _______________________________, which can result in death. An estimated 10 to 20 percent of these people will eventually die from complications related to anorexia.

   (a) will avoid food and taking in calories at all costs
   (b) would carefully adjust their daily caloric intake
   (c) could choose to eat food, and therefore calories
   (d) should maintain a bodyweight of around 80lbs

Answers

TEPS 독해 영역에 출제되었던 기출 문제를 자세한 설명과 함께 완전
히 이해하도록 하자.

1

Thanks to the World Wide Web, _______________________________. In fact, the idiom "at one's fingertips" is very vivid in illustrating how so much knowledge is shared and available to anyone that is interested. The advantage of having such data and tools in an electronic format over the Internet is the fact that it is easily accessible and convenient. Individuals can access such websites and information from any part of the world provided they have a computer and an Internet connection.

(a) it is possible to instantly send electronic mail anywhere
(b) instant messaging has become a cultural phenomenon
(c) the access to news and information has become readily available
(d) people can stay in touch with one another regardless of distance

해석 월드 와이드 웹 덕분에, 뉴스와 정보로의 접근은 즉시 이용 가능한 것이 되고 있다. 사실상, 관용어구인 '당장 이용할 수 있다'는 어떻게 많은 지식이 공유되고 관심 있는 사람에게 이용 가능하게 되는가를 매우 생생하게 묘사해주고 있다. 인터넷상에서 전자적인 형태로 그러한 데이터와 툴을 갖는 것의 장점은, 그것이 쉽게 접근 가능하고 편리하다는 데에 있다. 만약 개인이 컴퓨터와 인터넷 연결을 가지고 있다면, 그들은 세계 어떤 지역에서도 그러한 웹사이트와 정보에 접근할 수 있다.

해설 인터넷으로 인해 정보에 대한 접근이 더욱 용이해졌다는 내용의 지문이다. 빈칸이 지문의 제일 앞쪽에 있으므로 주제와 관련된 내용으로 빈칸을 채워야 한다. 따라서 정답은 (c)이다.

오답분석 (a) 어디에나 즉각적으로 전자우편을 보내는 것이 가능하다. – 이 지문이 말하고 있는 것은 전자우편에만 국한된 것이 아니라, 인터넷 전반에 대한 내용이다.
(b) 즉각적인 메시지는 문화적인 현상이 되어가고 있다. – 이 지문에서는 문화적 현상과 결부시켜 말하고 있지 않다.
(d) 사람들은 거리에 상관없이 다른 사람과 계속 연락할 수 있다. – 사람들간의 연락에 대한 내용은 언급되지 않았다.

어휘 **at one's fingertips** 즉시 이용할 수 있는, 곧 입수할 수 있는
accessible 접근하기 쉬운, 이용할 수 있는
convenient 편리한
phenomenon 현상

2

Anorexia is characterized by significant weight loss resulting from excessive dieting. Most women and an increasing number of men are motivated by the strong desire to be thin and a fear of becoming obese. Anorexics consider themselves to be fat, no matter what their actual weight is. Often anorexics do not recognize they are underweight and may still "feel fat" at 80 lbs. Anorexics close to death will show you on their bodies where they feel they need to lose weight. In their attempts to become even thinner, the anorexic _______________________________, which can result in death. An estimated 10 to 20 percent of these people will eventually die from complications related to anorexia.

(a) will avoid food and taking in calories at all costs
(b) would carefully adjust their daily caloric intake
(c) could choose to eat food, and therefore calories
(d) should maintain a bodyweight of around 80lbs

해석 거식증은 과도한 다이어트의 결과로 인한 눈에 띄는 체중의 감소로 특징지어진다. 대부분의 여성들과 점점 더 많은 수의 남성들은 날씬해지고자 하는 강한 열망과 비만이 되는 것에 대한 두려움으로 동기부여를 받는다. 거식증 환자들은 실제 체중이 얼마이든 간에 스스로가 뚱뚱하다고 여긴다. 때때로 거식증 환자들은 스스로가 체중 미달이라는 것을 깨닫지 못하고 80파운드의 체중에서도 '여전히 뚱뚱한' 것 같다고 생각한다. 너무 마른 거식증 환자들도 자신들이 살을 빼야 한다고 느끼는 신체 부위를 보여줄 것이다. 더 마르게 되려는 시도에서, 거식증 환자들은 어떤 대가를 치르고서라도 음식과 칼로리를 섭취하기를 피할 것이며, 이것은 죽음을 야기할 수도 있다. 이들 중10~20퍼센트는 이것에 관련된 합병증으로 죽게 될 것이라고 추정된다.

해설 anorexia라는 단어를 몰라도, 날씬해지고자 한다는 것과 체중 미달인데도 살을 빼야 한다고 믿는 것으로 보아 거식증에 대한 내용임을 유추할 수 있어야 한다. 따라서 정답은 (a)이다.

분섭 (b) 매일 매일의 칼로리 섭취를 조심스레 조정할 것이다. – 빈칸 뒤에서 죽음에 이를 수도 있다고 하였으므로 문맥상 맞지 않다.
(c) 음식을 먹음으로써 칼로리를 섭취할 것이다. – 더 마르게 되려고 한다고 했다.
(d) 80파운드 정도의 체중을 유지해야 한다. – 적정 체중을 말하는 것이 아니라 거식증 환자의 체중이 80파운드 정도라고 하였으므로 틀리다.

어휘 **anorexia** 식욕 감퇴, 거식증
anorexic 신경성 무식욕증 환자
lbs 1파운드 (= 1 pound = 453그램)
at all costs 기어코, 어떠한 희생·대가를 치르더라도

Answers:

1. (c) 2. (a)

 # Build Up 

▶▶ **Part I** Read the passage and choose the option that best fits the blank.

1. Many massage therapists are lobbying the government and strongly urging it to intervene in their industry. Various scandals and the increasing number of malpractice lawsuits have forced thousands of massage therapists to close their businesses. The concerned individuals are seeking for government assistance under the argument that their means for a livelihood has been taken away. As politicians at all levels agree that these massage therapists are in dire need of assistance, new legislation is expected to _______________________.

   (a) provide financial aid and other grants
   (b) close down any remaining businesses
   (c) suggest some massage therapy for relief
   (d) reform the universal health care system

2. A problem that usually affects colleges and universities is the issue of academic dishonesty. Numerous surveys indicate that approximately 50% of students have cheated in some manner during their stint at a post-secondary institution. Furthermore, results also suggested that the most common forms of academic dishonesty were plagiarism on written assignments, cheating during exams, and falsifying information. To discourage such practices, colleges and universities will often resort to severe, disciplinary actions. In fact, if a student is found guilty of academic dishonesty, the individual _______________________.

   (a) can be sentenced to a term in prison
   (b) has his parents notified of the incident
   (c) will be often suspended or even expelled
   (d) required to attend counseling sessions

3. The advertising industry's conduct, especially with respect to the targeting of children with junk food commercials, was thrown into sharp focus today by a report commissioned by congress which said that current food company marketing techniques were leading to a dramatic increase in childhood obesity and diabetes. The report was prepared by the Institute of Medicine, which also called on food manufacturers directly to produce and promote more healthy food than they do at present. They further pressed for congress to mandate a 2 year period during which food producing companies would be forced to comply or be barred from advertising via the media, particularly broadcast and cable TV.

   Q. What is the passage about?

      (a) Children's habit of watching too much television
      (b) The frequency of food advertisements on children's television
      (c) The detrimental effect of junk food advertising on children
      (d) Food advertisers taking steps toward self-regulation

4. Clement Marot is one of the most important figures in French poetry in the sixteenth century. He published intimate poetry, often in the forms of the ballade and the rondeau about his own mind, feelings, and habits. During the Renaissance, he mostly wrote about his love for Marguerite d'Angouleme, the king's sister, while later on in his life, he wrote about the horrors of war. In Flanders, he expressed his disgust for man's pursuit of power and his own attempt to detach himself from worldly things. However, the true genius of Marot is that in describing himself, he described all people.

   Q. What can be inferred about Marot according to the passage?

      (a) His emotional detachment kept him from pursuing power in the literary court.
      (b) His personal writings accurately portrayed the sentiment of war at the time.
      (c) He used self criticism as a means of critiquing humanity.
      (d) He ingeniously detailed common people's everyday lives during the Renaissance.

▶▶ **Part III** Identify the sentence that least fits the context of the passage.

5. Fermented drinks, also known as alcoholic beverages, are popular all over the world. (a) Most cultures have different methods of producing such drinks. (b) Chinese people make fermented drinks by mixing rice, honey and fruits, while those in the Middle East mix barley beer and grape wine. (c) These types of alcoholic beverages are not only fragrant but also nutritious for the body, but can be detrimental to the health if consumed in large amounts. (d) Storing alcohol drinks in bottles has always been the very best way to keep them from degenerating in quality.

정답: 212p

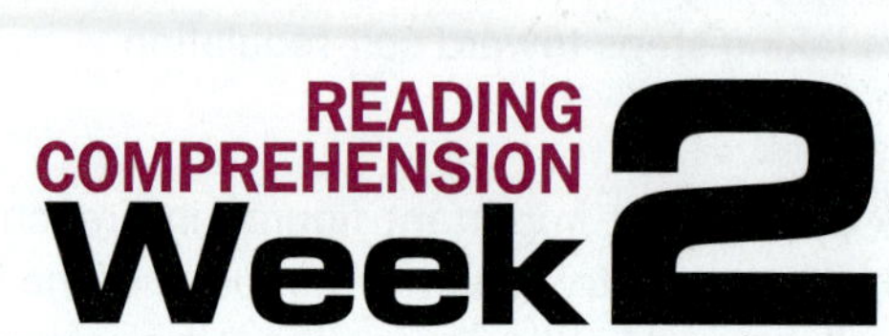
READING
COMPREHENSION
Week 2

Day 6

▶▶ 역접

유형정리 – 〈TEPS RC 지문 흐름 파악〉 역접

Catch Up – Part 1 빈칸 채우기

Day 7

▶▶ 예시

유형정리 – 〈TEPS RC 지문 흐름 파악〉 예시

Catch Up – Part 1 빈칸 채우기

Day 8

▶▶ Part 1 주제 관련 빈칸 채우기

유형정리 – 〈TEPS RC 지문 파트별 패턴 파악〉 Part 1 주제 관련
빈칸 채우기

Catch Up – Part 2 추론

Day 9

▶▶ Part 1 세부사항으로 빈칸 채우기

유형정리 – 〈TEPS RC 지문 파트별 패턴 파악〉 Part 1 세부사항으로
빈칸 채우기

Catch Up – Part 2 그 밖의 질문 유형

Day 10

▶▶ Part 1 추론이 필요한 빈칸 채우기

유형정리 – 〈TEPS RC 지문 파트별 패턴 파악〉 Part 1 추론이 필요한
빈칸 채우기

Catch Up – Part 3

Day 7
예시

예시는 글의 주제를 더욱 강화시키고 읽는 사람들로 하여금 쉽게 이해하도록 할 수 있다. 다소 어려운 주제를 다루고 있는 지문에서도 다양하고 구체적인 사례를 보여줌으로써 이해를 도울 수 있으며, 모호한 개념을 더욱 확실하게 알 수 있도록 한다.

따라서 TEPS 독해 지문에서 예시가 사용된 지문은 비교적 쉽게 이해할 수 있으며, Part 2의 주제를 고르는 유형의 문제에서는 지문을 끝까지 읽지 않고도 정답을 고를 수 있다. 또한, Part 1의 문제들에서는 예시들을 읽고 지문의 주제를 파악하여 정답을 고르거나 비슷한 예가 이어지는 것으로 정답을 고를 수 있어, 정답을 맞추는 데 큰 단서가 된다. 단, Part 2의 세부사항 확인 문제 유형 (Which is correct ~?)에서는 여러 예시들을 기억하고 있어야 하므로 체크하며 읽는 연습을 해야 한다.

다음의 예시와 같이 Part 3에서도 예시는 정답을 고르는 단서가 된다.

Example

There exists a certain type of flower suitable to every holiday, event and special occasion. (a) For example, soldiers that took part during World War II are commemorated by showy, red flowers called poppies. (b) Another type of red flower commonly used during the Christmas season is the poinsettia, while irises and lilies act as symbols of resurrection and life at burial sites. (c) An abundance of people proclaim roses to be the queen of all flowers due to its prickly thorns coupled with a strong heady scent. (d) During romantic occasions such as Valentine's Day, engagements, weddings and the like, roses are used as presents as a token of love.

첫 문장이 주제문으로, 각각의 명절이나 특별한 행사에 어울리는 꽃이 있다고 언급하고 있으며, 그 뒤로 이어지는 문장들은 이 주제문에 대한 예시들이다. 그런데 (c)의 queen of all flowers는 '꽃들의 여왕'이라는 어구이므로 특정한 날에 어울리는 꽃의 종류를 말하고 있지 않다는 것을 알 수 있으며, 따라서 이 지문에서 흐름에 어긋나는 문장으로 정답이 된다. 이와 같이 예시는 지문의 논지와 주제를 쉽게 파악하는 데 도움이 되며, 정답을 찾는 단서가 되므로 다소 어려운 지문에서도 예시를 잘 파악하면 지문 전체의 내용에 대해 감을 잡는 데 도움이 된다. 예시가 나오는 부분은 항상 표시하며 읽는 습관을 들이자.

해설: 222p

Catch Up

Part I Read the passage and choose the option that best fits the blank.

1. A common mistake people make is thinking that cults are purely religious groups. The modern definition of a "mind controlling cult" refers to all groups that use mind control and devious recruiting techniques that are invariably exposed. In a free society people can have faith in what they want, and most people would agree that it is wrong for anyone to try to trick and control others. Cults have millions of members around the world who once thought themselves immune, and still don't know they are in a cult. _______________, it's important to beware of assuming that you are immune from cult involvement.

   (a) In addition
   (b) Therefore
   (c) On the whole
   (d) In short

2. For the last few centuries, the overall climate of the world has been gradually becoming warmer. This is due to global warming which is the effect of the following: orbit of the earth around the sun, volcano eruptions and the concentration of greenhouse gases. Since the beginning of the 20th century, it has been observed that large glaciers have been melting at speeds greater than average. For example, the Muir Glacier in Alaska has contracted by two miles within the past ten years. _____________, the agricultural crop line in Canada has been shifting northward by approximately 10 to 50 miles. Moreover, trees such as birches and spruces have been withering in Eastern Canada due to the increase in temperature.

   (a) As a result
   (b) Nevertheless
   (c) Otherwise
   (d) On the contrary

Answers 

1

A common mistake people make is thinking that cults are purely religious groups. The modern definition of a "mind controlling cult" refers to all groups that use mind control and devious recruiting techniques that are invariably exposed. In a free society people can have faith in what they want, and most people would agree that it is wrong for anyone to try to trick and control others. Cults have millions of members around the world who once thought themselves immune, and still don't know they are in a cult. ____________, it's important to beware of assuming that you are immune from cult involvement.

(a) In addition
(b) Therefore
(c) On the whole
(d) In short

해석 사람들이 저지르는 흔한 실수는 신흥 종교들이 순수하게 종교적인 그룹이라는 생각이다. 현대적 정의로 '마음을 지배하는 신흥 종교'는 마음을 지배하는 기술을 사용하고, 늘 노출되게 마련인 새로운 신도를 모으는 데 빗나간 기술을 사용하는 모든 그룹을 지칭한다. 자유 사회에서 사람들은 자신이 원하는 것에 믿음을 가질 수 있으며, 누구든 다른 사람들을 속이고 지배하려는 것은 옳지 않다는 것에 동의할 것이다. 신흥 종교들에는 전 세계에 한때 자신들은 안전하다고 생각했고 여전히 신흥 종교에 속해 있음을 알지 못하는 몇 백만 명의 신도들이 있다. 그러므로, 신흥 종교에 연관되는 것으로부터 안전하다고 생각하는 것을 조심하는 것이 매우 중요하다.

해설 빈칸 바로 앞의 문장이 답을 고를 수 있는 직접적인 단서이다. 신흥 종교에 연관되는 것으로부터 안전하다고 생각하는 것을 조심해야 한다는 데에 대한 이유가 바로 앞 문장의 내용이므로, 두 문장을 적절히 이어주는 것은 (b) Therefore이다.

오답 분석
(a) 게다가 – 앞의 내용에 다른 내용을 추가할 때 쓴다.
(c) 전반적으로 볼 때 – 전반적인 상황을 정리할 때 쓴다.
(d) 간단히 말하면 – 앞의 내용을 종합, 정리할 때 쓴다.

어휘
cult (열광적) 신흥 종교
devious 빗나간
invariably 변함없이, 늘
immune 면제된, 면역이 있는

2

For the last few centuries, the overall climate of the world has been gradually becoming warmer. This is due to global warming which is the effect of the following: orbit of the earth around the sun, volcano eruptions and the concentration of greenhouse gases. Since the beginning of the 20th century, it has been observed that large glaciers have been melting at speeds greater than average. For example, the Muir Glacier in Alaska has contracted by two miles within the past ten years. _______________, the agricultural crop line in Canada has been shifting northward by approximately 10 to 50 miles. Moreover, trees such as birches and spruces have been withering in Eastern Canada due to the increase in temperature.

(a) As a result
(b) Nevertheless
(c) Otherwise
(d) On the contrary

해석 최근 1~2세기 동안, 세계의 전반적인 기후는 점차 따뜻해져왔다. 이것은 뒤에 나열된 것들의 결과인 지구 온난화 때문이다. 태양 주위를 돌 수밖에 없는 지구의 궤도, 화산 폭발, 그리고 온난화를 일으키는 가스들의 집중들이 그것이다. 20세기가 시작된 이래로, 거대한 빙하가 평균보다 빠른 속도로 녹고 있는 것이 관찰되어왔다. 예를 들어, 알래스카에 있는 Muir 빙하는 과거 10년 동안 2마일이나 줄어들었다. 그 결과, 캐나다의 농업 경계선은 북쪽으로 대략 10~50마일이나 이동해갔다. 게다가 자작나무와 전나무 같은 나무들은 온도의 상승 때문에 동부 캐나다에서 시들어가는 중이다.

해설 빈칸 앞의 문장에서 빙하가 줄어든다고 하였고, 캐나다 농업경계선이 북쪽으로 이동해 갔다고 하였으므로 인과관계임을 알 수 있다. 따라서 정답은 '(a) As a result – 그 결과'이다.

오답 분석　(b) 그럼에도 불구하고 – 앞의 내용으로부터 야기되는 결과로, 관련성이 없는 내용을 연출할때 쓴다.
(c) 그렇지 않으면 – 앞의 내용에 반대의 경우를 가정할 때 쓴다.
(d) 반면에 – 앞의 내용과 상반되는 내용을 연결한다.

어휘　**overall** 총체적인, 전반적인
orbit 궤도
eruption 폭발
approximately 대략
wither 시들다, 말라 빠지다

Answers:

1. (b)　2. (a)

Build Up

TEPS 독해 영역의 실전 문제와 가장 가까운 유형과 난이도의 예상 문제를 통해 실력을 쌓자.

Part I Read the passage and choose the option that best fits the blank.

1. The first branch of the Ku Klux Klan was established in Pulaski, Tennessee, in May, 1866. A year later a general organization of local Klans was established in Nashville in April, 1867. Most of the leaders were former members of the Confederate Army and the first Grand Wizard was Nathan Forrest, an outstanding general during the American Civil War. During the next two years Klansmen wearing masks, white cardboard hats and draped in white sheets, tortured and killed black Americans and sympathetic whites. Immigrants, who they blamed for the election of radical republicans, were also targets of their hatred. Between 1868 and 1870 the Ku Klux Klan _______________________________ in North Carolina, Tennessee and Georgia.

   (a) assisted in federal efforts toward desegregation
   (b) played an important role in restoring white rule
   (c) encouraged members of the public toward pragmatism
   (d) helped senior black citizens file for federal aid packages

Part II Choose the option that correctly answers the question.

2. Since the development of guns, a weapon which could deliver a continuous stream of fire was a highly attractive concept to gun manufacturers. Early designs basically copied the stationary gun, so a single trigger would provide the flash to ignite several barrels of a weapon at once. Whilst effective, the obvious drawback of the early devices was the prolonged loading and reloading, so alternatives were actively pursued. The first true machine-gun was invented by a dentist from North Carolina named Richard Gatling. His "Gatling Gun" revolutionized killing efficiency by delivering up to six hundred shots in two minutes. The key to his invention was the rotating 6-barrel cylinder.

   Q. What is the main idea of the passage?

   (a) Modern weapons are based on Richard Gatling's machine gun designs.
   (b) Early attempts at machine guns were ineffective.
   (c) Continuous fire is the key to killing efficiency.
   (d) The evolution of the machine gun hinged on Gatling's rotating barrel.

3. A trend that could be harmful to personal relationships and American society has been identified in a comprehensive new study by psychologists that showed that self-centeredness among today's students is on the rise. Researchers at San Diego State University assert that kids are already selfish enough, and to avoid having them grow into self-obsessed adults we need to stop endlessly telling children 'You're special' and having them repeat it back. The study measured people's level of narcissism and cited the responses of 16,475 college students nationwide. The results spanned the period from 1982 to 2006 and showed a distinct rise in narcissistic tendencies among the participants.

Q. Which of the following is correct according to the passage?

(a) The author is fully satisfied with parents' attitudes to their children.
(b) Parents have become better informed than in the past.
(c) Children should not exclusively receive positive reinforcement.
(d) The author defines the relationship between the self-centered parents and child.

4. Welcome to PLAN 101- Introduction to Urban Planning. In this course, we'll examine the history of urban planning by looking at early theories and practice since Rome. We will discuss planning theories that have stood the test of time and those that haven't, including the ones that failed to recognize the human need of 'sense of place.' We will also delve into pioneering architectural designs so as to have a complete understanding of how urban planning has developed into what it is today.

Q. What can be inferred from the notice?

(a) The professor disagrees with modern planning practice.
(b) Most of the lecture will focus on examples of bad planning.
(c) The objective of the class is to have an all-rounded understanding about urban planning
(d) None of the theory that will be studied in the class is fit for today's circumstances.

▶▶ Part III Identify the sentence that least fits the context of the passage.

5. If you're tired of the old dusty air, give your home the mountain fresh, clean air. (a) Air filters are a great addition to any household as they are able to cleanse the air of any bacteria, dust, pollen or mold. (b) Air conditioners and heaters also consist of air filters and help to keep the air fresh while dispensing that much needed cool or warm air. (c) Air fresheners are often used by people to hide foul odors in enclosed spaces. (d) Keeping air filters clean is a key to avoiding expensive maintenance bills and get clear air at the same time.

정답: 214p

READING
COMPREHENSION
Week 2

Day 6	▶▶ 역접
	유형정리 – 〈TEPS RC 지문 흐름 파악〉 역접
	Catch Up – Part 1 빈칸 채우기

Day 7	▶▶ 예시
	유형정리 – 〈TEPS RC 지문 흐름 파악〉 예시
	Catch Up – Part 1 빈칸 채우기

Day 8	▶▶ Part 1 주제 관련 빈칸 채우기
	유형정리 – 〈TEPS RC 지문 파트별 패턴 파악〉 Part 1 주제 관련 빈칸 채우기
	Catch Up – Part 2 추론

Day 9	▶▶ Part 1 세부사항으로 빈칸 채우기
	유형정리 – 〈TEPS RC 지문 파트별 패턴 파악〉 Part 1 세부사항으로 빈칸 채우기
	Catch Up – Part 2 그 밖의 질문 유형

Day 10	▶▶ Part 1 추론이 필요한 빈칸 채우기
	유형정리 – 〈TEPS RC 지문 파트별 패턴 파악〉 Part 1 추론이 필요한 빈칸 채우기
	Catch Up – Part 3

Day 8

Part 1 주제 관련 빈칸 채우기

TEPS 독해 영역의 1번에서 16번까지의 문제는 지문의 빈칸을 알맞은 보기로 채우는 빈칸 채우기 문제이다. 그 중에서도 빈칸이 지문의 제일 앞쪽이나 제일 뒤쪽에 있는 경우는 주제와 관련된 보기가 정답이 되는 경우가 많다. 영어는 두괄식이므로 지문의 제일 앞에 빈칸이 있는 문제는 곧 주제문에 빈칸이 있는 문제일 경우가 많으며, 지문의 제일 마지막 문장은 지문을 마무리하는 부분이기 때문에 주제와 관련된 언급으로 끝맺음을 하는 경우가 많기 때문이다.

Example

Thanks to the World Wide Web, ________________________________. In fact, the idiom "at one's fingertips" is very vivid in illustrating how so much knowledge is shared and available to anyone that is interested. The advantage of having such data and tools in an electronic format over the Internet is the fact that it is easily accessible and convenient. Individuals can access such websites and information from any part of the world provided they have a computer and an Internet connection.

(a) it is possible to instantly send electronic mail anywhere
(b) instant messaging has become a cultural phenomenon
(c) the access to news and information has become readily available
(d) people can stay in touch with one another regardless of distance

위의 예시는 지문의 제일 첫 문장에 빈칸이 있는 경우이다. 뒤에 이어지는 문장들에서 인터넷을 통해 정보에 쉽게 접근할 수 있다는 내용이 전개되고 있으며, 하이라이트 표시가 된 부분들이 정답이 되는 직접적인 단서들이다. 따라서 이 글의 주제이자 정답은 곧 '(c) 뉴스와 정보에 대해 즉시 접근할 수 있게 되었다'가 된다.

해설: 60p

Catch Up

Part II Choose the option that correctly answers the question.

1. Children acquire the basic social skills for life from parents and caregivers during their early stages of development. As they mature, they experience other emotional, social and cognitive encounters that are more difficult to negotiate. But the social rules that children learned through their initial interactions with adults become irrevelant as they form more multi-faceted relations with their peers. Consequently, young children often feel awkward and incompetent associating with children of their age. They would much rather affiliate with adults.

   Q. What can be inferred from the passage?

     (a) Children gain social security from peer relationships.
     (b) Children with siblings are better at adapting to new social situations.
     (c) Children who do not interact well with their parents tend to experience social withdrawal.
     (d) Children who are extroverted are more quickly accepted into social groups.

2. With the recently gathered public opinion, the city counsel has come to a final decision that the metal band GCC not be allowed to perform at any venue within city limits. The counsel recognizes that the band has had prior incidents with violence in other towns. Due to many safety concerns, the city feels that it should not take liability for any kind of problems that may occur. Furthermore, we should adhere to this position to avoid setting any precedent that will adversely affect the city in the future.

   Q. What can be inferred from the counsel's announcement?

     (a) The city has a history of legal problems with GCC.
     (b) The band, GCC, may put on a concert in the city at a later date.
     (c) The counsel is attentive to the cultural needs of citizens.
     (d) Other controversial bands will also be assessed by the counsel.

TEPS 독해 영역에 출제되었던 기출 문제를 자세한 설명과 함께 완전히 이해하도록 하자.

1

> Children acquire the basic social skills for life from parents and caregivers during their early stages of development. As they mature, they experience other emotional, social and cognitive encounters that are more difficult to negotiate. But the social rules that children learned through their initial interactions with adults become irrevelant as they form more multi-faceted relations with their peers. Consequently, young children often feel awkward and incompetent associating with children of their age. They would much rather affiliate with adults.
>
> **Q. What could be inferred from the lecture?**
>
> (a) Children gain social security from peer relationships.
> (b) Children with siblings are better at adapting to new social situations.
> (c) Children who do not interact well with their parents tend to experience social withdrawal.
> (d) Children who are extroverted are more quickly accepted into social groups.

해석 아이들은 발달 초기단계에서 부모님이나 돌봐주는 사람으로부터 삶에 대한 기본적인 사회적 기술을 얻는다. 그들이 성숙해져 갈 때, 그들은 처리하기에 좀 더 어려운 다른 감정적, 사회적, 인식적 측면들을 마주치게 된다. 그러나 아이들이 동년배들과 더 다방면에 걸친 관계를 형성해갈 때, 어른들과의 초기 상호작용을 통해 배웠던 사회적 규칙들은 존재하지 않는 것이 된다. 결과적으로, 어린 아이들은 종종 그들 또래의 아이들과 교제하는 중에 어색함과 무능함을 느낀다. 그들은 차라리 어른들과 교제하려 할 것이다.

해설 어른들과의 상호작용에서 배운 사회적 기술이 동년배들과 어울릴 때 별로 도움이 되지 않을 수 있다는 내용의 글이다. 따라서 또래들과 어울려본 아이들이 다른 또래들과 상호작용을 더 잘 할 것이므로 '(b) 형제, 자매가 있는 아이들이 새로운 사회적 상황에 더 잘 적응한다'를 유추할 수 있다.

오답 분석
(a) 아이들은 동년배와의 관계로부터 사회적인 안심을 얻는다. – 사회적 안심에 대해서는 지문에 언급된 바 없다.
(c) 그들의 부모와 상호작용을 잘 못한 아이들은 사회적으로 움츠려드는 경향이 있다. – 부모와 상호작용을 잘하면 사회적 관계에서 성공한다는 내용이 아니므로 정답이 될 수 없다.
(d) 외향적인 아이들은 좀 더 빠르게 사회 그룹에서 받아들여진다. – 사회적 작용의 조건으로 아이들의 외향성은 언급되지 않았다.

어휘
caregiver 돌보는 사람
cognitive 인식의
encounter 우연히 마주치다; 마주침
peer 동년배
awkward 어색한, 서투른
affiliate 교제하다, 친분을 맺다
incompetent 무능한
extroverted 외향적인

With the recently gathered public opinion, the city counsel has come to a final decision that the metal band GCC not be allowed to perform at any venue within city limits. The counsel recognizes that the band has had prior incidents with violence in other towns. Due to many safety concerns, the city feels that it should not take liability for any kind of problems that may occur. Furthermore, we should adhere to this position to avoid setting any precedent that will adversely affect the city in the future.

Q. What can be inferred from the counsel's announcement?

(a) The city has a history of legal problems with GCC.
(b) The band, GCC, may put on a concert in the city at a later date.
(c) The counsel is attentive to the cultural needs of citizens.
(d) Other controversial bands will also be assessed by the counsel.

해석 최근에 모인 여론과 함께, 도시 위원회는 메탈밴드인 GCC가 도시 안의 어떤 곳에서도 활동할 수 있도록 허용하지 않겠다는 마지막 결정을 내렸다. 도시 위원회는 그 밴드가 다른 마을에서 이전에 폭력과 연관된 사건들을 발생시켰다는 것을 알았다. 많은 안전에 대한 우려 때문에, 시는 발생할지도 모르는 어떤 종류의 문제들에 대한 책임을 질 수 없다고 생각한다. 나아가, 우리는 차후에 도시에 나쁘게 영향을 줄 어떤 선례가 자리 잡는 것을 피하기 위해 이러한 입장을 지켜야 한다.

해설 문제가 일어날 수 있기 때문에 GCC 밴드의 활동을 제한하겠다고 입장을 밝히며, 앞으로 이러한 입장을 지킬 것이라고 하였다. 따라서 시에 문제를 일으킬 소지가 있는 밴드의 방문을 허락하지 않을 것이라는 입장을 알 수 있으므로 '(d) 논쟁의 여지가 많은 다른 밴드 또한 법률 고문에 의해 평가될 것이다.'가 정답이 된다.

오답
분석 (a) 이 도시는 GCC에 대한 법률적인 문제점들의 역사를 가지고 있다. – 법률적 문제점은 언급되지 않았다.
(b) GCC는 아마도 나중에 도시에서 콘서트를 열 것이다. – 콘서트에 대한 계획은 언급되지 않았다.
(c) 도시 위원회는 시민들의 문화적 필요를 경청한다. – 이 지문의 내용으로는 알 수 없다.

어휘 **counsel** 법률고문, (행동의) 계획, 방침, 조언, 권고
venue 재판지, 행위의 현장, 발생지
liability 책임 있음, 책임, 불리한 일
precedent 전례, 종래의 관례
adversely 반대로, 적대적으로

Answers:

1. (b) 2. (d)

Build Up

TEPS 독해 영역의 실전 문제와 가장 가까운 유형과 난이도의 예상 문제를 통해 실력을 쌓자.

▶▶ **Part I** Read the passage and choose the option that best fits the blank.

1. The Australian Prime Minister, John Howard, has repelled pressure to apologize to aborigines for the dispossession of their land or to agree to reparations for the "stolen generations" of black children removed from their families in the 1940s and 1950s. Last year, more than 150,000 people marched across Sydney Harbor Bridge calling for reconciliation. The march was followed by a National Sorry Day during which white people signed books of atonement. Though Mr. Howard didn't participate in these movements, he _______________________________.

   (a) looked closely at apologizing process
   (b) apologized for the "hurt" of not apologizing
   (c) began to take a keen interest in the Sydney Harbor Bridge
   (d) apologized for previously having made an apology

▶▶ **Part II** Choose the option that correctly answers the question.

2. In today's day and age, far too many adolescents seem to take things for granted. Many of these young adults have no appreciation or even an idea of the work that is required to provide basic needs such as food and shelter. Since many of them have never had to grow crops or raise their own livestock for sustenance, this notion can be an unfamiliar one to them. Due to an utter and total dependence on technology in today's modern world, few adolescents can make the connection between production and consumption. Taking these facts into consideration, it would be wise to encourage students to participate in work seminars that examine the importance of work in their lives. Doing so would undoubtedly give them a better appreciation for all the products and services that are easily available to them.

   Q. What is the main idea of this passage?

   (a) The attitudes of today's young people are satisfactory.
   (b) Teenagers are better informed today than they were in the past.
   (c) Teenagers today should be more aware of the nature of work.
   (d) The relationship between production and technology should be taught at school.

3. The assumption that birds are the descendants of dinosaurs runs into a roadblock in the form of blood. Whilst it is widely believed that dinosaurs belonged to the reptile species and so were cold-blooded, therein lies the problem; birds are without dispute warm-blooded. This has led to a rethinking of whether dinosaurs were indeed cold-blooded or not. It has been suggested that they may have retained body heat, and therefore controlled their blood temperature because most dinosaurs had a distinctly upright posture, unlike modern reptiles like the crocodile which sprawl on the ground in order to absorb heat.

Q. Which of the following is correct about the passage?

(a) Dinosaurs' blood temperatures change very quickly.
(b) Most people believe dinosaurs were cold-blooded reptiles.
(c) Dinosaurs and birds share the same blood type.
(d) Crocodiles don't share any traits with upright dinosaurs.

4. *Faust: A Tragedy* is the title given for the masterpiece by Johann Wolfgang Von Goethe. Yet, many consider the play a musical comedy, in that it features many comic passages, songs, and lacks a tragic ending. The play's hero, Faust, is not a classic tragic figure either. The fact that he gains spiritual salvation after death has made it difficult for some people to regard it as tragic. In fact, his characteristic yearning for "divine knowledge" created a type for the romantic age still known as the Faustian hero.

Q. What can be inferred from the passage?

(a) We may think Goethe's Faust is somewhat contradictory.
(b) Faust concludes that one should strive to attain divine knowledge.
(c) We can explore the intellect of Goethe through Faust.
(d) Goethe's Faust emphasizes that life is tragic.

▶▶ **Part III** Identify the sentence that least fits the context of the passage.

5. If you are interested in experiencing foreign culture and want to earn money needed to finance your sojourn at the same time, then perhaps imparting your knowledge of the English language overseas would be apt for you. (a) Copious English-teaching positions are available all around the world, especially in China, Korea, Japan and Taiwan. (b) In order to take advantage of this once in a lifetime opportunity, all you need is parental permission and a high school diploma. (c) Couples that embark on a journey to work in a foreign country together more easily adapt to the chosen country than people who arrive at their destination alone. (d) Also, they are less prone to the severity of culture shock as the relationship itself acts partially as a "shock absorber."

정답: 217p

READING
COMPREHENSION
Week 2

Day 6	▸▸ 역접
	유형정리 – 〈TEPS RC 지문 흐름 파악〉 역접
	Catch Up – Part 1 빈칸 채우기

Day 7	▸▸ 예시
	유형정리 – 〈TEPS RC 지문 흐름 파악〉 예시
	Catch Up – Part 1 빈칸 채우기

Day 8	▸▸ Part 1 주제 관련 빈칸 채우기
	유형정리 – 〈TEPS RC 지문 파트별 패턴 파악〉 Part 1 주제 관련 빈칸 채우기
	Catch Up – Part 2 추론

Day 9	▸▸ Part 1 세부사항으로 빈칸 채우기
	유형정리 – 〈TEPS RC 지문 파트별 패턴 파악〉 Part 1 세부사항으로 빈칸 채우기
	Catch Up – Part 2 그 밖의 질문 유형

Day 10	▸▸ Part 1 추론이 필요한 빈칸 채우기
	유형정리 – 〈TEPS RC 지문 파트별 패턴 파악〉 Part 1 추론이 필요한 빈칸 채우기
	Catch Up – Part 3

Day 9

Part 1 세부사항으로 빈칸 채우기

▶▶ 지문의 가운데 부분에 빈칸이 있는 경우는 세부적인 사항으로 빈칸을 채워야 하는 문제일 경우가 많다. 세부사항으로 빈칸을 채우려면 앞과 뒤의 문맥에 잘 맞는 보기를 골라야 하므로 주제와 관련된 빈칸 채우기 문제보다 시간이 좀 더 걸리거나 난이도가 높다고 여겨질 수 있다. 그러나 지문의 가운데 부분에 빈칸이 있는 경우, 바로 앞 문장이나 바로 뒷문장에서 정답이 되는 정확한 단서를 찾을 수 있으므로 연습을 충분히 한다면 정답률을 높일 수 있다.

Example

Choosing a web host is one of the most important decisions facing every person who wishes to have their own web site for personal or business use. You need to look at price and dependability, keeping in mind the web host is someone you pay a fee to and in return he or she provides you with much space on their server in which to reliably store the files that make up your web site. ____________________ because you want to make sure you go with a web host that provides enough server space for you to grow your business at the rate you want.

(a) Stability is the most essential
(b) 3-dimensional graphics technology is a requisite
(c) Business expansion can be achieved
(d) Speed and support are also important

위의 예시에서 정답을 고르는 단서가 되는 부분은 빈칸 바로 뒷부분이다. 특히 이 문제에서는 '왜냐하면'으로 시작하고 있기 때문에 더욱 쉽게 정답을 고를 수 있다. 하이라이트 표시가 된 부분들에서 '충분한 서버 공간'과 '당신이 원하는 속도에 맞춰서'라고 언급되고 있으므로 정답은 '(d) 속도와 지원 또한 중요하다'임을 알 수 있다.

해설: 229p

Catch Up

Part II Choose the option that correctly answers the question.

1. The 17th annual Desmond G. Smith Honorary Service Award was once again held in the McArthur Auditorium of Johnson Hall. The recipient of this year's award was Fred Allison, a renowned philosophy professor. As it is customary for this honor, Allison also gave a lecture, titled "The Meaning of True Happiness," focused on people's never-ending quest to find true happiness. Allison began by addressing the fact that the struggle for material wealth, social status and interpersonal relationships is not necessarily linked to happiness. The reality of true happiness, Allison suggest, is acquired through self-realization and self-satisfaction.

   Q. What is the purpose of the passage?

   (a) To introduce a renowned philosophy scholar
   (b) To summarize a lecture that accompanied an award
   (c) To advertise an upcoming lecture by a philosopher
   (d) To state the current research trend in philosophy

2. Communicating positively with your children will not only build their self-esteem and inspire confidence but will also reinforce the good and eliminate the bad behavior. And it's easy once you get the hang of it. All children need to feel loved and accepted, and you can communicate those feelings with your children by the way you speak. The sense of positive self-esteem they learn through their interactions at home will then spill over as your children communicate in the outside world. Positive reinforcement will also help them immensely as they begin school when the self-esteem boost they have gained from home really starts to pay off.

   Q. How does the writer feel about positive reinforcement?

   (a) Enthusiastic
   (b) Apprehensive
   (c) Sensitive
   (d) Unapologetic

TEPS 독해 영역에 출제되었던 기출 문제를 자세한 설명과 함께 완전히 이해하도록 하자.

1

The 17th annual Desmond G. Smith Honorary Service Award was once again held in the McArthur Auditorium of Johnson Hall. The recipient of this year's award was Fred Allison, a renowned philosophy professor. As it is customary for this honor, Allison also gave a lecture, titled "The Meaning of True Happiness," focused on people's never-ending quest to find true happiness. Allison began by addressing the fact that the struggle for material wealth, social status and interpersonal relationships is not necessarily linked to happiness. The reality of true happiness, Allison suggest, is acquired through self-realization and self-satisfaction.

Q. What is the purpose of the passage?

(a) To introduce a renowned philosophy scholar
(b) To summarize a lecture that accompanied an award
(c) To advertise an upcoming lecture by a philosopher
(d) To state the current research trend in philosophy

해석 제17회 Desmond G. Smith 기념상이 존스 홀의 맥아더 기념관에서 다시 개최되었다. 올해의 수상자는 저명한 철학교수 Fred Allison이다. 이 영예에 대한 관행으로 Allison은 강연을 하였는데, 진정한 행복을 찾기 위한 사람들의 끝없는 추구에 초점을 맞춘 '진정한 행복의 의미'라는 제목의 강연이다. Allison은 물질적 부와 사회적 지위, 다른 사람들과의 관계를 위한 고군분투가 반드시 행복에 연결되어 있는 것은 아니라는 사실을 언급하며 시작했다. Allison은 진정한 행복의 실재는 자각과 자기만족을 통해 얻게 되는 것이라고 제시하였다.

해설 수상자의 수상 소식과 함께, 수상식에서의 강연이 어떤 내용이었는가를 말해주고 있는 글이다. 따라서 이 글의 목적은 '(b) 수상에 동반된 강의를 요약해주기 위해'이다.

오답 분석
(a) 저명한 철학자를 소개하기 위해 – 저명한 철학자 Allison의 수상 소식을 알리고 있는 글이다.
(c) 철학자에 의해 시작되는 강의를 홍보하기 위해 – 이 지문은 광고글이라고 볼 수 없다.
(d) 철학에서 현재 연구 경향을 언급하기 위해 – 이 글은 철학 전반에 대한 내용을 다루고 있지 않다.

어휘 **recipient** 수납자, 수령인
customary 습관적인, 통례의; 관례에 의한, 관습상의
accrue (저절로) 생기다
forge 합의·친교 등을 맺다

Communicating positively with your children will not only build their self-esteem and inspire confidence but will also reinforce the good and eliminate the bad behavior. And it's easy once you get the hang of it. All children need to feel loved and accepted, and you can communicate those feelings with your children by the way you speak. The sense of positive self-esteem they learn through their interactions at home will then spill over as your children communicate in the outside world. Positive reinforcement will also help them immensely as they begin school when the self-esteem boost they have gained from home really starts to pay off.

Q. How does the writer feel about positive reinforcement?

(a) Enthusiastic
(b) Apprehensive
(c) Sensitive
(d) Unapologetic

해석 아이들과 긍정적으로 소통하는 것은 아이들의 자부심을 쌓아주고 자신감을 불어넣어줄 뿐 아니라 좋은 행동을 강화시켜주고 나쁜 행동을 제거해줄 것이다. 그리고 일단 요령을 터득하기만 하면 매우 쉬운 일이다. 모든 아이들은 사랑 받고 있으며 인정받고 있다는 느낌을 가져야 하며, 아이들에게 이야기하는 방식을 통해 이러한 감정을 전달할 수 있다. 집에서의 상호작용을 통해 아이들이 배우는 긍정적인 자부심은 아이들이 집 밖의 세상에서 소통을 할 때에도 자연스럽게 발현될 것이다. 긍정적 강화는 아이들이 학교에 다니기 시작할 때에도 크게 도움이 된다. 이 때 집에서 얻은 자부심의 향상이 긍정적인 효과를 내기 시작하기 때문이다.

해설 화자가 긍정적 강화에 대해 어떻게 느끼고 있는가를 묻고 있다. 이 글에서 긍정적 강화가 아이들이 의사소통에 좋게 작용하며 매우 중요하다고 하였으므로 정답은 '(a) 열심인, 열중한'이 정답이 된다.

오답
분석
(b) 이해가 빠른, 감지하는 – 이 글에서는 긍정적 강화를 인지하는 것에서 나아가 중요성을 역설하고 있다.
(c) 예민한, 민감한 – 긍정적 강화에 대해 민감한 것이 아니라 중요성을 강조하고 있다.
(d) 인정하지 않는 – 긍정적 강화가 중요하다고 하였으므로 정반대의 의미이다.

어휘 **self-esteem** 자부심, 자신감
eliminate 제거하다, 없애다
get the hang of 요령을 터득하다
reinforcement 보강, 강화
pay off 성과가 나다, 잘 되어가다

Answers:

1. (b) 2. (a)

Build Up

TEPS 독해 영역의 실전 문제와 가장 가까운 유형과 난이도의 예상 문
제를 통해 실력을 쌓자.

▶▶ Part I Read the passage and choose the option that best fits the blank.

1. Ultrasound scanners consist of a computer and electronics control console, a video display screen and a________________________________. This is a small hand-held device that resembles a microphone attached to the scanner by a cord. A returning sound wave or "echo" is picked up by the transducer after it sends out a high frequency sound wave. The ultrasound image is visible real-time on a nearby screen that looks a lot like a small television or computer monitor. The image is created based on the amplitude, frequency and time it takes for the sound signal to return from the patient to the transducer.

   (a) a transducer that is used to scan the body
   (b) foot, ankle and knee restraint made from spandex
   (c) large piece of digital electronic medical equipment
   (d) comprehensive set of instructions written underneath

▶▶ Part II Choose the option that correctly answers the question.

2. Parents often tend to focus too much on how well their children do in school. Giving too much praise to students for getting good grades may mislead students into thinking that results are all that really matters in life. Instead, we should nurture students to develop practical life skills such as cooperation and independent thinking. To reinforce these characteristics, positive feedback should be given when they collaborate well in a group setting and are seen dividing up the work evenly among themselves.

   Q. What is the topic of the passage?

   (a) Continuing to praise students who excel in school
   (b) Constructive criticism and positive reinforcement regarding classroom behavior
   (c) Complimenting on students' cooperative behavior in order to foster life skills
   (d) Encouraging students to achieve goals through discipline

3. New computer monitor displays employ an integral-type imaging system that reproduces light beams similar to those produced by a real object and not its visual representation. This overcomes the main problem with a flatbed display: distance. The difference in the distance from the eye to the center of a display and to the display's edges and corners is greater for a flatbed than for a standard upright display. To solve this problem, flatbeds produce 3-D images with a wide viewing angle by using multiple live-action or CG images.

Q. Which of the following is correct according to the passage?

(a) The development of a true 3D image application for monitors has yet to occur.
(b) 3D viewing on a flatbed monitor will not be available commercially for 10 to 20 years.
(c) The technology used to create a 3D image is unrelated to that used for a flatbed display.
(d) 3D technology is reproducing similar light beams to those produced by a real object.

4. At the moment online banking has attracted around 23 million users, a figure which is projected to rise by nearly 300% by the year 2012. The main barrier to achieving this growth is not the reluctance of consumers to adopt non-traditional approaches to banking but existing financial institutions themselves. For instance, most still do not offer simple account opening procedures or real-time account credit and debit facilities both stumbling blocks toward their future growth. The whole situation is expected to change as the world's major banks enhance their investment in online product development in an effort to boost business efficiency.

Q. What can be inferred from the passage?

(a) Explosive growth is predicted in the retail banking sector.
(b) Increased investment in online banking will lead to greater product availability.
(c) Current online banking services are expected to continue to dominate the market.
(d) By 2012 few customers are expected not to be using banks.

▶▶ **Part III** Identify the sentence that least fits the context of the passage.

5. There exists a certain type of flower suitable to every holiday, event and special occasion. (a) For example, soldiers that took part during World War II are commemorated by showy, red flowers called poppies. (b) Another type of red flower commonly used during the Christmas season is the poinsettia, while irises and lilies act as symbols of resurrection and life at burial sites. (c) An abundance of people proclaim roses to be the queen of all flowers due to its prickly thorns coupled with a strong heady scent. (d) During romantic occasions such as Valentine's Day, engagements, weddings and the like, roses are used as presents as a token of love.

정답: 220p

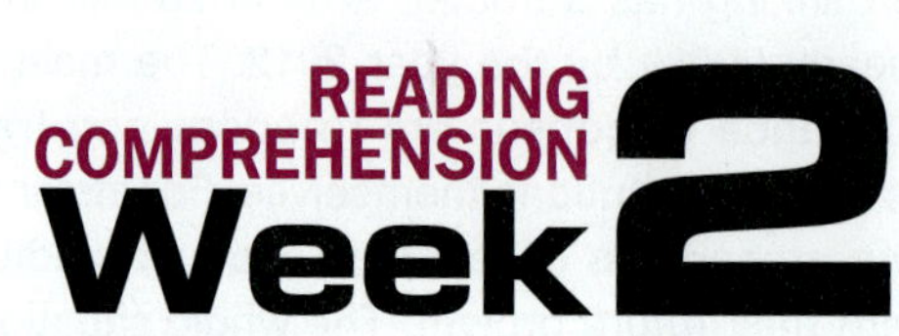

READING
COMPREHENSION
Week 2

Day 10

Part 1 추론이 필요한 빈칸 채우기

▶▶ 빈칸 채우기 문제들 중에서도, 지문에 언급된 내용을 직접적으로 정답으로 고를 수 있는 것이 아니라 약간의 추론이 필요한 경우가 있다. 그러나 '추론'이라는 것은 지문에 언급된 내용을 바탕으로 아주 당연하게 나올 수 있는 정도의 추론이지, 두세 단계씩 멀리 나아간 추론이 아니라는 것을 반드시 기억해야 한다. 아래의 예시를 통해 더욱 자세히 알아보도록 하자.

Example

The Australian Prime Minister, John Howard, has **repelled pressure to apologize** to aborigines for the dispossession of their land or to agree to reparations for the "stolen generations" of black children removed from their families in the 1940s and 1950s. Last year, more than 150,000 people marched across Sydney Harbor Bridge calling for reconciliation. The march followed by a National Sorry Day during which white people signed books of atonement. Though, Mr. Howard didn't participate in these movements, he _______________________________.

(a) looked closely at apologizing process
(b) apologized for the "hurt" of not apologizing
(c) began to take a keen interest in the Sydney Harbor Bridge
(d) apologized for previously having made an apology

첫 문장에서, '사과하라는 압력을 물리쳤다'고 하였고, 빈칸이 있는 마지막 문장은 '비록 Howard가 이러한 움직임에는 동참하고 있지 않고 있다해도'라고 시작하고 있다. 그렇다면 우리는 여기에서 'John Howard는 사과하지는 않았지만 ~ 하였다'라는 문맥임을 알 수 있다. 이렇게 전체적인 문맥을 파악하고 나면, 보기 중 빈칸에 어울리는 것은 'John Howard는 사과하지는 않았지만 사과하지 않은 것의 상처에 대해서는 사과했다'가 된다는 것을 알 수 있다.

이와 같이, 추론이 필요한 빈칸 채우기 문제들에서는 전체적인 지문의 흐름을 이해하고 그에 따라 어떤 내용으로 빈칸을 채우면 가장 문맥상 자연스러운가를 따져보면 정답을 찾을 수 있다.

해설: 217p

Catch Up

TEPS 독해 영역에 출제되었던 문제를 풀어봄으로써 실전 문제 유형
을 확실하게 파악해두자.

Part III Identify the sentence that least fits the context of the passage.

1. William Faulkner, a great American writer, set a fictional county named 'Yoknapatawpha County' to depict social changes in 19th through 20th century and people at that times. (a) All the names of the places within his works were mainly senseless, long, five syllable blurbs. (b) While some of his characters were based on real people, fictional families such as the Compsons, Snopes and Sartoris were also created and used in many of his works. (c) Profound truths regarding the South and the nature of humans were revealed through these fictional characters. (d) This can be found throughout his stories, most notably in *The Sound and the Fury* and *Light in August*.

2. There are many practical advantages to renting household appliances from Switchin' Kitchens. (a) During relocation, it would be unnecessary to try to sell or throw out your unwanted appliances as our company will just recall any of those items. (b) At Switchin' Kitchens, we also provide 24 hours online support for those that need help repairing their appliances. (c) But many people prefer purchasing more technologically advanced appliances rushing to the market with every passing day to repairing the old ones. (d) Best of all, Switchin' Kitchens is willing to replace any reasonably unsatisfied rentals and we deliver for free!

TEPS 독해 영역에 출제되었던 기출 문제를 자세한 설명과 함께 완전히 이해하도록 하자.

1

William Faulkner, a great American writer, set a fictional county named 'Yoknapatawpha County' to depict social changes in 19th through 20th century and people at that times. (a) All the names of the places within his works were mainly senseless, long, five syllable blurbs. (b) While some of his characters were based on real people, fictional families such as the Compsons, Snopes and Sartoris were also created and used in many of his works. (c) Profound truths regarding the South and the nature of humans were revealed through these fictional characters. (d) This can be found throughout his stories, most notably in *The Sound and the Fury* and *Light in August.*

해석 미국의 위대한 작가인 William Faulkner는 19세기부터 20세기까지의 사회적인 변화와 그 시대의 사람들을 묘사하기 위해 Yoknapatawpha County라는 이름이 붙여진 허구적인 마을을 설정하였다. (a) 그의 작품에 나온 장소들의 모든 이름들은 주로 무감각하고, 길고, 5음절의 짧고 과장된 광고 같았다. (b) 등장인물의 몇몇이 실제 사람들에게 기반을 두었지만, Compsons, Snopes, Sartoris 같은 소설의 가족들은 만들어진 것으로, 그의 많은 작품에 쓰였다. (c) 미국 남부와 인간의 본성에 관한 깊은 진실들이 이러한 허구적 등장인물들을 통해서 드러났다. (d) 이러한 점은 그의 소설들을 통해서 발견할 수 있는데, 〈The sound and the Fury〉와 〈Light in August〉에서 가장 두드러진다.

해설 윌리엄 포크너의 작품에 대한 글로, 배경이 되는 허구적 마을과 그 마을의 사람들에 대한 것을 언급하고 있다. (a)는 그의 작품 속의 지명이 과대광고와 같다고 언급하고 있는데, 이 내용을 뒷받침해주는 문장이 이어지지 않고 있으므로 문맥상 없어져야 할 문장이다.

오답 분석 (b)는 윌리엄 포크너의 작품에 등장하는 인물들, (c)는 그러한 인물들을 통해 작가가 나타낸 점, (d)는 이러한 점을 잘 나타내고 있는 작가의 다른 작품들에 대한 언급이므로, 유기적으로 연결되어 있다.

어휘 **syllable** 음절
blurb 과대선전
fictional 꾸며낸, 허구의; 소설적인, 소설의
notably 현저하게, 두드러지게; 특히

2

There are many practical advantages to renting household appliances from Switchin' Kitchens. (a) During relocation, it would be unnecessary to try to sell or throw out your unwanted appliances as our company will just recall any of those items. (b) At Switchin' Kitchens, we also provide 24 hours online support for those that need help repairing their appliances. (c) But many people prefer purchasing more technologically advanced appliances rushing to the market with every passing day to repairing the old ones. (d) Best of all, Switchin' Kitchens is willing to replace any reasonably unsatisfied rentals and we deliver for free!

해석 Switchin' Kitchens에서 가정용 기구를 빌리는 것에는 많은 실용적인 장점이 있습니다. (a) 우리 회사에서 물품을 회수할 것이기 때문에, 이사를 갈 때 당신은 원치 않는 기구들을 팔거나 버리려는 노력을 하지 않아도 될 것입니다. (b) Switchin' Kitchens에서는 가전제품들을 고치는 데 도움이 필요한 사람들을 위해 24시간 온라인 지원을 제공합니다. (c) 그러나 많은 사람들은 오래된 것을 고치는 것보다 날마다 시장으로 쏟아져 나오는 기술적으로 더욱 진보된 가전제품을 구매하는 것을 선호합니다. (d) 무엇보다도, Switchin' Kitchens는 정당하게 불만족스러운 대여 제품들을 기꺼이 바꾸어주며 우리는 무료로 배달도 해드립니다!

해설 Switchin' Kitchens가 여러 가지 장점을 설명하며 회사를 홍보하고 있는 글이다.
(c)는 일반적인 사람들에 대한 내용이며 Switchin' Kitchens에 대한 내용이 아니므로 이 글의 응집성을 해치고 있는 문장이다.

오답 분석 첫 문장에서 '많은 실용적인 장점'이 있다고 언급하고, (a), (b), (d)에서 어떠한 장점들이 있는지를 구체적으로 밝히며 뒷받침해주고 있다.

어휘 **appliance** 기계, 기구, 용구; 가정용 전기기구
recall 상기하다, 회상하다, 회수하다
reasonably 도리에 맞게, 합리적으로, 온당하게

Answers:

1. (a) 2. (c)

Build Up

TEPS 독해 영역의 실전 문제와 가장 가까운 유형과 난이도의 예상 문
제를 통해 실력을 쌓자.

▶▶ **Part I** Read the passage and choose the option that best fits the blank.

1. Though it has had various nicknames over time, the United States has often been
   referred to as a "Melting Pot." This particular term is derived from the fact that although
   the demographic make-up of the country entails a diverse variety of races and cultures,
   they often end up blending in with American culture. In fact, it can be argued that a form
   of cultural assimilation takes place as immigrants will eventually __________________
   and adopt the ways of their new host country.

   (a) make many new friends and acquaintances
   (b) experience severe culture shock and homesickness
   (c) totally forget all about their country of birth
   (d) abandon their original customs and cultures

▶▶ **Part II** Choose the option that correctly answers the question.

2. Gallstones develop in the gallbladder, a small pear-shaped organ located beneath the
   liver on the right side of the abdomen. The gallbladder is about 3 inches long and 1 inch
   wide at its thickest part. Gallstones can form when people who are obese produce bile
   containing a higher level of cholesterol than can be dissolved. When this happens, they
   may also develop swollen gallbladders that do not empty normally or completely. Some
   studies have shown that men and women who carry fat around their midsections may be
   at a greater risk for developing gallstones than those who carry fat around their hips and
   thighs.

   Q. What can be inferred from this passage?

   (a) A prevalence of gallstones has been found to exist in the obese.
   (b) The anatomical position of the gallbladder affects obesity.
   (c) Reducing ones body weight causes a consequent reduction in gallstones.
   (d) Appetite control is an effective treatment for gallstones.

3. Globalization has produced migrations of people domestically and internationally. For example, as a matter of economic survival, rural dwellers, through the loss of their traditional forms of income and opportunities, have been forced to leave their villages and join a rural drift to urban centers. Global agri-business corporations have used advances in technology to reduce the need for a large manual workforce. One of the most dramatic changes is in Asia where the rapid adoption of technology has further displaced rural workers.

Q. Which of the following is correct according to the passage?

(a) Global agri-business has replaced rural dwellers' lost incomes.
(b) A great number of jobs in the rural sector have been recently created.
(c) A major cause of rural drift has been the mechanization of farms.
(d) Human migration from urban areas is mainly caused by advanced technology.

4. Many of us have great interest in astronomy and more often, an irresistible worship for astrology. While some of us are more fascinated than others by the wonders of the night scene, most of us have trouble if we were asked to locate our favorite stars in the sky. In the northern hemisphere, the star most commonly recognized is Polaris, which is about 15 light years from the Earth, and is located on the edge of the constellation, Ursa Minor. Interestingly enough, although its scientific name is Polaris, most people know it as the Northern Star.

Q. Which of the following would follow this passage?

(a) Group of stars of the Ursa Minor constellation
(b) Wrongly recognized names of stars in the northern hemisphere
(c) Why people are more familiar with 'Northern star' than 'Polaris'
(d) Scientific names and common names of stars

▶▶ **Part III** **Identify the sentence that least fits the context of the passage.**

5. World War I and World War II had an immense influence on the traditional representation of female figures and their roles in society. (a) Prior to the wars, women were often viewed as being inferior to men although female characters still managed to play crucial roles that affected the lives of the people around them. (b) It is undoubtedly certain that men are superior to women in terms of physical strength. (c) During the war periods, while the men were serving, the women were in charge of 'bringing home the bacon' as well as fulfilling their domestic roles. (d) During the post war years, even though some still viewed females as second-rate citizens, their social status had become equal to that of men.

정답: 222p

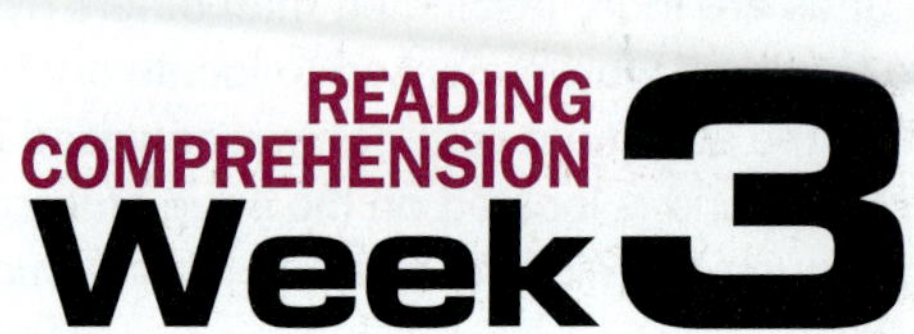
READING
COMPREHENSION
Week 3

Day 11

Part 1 접속사로 빈칸 채우기

TEPS 독해 영역의 Part1 빈칸 채우기 문제 16개 중에, 마지막 15번과 16번은 항상 접속사로 빈칸 채우기 문제들이다. 접속사 문제를 잘 맞추기 위해서는 이 유형의 문제들을 많이 풀어보는 연습도 물론 중요하지만, 각각의 접속사가 정확히 어떤 의미를 가지며, 어떤 경우에 사용되는가를 파악하는 것이 무엇보다도 선행되어야 한다.

따라서 독해 지문에 등장하는 접속사들을 항상 주목해서 보는 것이 효과적이다. 지문을 읽을 때 항상 접속사를 중심으로 그 앞과 뒤에 어떤 논리로 문장들이 이어지고 있는지를 확인해보는 습관을 들이면, 접속사들의 정확한 쓰임새를 알 수 있어 접속사 문제의 정답을 쉽게 고를 수 있는 훈련이 된다.

Example

For the last few centuries, the overall climate of the world has been gradually becoming warmer. This is due to global warming which is the effect of the following: orbit of the earth around the sun, volcano eruptions and the concentration of greenhouse gases. Since the beginning of the 20th century, it has been observed that large glaciers have been melting at speeds greater than average. For example, the Muir Glacier in Alaska has contracted by two miles within the past ten years. ______________, the agricultural crop line in Canada has been shifting northward by approximately 10 to 50 miles. Moreover, trees such as birches and spruces have been withering in Eastern Canada due to the increase in temperature.

(a) As a result
(b) Nevertheless
(c) Otherwise
(d) On the contrary

위의 지문은 최근 전반적인 기온이 점차 올라가게 되면서 지구 온난화로 인해 빙하가 녹고 있다는 내용이다. 빈칸 뒤의 내용은 캐나다의 농업이 그로 인해 어떻게 변화하게 되었는지를 언급하고 있으므로, 앞의 내용과 인과관계를 이루고 있다는 것을 알 수 있다. 따라서 빈칸에는 '(a) 그 결과' 가 들어가는 것이 알맞다.

해설: 69p

Catch Up

TEPS 독해 영역에 출제되었던 문제를 풀어봄으로써 실전 문제 유형
을 확실하게 파악해두자.

Part I Read the passage and choose the option that best fits the blank.

1. Children exposed to high levels of testosterone in the womb showed more autism-related traits later in life, according to findings that suggest the male hormone may_____________________________. The results support a hypothesis that higher levels of testosterone may contribute to autism and reinforce findings from tests on animals. The findings of the ongoing research were described as promising but contained a caution that a direct link between autism and testosterone was not proven and that other factors could be involved.

   (a) produce results experts expect from the disorder
   (b) indicate where you should diagnose the disease
   (c) play a key role in the complex brain disorder
   (d) make some people acquire friends more easily

2. Whether it is the school playground or classroom, the world in which children coexist with one another is a rather complex one. The nature of the interactions between male and female students has been the subject of studies in the past for there is a lot to be learned. It is important to understand the relationships between boys and girls in addition to their roles as students and members of society. By exploring this matter and the questions involved, some theories and insights might be made _______________________ __________ within a school environment.

   (a) that will show the female students' priority to male students
   (b) that will help teachers deal with male and female relationships better
   (c) that let parents put more emphasis on academics and learning
   (d) that will reveal the different eating patterns of male and female students

TEPS 독해 영역에 출제되었던 기출 문제를 자세한 설명과 함께 완전히 이해하도록 하자.

1

Children exposed to high levels of testosterone in the womb showed more autism-related traits later in life, according to findings that suggest the male hormone may ___________________________. The results support a hypothesis that higher levels of testosterone may contribute to autism and reinforce findings from tests on animals. The findings of the ongoing research were described as promising but contained a caution that a direct link between autism and testosterone was not proven and that other factors could be involved.

(a) produce results experts expect from the disorder
(b) indicate where you should diagnose the disease
(c) play a key role in the complex brain disorder
(d) make some people acquire friends more easily

해석 남성 호르몬이 복잡한 뇌의 장애에 대해 중심적 역할을 한다는 것을 제시한 연구 결과에 따르면, 자궁에서 높은 수치의 남성 호르몬에 노출된 아이들은 나중에 자폐증에 관련된 성질을 더 많이 보여준다고 한다. 이 결과는 더 높은 수치의 남성 호르몬이 자폐증에 영향을 미친다는 가설을 지지해주며, 동물 시험으로부터의 결과를 더욱 강화시켜준다. 진행되고 있는 연구에서 발견된 것들은 믿음직한 것으로 보이지만, 자폐증과 남성 호르몬 사이의 직접적인 연관성은 밝혀지지 않았으며 다른 요소들이 개입될 수도 있다는 경고를 포함한다.

해설 빈칸이 있는 문장 바로 뒤에 나온 문장에서 정답에 대한 단서를 찾을 수 있다. 남성 호르몬이 자폐증에 영향을 미친다는 가설을 지지해준다고 하였으므로 정답은 (c)가 된다.

오답 분석 (a) 전문가들이 장애로부터 예측한 결과를 만들어낸다. – 남성 호르몬이 어떠한 결과를 생산해낸다는 것은 문장의 의미상 맞지 않다.
(b) 어디에서 질병을 진단해야 하는가를 나타내준다. – 이 지문은 질병의 진단에 대한 내용이 아니다.
(d) 몇몇 사람들이 친구를 더 쉽게 얻을 수 있도록 해준다. – 친구에 대한 내용은 지문에 언급되지 않았다.

어휘 **testosterone** 남성 호르몬
womb 자궁
autism 자폐증
hypothesis 가설, 가정, 추측
promising 가망 있는, 유망한, 믿을 만한

2

Whether it is the school playground or classroom, the world in which children coexist with one another is a rather complex one. The nature of the interactions between male and female students has been the subject of studies in the past for there is a lot to be learned. It is important to understand the relationships between boys and girls in addition to their roles as students and members of society. By exploring this matter and the questions involved, some theories and insights might be made ____________________ within a school environment.

(a) that will show the female students' priority to male students
(b) that will help teachers deal with male and female relationships better
(c) that let parents put more emphasis on academics and learning
(d) that will reveal the different eating patterns of male and female students

해석 학교 운동장이든, 교실이든, 아이들이 서로서로 공존하는 세계는 좀 복잡한 곳이다. 배울 것이 많았기 때문에 남학생과 여학생 사이의 상호관계의 본질은 과거부터 연구의 주제가 되어왔다. 남학생들과 여학생들의 사회 구성원으로서의 역할과 학생으로서의 역할에 더해, 그들 사이의 관계를 이해하는 것도 중요하다. 이러한 문제와 이에 관련된 질문들을 탐구해봄으로써, 학교 환경에서 선생님들이 남자와 여자의 관계들을 더 잘 다룰 수 있게 도와줄 이론들과 통찰력이 생길 수 있을 것이다.

해설 학교에서의 남자 아이들과 여자 아이들 사이의 상호관계와 역할에 대한 내용을 다루고 있으므로 정답은 (b)가 된다.

오답
분석
(a) 남학생들에 대한 여학생들의 우월성을 보여주는 – 남학생과 여학생 중 누가 더 우월한가는 지문에 언급되지 않았다.
(c) 부모들이 학문적 측면과 배움에 더욱 강조를 두도록 하는 – 부모에 대한 내용은 지문에 언급되지 않았다.
(d) 남학생들과 여학생들의 다른 식습관을 드러내주는 – 식습관에 대한 내용은 지문에 언급되지 않았다.

어휘 **coexist** 동시에 존재하다, ~과 공존하다
explore 탐험하다, (문제 등을) 탐구하다, 조사하다
insight 통찰, 간파; 통찰력

Answers:

1. (c) 2. (b)

 ## Build Up 

TEPS 독해 영역의 실전 문제와 가장 가까운 유형과 난이도의 예상 문
제를 통해 실력을 쌓자.

▶▶ Part I Read the passage and choose the option that best fits the blank.

1. The "Third World" is a commonly used term that has been the subject of much controversy and discussion since ________________________. During the period of the Cold War, the "Third World" was defined as those countries that were not ideologically aligned with either the "First World" or "Second Worlds" which comprised of the United States and the Soviet Union respectively. Today, the more common interpretation of the term is that it consists of the developing and underdeveloped countries of Asia, Latin America, and Africa.

   (a) it represented the ideological conflicts during the Cold War
   (b) it has been employed to mark a geographic territory
   (c) it has been interpreted in different ways
   (d) it presented a highly disputable scientific theory

2. Though there have been many major battles in Roman history, the Battle of the Teutoberg Forest is certainly one of the most famous ones. This battle had many ramifications for Rome and also played a big factor in changing the course of European history. From a historian's point of view, the Battle of the Teutoberg Forest was a fascinating event and still continues to be the topic of much study and research. Aside from military knowledge, much can also be learned about Roman society from this conflict. Clearly, this battle is a valuable resource because of the significant insights and understanding it provides pertaining to ____________ in Roman history.

   (a) the roles of war and society
   (b) the sway and influence of scholars
   (c) the lavish lifestyles of Caesars
   (d) the appeal of gladiators

3. If you know you are being bullied, ask a potential counselor you are considering if he or she knows what psychological violence or bullying in the workplace is, and don't hesitate to ask them questions to ascertain their expertise. A good counselor will know that many commonly held facets about personality conflicts are tough to handle, and that his or her solutions may not apply to your situation. If your counselor does not have the skills to identify the differences, then the bully may spot further vulnerability which could lead to his discovering other ways to impair your health and employment.

   Q. Which of the following is correct according to the passage?

      (a) Sometimes you should change a counselor for the sake of your job.
      (b) You should never sympathize with an employer who yells at employees.
      (c) If you confront the workplace bully, you will probably back down.
      (d) A counselor's experience is one key to understanding your situation.

4. The 16th "Annual Reading for the Love of It Conference" will be held this year in Toronto, Canada from April 25th to 29th. Some of the most renowned authors and guest lecturers will be in attendance. Please note that the conference does not offer discounted conference rates. However, register before March 31st, and you will get a free conference package that includes Gabbi Mann's latest research on dyslexia and other learning disabilities, as well as a full description of the attending speakers.

   Q. What could be inferred from the conference notice?

      (a) Medical experts will attend for a tutorial in learning disabilities.
      (b) Attendees who register early will get a discount.
      (c) The conference is a national event held in Canada every year.
      (d) The conference will deal with those who have trouble in learning.

▶▶ **Part III** Identify the sentence that least fits the context of the passage.

5. The study of women's history in East Asia is a complex yet fascinating topic that is quite relevant in the academic field of gender studies. (a) Molly Beaulac, a university professor, is considered one of the leading scholars in the field of gender studies in the history of pre-modern China. (b) Her book, *The Lives of Chinese Women in the Sung Period*, explores the lives of Chinese women during the period of the Sung Dynasty. (c) Beaulac's work is undoubtedly a valuable resource for scholars interested in the study of women in China. (d) To this day, many women in China still enjoy reading historical journals about Sung Dynasty.

정답: 225p

READING
COMPREHENSION
Week 3

Day 12

Part 2 주제 찾기

TEPS 독해 영역의 17번부터 37번까지는 질문에 답하는 유형인 Part2 중에서, 주제 찾기 문제는 주로 앞쪽에 7~8문제 정도 출제된다. 지문의 전체적인 주제를 찾는 문제이기 때문에 모든 독해 문제 유형들 중 가장 기본적인 것이라고 볼 수 있다.

그러나 주제 찾기 문제의 정답률이 80퍼센트가 넘지 않으면, 빈칸 채우기 유형이나 추론 유형 등의 문제들의 정답률도 향상되지 않을 것이므로 독해 영역에서 고득점을 노릴 수가 없다. 보통 오답함정이 되는 보기들은 주제가 아닌 그 지문의 소재를 이용한 보기인 경우가 많다. 글의 소재와 주제를 구별하여 오답함정에 속지 않도록 주의하고, 가장 기본적인 유형인만큼 중요하다는 것을 인지해야 한다.

Example

Parents often tend to focus too much on how well their children do in school. Giving too much praise to students for getting good grades may mislead students into thinking that results are all that really matters in life. Instead, **we should nurture students to develop practical life skills such as cooperation and independent thinking.** To reinforce these characteristics, positive feedback should be given when they collaborate well in a group setting and are seen dividing up the work evenly among themselves.

Q. What is the topic of the passage?

(a) Continuing to praise students who excel in school
(b) Constructive criticism and positive reinforcement regarding classroom behavior
(c) Complimenting on students' cooperative behavior in order to foster life skills
(d) Encouraging students to achieve goals through discipline

위의 지문은 부모님들이 아이들이 학교에서 얼마나 잘하는가에 너무 초점을 맞추는 경향이 있는데, 삶에 필요한 기술을 발전시키는 것에 중점을 두어야 한다는 내용이다. 따라서 주제는 '(c) 삶에 필요한 기술을 키우기 위해 학생들의 협동적 행동에 대해 칭찬하기'가 된다.

해설: 220p

Catch Up

Part I Read the passage and choose the option that best fits the blank.

1. Over the years, the Canadian government has not been able to develop the Northwest Territories into a successful and independent area able to economically thrive on its own. Despite the vast potential of this region as well as the good intentions behind various projects and initiatives, the territory has failed to flourish both economically and socially. Furthermore, an alarming trend in the territory's demographic structure has developed. The number of young people in the Northwest Territories is significantly high while the number of those that have completed high school is a relatively small figure. Unless strong measures are taken, the region will _______________________________.

   (a) be sold to the highest bidder in an online auction
   (b) immediately begin to proper and thrive economically
   (c) adopt Communism as its new political ideology
   (d) continue to lack any economic and social success in the future

2. Overpopulation is regarded as a serious problem in major cities. If a city has more people than it has the capacity to provide for, the quality of health care usually diminishes or even becomes non-existent as some people lack access to it. Furthermore, another issue this problem creates is _______________________. With overpopulation, this presumably means that the labor force is most likely going to be greater than the jobs that are available. As a result of such a scenario, wages will probably decrease and it is possible that employers might exploit workers due to the abundant labor force and the high levels of competition between people for the same jobs.

   (a) air pollution
   (b) job availability
   (c) effects of religion
   (d) economic crisis

Answers

1

Over the years, the Canadian government has not been able to develop the Northwest Territories into a successful and independent area able to economically thrive on its own. Despite the vast potential of this region as well as the good intentions behind various projects and initiatives, the territory has failed to flourish both economically and socially. Furthermore, an alarming trend in the territory's demographic structure has developed. The number of young people in the Northwest Territories is significantly high while the number of those that have completed high school is a relatively small figure. Unless strong measures are taken, the region will _______________________________.

(a) be sold to the highest bidder in an online auction
(b) immediately begin to proper and thrive economically
(c) adopt Communism as its new political ideology
(d) continue to lack any economic and social success in the future

해석 과거에, 캐나다 정부는 서북부 지역을 스스로 경제적으로 번성할 수 있는 성공적이고 독립적인 지역으로 발전시켜오지 못했다. 이 지역의 거대한 잠재력 그리고 다양한 프로젝트와 독창력을 뒷받침해주는 좋은 의도에도 불구하고, 그 영토는 경제적, 사회적으로 번성하는 데 실패해 왔다. 더욱이, 이 지역에서의 인구통계 구조는 걱정스러운 경향을 나타내고 있다. 서북부 영토들에 젊은이의 수는 매우 많지만 고등학교를 마친 젊은이들은 상대적으로 적다. 어떤 조치가 취해지지 않는다면, 이 지역은 앞으로도 계속해서 경제적, 사회적 성공에 실패할 것이다.

해설 지문의 앞부분에서 캐나다 서북부 지역의 여러 문제점들을 열거하였다. 그러므로 정답은 (d)가 된다.

오답 (a) 온라인 경매에서 가장 높은 가격 입찰자에게 팔린다. – 경매에 대한 내용은 관계가 없다.
분석 (b) 즉각 경제적인 번영을 시작한다. – 빈칸 바로 앞의 내용과 문맥상 맞지 않는다.
(c) 그것의 새로운 정치적인 이데올로기로서 공산주의를 채택한다. – 정치적 체제에 대한 내용은 언급되지 않았다.

어휘 **territory** 영토, 구역
intention 의향, 의도, 목적
initiative 시작; 솔선 ; 독창력
flourish 번영하다
demographic 인구통계학의
alarming 놀라운, 걱정스러운

Overpopulation is regarded as a serious problem in major cities. If a city has more people than it has the capacity to provide for, the quality of health care usually diminishes or even becomes non-existent as some people lack access to it. Furthermore, another issue this problem creates is ___________________. With overpopulation, this presumably means that the labor force is most likely going to be greater than the jobs that are available. As a result of such a scenario, wages will probably decrease and it is possible that employers might exploit workers due to the abundant labor force and the high levels of competition between people for the same jobs.

(a) air pollution
(b) job availability
(c) effects of religion
(d) economic crisis

해석 인구 과잉은 주요 도시에서 심각한 문제로 간주된다. 만약 도시에 수용할 수 있는 능력보다 더 많은 사람들이 거주한다면, 건강 관리의 질이 보통 떨어지거나, 심지어 그것에 접근이 용이하지 않은 사람에게는 존재하지 않게 된다. 더 나아가, 이 문제가 발생시키는 다른 쟁점은 직업 유용성이다. 인구가 과잉인 도시에서, 이것은 아마도 노동력이 이용 기능한 직업보다 더 많아진다는 것을 의미한다. 이런 시나리오의 결과, 동일한 직업들에 대한 사람들의 경쟁은 높아지고 노동력이 풍부해져서, 임금은 감소하고 고용주가 노동자들을 착취할 것이다.

해설 지문의 후반부는 일자리보다 노동력이 더 많을 경우의 문제점에 대한 내용이므로 정답은 (b)가 된다.

오답 (a) 공기 오염 – 지문에서 오염에 대한 내용은 나오지 않았다.
분석 (c) 종교의 영향 – 종교에 대한 내용은 언급되지 않았다.
　　 (d) 경제적 위기 – 일자리의 부족에 대한 내용이므로, 경제적 위기는 너무 광범위한 내용이다.

어휘 overpopulation 인구 과잉
　　 diminish 줄이다, 감소하다
　　 presumably 아마, 생각건대
　　 exploit 자원을 개발하다, 노동력을 착취하다

Answers:

1. (d) **2.** (b)

Build Up 

TEPS 독해 영역의 실전 문제와 가장 가까운 유형과 난이도의 예상 문제를 통해 실력을 쌓자.

▶▶ Part I Read the passage and choose the option that best fits the blank.

1. In 1995 the U.S. Department of Agriculture and a pharmaceutical research firm received a patent on a technique to extract an anti-fungal agent from the Neem tree, or Azadirachta indica, which grows throughout India; Indian villagers have long understood the tree's medicinal value. Although the patent had been granted on an extraction technique, the Indian press described it as a patent on the Neem tree itself and the result was widespread public outcry, which was echoed throughout the developing world. _______________________________________, with the patent eventually being overturned in 2005.

   (a) Legal action by the American government followed
   (b) The Indian government assented to the US rights
   (c) The anti-fungal agent proved to be wholly ineffectual
   (d) Legal action by the Indian government followed

2. In Georgetown, a group of young men broke into a local discount clothing store. Only minutes after, an anonymous person made a phone call to the Georgetown police notifying them of the situation and officers rushed off to the reported area. Upon their arrival at the scene, the group of allegedly armed young men tried to flee in a car they had stolen a couple of days ago in Carbon City and reportedly fired several times at the police cars chasing behind them. __________, the police were eventually able to arrest all the members of the group without any injuries on either party.

   (a) Accordingly
   (b) Nevertheless
   (c) Although
   (d) In addition

3. Dispute resolution laws in Australia provide mechanisms at both State and Federal levels covering relationship breakups or periods of crisis. Heterosexual and de facto relationships have been recognized by these laws yet relationships between same sex couples have not, even though such relationships have been deemed lawful. To address this anomaly, an amendment was passed by the New South Wales parliament in 1999 extending the definition of a de facto couple to include same sex and other domestic partnerships. Other acts have to be amended to ensure a dovetailing of current laws, particularly in the areas of inheritance, compensation and guardianship.

   Q. Which of the following is correct according to the passage?

   (a) Heterosexual married couples do not receive legal recognition.
   (b) De facto couples are defined as those facing crises or a break up.
   (c) Divorced couples did not receive legal protection in Australia before 1999.
   (d) Gay and lesbian relationships have been legally recognized since 1999.

4. The Lord David Cecil's essay, *Fits of Despair*, examined in many college courses is the biographical study of the lawyer and poet William Cowper. The essay praises Cowper as a precursor of the English Romantic Movement represented by Wordsworth. The essay certainly gives us a great introduction to his wonderful, though tragic work. Also, there are many life lessons to be learned from Cowper's lifelong struggle with depression in this essay. But Cecil adjudicates others' commentary on Cowper rather than initiates in much of it. Indeed, his essay often reads as a critique of other critics.

   Q. What could be inferred from the passage?

   (a) Cecil drew criticism of other critics for his study of Cowper.
   (b) Cowper is not as gifted as scholars once assumed.
   (c) Cecil's work on Cowper has received undue criticisms from many.
   (d) *Fits of Despair* fails to portray the real Cowper as a poet.

▶▶ **Part III** Identify the sentence that least fits the context of the passage.

5. Anxiety disorders that are the result of a traumatic experience are referred to as a post-traumatic stress disorder. (a) STD is the abbreviation for sexually transmitted diseases; thus, the abbreviation for post-traumatic stress disorder is PPSD. (b) Post-traumatic disorders can result from warfare, the death of someone close or other dire events that can lead to severe psychological traumas. (c) Symptoms consist of insomnia, flashbacks, emotional detachment, loss and many others. (d) During World War II, many soldiers were diagnosed with this anxiety disorder due to the constant exposure to violent warfare and may still be trying to recover from it as of today.

정답: 227p

READING
COMPREHENSION
Week 3

Day 11	▶▶ Part 1 접속사로 빈칸 채우기
	유형정리 – 〈TEPS RC 지문 파트별 패턴 파악〉 Part 1 접속사로 빈칸 채우기
	Catch Up – Part 1 빈칸 채우기

Day 12	▶▶ Part 2 주제 찾기
	유형정리 – 〈TEPS RC 지문 파트별 패턴 파악〉 Part 2 주제 찾기
	Catch Up – Part 1 빈칸 채우기

Day 13	▶▶ Part 2 세부사항 확인하기
	유형정리 – 〈TEPS RC 지문 파트별 패턴 파악〉 Part 2 세부사항 확인하기
	Catch Up – Part 2 주제 찾기

Day 14	▶▶ Part 2 추론
	유형정리 – 〈TEPS RC 지문 파트별 패턴 파악〉 Part 2 추론
	Catch Up – Part 2 세부사항 확인

Day 15	▶▶ Part 2 글의 목적
	유형정리 – 〈TEPS RC 지문 파트별 패턴 파악〉 Part 2 글의 목적
	Catch Up – Part 3

Day 13

Part 2 세부사항 확인하기

세부사항을 확인하는 문제는 독해 문제 40개 중 8~9개 정도로 많이 출제되는 유형이다. 세부사항을 확인하여 지문의 내용과 맞는 것이나 맞지 않는 것을 고르는 유형인데, TEPS 시험의 특성상 시간이 부족하기 때문에 세부사항을 확인하기 위해 보기와 독해지문을 두세 번씩 반복해서 맞춰보며 읽다 보면 뒷부분의 많은 문제들을 시간 내에 풀 수 없다.

따라서 세부사항 확인문제들은 TEPS 독해 부분의 시간 관리에 큰 영향을 미치므로, 집중하여 지문을 한 번 읽고 세부사항들을 기억하여 정답을 맞추는 집중력 연습을 해야 한다. 또한, 구체적인 지명이나 인명, 연도 등의 세부사항이 여러 개 나열되어 기억해야 할 정보가 많을 경우에는 항상 펜으로 체크해 두고 보기에 언급된 부분을 지문에서 바로 찾을 수 있도록 연습해야 한다.

Example

The New York State Assembly has passed legislation that would make it illegal for employers to require nurses to work overtime. The action was applauded by the New York State Nurses Association (NYSNA), which had proposed and promoted the legislation. Research has shown that when nurses work mandatory overtime, patients are at greater risk for medical errors. In addition, nurses who are required to work overtime are more likely to develop injuries that take them out of the workforce and exacerbate the nursing shortage. Mandatory overtime also costs hospitals money in the form of increased nursing turnover. The bill is on the State Senate calendar and nurses are urging Senators to approve it before the end of session. Similar legislation already exists in 11 other states.

Q. Which of the following is correct according to the report?

(a) New York is the first state to adopt such legislation.
(b) Doctors make more mistakes if nurses work overtime.
(c) Mandatory overtime is now a choice for nurses in New York State.
(d) New York has become the twelfth state to adopt the new law.

위의 지문은 뉴욕 주에서 간호사들의 초과 근무를 불법으로 규정하는 새로운 법에 대한 내용이다. 지문의 가장 마지막 부분에서 11개의 다른 주들에서도 비슷한 법이 존재한다고 하였으므로 지문의 내용과 맞는 것은 '(d) 뉴욕은 이 새로운 법을 채택한 12번째 주가 되었다'이다. 이처럼 지문에 나온 단어와 어구를 그대로 쓰지는 않았지만 내용은 그대로 유지되는 paraphrasing에 유의하면 세부사항 문제의 정답률을 높일 수 있다.

해설: 164p

Catch Up

TEPS 독해 영역에 출제되었던 문제를 풀어봄으로써 실전 문제 유형
을 확실하게 파악해두자.

Part II Choose the option that correctly answers the question.

1. For many who lead today's busy lifestyle, breakfast may only be a luxury item on their grocery list. For others, cereal is the healthiest option in the morning. However, while some breakfast cereals claim to be healthy from the ingredient labeling on the package, not all of them are. Most breakfast cereals are made with processed sugars and refined white flour. Even with reduced sugar content, they are still high in simple carbohydrates. Therefore, they are not what they seem! That is why it is very important to check the ingredient contents carefully. If it is not labeled as containing low sugar or made with whole grain, then it is probably not healthy for you.

   Q. What is the main point of the passage?

   (a) Most breakfast cereals are good for your health.
   (b) Healthy people prefer processed sugars and refined white flour.
   (c) Simple carbohydrates are healthier for you in the long run.
   (d) You should check carefully before you decide on a cereal.

2. Western people have always had superstitious beliefs about numbers, especially about the number 13. There are many controversies about why the number 13 has a reputation for being unlucky. Many people associate the number with the Last Supper from the Bible, in which Judas, the betrayer, was the 13th guest. However, there is an evidence that the number 13 was considered unlucky prior to the Christian era; it comes after 12, which was once believed to be the perfect number.

   Q. What is the main topic of the passage?

   (a) Superstitions in the pre-Christian era
   (b) Superstitious beliefs in the bible related to numbers
   (c) Different beliefs about why the number 13 has been associated with bad luck
   (d) The relationship between the number 13 and Christianity

Answers

TEPS 독해 영역에 출제되었던 기출 문제를 자세한 설명과 함께 완전
히 이해하도록 하자.

1

For many who lead today's busy lifestyle, breakfast may only be a luxury item on their grocery list. For others, cereal is the healthiest option in the morning. However, while some breakfast cereals claim to be healthy from the ingredient labeling on the package, not all of them are. Most breakfast cereals are made with processed sugars and refined white flour. Even with reduced sugar content, they are still high in simple carbohydrates. Therefore, they are not what they seem! That is why it is very important to check the Ingredient contents carefully. If it is not labeled as containing low sugar or made with whole grain, then it is probably not healthy for you.

Q. What is the main point of the passage?

(a) Most breakfast cereals are good for your health.
(b) Healthy people prefer processed sugars and refined white flour.
(c) Simple carbohydrates are healthier for you in the long run.
(d) You should check carefully before you decide on a cereal.

해석 오늘날 바쁜 생활 패턴으로 사는 많은 사람들에게 아침식사는 아마도 그들의 식단 목록의 사치스러운 품목일 것이다. 다른 사람들에게 있어서는, 시리얼이 아침식사로 가장 건강한 선택이다. 그러나 아침식사용 시리얼이 포장에 영양성분 표시를 붙여 건강에 좋다고 주장하지만, 모두 그러한 것은 아니다. 대부분의 아침 시리얼은 가공된 설탕과 정제된 하얀 밀가루로 만들어진다. 설탕 성분은 감소되었다고 할지라도, 그것들은 여전히 단순 탄수화물 함량이 높다. 그러므로 시리얼은 보이는 그대로가 아니다! 바로 그렇기 때문에 성분 함량을 살펴보는 것이 중요하다. 만약 설탕 함량이 낮음, 또는 통곡물 함유라는 라벨이 없다면 아마도 건강에 좋지 않을 것이다.

해설 시리얼이 보이는 것보다 건강에 좋지 않을 수도 있기 때문에 성분 함량을 잘 살펴보아야 한다는 내용의 지문이다. 그러므로 정답은 '(d) 시리얼을 선택하기 전에 신중하게 살펴보아야 한다.' 이다.

오답
분석
(a) 대부분의 아침 시리얼은 건강에 좋다. – 그렇지 않을 수도 있다고 지문에 언급되었다.
(b) 건강한 사람들은 가공된 설탕과 정제된 하얀 밀가루를 좋아한다. – 대부분의 시리얼이 가공된 설탕과 하얀 밀가루로 이루어져 있다고만 언급했으므로 정답이 될 수 없다.
(c) 단순 탄수화물은 장기적으로 건강에 좋다. – 단순 탄수화물의 함량이 높은 것이 문제가 되고 있기 때문에 건강에 좋다고 볼 수 없다.

어휘 **ingredient** 식품 성분표, 영양 성분표
refine 정제하다

2

Western people have always had superstitious beliefs about numbers, especially about the number 13. There are many controversies about why the number 13 has a reputation for being unlucky. Many people associate the number with the Last Supper from the Bible, in which Judas, the betrayer, was the 13th guest. However, there is an evidence that the number 13 was considered unlucky prior to the Christian era; it comes after 12, which was once believed to be the perfect number.

Q. What is the main topic of the passage?

(a) Superstitions in the pre-Christian era
(b) Superstitious beliefs in the bible related to numbers
(c) Different beliefs about why the number 13 has been associated with bad luck
(d) The relationship between the number 13 and Christianity

해석 서양 사람들은 항상 숫자에 관한, 특별히 숫자 13에 관한 미신적인 믿음을 가지고 있었다. 왜 숫자 13이 불운의 명성을 가지고 있는가에 대해 많은 논쟁이 있었다. 많은 사람들은 성경에서 나온 최후의 만찬과 그 숫자를 연결시키는데, 그 만찬에서 배반자인 Judas는 13번째 손님이었다. 그러나 숫자 13이 기독교 시대 이전에 불운의 숫자라고 생각되었다는 증거가 있다. 13은 12의 다음에 오는 숫자인데, 12는 한때 완벽한 숫자라는 믿음이 있었기 때문이다.

해설 13이라는 숫자가 왜 불운하다고 여겨지게 되었는가에 대한 내용의 지문으로, 각기 다른 두 가지 이유를 들어 보여주고 있다. 따라서 정답은 '(c) 왜 13이 불운과 연관되어 있는가에 대한 다른 믿음' 이다.

오답 (a) 기독교 시대 이전 시기의 미신 – 기독교 시대의 미신들에 대해서는 언급되지 않았다.
분석 (b) 성경에 관련된 숫자에 대한 미신적인 믿음 – 이 글의 소재는 성경에 관련된 숫자가 아니라 숫자 13이다.
(d) 숫자 13과 기독교 사이의 관계 – 숫자 13에 대한 기독교적인 관점만 소개된 것이 아니므로 정답이 될 수 없다.

어휘 **superstitious** 미신의, 미신에 관한, 미신에 사로잡힌
reputation 평판, 명성
betrayer 배신자, 매국노

Answers:

1. (d) 2. (c)

Build Up

TEPS 독해 영역의 실전 문제와 가장 가까운 유형과 난이도의 예상 문제를 통해 실력을 쌓자.

▶▶ **Part I** Read the passage and choose the option that best fits the blank.

1. Choosing a web host is one of the most important decisions facing every person who wishes to have their own web site for personal or business use. You need to look at price and dependability, keeping in mind the web host is someone you pay a fee to and in return he or she provides you with much space on their server in which to reliably store the files that make up your web site. _________________ because you want to make sure you go with a web host that provides enough server space for you to grow your business at the rate you want.

    (a) Stability is the most essential
    (b) 3-dimensional graphics technology is a requisite
    (c) Business expansion can be achieved
    (d) Speed and support are also important

▶▶ **Part II** Choose the option that correctly answers the question.

2. Getting an important promotion may hinge more on your ability to avoid the gossip trap than your qualifications and job skills. A positive atmosphere at work is generated by the staff and how well they get along together, so employees who make more of an effort to get along and be friendly will usually lead to their climbing the corporate ladder faster. Conversely, employees who engage in gossip risk damage not only to their reputation at work, but are also more unlikely to get ahead. Good advice to avoid the gossip trap includes searching for subjects other than co-workers to talk about and setting a time limit on conversations with colleagues.

    Q. What is the main idea of the passage?
        (a) You're less likely to be promoted at work if you eschew gossip.
        (b) You're more likely to be promoted at work if you eschew gossip.
        (c) Creating a positive atmosphere in the workplace leads to promotion.
        (d) Talking about colleagues will enhance your prospects of promotion.

3. Modern day technology allows several methods to safeguard aircrafts from lightning. One of the most commonly employed methods are to combine aluminum with other materials containing layers of conductive fibers designed to carry lightning currents. In the case that lightning strikes, the currents travel along the exterior as these aircrafts are designed to have no gaps in conductive paths, and the tail would act as an outlet for the current to flow out.

Q. Which is correct according to the passage?

(a) Conductive paths are engineered without gaps.
(b) Aircraft skins are designed to withstand electric currents.
(c) Very few aircrafts are constructed with aluminum exteriors.
(d) Lightning currents cannot reach the interiors of the aircraft.

4. The National Sleep Foundation says sleeping habits are a key factor in weight loss. People who get a recommended 7-9 hours of sleep daily weigh less on average than those who do not. The majority of obese people falls into the category of sleep deprived. It is estimated that only 25% of Americans currently get enough sleep, causing the majority to suffer at least some endocrine system problems leading to fluctuations in insulin production. This causes a breakdown of the body's ability to metabolize sugar and can lead to diabetes. Sleep apnea is another condition caused largely by obesity, and although most sufferers show lighter symptoms such as interrupted breathing patterns, it can be fatal.

Q. What can be inferred from the passage?

(a) Getting enough sleep daily is the key to becoming obese.
(b) Diabetes is caused directly by sleep deprivation.
(c) A link between obesity and sleeping habits is unproven.
(d) Getting 7-9 hours of sleep each day can control weight.

▶▶ **Part III** Identify the sentence that least fits the context of the passage.

5. Football, more commonly referred to as soccer, is a sport copious amounts of people all over the world are enthused with. (a) In every continent, there are people that spend their waking moments thinking about soccer, watching soccer and playing soccer. (b) For many soccer fans, this renowned sport is not just a favorite pastime, but a passion; a way of life. (c) Although many people are enthusiastic about soccer, they frown at the astronomical figures of money star players acquire. (d) To further attest to the popularity soccer, many individuals take great pleasure in watching soccer games on the "tube" and are overexcited when the time comes for the World Cup to occur.

정답: 229p

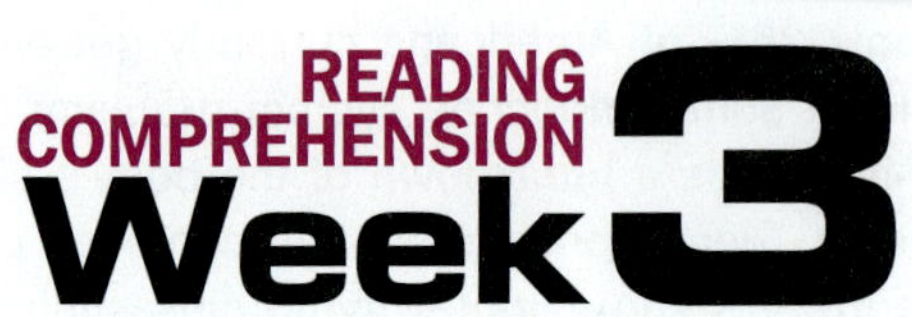

READING
COMPREHENSION
Week 3

| **Day 11** | ▶▶ Part 1 접속사로 빈칸 채우기 |
유형정리 – 〈TEPS RC 지문 파트별 패턴 파악〉 Part 1 접속사로
빈칸 채우기
Catch Up – Part 1 빈칸 채우기

| **Day 12** | ▶▶ Part 2 주제 찾기 |
유형정리 – 〈TEPS RC 지문 파트별 패턴 파악〉 Part 2 주제 찾기
Catch Up – Part 1 빈칸 채우기

| **Day 13** | ▶▶ Part 2 세부사항 확인하기 |
유형정리 – 〈TEPS RC 지문 파트별 패턴 파악〉 Part 2 세부사항 확인하기
Catch Up – Part 2 주제 찾기

| **Day 14** |  Part 2 추론 |
유형정리 – 〈TEPS RC 지문 파트별 패턴 파악〉 Part 2 추론
Catch Up – Part 2 세부사항 확인

| **Day 15** |  Part 2 글의 목적 |
유형정리 – 〈TEPS RC 지문 파트별 패턴 파악〉 Part 2 글의 목적
Catch Up – Part 3

Day 14

Part 2 추론

추론 문제는 TEPS 독해 영역의 Part 2의 뒷부분에 4~5문제 정도 출제되는데, 보통 시간이 모자라서 추론 문제를 풀지 못하거나 혹은 추론 문제는 어렵다는 고정관념 때문에 시도조차 하지 않는 경우가 많다. 그러나 추론 문제는 정답이 나오는 원리만 파악하면 그리 어렵지 않게 맞출 수 있는 부분이므로, 오히려 세부사항을 확인하는 문제에서 시간 관리를 잘 못하고 많은 시간을 보내는 경향이 있는 수험자들은 추론 문제를 푸는 것이 시간 관리와 점수를 올리는 것 두 가지 모두에 더 효율적일 수 있다.

앞서 〈Day 10. 추론이 필요한 빈칸 채우기〉에서도 언급했듯이, 추론 문제에서는 두세 단계씩 멀리 나아간 추론이 정답이 되는 것이 아니라 지문의 내용에서 한 단계만 추론된 것이 정답이 된다. 즉, 지문의 주제를 정확하게 파악하고 지문의 내용을 기반으로 하여 한 발짝만 나아간 것이 정답이라고 생각하면 오답 함정을 피해갈 수 있다.

Example

The best satire seeks to administer a shock to an audience when they recognize a joke that deals with a vice. It doesn't necessarily exist to create harm or ridicule, but it does seek to damage the structure of the vice. A satire's job is to expose the vice in all its repulsiveness with the aim to eradicate it from a person or society. Bitter medicine followed by candy is a time-honored formula for relief from sickness, and so does satire work by sweetening the barb of wit with laughter. Satirists are often portrayed as constructive critics; far from being destructive, they often depict themselves as redeemers to society from its ills.

Q. What can be inferred from the passage?

(a) Satire plays a role in making people recognize bad practices.
(b) Satire should not be taken seriously because it's only for fun.
(c) Satirists have proven to be very efficient in spreading vices.
(d) Most satire tends to ignore issues related to everyday life.

위의 지문은 풍자의 역할에 대한 글이다. 첫 문장이 이 지문의 주제문이며, 하이라이트 표시가 된 부분은 모두 주제문인 첫 문장을 뒷받침해주는 부연설명 부분들 중 가장 중요한 단서가 되는 부분들이다. 가장 좋은 풍자는 관객이 악덕을 다루는 농담을 인지할 때 충격을 주는 것, 즉 악덕의 구조에 손상을 가하여 사회로부터 악덕을 근절시키려는 목적을 가지는 것이다. 따라서 정답은 '(a) 풍자는 사람들이 나쁜 풍습을 깨닫도록 하는 역할을 한다.'가 된다.

해설: 246p

Catch Up

TEPS 독해 영역에 출제되었던 문제를 풀어봄으로써 실전 문제 유형
을 확실하게 파악해두자.

Part II Choose the option that correctly answers the question.

1. The most recent of the 'Die Hard' series, 'Live Free or Die Hard' will not appeal to everyone. If you want to watch a tense game of cat and mouse and see the good guy win against impossible odds, this movie is for you. While that's a bit of a simplification of the plot, it's actually quite accurate. The plot is extremely simple with some well-drawn characters. The director of this film, McTiernan managed to fill his film with intriguing visuals, keeping the film running at a hyperactive pace, ensuring there isn't one dull moment. But with a critical look at it, the way the hero of this film settles both national crisis and personal problem definitely lacks probability.

    Q. Which is correct about the movie, 'Live Free or Die Hard' according to the review?

    (a) It is based on a fictional novel.
    (b) It is a thrill ride at a breakneck pace.
    (c) It has an elaborate story line.
    (d) It features a good guy who is clever at disguising himself.

2. Our body has many ways to restore its own balance when there is an intrusion from outside. When a foreign cell such as a dangerous organism or virus enters our body, our immune system identifies it by looking for tall-tale signs on its surface structure. These identifying signs are called antigens. Foreign cells, whether it be bacteria, viruses, or allergen, have distinctive antigens that distinguish them from our own cells. When our immune system finds cells with these antigens, it attacks them.

    Q. Which is correct according to the lecture?

    (a) Antigens prevent organisms from developing infections.
    (b) Bacteria attack the human body with antigens.
    (c) Antigens are our immune system's means of foreign identification.
    (d) Antigens enter our body after bacteria is recognized in our immune system.

Answers

TEPS 독해 영역에 출제되었던 기출 문제를 자세한 설명과 함께 완전
히 이해하도록 하자.

1

> The most recent of the '*Die Hard*' series, '*Live Free or Die Hard*' will not appeal to
> everyone. If you want to watch a tense game of cat and mouse and see the good
> guy win against impossible odds, this movie is for you. While that's a bit of a
> simplification of the plot, it's actually quite accurate. The plot is extremely simple
> with some well-drawn characters. The director of this film, McTiernan managed to fill
> his film with intriguing visuals, keeping the film running at a hyperactive pace,
> ensuring there isn't one dull moment. But with a critical look at it, the way the hero of
> this film settles both national crisis and personal problem definitely lacks probability.
>
> **Q.** Which is correct about the movie, '*Live Free or Die Hard*' according to the review?
>
> (a) It is based on a fictional novel.
> **(b) It is a thrill ride at a breakneck pace.**
> (c) It has an elaborate story line.
> (d) It features a good guy who is clever at disguising himself.

해석 다이하드 시리즈의 가장 최신작 〈Live free or Die Hard〉는 모든 사람에게 와 닿지는 않을 것이다. 만약 당신이 고양이와 쥐의 긴장된
게임을 보기 원하고, 승산이 없는 불가능에 맞서 이기는 멋진 사람을 보기 원한다면, 이 영화는 당신에게 잘 맞는다. 이것이 줄거리를 좀
단순화시킨 것이긴 하지만, 사실상 꽤 정확하기도 하다. 영화의 줄거리는 몇몇 잘 그려진 캐릭터들로 매우 간단하다. 이 영화의 감독인
McTiernan은 매우 활동적인 속도로 영화가 진행되게 하고 단 한 순간도 지루하지 않게 하면서, 흥미를 유발시키는 시각적 효과로 이 영
화를 가득 채웠다. 그러나 비판적 시각으로 보면, 이 영화의 영웅이 국가적 위기와 개인적 문제를 해결하는 과정은 확실히 개연성이 떨어
진다.

해설 지문에 언급된 영화는 매우 빠른 속도로 진행되고 있다고 하였으므로 정답은 '(b) 매우 빠른 속도로 진행되는 스릴 넘치는 놀이기구를 타
는 것과 같다.'가 된다.

오답
분석
(a) 이 영화는 허구적인 소설에 기반을 두고 있다. – 원작이 소설이라는 내용은 언급되지 않았다.
(c) 이 영화는 정밀한 이야기 구조를 가지고 있다. – 마지막에서 개연성이 떨어진다고 하였으므로 지문의 내용과 반대이다.
(d) 변장에 능한 영웅을 보여준다. – 변장에 대한 내용은 언급되지 않았다.

어휘 **odds** 승산, 가능성
hyperactive 지나치게 활동적인
probability 개연성
breakneck (목이 부러질 정도로) 위험하기 짝이 없는, 몹시 가파른
disguise 변장, 가장, 분장

Our body has many ways to restore its own balance when there is an intrusion from outside. When a foreign cell such as a dangerous organism or virus enters our body, our immune system identifies it by looking for tall-tale signs on its surface structure. These identifying signs are called antigens. Foreign cells, whether it be bacteria, viruses, or allergen, have distinctive antigens that distinguish them from our own cells. When our immune system finds cells with these antigens, it attacks them.

Q. Which is correct according to the lecture?

(a) Antigens prevent organisms from developing infections.
(b) Bacteria attack the human body with antigens.
(c) Antigens are our immune system's means of foreign identification.
(d) Antigens enter our body after bacteria is recognized in our immune system.

해석 우리의 신체는 외부로부터의 침입이 있을 때 균형을 되찾는 많은 방법들을 가진다. 위험한 생명체 또는 바이러스 같은 외래 세포가 우리 몸에 들어올 때, 면역 시스템은 표면 구조에서 암시하는 사인을 찾음으로써 그것을 식별한다. 이 식별하는 사인들을 항원이라고 부른다. 그것이 박테리아든, 바이러스든, 알레르기 항원이든, 외래 세포는 우리의 세포들로부터 나온 그것들과 구별되는 독특한 항원을 가지고 있다. 우리의 면역 시스템이 이런 항원들을 가지고 있는 세포들을 찾았을 때, 면역 시스템은 세포들을 공격한다.

해설 두 번째와 세 번째 문장에서 면역 시스템이 외래 세포를 확인하는 사인들이 항원이라고 하였으므로 정답은 '(c) 항원들은 외부 식별에 대한 우리의 면역 시스템 수단이다.'가 된다.

오답 (a) 항원들은 생명체를 교차 감염으로부터 막는다. – 교차 감염은 지문에 언급되지 않았다.
분석 (b) 박테리아는 항원들을 가지고 있는 인체를 공격한다. – 지문에 언급되지 않은 내용이다.
　　(d) 항원들은 박테리아가 우리의 면역 시스템에 인지된 후, 우리 몸에 들어간다. – 항원은 우리 신체에도 있는 것이다.

어휘 **intrusion** 침입, 방해
　　tell-tale 암시하는, 증거를 보여주는
　　antigen 항원

Answers:

1. (b) 2. (c)

Build Up

▶▶ **Part I** Read the passage and choose the option that best fits the blank.

1. In exploring morality in context one starting point may be the change in the socio-structural and socio-cultural conditions of modern societies. This involves change in the social demand on morality and in the empirical conditions of moral action. New perspectives emerge and problems are observed as these changes are accounted for and analyzed in the social sciences. Philosophers and social scientists can cooperate to solve these problems; the 'placeholder' function of philosophy is served by data from social scientists, and _________________________________ is provided by the philosopher.

    (a) essential philosophical and theological directions
    (b) social changes asked for by the social activist
    (c) political, law enforcement and welfare roles
    (d) conceptual clarity required by the social scientist

▶▶ **Part II** Choose the option that correctly answers the question.

2. How can one distinguish between a regular person and a criminal? Certainly, one cannot determine this based on an individual's appearance or other physical characteristics. Unfortunately, there is no foolproof way to determine whether a particular person is susceptible to engaging in violent, criminal activities. However, some methods to identify individuals with potential criminal characteristics exist. For example, a common technique used to identify serial killers and terrorists is profiling. Due to its effectiveness, it has even begun to be commonly used by most law enforcement agencies. Some schools also try using this method as a form of early detection to identify any troubled children whose aggressive traits might result in future criminal behavior.

    Q. What is the main idea of the passage?

    (a) Criminal behavior is seldom predictable.
    (b) Serial killers and terrorists often fit into certain profiles.
    (c) Methods such as profiling exist that are used to try and identify the criminal mind.
    (d) Criminals do not possess any different physical characteristics.

3. Welcome to New Zealand's Whakairo Visitor's Center. The Whakairo Center offers many attractions from lush tropical rainforests to waterfalls to white sandy beaches, but nothing is as spectacular as the Maori cultural demonstrations. Five times each afternoon, the villagers will put on a demonstration that explains the symbolic significance of their unique carvings, as well as their Haka dance. Kids will enjoy learning to play a traditional Maori stick game, called the Tititorea, as well as getting facial tattoos at the front porch.

Q. Which is correct according to the passage?

(a) Whakairo's main attraction is its white sandy beaches
(b) Whakairo is the world's largest tropical rainforest region.
(c) Whakairo offers evidence of Maori settlement and cultivation.
(d) Whakairo's Visitor's Center is as popular as the waterfalls

4. Auto-plagiarism is defined as an author republishing or reusing the same piece of writing without citing the initial publication. The practice is prohibited by colleges and universities because the refereed journals they produce require that material had not been published elsewhere. Even a student who hands in the same essay paper in two different classes without permission is guilty of auto-plagiarism. Unethical faculty members have been paid for submitting the same literature to multiple organizations and therefore, defraud journals, publishers and universities.

Q. What can be inferred from the passage?

(a) Some professors and students claim unpublished work as originally their own.
(b) Corrupt faculty members take student's work and publish it as their own.
(c) Corrupt students take faculty members' work and publish it as their own.
(d) Some students and professors claim work as original that has been previously published.

▶▶ **Part III** Identify the sentence that least fits the context of the passage.

5. In many households, pets are cherished and even considered as part of the family. (a) Thus, it's not too much to say that starting a pet grooming business may be the best way to "reel in the dough." (b) One thing to know before starting the business is that it may be necessary to tend to those pets in the comfort of their own homes. (c) Pet owners don't like animals that are too big since they will be quite heavy to carry around. (d) This will allow pet owners to have more free time to complete other tasks as care-giving responsibility for their pets is very time consuming.

정답: 232p

READING
COMPREHENSION
Week 3

Day 11　▶▶ Part 1 접속사로 빈칸 채우기
유형정리 – 〈TEPS RC 지문 파트별 패턴 파악〉 Part 1 접속사로
　　　　　빈칸 채우기
Catch Up – Part 1 빈칸 채우기

Day 12　▶▶ Part 2 주제 찾기
유형정리 – 〈TEPS RC 지문 파트별 패턴 파악〉 Part 2 주제 찾기
Catch Up – Part 1 빈칸 채우기

Day 13　▶▶ Part 2 세부사항 확인하기
유형정리 – 〈TEPS RC 지문 파트별 패턴 파악〉 Part 2 세부사항 확인하기
Catch Up – Part 2 주제 찾기

Day 14　▶▶ Part 2 추론
유형정리 – 〈TEPS RC 지문 파트별 패턴 파악〉 Part 2 추론
Catch Up – Part 2 세부사항 확인

Day 15　▶▶ Part 2 글의 목적
유형정리 – 〈TEPS RC 지문 파트별 패턴 파악〉 Part 2 글의 목적
Catch Up – Part 3

Day 15
Part 2 글의 목적

글의 목적을 고르는 문제는 보통 독해 영역 한 세트에서 한 문제 정도 출제되는데, 그리 어렵지 않게 정답을 고를 수 있는 경우가 많다.

어떤 용도를 위해 이 글이 쓰여졌는가를 묻는 것이기 때문에, 그 지문이 광고나 공지글인지 (to advertise, to notify) 아니면 정보를 주기 위한 것인지 (to inform) 혹은 경고나 비판을 하기 위해서인지 (to warn, to criticize)를 파악하면, 지문의 내용을 100퍼센트 이해하지 못했다 하더라도 정답을 고를 수 있다.

Example

The 17th annual Desmond G. Smith Honorary Service Award was once again held in the McArthur Auditorium of Johnson Hall. The recipient of this year's award was Fred Allison, a renowned philosophy professor. As it is customary for this honor, Allison also gave a lecture titled "The Meaning of True Happiness," focused on people's never-ending quest to find true happiness. Allison began by addressing the fact that the struggle for material wealth, social status and interpersonal relationships is not necessarily linked to happiness. The reality of true happiness, Allison suggest, is acquired through self-realization and self-satisfaction.

Q. What is the purpose of the passage?

(a) To introduce a renowned philosophy scholar
(b) To summarize a lecture that accompanied an award
(c) To advertise an incoming lecture by a philosopher
(d) To state the current research trend in philosophy

위의 지문은 수상자의 연설이 어떤 내용이었는가를 간략하게 소개하고 있는 글이므로 정답은 '(b) 수상에 따른 강연을 요약하는 것' 이다.

해설: 84p

Catch Up

Part III Identify the sentence that least fits the context of the passage.

1. A new planet, approximately the same size as Jupiter, was discovered orbiting around a star in a triple-star system in the constellation Cygnus. (a) The discovery sparked a great deal of interest among scientists. (b) This sighting was considered an astronomical breakthrough because the planet exists in a multiple-star system which challenged the current theory of orbital migration. (c) The Sun is the only star in Earth's single-star system. (d) More than 100 planets have been found in recent years, but most have been located in single-star systems.

2. Teachers and parents often try instill in newer generations that pop culture can be detrimental toward the development of the intellect. (a) However, Steven Johnson doesn't seem to think so in his book: *How Pop Culture Makes Us Smarter.* (b) In this book, he argues that popular culture is responsible for the gradual increase in IQ scores. (c) Pop culture is often recognized as rebellious to the older generation and even as instilling decadence to the younger generation. (d) Johnson's standpoint has received many criticisms as well as praise; it is the first audacious book to argue the positive effect of pop culture so convincingly.

Answers

TEPS 독해 영역에 출제되었던 기출 문제를 자세한 설명과 함께 완전
히 이해하도록 하자.

1

A new planet, approximately the same size as Jupiter, was discovered orbiting around a star in a triple-star system in the constellation Cygnus. (a) The discovery sparked a great deal of interest among scientists. (b) This sighting was considered an astronomical breakthrough because the planet exists in a multiple-star system which challenged the current theory of orbital migration. (c) The Sun is the only star in Earth's single-star system. (d) More than 100 planets have been found in recent years, but most have been located in single-star systems.

해석 백조자리의 세 개의 항성이 있는 태양계에서 그 중 하나의 항성을 궤도를 그리며 도는, 목성과 크기가 비슷한 새로운 행성이 발견되었다. (a) 이 발견은 과학자들 사이에 큰 반향을 불러일으켰다. (b) 그 행성은 현재의 궤도 이동 이론에 도전장을 던지는, 여러 개의 항성이 있는 태양계에 존재하기 때문에 이 관찰은 천문학적인 돌파구로 생각되었다. (c) 태양은 지구의 하나의 항성이 있는 태양계에서 하나뿐인 항성이다. (d) 100개 이상의 행성이 최근에 발견되었지만 대부분은 하나의 항성이 있는 태양계에 위치해 있다.

해설 항성이 세 개인 태양계의 행성이 발견되었으며, 그 발견이 의미하는 바를 설명하고 있는 글이다. (c)는 지구의 태양계에 대한 내용이므로 이 글의 흐름에서 벗어난다.

오답 분석 (c)를 제외하고, (a), (b), (d)는 이 지문에서 다루고 있는 행정의 발견이 어떤 의미를 지니며, 왜 의미가 있는지를 글의 흐름에 따라 일관성 있게 설명하고 있다.

어휘 **constellation** 별자리, 성좌
astronomical 천문학의, 천문학적인, 거대한
breakthrough 큰 발전, 돌파구, 약진
orbit 궤도

2

Teachers and parents often try instill in newer generations that pop culture can be detrimental toward the development of the intellect. (a) However, Steven Johnson doesn't seem to think so in his book: *How Pop Culture Makes Us Smarter.* (b) In this book, he argues that popular culture is responsible for the gradual increase in IQ scores. (c) Pop culture is often recognized as rebellious to the older generation and even as instilling decadence to the younger generation. (d) Johnson's standpoint has received many criticisms as well as praise; it is the first audacious book to argue the positive effect of pop culture so convincingly.

해석 선생님과 부모님들은 종종 어린 세대들에게 팝 문화는 지적 능력의 발달에 유해한 영향을 미칠 수 있다는 것을 주입하려 한다. (a) 그러나 Steven Johnson은 그의 책 〈팝 문화가 어떻게 우리를 더욱 똑똑하게 만들어 주는가〉에서 다른 견해를 보이고 있다. (b) 이 책에서, 그는 팝 문화가 IQ 수치의 점진적 상승에 원인이 된다고 주장한다. (c) 팝 문화는 종종 기성세대에게 반항적이며 심지어 어린 세대에게 퇴폐성을 주입하고 있다고 여겨진다. (d) 이것은 팝 문화의 긍정적 효과를 매우 확신 있게 주장하고 있는 대담한 첫 번째 책이기 때문에 Johnson의 관점은 칭찬뿐 아니라 많은 비판도 받아왔다.

해설 스티븐 존슨의 책이 팝 문화의 긍정적 영향에 대해 주장하고 있다는 내용의 글이다. 팝 문화의 긍정적 효과가 이어져야 하는 위치에 (c)문장은 팝 문화에 대한 부정적 견해들을 이야기하고 있으므로 앞뒤의 문장과 연결되지 않는다.

오답 분석 첫 문장에서는 팝 문화에 대한 편견으로 도입부에 속하며, (a)문장은 그에 반대하는 스티븐 존슨의 책에 대한 언급을 하고 있으므로 주제문이 된다. (b)문장은 (a)를 뒷받침하는 내용이고, (d)문장은 스티븐 존슨의 책에 대한 사람들의 반응이므로 모두 유기적으로 연결되어 있다.

어휘 **instill** 주입하다, 불어넣다
detrimental 유해한, 해로운
rebellious 반항적인, 다루기 힘든
decadence 퇴폐, 타락, 방종
standpoint 관점, 입장, 견지
audacious 대담한, 무례한
convincingly 설득력 있게

Answers:

1. (c) 2. (c)

Build Up 

▶▶ Part I Read the passage and choose the option that best fits the blank.

1. Mary Shelley's *Frankenstein* is arguably one of the most popular and influential novels of the early 20th Century. Infused with elements from Romanticism as well as Gothic Horror, the novel has had _______________ in contemporary popular culture. At a first glance, Shelley's work appears to be a straightforward gothic horror novel based on the premise of a monster. However, the many themes and messages in the novel hint at the actual complexity of the story. In fact, part of the novel's appeal has been the fact that the story is so rich with metaphors and allegories that can be interpreted in many ways.

(a) its fair share of critics
(b) a significant influence
(c) a negative response
(d) no impact whatsoever

▶▶ Part II Choose the option that correctly answers the question.

2. Ratings juggernaut *CSI: Crime Scene Investigation* has invited Rolling Stones' lead guitarist Ron Wood to appear as a guest star as a safecracker. But he, after being warned by Daltrey that producers were extremely demanding, turned down the opportunity to be in *CSI*. Roger Daltrey, another famed musician of *The Who*, coincidentally the band who recorded the *CSI* main theme, made an appearance as a back-from-the-dead gangster. But after that he was required to act as five different characters; the roles apparently stretching his talents to their limit.

Q. What is the main idea of the passage?

(a) Roger Daltrey is shortly to appear in a cameo role on CSI.
(b) Ron Wood advised his old friend Roger not to appear on CSI.
(c) A rock musician has refused an offer to appear on CSI.
(d) The Rolling Stones will soon record a new CSI theme tune.

3. We owe to our students, interns, and trainees, nondiscriminatory access to education and training. We shall provide education and training that is relevant, informed and accurate with respect to the needs of our student body. We recognize the need to responsibly mentor our students in their professional and academic development. We are committed to continuing education in order to improve and expand our skills and knowledge, and our onus to inform students of their ethical responsibilities. Students can be assured that their contributions to our professional activities, including research and publication, will be appropriately recognized.

Q. According to the passage, which of the following statements is NOT true?

(a) Careful monitoring of student progress is a key area of responsibility.
(b) The needs of students engaged in continuing education take precedence.
(c) It is important that student's research be properly acknowledged.
(d) One key goal is to utilize unbiased criteria for entry to education.

4. There used to be the world's largest and most successful tuna fishing fleet in San Diego until the 1980's. However, in more recent years, tuna fishing has been proven to be harder as migratory tuna have deviated from their usual migratory route. Representatives of San Diego's tuna fishing industry announced that tuna used to only follow warm currents but accelerating global warming is causing the melting of northern glaciers, producing cold water currents and driving the fish deeper and farther offshore, making them much more difficult to catch.

Q. What can be inferred from the news report?

(a) San Diego's tuna fishing industry will not last long.
(b) The temperature of San Diego's coastal waters has risen.
(c) The recent pattern in tuna migration is bound to continue in the next few years.
(d) Tuna migration has not been effected by sea level rise.

▶▶ **Part III** Identify the sentence that least fits the context of the passage.

5. Pilates is a form of physical exercise developed by Joseph Pilates in the early 20th century. (a) It is a form of fitness that teaches accurate methods of breathing and aligning the spine in order to promote a healthy lifestyle while avoiding severe back pains. (b) Pilates and yoga are two different names for the same form of fitness. (c) Extreme concentration is needed to help keep the body balanced and to pay attention to the body while continuing to perform controlled breathing. (d) Precision is also heavily emphasized as each Pilate form requires precise and perfected movement which, when practiced enough, eventually becomes second nature to our everyday lives.

정답: 234p

READING
COMPREHENSION
Week 4

Day 16

Part 2 뒤에 이어질 내용 고르기

▶▶ 지문의 뒤에 이어질 내용을 고르는 문제는 TEPS 독해 영역에서 한 문제 정도 출제되나, 매회 출제되는 것은 아니다. 그러나 기출 유형이므로 정답을 고르는 요령을 알아두어야 한다.

보통 지문의 가장 마지막 문장을 보면 그 뒤에 이어질 내용을 알 수 있지만, 가장 마지막 부분과 연결되는 보기를 찾을 수 없을 때에는 지문의 제일 앞쪽 주제문을 찾아보아야 한다. 주제문에서 A와 B에 대해 다루겠다고 하였는데 그 지문에서 A에 대한 내용만이 언급되었다면, 뒤에 이어질 내용은 B에 대한 내용이 될 것이기 때문이다.

지문 전체의 흐름을 읽을 수 있으면 지문 뒤에 이어질 내용도 알 수 있다

Example

Many of us have great interest in astronomy and more often, an irresistible worship for astrology. While some of us are more fascinated than others by the wonders of the night scene, most of us have trouble if we were asked to locate our favorite stars in the sky. In the northern hemisphere, the star most commonly recognized is Polaris, which is about 15 light-years from the Earth, and is located on the edge of the consolation, Ursa Minor. Interestingly enough, although its scientific name is Polaris, most people know it as the Northern Star.

Q. Which of the following would follow this passage?

(a) Group of stars of the Ursa Minor consolation
(b) Wrongly recognized names of stars in the northern hemisphere
(c) Why people are more familiar with 'Northern star' than 'Polaris'
(d) Scientific names and common names of stars

위의 지문은, 우리가 천문학이나 점성술에 대해 가지고 있는 관심에 비해 별을 알아보는 데에는 매우 서툴다는 내용의 지문이다. 제일 마지막 문장에서, 우리가 가장 흔히 알아볼 수 있는 별은 북극성(Polaris)인데, 그 이름을 우리가 Northern Star라고 알고 있는 경우가 많다고 하였다. 이 마지막 문장을 Interestingly enough(충분히 흥미롭게도)로 시작하고 있다는 것도 하나의 단서가 되며, 따라서 북극성의 이름의 유래에 대한 내용이 이어질 것임을 알 수 있다.

해설: 224p

Catch Up

TEPS 독해 영역에 출제되었던 문제를 풀어봄으로써 실전 문제 유형
을 확실하게 파악해두자.

Part I Read the passage and choose the option that best fits the blank.

1. Manila is one of East Asia's oldest cities as written records of its origin can be traced as far back as 1571 when it was under the rule of Spanish conquistadors. Though the city had existed prior to the advent of Europeans, that pre-Hispanic culture and way of life disappeared under the rule of the Spaniards. After Spain ceded the Philippines to the United States in 1898, the city of Manila was colonized by the Americans and subject to its influence for the next forty years. Years later, the region would finally gain its own autonomy and become independent. The years of rule under several different countries explains why the city of Manila is _________________.

   (a) such a rapidly growing and thriving environment
   (b) so diverse and heavily influenced by other cultures
   (c) such a highly unpopular tourist travel destination
   (d) heavily affected by overpopulation and other problems

2. GIS, also known as geographic information systems, is comprised of a series of systems used to record, analyze, and interpret information of a geographic nature. It is composed of the following components: hardware, software, data, people, and methods. An advantage of using GIS is the improved efficiency in dealing with geographically-referenced data. There is also a greater consistency in recording statistics and more accurate information analysis for users and decision makers. _________________, there are many benefits to using GIS.

   (a) In spite of the systemic defects
   (b) Due to its useful and diverse nature
   (c) Although there is a lack of experience using GIS
   (d) Due to the complexity of manual functions

Answers

TEPS 독해 영역에 출제되었던 기출 문제를 자세한 설명과 함께 완전히 이해하도록 하자.

1

> Manila is one of East Asia's oldest cities as written records of its origin can be traced as far back as 1571 when it was under the rule of Spanish conquistadors. Though the city had existed prior to the advent of Europeans, that pre-Hispanic culture and way of life disappeared under the rule of the Spaniards. After Spain ceded the Philippines to the United States in 1898, the city of Manila was colonized by the Americans and subject to its influence for the next forty years. Years later, the region would finally gain its own autonomy and become independent. The years of rule under several different countries explains why the city of Manila is _______________.
>
> (a) such a rapidly growing and thriving environment
> **(b) so diverse and heavily influenced by other cultures**
> (c) such a highly unpopular tourist travel destination
> (d) heavily affected by overpopulation and other problems

해석 마닐라는 그 기원에 관한 기록이 스페인 정복자의 통치 아래 있었던 1571년으로 거슬러 올라갈 수 있었기 때문에, 동아시아의 가장 오래된 도시 중 하나이다. 비록 그 도시가 유럽인들의 출현 이전에도 존재했었지만, 스페인계 이전의 문화와 삶의 방식은 스페인 사람의 통치 아래에서 사라졌다. 스페인이 필리핀을 미국에 양도한 1898년 이후, 마닐라라는 도시는 미국에 의해 식민지화되었고 40년 동안 미국의 영향력 하에 있었다. 시간이 흐른 후, 그 지역은 마침내 자치권을 얻고 독립하게 되었다. 여러 다른 국가들 하에서 통치된 세월은 왜 마닐라라는 도시가 그렇게 다양하면서도 크게 다른 문화에 의해 영향을 받았는지를 설명해준다.

해설 마닐라가 스페인과 미국에 의해 통치 받았던 것을 설명하고 있다. 따라서 정답은 (b)가 된다.

**오답
분석** (a) 급속한 성장과 번화한 환경인지 – 다른 나라들에 의해 통치를 받았다는 내용이므로 성장에 대한 것은 정답이 될 수 없다.
(c) 관광객의 여행 목적지로 많이 인기 없는지 – 관광에 대한 내용은 지문에 언급되지 않았다.
(d) 인구 과잉과 다른 문제들로 심하게 영향을 받는지 – 마닐라라는 도시의 문제점은 언급되지 않았다.

어휘 **conquistador** 정복자
advent 출현, 도래
cede (권리를) 양도하다; (영토를) 할양하다
autonomy 자치; 자치권

2

GIS, also known as geographic information systems, is comprised of a series of systems used to record, analyze, and interpret information of a geographic nature. It is composed of the following components: hardware, software, data, people, and methods. An advantage of using GIS is the improved efficiency in dealing with geographically-referenced data. There is also a greater consistency in recording statistics and more accurate information analysis for users and decision makers. ___________________________, there are many benefits to using GIS.

(a) In spite of the systemic defects
(b) Due to its useful and diverse nature
(c) Although there is a lack of experience using GIS
(d) Due to the complexity of manual functions

해석 지리 정보 시스템인 GIS에는 자연 지형의 정보를 기록, 분석, 해석하는 데 쓰여진 여러 개의 시스템이 포함되어 있다. 그것은 다음과 같은 구성요소로 이루어져 있는데, 하드웨어, 소프트웨어, 데이터, 사람, 그리고 방법이다. GIS를 사용하는 이점은 지형적인 참고자료를 다루는 데에 있어서 향상된 효율이다. 또한 사용자와 결정권자들을 위한 통계자료의 기록과 좀 더 정확한 정보 분석에 큰 일관성을 지닌다. 그것의 유용성과 다양한 성질 때문에 GIS를 사용하는 것은 많은 장점이 있다.

해설 GIS의 구성 요소와 쓰임새에 대해 설명하고 있는 글이다. 지문의 마지막 문장에 빈칸이 있으므로 이 지문의 내용을 정리하는 문장이다. 따라서 정답은 '(b) 유용성과 다양성 때문에'가 된다.

오답 분석 (a) 시스템적인 결함에도 불구하고 – 결함에 대한 내용은 지문에 언급되지 않았다.
(c) GIS 사용의 경험이 부족함에도 불구하고 – 이 지문은 사용 경험의 유무에 따른 장점을 언급하고 있지 않다.
(d) 수동 기능의 복잡성 때문에 – GIS의 복잡성은 언급되지 않았다.

어휘 comprise 포함하다.
compose 조립하다, 구성하다; 만들다
consistency 일관성
accurate 정확한, 한 치의 오차도 없는

Answers:

1. (b) 2. (b)

Build Up

▶▶ Part I Read the passage and choose the option that best fits the blank.

1. In terms of cancer and nutrition, it is said that there are some foods geared towards cancer prevention but others detrimental to our health. To defend against our health from cancer, it is important to reduce the intake of dietary saturated and unsaturated fat by approximately 30 to 40 percent. Many experts have undergone experiments with the hopes to prove that fiber can lead the fight for the prevention of cancer. They hypothesized that fiber may reduce the risk of cancer by slowing down and inactivating the effect of carcinogens. ____________, even though many believe in this theory, studies of the fiber-cancer connection have been inconsistent and controversial.

   (a) However
   (b) Moreover
   (c) Otherwise
   (d) Indeed

▶▶ Part II Choose the option that correctly answers the question.

2. The history of today's simple mechanical devices goes back in time to ancient Greece. For example, Archimedes, a Greek mathematician, physicist and engineer, who lived some two thousand two hundred years ago, was one of the leading scientists in mechanics. Archimedes is known to us today for his innovative machines and simple devices such as the lever. While Archimedes did not invent the lever, he was the first to understand the principle involved. To explain the principle of levers, he once designed pulley systems that allowed sailors enabled to move a large ship by themselves.

   Q. What is the topic of the passage?

   (a) The history and science of mechanical devices
   (b) The beginnings of Greek mathematics
   (c) The various uses of levers in ancient Greece
   (d) The influence of Greek mathematicians on physics

3. The latest step toward greater realism in virtual reality comes in the form of a unique pressure vest, which allows the wearer to experience the physical sensation caused by a blow from being struck by a fist or weapon, a crashing vehicle or falling down. The 3rd Space vest, as it has been named, was developed from a medical device designed to allow doctors to more accurately remote-diagnose patient illnesses. While still currently pending approval from the US Food and Drug Administration the vest is expected to complement existing sensor gloves and virtual headsets in the lucrative first-person shooter computer game market.

Q. Which is correct about the passage?

(a) The market for first-person shooter computer games is expanding.
(b) The FDA will approve the vest if it is found to be safe.
(c) The computer game market is about to get another exciting accessory.
(d) Doctors can now diagnose patient illnesses without being there.

4. The word subculture suggests that there is a separate entity within a larger society with which the larger society must contend. In other words, a subculture is a socio-cultural formation that exists as a sort of enclave or island within the larger society. Subcultures constitute meaningful systems and modes of expression or life styles developed by subordinately positioned groups in response to the dominant systems. They reflect the attempt to solve structural contradictions arising from the wider societal context.

Q. What can be inferred from the passage?

(a) Cultures and subcultures exist for one and the same purpose.
(b) A subculture helps to provide an important public service.
(c) Subcultures exist to counterpoint a larger society's contradictions.
(d) Subcultures are necessary to maintain a well-functioning wider society.

▶▶ **Part III** Identify the sentence that least fits the context of the passage.

5. As pollution is one of key concerns of the people all over the world, it's important to search for ways to help the environment. (a) Using tactful techniques to remove carbons from the atmosphere is one way of reaching this goal. (b) Also, replanting trees and ceasing or at least reducing deforestation can be another way to save our environment. (c) Increasing the usage of toxic products containing chlorofluorocarbons or CFCs, which exist in common household items such as hair sprays, is the culprit for the destruction of the ozone layer. (d) Recycling and using environmentally-friendly materials can also give mother earth a helping hand.

정답: 237p

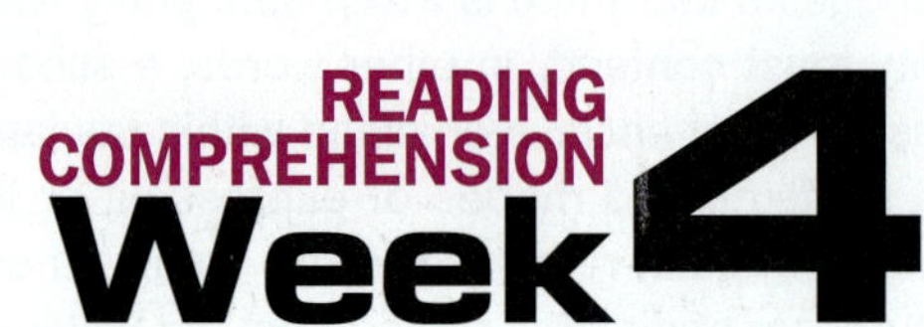
READING
COMPREHENSION
Week 4

Day 17

Part 2 화자의 어조

TEPS 독해 영역에서 화자의 어조를 묻는 지문도 한 문제 정도 출제된다.
화자의 어조를 고르는 문제는 전반적인 글의 뉘앙스를 파악하면 세부적인 내용을 전부 다 이해하지 못했다고 할지라도 그리 어렵지 않게 맞출 수 있다. 글쓴이가 지문에서 언급하고 있는 대상에 대해 어떤 태도를 가지고 있는가를 알아보고, 보기로 출제되는 단어들을 정확하게 알아두어야 한다.

Example

Communicating positively with your children will not only build their self-esteem and inspire confidence but will also reinforce the good and eliminate the bad behavior. And it's easy once you get the hang of it. All children need to feel loved and accepted, and you can communicate those feelings with your children by the way you speak. The sense of positive self-esteem they learn through their interactions at home will then spill over as your children communicate in the outside world. Positive reinforcement will also help them immensely as they begin school when the self-esteem boost they have gained from home really starts to pay off.

Q. How does the writer feel about positive reinforcement?

(a) Enthusiastic
(b) Apprehensive
(c) Sensitive
(d) Unapologetic

위의 지문은 긍정적 강화가 아이들에게 좋은 영향을 끼친다는 내용이다. 첫 문장에서 지문의 주제와 함께 중요한 내용을 거의 모두 언급하고 있으며, 뒤에 이어지는 내용은 어떤 방식으로 긍정적 강화를 줄 수 있는가를 설명하고 있다. 하이라이트 표시가 된 부분은 '긍정적 강화는 아이들에게 엄청나게 도움이 된다' 라고 언급하며 지문을 마무리하고 있으므로 정답 '(a) 열정적인' 으로 가는 직접적인 단서가 된다.

해설: 85p

Catch Up

TEPS 독해 영역에 출제되었던 문제를 풀어봄으로써 실전 문제 유형
을 확실하게 파악해두자.

Part I Read the passage and choose the option that best fits the blank.

1. The late Giovanni Boccaccio was an Italian writer who was predominantly known for his witty stories. Many of his works were wondrously written, but it was the creation of *The Decameron* that led others to give him the nickname "Father of Italian Prose." More prominently, he stressed the importance of education by being the first Italian in seven centuries to learn how to read classical Greek. ___________, he aided in the search for and identification of the lost writings of ancient literature. Not long after, hundreds of eager scholars were engaged in the task of spreading abroad the new findings, with all sorts of unsettling results.

   (a) Nonetheless
   (b) Furthermore
   (c) On the other hand
   (d) In general

2. The subjects of archaeologists' study are buried and can be unearthed from the ground; they can be touched, felt and observed. Historians research documents and pictographs, sometimes written several thousand years ago. On the other hand, unlike other scholars, astronomers cannot control any object or phenomenon they investigate because astronomy encompasses the collection and analysis of light gathered from objects that are not from Earth. ___________, in most cases astronomers cannot watch the birth and death of the subject of their study because stars live at least a million to a trillion times longer than humans.

   (a) In particular
   (b) In contrast
   (c) Indeed
   (d) In comparison

Answers

TEPS 독해 영역에 출제되었던 기출 문제를 자세한 설명과 함께 완전
히 이해하도록 하자.

1

The late Giovanni Boccaccio was an Italian writer who was predominantly known for his witty stories. Many of his works were wondrously written, but it was the creation of *The Decameron* that led others to give him the nickname "Father of Italian Prose." More prominently, he stressed the importance of education by being the first Italian in seven centuries to learn how to read classical Greek. __________, he aided in the search for and identification of the lost writings of ancient literature. Not long after, hundreds of eager scholars were engaged in the task of spreading abroad the new findings, with all sorts of unsettling results.

(a) Nonetheless
(b) Furthermore
(c) On the other hand
(d) In general

해석 고(古)Giovanni Boccaccio는 재치 있는 이야기로 잘 알려진 이탈리아 작가이다. 그의 작품의 대다수가 놀랄 만한 것들이지만, 사람들이 그에게 "이탈리아 산문의 아버지" 라는 별명을 주게끔 이끌었던 것은 바로 '데카메론' 의 창작이었다. 더욱 두드러지게, 그는 7세기 만에 고대 그리스어를 읽는 방법을 배운 첫 번째 이탈리아 사람이 됨으로써 교육의 중요성을 강조했다. 더 나아가, 그는 잃어버린 고대 문학 작품을 찾고 확인하는 것을 도왔다. 오래지 않아, 열정적인 수백 명의 학자들이 새로운 발견들을 널리 퍼뜨리는 임무에 종사하였고, 많은 동요시키는 결과들을 낳았다.

해설 Boccaccio의 업적에 대한 내용의 글이다. 빈칸 뒤에서 또 다른 업적을 덧붙이고 있으므로, 정답은 '(b) Furthermore 더군다나, 더 나아가' 가 된다.

오답
분석
(a) 그럼에도 불구하고, 그렇지만 – 양보나 역접의 의미로 쓰인다.
(c) 다른 한편으로, 이와 반대로 – 앞에 나온 것과 반대가 되거나 대립항에 있는 것을 언급할 때 쓴다.
(d) 일반적으로 – 일반론을 펼 때 쓴다.

어휘
predominantly 뛰어나게, 널리, 우세하게
wondrously 놀랄 만큼, 불가사의 하게
prominently 두드러지게
identification 동일함, 동일하다는 증명[확인, 감정]
eager 열망하는
unsettling 동요시키는, 심란하게 하는

2

The subjects of archaeologists' study are buried and can be unearthed from the ground; they can be touched, felt and observed. Historians research documents and pictographs, sometimes written several thousand years ago. On the other hand, unlike other scholars, astronomers cannot control any object or phenomenon they investigate because astronomy encompasses the collection and analysis of light gathered from objects that are not from Earth. _________, in most cases astronomers cannot watch the birth and death of the subject of their study because stars live at least a million to a trillion times longer than humans.

(a) In particular
(b) In contrast
(c) Indeed
(d) In comparison

해석 고고학자들의 연구 대상은 매장되어 있고 발굴할 수 있기 때문에, 그 내용물들을 만지고 느끼고 관찰할 수 있다. 그리고 역사학자들은 때때로 몇 천 년 전에 쓰여진 문서들이나 상형문자들을 연구한다. 반면에, 다른 학자들과 달리 천문학자들은 그들이 관찰하는 물체나 현상을 조절할 수 없다. 왜냐하면 천문학은 지구에 있지 않은 물체로부터 모은 빛의 분석과 수집을 포함하기 때문이다. 사실상, 별은 인간보다 최소한 백만 년에서 1조 년을 더 살기 때문에, 대부분의 경우 천문학자들은 연구 대상의 탄생과 소멸을 관찰할 수 없다.

해설 천문학 연구가 다른 학문의 연구와 다른 점들을 설명하고 있는 글이다. 빈칸이 있는 문장은 앞 문장의 내용과 관련된 내용을 계속해서 설명하고 있기 때문에 정답은 (c) indeed가 된다.

오답 (a) 특히 – 특정하게 한 가지만 집어서 말할 때 쓴다.
분석 (b) 대조적으로 – 앞의 내용과 대조를 이루는 반대의 내용이 나올 때 쓴다.
(d) 비교하면 – 앞의 내용과 다른 것을 비교할 때 쓴다.

어휘 **unearth** 발굴하다, 파내다
pictograph 상형문자
encompass 둘러싸다, 포위하다; ~을 포함하다. 싸다
gather 모으다; 따다, 채집하다
occupation 직업, 업무

Answers:

1. (b) 2. (c)

Build Up 

TEPS 독해 영역의 실전 문제와 가장 가까운 유형과 난이도의 예상 문제를 통해 실력을 쌓자.

▶▶ **Part I** Read the passage and choose the option that best fits the blank.

1. Dear Sir,

   I'm writing this letter of appreciation on behalf of the entire crew of flight attendants working with XYZ International Airlines for providing us with newly designed uniforms. We are very grateful to be working at such a wonderful company that consists of team-oriented people and are now in high spirits at how befitting and spectacular the new uniforms turned out to be. We all agree that this innovative design is more comfortable, allowing for more movement. ___________, on behalf of all of the flight attendants, I would like to tell you that we cannot thank enough for making such an incredibly great design!

   (a) In fact
   (b) Therefore
   (c) However
   (d) Similarly

▶▶ **Part II** Choose the option that correctly answers the question.

2. *Lara Croft: Tomb Raider* is a film highly recommended by many who consider it a great achievement to make a live action film look like a video game. However, I don't see anything remarkable in this, nor as any reason to celebrate. Live action that is indistinguishable from animation, does not make films more real for us; rather, it makes it hyper illusive. Furthermore, director Simon West's overuse of visual effects in *Lara Croft: Tomb Raider* diverts the viewers' attention from the storyline. What many of us should realize is that what he gives us is an over-fantasized world of violence to improve the heroine's aggression skills.

   Q. Which best summarizes the writer's opinion of the film *Lara Croft: Tomb Raider*?

   (a) It distorts the legend of the video game for the purpose of film making.
   (b) It fails in using live action in a contemporary setting.
   (c) It misrepresents the main character with underlying sarcasm.
   (d) It compounds live action film inaccuracies with excessive visual effects.

3. Malaria is a parasitic disease which affects over 300 million people globally and is fatal to between 1 and 1.5 million people annually. Though malaria was once spread wherever mosquitoes existed, recently it has been confined to Africa, South America and Southeast Asia. It is carried by only the female mosquito, whilst the male only feeds on plant juices and so presents no threat of disease transmission to humans. As the infected insect bites it injects the contents of its guts, thereby transporting the parasite to a new victim. The parasite then makes its way to the liver of its new host where it destroys red blood cells causing anemia. If untreated, the parasite spreads to other organs leading to death.

Q. Which is correct about the passage?

(a) The gut contents of the female mosquito contain the malaria parasite.
(b) Malaria, despite its containment, continues to be a fatal problem.
(c) Male mosquitoes are not part of the malaria problem.
(d) Malaria spreads to wherever mosquitoes live.

4. Rudeness is not usually considered a crime, but "flames" – angry or heated messages exchanged online – may be considered out of bounds by law. For psychologists, the phenomenon individuals anonymously post insulting messages on the Internet is a new area of interest. "Flaming" is not simply because of individual personality traits, but is largely due to the way the human brain is shaped. In face to face encounters, people experience an array of stimuli such as vocal tone and facial expressions. With online text-only communications, these stimuli are luxury items.

Q. What could be inferred from the lecture?

(a) Poor communication skills lead to flaming.
(b) Sensory input may work to inhibit flaming.
(c) Impulsive behavior is not innate but learned.
(d) Internet flamers are typically jealous of others.

▶▶ Part III Identify the sentence that least fits the context of the passage.

5. Halloween is a popular holiday that is celebrated by North Americans every year on October 31. (a) Though its origin stems from religious roots, it has become the most commercialized holidays in the present day. (b) The jack-o-lantern, a carved pumpkin, is often synonymous with this particular tradition. (c) Children dress up in costumes of their favorite heroes or comic book characters and go from door to door 'trick or treating.' (d) This tradition is fun for children, but in terms of industry, the costumes and sweets are actually a good means to make people spend extra money.

정답: 239p

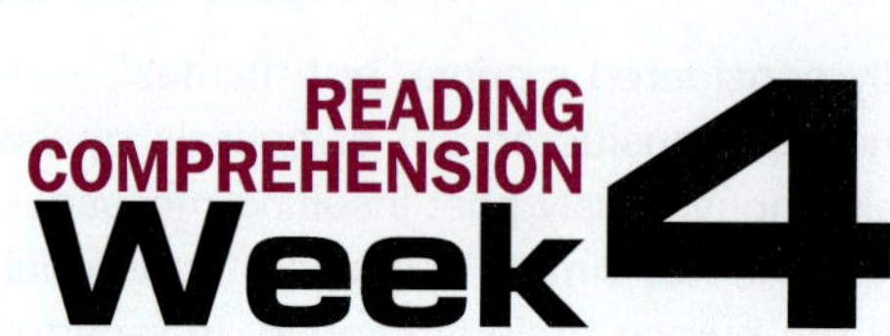

READING
COMPREHENSION
Week 4

Day 18
Part 3 소재에서 벗어난 문장 고르기

TEPS 독해 영역에서 글의 흐름상 어색한 문장을 고르는 Part 3 유형의 문제는 가장 마지막에 세 문제가 출제된다. 수적으로 적은 문항 수를 차지하지만 배점이 높은 문제들이며, 정답을 고르는 요령을 터득하면 빠른 시간 안에 풀 수 있는 문제들이므로 충분한 연습을 통해 실전에 대비해두어야 한다.

흐름상 어색한 문장이란 지문의 흐름을 해치기 때문에 지문에서 제외시켜야 하는 문장을 뜻하므로, 지문에서 다루고 있는 소재에서 벗어난 문장이 섞여 있는 경우 쉽게 정답을 고를 수 있다.

When land surveyors first began measuring a peninsula, they were unable to collect accurate measurements during winter. (a) This was discovered when measurements taken during winter differed greatly from those collected during summer. (b) The measurement is much more accurate these days because the average temperature has risen due to global warming. (c) The surveyors used long metal chain like a ruler that stretched across forests and swamps. (d) After some time, they realized the source of the inaccurate measurements, the long metal chain because metals contract under severely cold temperatures.

위의 지문은 과거 겨울에 토지를 측정할 때 금속 측정 도구의 길이가 줄어들어 정확한 측정이 어려웠다는 내용이다. 그러나 (b)는 요즈음의 토지 측정에 대한 내용이므로 이 글에서 다루고 있는 소재에서 완전히 벗어나 있다. 이렇게 소재에서 벗어난 문장이 섞여 있는 경우가 Part 3 문제들 중 가장 쉬운 유형이다.

해설: 53p

Catch Up

TEPS 독해 영역에 출제되었던 문제를 풀어봄으로써 실전 문제 유형
을 확실하게 파악해두자.

Part II Choose the option that correctly answers the question.

1. As a senior, you want to feel like you are independent. And an important part of that
    independence is feeling like you are still able to drive. While many senior citizens strive
    to keep their driving privileges, some sections of the community are now calling for the
    mandatory examination of senior citizen's vision, following a series of accidents
    involving seniors over the past few months. One suggestion was that drivers over 70
    years of age should go through a driving test each year in order to keep their driver's
    license valid.

    Q. What can be inferred from the passage?

    (a) Communities should take actions to improve the senior citizens' vision.
    (b) People blamed senior citizens for a series of road accidents.
    (c) Senior citizens regard a driver's license as a symbol of youth.
    (d) Senior citizens' driving skills should be reassessed regularly to ensure road
        safety.

2. During the sixteenth and seventeenth centuries, several thousand crypto-Jews or secret
    Jews emigrated from Spain and Portugal to the Indies. Crypto-Jews are Jewish
    descendents who secretly maintain Jewish traditions, often while adhering to other
    faiths, such as Catholicism as they were not allowed to practice their own religion, but
    instead were forced to practice Catholicism. However, the reason for emigration of some
    Jews had little to do with religion, but mostly to do with better material circumstances. In
    other words, they sought wealth rather than freedom of religion.

    Q. What can be inferred about Crypto-Jews?

    (a) Most of them were forced to make decision between the traditional religion and
        death.
    (b) Many suffered under poor living conditions in Portugal.
    (c) They absorbed their new religion, Catholicism with ease.
    (d) Some of them thought Spain and Portugal offered them wealthier living
        environments.

Answers

1

As a senior, you want to feel like you are independent. And an important part of that independence is feeling like you are still able to drive. While many senior citizens strive to keep their driving privileges, some sections of the community are now calling for the mandatory examination of senior citizen's vision, following a series of accidents involving seniors over the past few months. One suggestion was that drivers over 70 years of age should go through a driving test each year In order to keep their driver's license valid.

Q. What can be inferred from the passage?

(a) Communities should take actions to improve the senior citizens' vision.
(b) People blamed senior citizens for a series of road accidents.
(c) Senior citizens regard a driver's license as a symbol of youth.
(d) Senior citizens' driving skills should be reassessed regularly to ensure road safety.

해석 고령자로서, 당신은 자신이 독립적이라고 느끼고 싶어한다. 그리고 그러한 독립의 중요한 부분은 당신이 여전히 운전할 수 있다고 느끼는 것이다. 많은 고령자 시민들은 그들의 운전 특권을 유지하려고 노력하지만, 지난 몇 달 동안의 고령자들이 관련된 일련의 사고에 따라, 사회의 일부에서는 이제 고령자 시민의 의무적인 시력검사를 요구하고 있다. 70세가 넘는 운전자들은 그들의 운전면허증의 유효성을 유지하기 위해 매년 운전 테스트를 받아야 한다는 한 가지 제안이 나왔다.

해설 고령자 시민들에 의한 사고의 위험성이 있기 때문에, 고령자들은 운전 특권을 유지하기 위해서 테스트를 받게 되었다는 내용의 글이다. 따라서 정답은 '(d) 고령 시민의 운전 기술은 도로 안전을 확보하기 위해 주기적으로 재평가되어야 한다.'이다.

**오답
분석** (a) 사회에서 고령 시민의 시력을 향상시키기 위한 조치를 취해야 한다. – 지문에서는 시력 검사를 실시한다고 하였으므로 정답이 될 수 없다.
(b) 사람들은 도로 사고에 대해 고령 시민을 책망한다. – 시민들의 반응은 언급되지 않았다.
(c) 고령 시민들은 운전면허를 젊음의 상징으로 간주한다. – 지문에 언급되지 않은 내용이다.

어휘 **senior** 고령자, 상위의, 선임의
strive 노력하다, 애쓰다
privilege 특권
mandatory 명령의;강제의, 의무의
valid 유효한

2

During the sixteenth and seventeenth centuries, several thousand crypto-Jews or secret Jews emigrated from Spain and Portugal to the Indies. Crypto-Jews are Jewish descendents who secretly maintain Jewish traditions, often while adhering to other faiths, such as Catholicism as they were not allowed to practice their own religion, but instead were forced to practice Catholicism. However, the reason for emigration of some Jews had little to do with religion, but mostly to do with better material circumstances. In other words, they sought wealth rather than freedom of religion.

Q. What can be inferred about Crypto-Jews?

(a) Most of them were forced to make decision between the traditional religion and death.
(b) Many suffered under poor living conditions in Portugal.
(c) They absorbed their new religion, Catholicism with ease.
(d) Some of them thought Spain and Portugal offered them wealthier living environments.

해석 16세기와 17세기에 수천의 비밀 유대인 또는 은둔 유대인들은 스페인, 포르투갈, 인도로까지 이주했다. 비밀 유대인은 종종 자신의 종교를 실천하도록 허용받지 못하고, 대신에 카톨릭을 믿으라고 강요받았기 때문에 카톨릭과 같은 다른 종교를 따르기도했지만, 유대인의 전통을 비밀리에 유지하고 있는 유대의 후손들이다. 그러나 어떤 유대인들에게 있어 이주의 이유는 종교와 거의 연관이 없고 대부분은 더 나은 물질적 환경과 관련되어 있다. 다른 말로 하자면, 그들은 종교적 자유보다는 부유한 삶을 추구하였던 것이다.

해설 지문에서 유대인들 중 일부는 부유한 삶을 위해 이주해 갔다고 하였으므로, 이 글로부터 추론할 수 있는 바는 '(d) 그들 중 일부는 스페인과 포르투갈이 부유한 생활환경을 제공할 것이라고 생각했다'이다.

오답 분석 (a) 그들 중 대부분은 전통적 종교와 죽음 중 결정을 내리도록 강요당했다. - 죽음에 대한 내용은 지문에 언급되지 않았다.
(b) 포르투갈에서 많은 사람들이 빈곤한 생활환경으로 고통 받았다. - 포르투갈에서 빈곤한 생활을 한 것이 아니라, 빈곤한 생활을 피해 포르투갈로 이주한 사람들도 있었다고 하였다.
(c) 그들은 쉽게 새 종교 카톨릭을 흡수하였다. - 쉽게 카톨릭을 받아들였다는 내용은 지문에 언급되지 않았다.

어휘 **crypto** 비밀 당원, 비밀 동조자
emigrate 타국으로 이주하다
descendent 후손

Answers:

1. (d) 2. (d)

Build Up

TEPS 독해 영역의 실전 문제와 가장 가까운 유형과 난이도의 예상 문제를 통해 실력을 쌓자.

▶▶ Part I Read the passage and choose the option that best fits the blank.

1. A "fringe benefit" is a payment to an employee, but ______________________________.
   Both the terms benefit and fringe benefit have broad meanings for Fringe Benefit Taxation purposes. Benefits wholly include rights, privileges or services associated with a company and the employees' position within it, including fringe benefits. Examples of fringe benefits may include allowing an employee to use a work car for private purposes, reimbursing an expense incurred by an employee, such as school fees, or providing entertainment by way of free tickets to concerts.

   (a) not everyone can take it
   (b) allows two weeks of unpaid leave
   (c) in a different form to salary or wages
   (d) in a restricted form of bonus

▶▶ Part II Choose the option that correctly answers the question.

2. In today's modern society, leisure is defined as free time that is used for recreational purposes and fun. However, that was not always the case, as perceptions of this word have had different meanings and interpretations over time. This often depended on specific groups of people from particular periods in time. One notable example is that of the ancient Greek philosophers who considered leisure to be a form of mental work. In fact, they believed that this notion encompassed studying and focusing on academia in order to develop their intellect through an exertion of the mind. As a result, philosophy and the concept of debates originated from the Greek's use of leisurely time.

   Q. What is the main idea of this passage?

   (a) Many people today regard the main goal of leisure as educating themselves.
   (b) The body as well as the mind was emphasized by many Greek philosophers.
   (c) The concept and interpretation of leisure has varied depending on different time periods.
   (d) Leisure is more important in the present day than it was during ancient Greece.

3. The issue of language in schools is a key issue for many political groups in Malaysia. Although private schools using the Tamil and Chinese languages are allowed, the United Malays National Organization has championed the cause of Malay language usage in schools. As a reflection of this movement, there are now two groups of schools; the private schools are referred to only as national-type schools, whereas public schools that use Malay language receive the title of a national school. English-medium schools, which no longer exist in Malaysia, would have been referred to as national-type schools.

Q. Which of the following is correct according to the passage?

(a) Schools in Malaysia adopting Malay lauguage can be entitled as national schools.
(b) Tamil, Malay and English-medium schools coexist with official recognition in Malaysia.
(c) English-medium schools comprise international and returnee students.
(d) Students who do not speak Chinese must attend a Malay or English-medium school.

4. If you're doing web work you should have a website, because without a website you are invisible to your core audience. A website serves two main purposes. First, a page should display your skills with a few clear and simple examples of your work. This isn't for the accidental visitor to your site who might just hire you, but to increase your network of valuable contacts. The second key purpose of a website is to keep you visible by updating your network on your interests, completed works, and works-in-progress.

Q. What can be inferred from the passage?

(a) The target of this passage is a web-freelancer.
(b) The writer is a web page designer.
(c) Web related job opportunities are scarce.
(d) Maintaining a web site is a very demanding job.

▶▶ **Part III** Identify the sentence that least fits the context of the passage.

5. For over 30 years, Greenpeace has committed themselves to the protection and conservation of the earth while using non-violent methods to promote peace. (a) The organization is geared towards solving problems "from the gecko"; where they start. (b) Among other things, they demote the usage of chemicals hazardous to our environment by promoting products that are environmentally safer. (c) Hairspray causes the ozone layer to thin out, plastic bags remain in the soil without degrading for several decades, and many foods we take in everyday contain chemicals that eventually do harm to our health. (d) They also seek to cease climate change, to protect and defend oceans and forests as well as the animals in danger of extinction.

정답: 242p

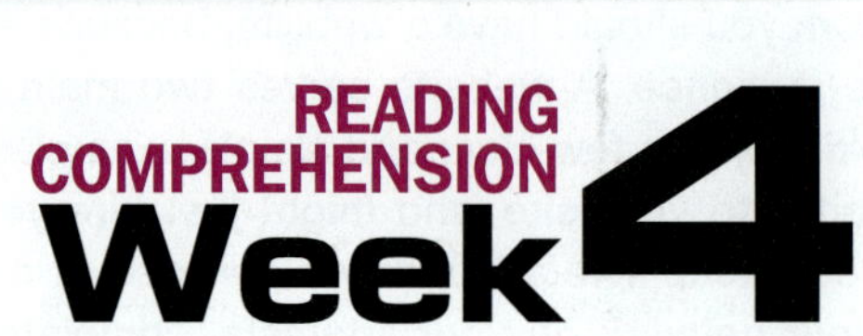
READING
COMPREHENSION
Week 4

Day 19

Part 3 주제에서 벗어난 문장 고르기

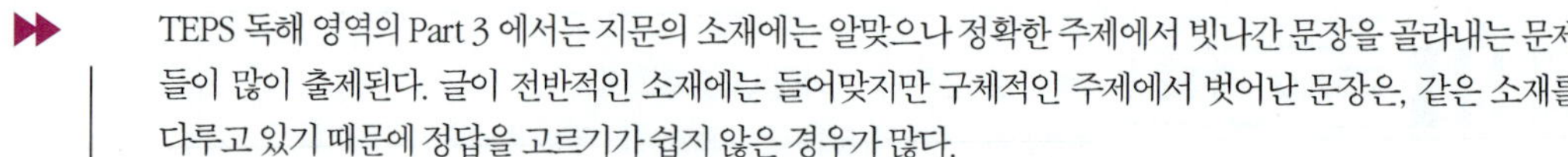

▶▶ TEPS 독해 영역의 Part 3 에서는 지문의 소재에는 알맞으나 정확한 주제에서 빗나간 문장을 골라내는 문제들이 많이 출제된다. 글이 전반적인 소재에는 들어맞지만 구체적인 주제에서 벗어난 문장은, 같은 소재를 다루고 있기 때문에 정답을 고르기가 쉽지 않은 경우가 많다.

그러나 지문의 주제를 정확히 파악하고 앞 뒤 문장들 간의 흐름을 생각하며 읽는 연습을 하다 보면 정답을 고르는 요령을 터득할 수 있다.

Example

Teachers and parents often try to instill to newer generations that pop culture can be detrimental towards the development of the intellect. (a) However, Steven Johnson doesn't seem to think so in his book: *How Pop Culture Makes Us Smarter*. (b) In this book, he argues that popular culture is responsible for the gradual increase in IQ scores. (c) Pop culture is often recognized as rebellious to the older generation and even as instilling decadence to the younger generation. (d) Johnson's standpoint has received many criticisms as well as praise; it is the first audacious book to argue the positive effect of pop culture so convincingly.

위의 지문은 고정관념과 달리, 대중문화가 우리를 더 영리하게 만들어 준다는 스티븐 존슨의 주장을 다루고 있는 글이다. 그러나 (c)는 대중문화가 젊은 층에게 반항적이고 퇴폐적인 면을 조장하는 영향을 끼친다는 내용이므로, 이 글의 소재인 '대중문화'에 대해 다루고 있기는 하지만 주제인 '대중문화의 긍정적 영향'에는 벗어나는 내용이다. 따라서 이 문제의 정답은 (c)가 된다.

지문의 첫 문장에서 대중문화가 해로울 수 있다는 내용이 언급되었기 때문에 빨리 지문을 읽다 보면 (c)문장이 흐름에 어울리는 문장으로 보일 수 있지만, (a)문장에서 역접을 통해 주제문을 강조하고 있으므로 (c)문장이 흐름상 어색한 것임을 확인할 수 있다.

해설: 133p

Catch Up

TEPS 독해 영역에 출제되었던 문제를 풀어봄으로써 실전 문제 유형
을 확실하게 파악해두자.

Part II Choose the option that correctly answers the question.

1. The New York State Assembly has passed legislation that would make it illegal for employers to require nurses to work overtime. The action was applauded by the New York State Nurses Association (NYSNA), which had proposed and promoted the legislation. Research has shown that when nurses work mandatory overtime, patients are at greater risk for medical errors. In addition, nurses who are required to work overtime are more likely to develop injuries that take them out of the workforce and exacerbate the nursing shortage. Mandatory overtime also costs hospitals money in the form of increased nursing turnover. The bill is on the State Senate calendar and nurses are urging Senators to approve it before the end of session. Similar legislation already exists in 11 other states.

    Q. Which of the following is correct according to the report?

    (a) New York is the first state to adopt such legislation.
    (b) Doctors make more mistakes if nurses work overtime.
    (c) Mandatory overtime is now a choice for nurses in New York State.
    (d) New York has become the twelfth state to pass the new bill.

2. With Kazakhstan's gas pipe lines continuing to be built after a decade of development, global companies are examining opportunities to further expand their oil and gas prospects in the region. Their projects will be the most capital intensive in the world, bound to create tremendous business opportunities in the near future. Don't miss the Canadian Energy Institute-sponsored conference on opportunities in Kazakhstan oil and gas at the Convention Center in Toronto. Leading oil industry decision makers will be in attendance. Register for this great opportunity now.

    Q. Which is correct according to the conference notice?

    (a) More capital is needed to expand oil prospects in the Kazakhstan region.
    (b) Business opportunities in Kazakhstan will increase in the future.
    (c) Toronto companies are sponsoring Kazakhstan businesses.
    (d) International companies will share business strategies.

Answers

1

> The New York State Assembly has passed legislation that would make it illegal for employers to require nurses to work overtime. The action was applauded by the New York State Nurses Association (NYSNA), which had proposed and promoted the legislation. Research has shown that when nurses work mandatory overtime, patients are at greater risk for medical errors. In addition, nurses who are required to work overtime are more likely to develop injuries that take them out of the workforce and exacerbate the nursing shortage. Mandatory overtime also costs hospitals money in the form of increased nursing turnover. The bill is on the State Senate calendar and nurses are urging Senators to approve it before the end of session. Similar legislation already exists in 11 other states.
>
> **Q.** Which of the following is correct according to the report?
>
> (a) New York is the first state to adopt such legislation.
> (b) Doctors make more mistakes if nurses work overtime.
> (c) Mandatory overtime is now a choice for nurses in New York State.
> (d) New York has become the twelfth state to pass the new bill.

해석 뉴욕 주 의회는 고용주들이 간호사들로 하여금 시간 외 근무를 하도록 요구하는 것을 불법으로 하는 법안을 통과시켰다. 이 법안을 제안하고 장려한 뉴욕 주 간호사 협회는 이러한 조치에 성원을 보냈다. 간호사들이 강제적인 초과근무를 하게 되면 환자들이 의학적 실수에 대한 엄청난 위험에 처한다는 것을 조사 결과에서 볼 수 있다. 게다가 초과근무를 하는 간호사들은 상해를 입을 가능성이 더 커지게 되어 일을 할 수 없게 되고, 간호사의 부족을 더욱 악화시키게 된다. 의무적 초과근무는 또한, 간호사들의 교대 시간을 더 늘이게 되므로 병원들의 비용이 들게 한다. 이 법안은 주 의회 일정표에 올랐으며, 간호사들은 상원의원들이 법의 개정이 끝나기 전에 이 법안을 승인할 것을 촉구하고 있다. 비슷한 법률이 이미 11개의 다른 주들에도 존재한다.

해설 지문의 마지막 문장에서 11개의 다른 주에서 이 법률이 존재한다고 하였으므로 '(d) 뉴욕 주는 이 새로운 법안을 통과시킨 열두 번째 주가 되었다.'가 지문의 내용과 맞는 내용이다.

오답 분석 (a) 뉴욕 주는 이러한 법안을 채택한 첫 번째 주이다. – 지문의 마지막 문장에서 다른 11개의 주에 이러한 법률이 있다고 하였다.
(b) 간호사들이 초과근무를 하면 의사들이 더 많은 실수를 저지른다. – 지문에 의사들에 대한 내용은 언급되지 않았다.
(c) 의무적 초과근무는 이제 뉴욕 주에서 간호사들에게 선택사항이다. – 선택적이지 않은, 의무적인 초과근무이기 때문에 여러 문제들이 발생한다고 하였으며 법안은 아직 승인되지 않은 상태이다.

어휘 **applaud** 성원하다, 박수 갈채를 보내다, 칭찬하다
exacerbate 악화시키다
turnover 교대
session 의회의 개회, 법정의 개정

With Kazakhstan's gas pipe lines continuing to be built after a decade of development, global companies are examining opportunities to further expand their oil and gas prospects in the region. Their projects will be the most capital intensive in the world, bound to create tremendous business opportunities in the near future. Don't miss the Canadian Energy Institute-sponsored conference on opportunities in Kazakhstan oil and gas at the Convention Center in Toronto. Leading oil industry decision makers will be in attendance. Register for this great opportunity now.

Q. Which is correct according to the conference notice?

(a) More capital is needed to expand oil prospects in the Kazakhstan region.
(b) Business opportunities in Kazakhstan will increase in the future.
(c) Toronto companies are sponsoring Kazakhstan businesses.
(d) International companies will share business strategies.

해석 10년간의 발전 후에 계속해서 건설되고 있는 카자흐스탄의 가스파이프 라인과 함께 전 세계의 회사들은 그 지역에서 석유와 가스에 대한 전망을 좀 더 확장하기 위한 기회를 검토하고 있습니다. 그들의 프로젝트는 세계에서 가장 자본 집약적이고, 멀지 않은 미래에 반드시 엄청난 사업 기회들을 창조하게 될 것입니다. 캐나다 에너지 회사가 지원하며 토론토 컨벤션 센터에서 열리는 카자흐스탄 석유와 가스에 관한 컨퍼런스를 놓치지 마십시오. 석유산업을 선도하는 사람들이 참석할 것입니다. 이 큰 기회에 지금 등록하세요.

해설 지문에서, 카자흐스탄 지역에서는 멀지 않은 미래에 엄청난 사업 기회들이 있을 것이라고 언급하였으므로 정답은 '(b) 미래에 카자흐스탄에서 사업 기회들이 많아질 것이다.'가 된다.

오답 분석 (a) 카자흐스탄 지역의 가능성을 넓히려면 좀 더 많은 자본이 필요하다. – 카자흐스탄 지역은 가능성은 이미 충분하며, 자본이 집약될 것이라고 하였다.
(c) 토론토의 회사들은 카자흐스탄 사업을 지원하고 있다. – 토론토는 컨퍼런스가 열리는 곳이다.
(d) 다국적 회사는 사업 전략들을 나눌 것이다. – 지문에서 언급되지 않은 내용이다.

어휘 **prospect** 전망, 가능성
bound to 꼭 ~하게 되어 있는

Answers:

1. (d) 2. (b)

TEPS 독해 영역의 실전 문제와 가장 가까운 유형과 난이도의 예상 문제를 통해 실력을 쌓자.

▶▶ **Part I** Read the passage and choose the option that best fits the blank.

1. Canada is one of the few countries that provide free heath care to its citizens. However, the nation's universal health care system has been _________________ in recent years. Arguably, big factors in all the upheaval and change have been the cost of funding this service and the decrease in federal transfers. Is it feasible to continue providing free health care for everyone? Have recent reforms affected the quality of health care that is provided? Many issues have been raised over whether such cutbacks and decreases in federal funding will affect the accessibility of health care to the Canadian public

(a) a privately funded public campaign
(b) the subject to various reforms
(c) gaining more popularity and support
(d) modeled after by less liberal countries

▶▶ **Part II** Choose the option that correctly answers the question.

2. Each child develops in a unique way, and some develop language more quickly than others. Typically, during the infancy period of up to 12 months of age, the child is getting ready to talk, responding to noises and babbling. At 18 months of age, you can expect a significant increase in language development, as toddlers reach the third stage of language development. During this period, babies are able to communicate using telegraphic sentences comprised primarily of nouns. For example, a baby might say, "Mommy, no sleep" rather than "Mommy, I don't want to sleep yet." Children in this stage of language development will often repeat the same words of a phrase, because their vocabulary is still developing.

Q. What is the main topic of the lecture?

(a) Typical problems with telegraphic communication for children
(b) Aspects of the third stage of childhood language development
(c) Communication with mothers and its relationship with children's language development
(d) The importance of repetition in increasing children's vocabulary

3. There's nothing more spectacular than a sunrise or sunset over the mountainous Caribbean forest, surrounded by the crystal-clear waters of the sea. However, in order to experience the true panoramic splendor of the Caribbean, you need to see the drenching slopes of the forests when it rains. Over 200 inches of rain fall on the forest each year amounting to an astounding 100 billion gallons of water. Mild temperatures combined with this abundant moisture from the rain, create ideal tropical conditions for the forest's various exotic flora and fauna including the nearly extinct Puerto Rican parrot.

Q. Which is correct about the Caribbean natural forest?

(a) It rains for more than 200 days a year.
(b) It has numerous species of endangered animals.
(c) It has mild temperatures.
(d) It has 200 different kinds of tropical plants.

4. The best satire seeks to administer a shock to the audience when they recognize a joke that deals with a vice. It doesn't necessarily exist to harm or ridicule, but it does seek to damage the structure of the vice. A satire's job is to expose the vice in all its repulsiveness with the aim to eradicate it from a person or society. Bitter medicine followed by candy is a time-honored formula for relief from sickness, and so does satire work by sweetening the barb of wit with laughter. Satirists are often portrayed as constructive critics; far from being destructive, they often depict themselves as redeemers of society from its ills.

Q. What can be inferred from the passage?

(a) Satire plays a role in making people recognize bad practices.
(b) Satire should not be taken seriously because it's only for fun.
(c) Satirists have proven to be very efficient in spreading vices.
(d) Most satire tends to ignore issues related to everyday life.

▶▶ **Part III** Identify the sentence that least fits the context of the passage.

5. Popeye, the Sailor, first starred in the cartoon strip *Thimble Theatre* in 1929. (a) Popeye was created by a man named Elzie Crisler Segar and eventually became a popular animated cartoon series. (b) The title of the comic strip officially modified to being called Popeye, after the death of Segar, by those that continued his work on the cartoon. (c) In the series, in order to defeat villains, Popeye, the Sailor, had to consume spinach and gain physical power. (d) This boosted the sales of spinach by 50 percent, but it didn't last long because kids' interest moved to other cartoon heroes.

정답: 244p

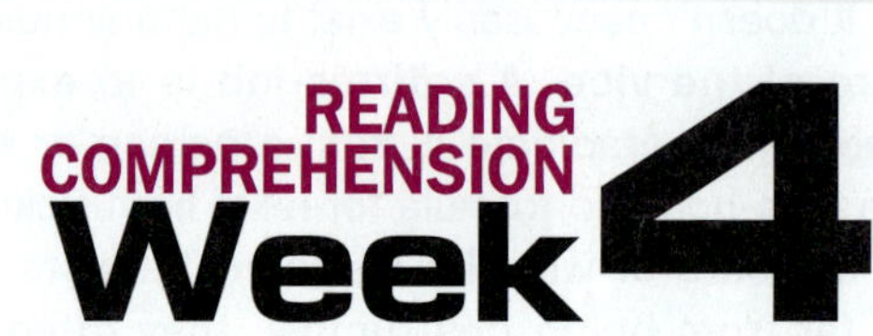
READING
COMPREHENSION
Week 4

<table>
<tr><td>Day 16</td><td>▶▶ Part 2 뒤에 이어질 내용 고르기
유형정리 – 〈TEPS RC 지문 파트별 패턴 파악〉 Part 2 뒤에 이어질 내용 고르기
Catch Up – Part 1 빈칸 채우기</td></tr>
<tr><td>Day 17</td><td>▶▶ Part 2 화자의 어조
유형정리 – 〈TEPS RC 지문 파트별 패턴 파악〉 Part 2 화자의 어조
Catch Up – Part 1 빈칸 채우기</td></tr>
<tr><td>Day 18</td><td>▶▶ Part 3 소재에서 벗어난 문장 고르기
유형정리 – 〈TEPS RC 지문 파트별 패턴 파악〉 Part 3 소재에서 벗어난 문장 고르기
Catch Up – Part 2 추론</td></tr>
<tr><td>Day 19</td><td>▶▶ Part 3 주제에서 벗어난 문장 고르기
유형정리 – 〈TEPS RC 지문 파트별 패턴 파악〉 Part 3 주제에서 벗어난 문장 고르기
Catch Up – Part 2 세부사항 확인</td></tr>
<tr><td>Day 20</td><td>▶▶ Part 3 세부적 내용이 틀린 문장 고르기
유형정리 – 〈TEPS RC 지문 파트별 패턴 파악〉 Part 3 세부적 내용이 틀린 문장 고르기
Catch Up – Part 3</td></tr>
</table>

Day 20

Part 3 세부적 내용이 틀린 문장 고르기

▶▶ 지문의 흐름상 세부적인 내용이 틀린 문장을 고르는 문제는 지문의 소재에 대해 다루고 있으나 세부적인 내용상 오류가 있는 문장을 골라야 하는 문제이다. 따라서 주제에서 빗나간 문장들을 고를 때와 같이 빨리 읽다 보면 정답이 되는 문장을 놓칠 수 있다.

지문의 주제를 정확히 파악하고 앞 문장과 어떠한 관계로 이어지고 있는가를 따지면서 읽으면 지문의 유기적 흐름을 파악할 수 있으므로, 내용상의 오류를 발견할 수 있다. 빠른 시간에 정답을 찾아야 하므로 항상 문장 간의 관계를 따지며 읽는 연습을 하는 것이 필요하다.

Example

William Faulkner, a great American writer, set a fictional county named 'Yoknapatawpha County' to depict social changes in 19th through 20th century and people at that times. (a) All the names of the places within his works were mainly senseless, long, five syllable blurbs. (b) While some of his characters were based on real people, fictional families such as the Compsons, Snopes and Sartoris were also created and used in many of his work. (c) Profound truths regarding the South and the nature of humans were revealed through these fictional characters. (d) This can be found throughout his stories, most notably in *The Sound and the Fury* and *Light in August*.

위의 지문의 William Faulkner의 작품에 등장하는 가상의 마을과 그 마을의 가상의 인물들에 대한 내용이다. 가상의 마을과 가상의 인물들을 통해 William Faulkner는 인간사에 대한 심오한 진실을 전달하고 있다고 하였다.

그런데 (a)문장은 Faulkner의 작품에 등장하는 지명들이 너무 길고 터무니없으며 마치 광고 문구와 같다는 내용을 언급하고 있다. 이 문장은 Faulkner의 작품에 언급된 지명에 대한 내용인 듯하여 소재와 주제에 모두 적합한 문장으로 보일 수 있지만, 사실상 지문의 전반적인 내용과 전혀 관련이 없는 문장이다.

이렇게 세부적인 내용이 지문의 흐름상 오류가 되는 경우는 앞 뒤 문장을 연결하며 지문을 끝까지 읽어보아야 한다.

해설: 92p

Catch Up

Part III Identify the sentence that least fits the context of the passage.

1. Since the discovery of the reed pen by Egyptians, today's commonly used stationery has been evolving at a leisurely pace. (a) The pen has gone through many transformations and has been continually improved to control the flow of ink amongst other things. (b) The roller ball pen, consisting of a mobile ball and liquid ink, was created in order to produce smoother lines and was continually tweaked since its birth in the 1980s. (c) Plans are afoot to convert the humble writing instrument into a wireless digital device. (d) Eventually, the porous point pen was introduced to solve the problem of the pen tip broadening under applied pressure in the 1990s.

2. Pterodactyls are commonly referred to as dinosaurs; however, it can be said that this is quite incorrect. (a) Although the Greek word pterodactyl is the more popular way of distinguishing the "flying dinosaur," it is actually called a pterosaur, meaning "winged lizard." (b) As the direct translation of the word may suggest, the pterosaur is indeed a large lizard that evolved flight, and is the first vertebrate to do so. (c) The wings were formed by muscle tissue, skin and fifty-six extra bones. (d) The term "dinosaurs" describes a group of terrestrial reptiles that possess a unique upright stance; therefore excluding the pterosaur and putting it in a category of its own.

Answers

1

> Since the discovery of the reed pen by Egyptians, today's commonly used stationery has been evolving at a leisurely pace. (a) The pen has gone through many transformations and has been continually improved to control the flow of ink amongst other things. (b) The roller ball pen, consisting of a mobile ball and liquid ink, was created in order to produce smoother lines and was continually tweaked since its birth in the 1980s. (c) Plans are afoot to convert the humble writing instrument into a wireless digital device. (d) Eventually, the porous point pen was introduced to solve the problem of the pen tip broadening under applied pressure in the 1990s.

해석 이집트인에 의해 갈대 펜이 발견된 이후로, 오늘날 일반적으로 사용되는 문구류는 천천히 진화를 거듭해오고 있다. (a) 펜은 많은 변형을 겪었고, 다른 요소들 중에서도 잉크의 유입량을 조절하는 것이 끊임없이 향상되어왔다. (b) 움직이는 볼과 액체 잉크로 구성된 롤러 볼펜은 부드러운 선을 그리기 위해 생산되었고, 그것은 1980년대에 만들어진 이래로 끊임없이 개조되어 왔다. (c) 단순한 쓰기 도구를 선 없는 디지털 장치로 변환시키려는 계획이 진행 중이다. (d) 마침내 1990년대에 침투성 펜이 실질적인 압력 하에서 발생하는 펜 끝의 무뎌짐을 해결하기 위해 도입되었다.

해설 펜의 발전에 대한 내용의 글이다. 현재까지 어떻게 펜이 진보해오고 있는가를 설명하는 가운데, 80년대와 90년대의 진보 사이에 앞으로의 계획을 밝히고 있으므로 (c)가 정답이 된다.

오답 분석 (a)는 첫 문장에 대한 부연 설명의 기능을 하고 있으며, (b)와 (d)는 그에 대한 세부적인 예시의 기능을 하고 있으므로 유기적으로 연결되고 있다. (c)의 디지털 장치는 앞뒤 문장과 연결되지 않는 내용이다.

어휘
stationery 문구
leisurely 천천히, 유유히
tweak 개조하다
smoother 부드럽게 하는 기구
afoot 진행 중인, 일이 벌어지고 있는
convert 변하게 하다, 전환시키다
humble 겸손한, 낮은
porous 스며드는, 침투성의, 구멍이 많은

Pterodactyls are commonly referred to as dinosaurs; however, it can be said that this is quite incorrect. (a) Although the Greek word pterodactyl is the more popular way of distinguishing the "flying dinosaur," it is actually called a pterosaur, meaning "winged lizard." (b) As the direct translation of the word may suggest, the pterosaur is indeed a large lizard that evolved flight, and is the first vertebrate to do so. (c) The wings were formed by muscle tissue, skin and fifty-six extra bones. (d) The term "dinosaurs" describes a group of terrestrial reptiles that possess a unique upright stance; therefore excluding the pterosaur and putting it in a category of its own.

해석 익수룡은 흔히 공룡이라고 불리우지만, 이것은 부정확하다고 볼 수 있다. (a) 그리스어인 익수룡이 '날아다니는 공룡'을 구별하는 데 더욱 많이 쓰이는 방법이기는 하지만, 사실상 '날개 달린 도마뱀'을 의미하는 '익룡'이라고 불리는 것이 맞다. (b) 이 단어의 직역이 보여주듯이, 익룡은 사실 비행을 진화시킨 커다란 도마뱀이며, 척추동물로서 처음이었다. (c) 날개는 근육 조직, 피부, 그리고 56개의 별도의 뼈들로 이루어져 있었다. (d) '공룡'이라는 용어는 직립 자세를 특징으로 갖는 뭍에 사는 파충류의 그룹으로 묘사되며, 그러므로 익수룡은 제외되고 그 자신만의 범주를 갖게 된다.

해설 (c)는 pterodactyl(익수룡)과 pterosaur(익룡)에 대한 내용이 아니라, '날개' 자체에 대한 내용이므로 이 글의 흐름에서 벗어난 문장이다.

오답 분석 pterodactyl(익수룡)과 pterosaur(익룡)이 서로 다르다는 것을 말해주면서 pterodactyl은 dinosaur(공룡)의 범주에 포함되지 않는다는 것을 제시하고 있다. (b)문장과 (d)문장을 이어보면 '익룡'이라는 것은 비행을 할 수 있었던 도마뱀이며 '익수룡'은 공룡이 아니라 그 자신만의 범주에 포함된다는 내용이므로 서로 연결되어 있다는 것을 알 수 있다.

어휘 **pterodactyl** 익수룡
pterosaur 익룡
vertebrate 척추동물
terrestrial 지구상의, 지상의, 뭍의, 흙의
upright 직립한, 곧은, 똑바로 선
stance 자세, 위치

Answers:

1. (c) 2. (c)

Build Up

TEPS 독해 영역의 실전 문제와 가장 가까운 유형과 난이도의 예상 문제를 통해 실력을 쌓자.

▶▶ **Part I** Read the passage and choose the option that best fits the blank.

1. One of the most important events in China's history was the Chinese May Fourth Movement in 1919. It was the first mass movement in modern Chinese history as it occurred during the early 20th Century. Basically, the intellectuals and students of the nation rallied together in an anti-foreign movement and protest of the Treaty of Versailles. However, the magnitude of this event went far beyond that of a mere mass. The Chinese May Fourth Movement was an epic event in modern Chinese history ______________________________ as evidenced by the changes in the nation's social, political, and cultural way of life.

   (a) as the nation adopted some capitalist principles
   (b) as popular leaders appeared to change the nation's practices
   (c) as it began the shift away from classical tradition
   (d) as people realized the importance of participation

▶▶ **Part II** Choose the option that correctly answers the question.

2. Heisenberg argued that it's impossible to measure a system without interfering with that system. That is, the method of observation we use essentially changes the system's dimensions. If you wish to look at a subatomic particle, you have to bounce another particle off it for it to appear; thus its motion will be altered during the process of observation. In measuring the position of an electron, for example, its speed will be changed. However, as a consequence of this change in speed its position is no longer certain. This explains the basis for Heisenberg's Uncertainty Principle.

   Q. What is the best title for the passage?

   (a) How to Measure Particle Velocity Successfully
   (b) Heisenberg and the Nobel Prize
   (c) The Uncertainty of the Velocity of a Particle
   (d) The Heisenberg Experiment: Changing the Speed of Particles

3. The World Wildlife Fund's job is to safeguard hundreds of species around the world and pay special attention to flagship species such as pandas, tigers and whales. Flagship species commonly serve as umbrella species, helping other species that live in the same habitats, and thus require extra protection. In addition to these flagship species, the fund works to protect other species in peril that live within priority eco-regions. Animals that live in these eco-regions, such as grizzly bears and songbirds, depend on the fund's conservation efforts to ensure their future.

   Q. Which of the following is correct according to the article?

   (a) Less effort is going to the protection of flagship species than umbrella species.
   (b) The World Wildlife Fund thinks seriously about the future of its priority eco-regions.
   (c) Grizzly bears are highly protected and their numbers are increasing rapidly.
   (d) There used to be many more forms of protection in priority eco-regions than at present.

4. Freedom of the press is a tenet central to most nations claiming adherence to democracy. However, the following example shows how that very freedom may be abused. In 1993, The Sunday Sport paid substantial amount of money out of court damages to a police officer who had been acquitted of assault. Although exonerated, the officers' reputation remained besmirched because the paper failed to mention the alleged victims' weak testimony. The Sunday Sport should have reported a fair and balanced account of the event.

   Q. Which of the following is correct according to the passage?

   (a) Freedom of the press in the U.S.A. has been a declared civil right since the 20th century.
   (b) A free press has been taken for granted in most European countries since the late 1700s.
   (c) Freedom of the press, however vital, does not constitute license to misreport.
   (d) The Sunday Sport, notwithstanding the judgment against them, reported the case fairly.

▶▶ **Part III** Identify the sentence that least fits the context of the passage.

5. Through various studies, it has been observed that the sense of smell is of great importance in attracting the opposite sex. (a) For example, in an experiment by a research team from the University of Toronto, some men and women were put in a single room to mingle. (b) After choosing an individual they felt most attracted to, the women were blindfolded and asked to smell the clothing of various men in order to find the one they felt had the "preferred" scent. (c) Before the experiment, women felt that they were attracted to handsome men who possess musky scents. (d) Putting their sense of smell to good, each woman was able to choose the same man selected during the mingling time, by olfactory skills alone.

정답: 247p

FINAL CHECK

READING
COMPREHENSION

DIRECTIONS

The part of the exam tests your ability to comprehend reading passages.
You will have 45 minutes to complete the 40 questions. Be sure to follow
the directions given by the proctor.

1. The radio is one of the oldest, yet most widely distributed inventions of all time. Its versatility stems not only from its availability all around the world but also from its useful application in many areas. The radio can be turned on to catch "up to the minute" newscasts, listen to music and even to check the weather or traffic reports. History demonstrates how valuable access to a radio has been over the years. Even with the growing popularity of the Internet along with other forms of communication and entertainment; the radio will most likely ___________________________.

   (a) continue to have a place in society
   (b) become banned from households
   (c) become utterly obsolete and fogotten
   (d) cater to an exclusive, niche audience

2. Anaheim, California has been synonymous with Walt Disney World since its opening in 1955 and spectacular success. Its sibling, however, has not fared so well. California Adventure, founded in 2001 as a younger, more street-hip alternative to the stayed family image of its elder brother is about ____.
   The retooling and expansion plans include a complete revamp of the amusement areas and rides, as well as a major hotel and condominium construction project to encourage more long-term guests.

   (a) to undergo a transformation to counter falling gate revenues
   (b) to receive a federal grant to stave off impending insolvency
   (c) 20 miles by road across the county from Walt Disney World
   (d) to get a name-change to Walt Disney World II

3. France's national transport network has been paralyzed by a major strike involving most of
the country's rail federations. Officials said routes in and around most major cities have
been ____, showing a worry for this weekend's
soccer fans hoping to get to Paris for the World Cup Final. France's President, Nikolas
Sarkozy is, however, resolute in his determination to restructure the nation's transport
sector, citing general waste, overstaffing and unaffordable retirement benefits as key issues
to be addressed. Public concern is also mounting with some calling the union's demands
infuriating, unrealistic and greedy.

(a) renovated recently in the hopes of more users
(b) dilapidated and are not expected to be fixed
(c) closed or are running at minimum capacity
(d) cleared and are running at full capacity

4. Too often twins are defined only by their being a part of a whole, rather than by their own
identity. This can be especially damaging during the time children are struggling to
establish their own self worth and place in the world. One of the most important things that
parents of twins should do when their children are still young is to foster independence. As
parents, they will find their children heavily dependent on each other. While it is important
for the twins to draw on each other's support throughout their early stages of development,
parents should also make sure that they are fostering a comfortable atmosphere to
______________________.

(a) be separated from each other at an early age
(b) be together in their early years
(c) encourage the development of their own interests
(d) amend each other's differences through strict discipline

5. Women are freezing their eggs ____ in greater and greater numbers. Controversy surrounds the practice because many clinics, even though they are government approved and licensed, do not fully inform their clients of the risks associated with the procedure. Not only are the chances of becoming pregnant after 40 much smaller than those in their 20s, but also the chances of retaining the structure of eggs in a long-term frozen state are minimal. Despite these factors contributing to a high failure rate for in-vitro procedures, previously popular for women suffering an illness or perhaps undergoing a course of chemotherapy, some clinics have begun to market their services to otherwise healthy women.

(a) because later they will produce them
(b) in the hope of using them later in life
(c) expecting to have healthy babies
(d) in competition with other women

6. Former Pakistani President Benazir Bhutto returned home today after years in exile and the whole of Karachi ground to a halt as she made her way from the airport to her residence on the outskirts of the city that was once her power base. Cheering spectators lined the streets and flags waved in honor of Bhutto, unseated by Pervez Musharraf in a military coup almost a decade ago. Returning to Pakistan in political turmoil, she is expected to seek some form of power-sharing agreement with Musharraf, yet no definite plans have been drawn up. At the moment in Pakistani politics, _________________________________.

(a) Benazir Bhutto will definitely regain her former power
(b) the settled situation looks sure to continue
(c) the only certain thing seems to be the uncertainty
(d) Pervez Musharraf will win his court case conclusively

7. Do you need another reason to switch to green tea? Aside from fighting Alzheimer's and Parkinson's disease, researchers have found that drinking green tea may also ___________________. The findings built on evidence from lab experiments show that certain compounds in green tea, called catechins help burn calories and lower LDL cholesterol, therefore mildly reducing body fat. The results also suggest that catechins in green tea contribute to the prevention of and improvement in various lifestyle-related diseases, particularly obesity.

(a) allow you to look more youthful and well-rested
(b) help you have a slender figure
(c) help you live longer than others
(d) have a lesser risk of mental diseases such as dementia

8. Toyota has lost its aura of invincibility in the North American market, with the release this week of the 2007 automobile reliability and safety rankings. In the list, compiled by the magazine *Consumer Report*, since 1996 this year is the first that Toyota has not been included in the recommended vehicle listing. So long the pretender to the perennially top-ranked Ford's throne, the Japan-based Toyota Motor finally took top spot this year to become the world's largest automaker. But a rash of recalls on its vehicles has tarnished its new crown and ______________________. Reaction in Tokyo to the news was swift; the chief executive reportedly demanded the immediate resignation of a number of senior executives.

(a) had them take the responsibility of accidents
(b) subsequently caused a sharp slide in sales
(c) was forced to apologize for the recalls
(d) prompted the withdrawal from the North American market

9. Now you can prepare and register your last will and testament online at a far lower cost than that of the usual route of signatories and attorney witnesses, all of whom charge a substantial fee for their services. A last will prepared for you by a lawyer could, for an average-size estate, cost up to $1,000. Now experience the online service running at around $70 and you will also find _______________________________. Just last year the downloadable DIY form of one web-will provider registered a massive 33% increase yet seems to represent only the tip of a very large iceberg.

(a) a heavily discounted product being offered by the legal community
(b) it difficult to imagine how an attorney could match such a good price
(c) the usual fee calculated by dividing by ten, then less another thirty dollars
(d) it easy to see why consumers prefer their testament with their computer mouse

10. There has never been a greater need to stay alert and informed, as our fast-paced and technological society requires us to make quick and smart decisions everyday. The celebrated speaker Matthias Large is famous for saying that it is in your short moments of decisions that your life is shaped. Trivial or profound, our everyday decisions tweak our pathway in lives in a positive or negative direction. While our brain cells crackle to deal with the many choices in life that we have to make, we need to act shrewdly to

_______________________.

(a) succeed in forming our pathway in life
(b) debate about our lives' decisions with others
(c) keep up with the smart decisions being made
(d) get rid of the stress with your poor decision-making skills

11. Municipal shelters have traditionally provided a service to lost pet owners in reuniting them with their lost dog, cat or other treasured family pet but so-called Private Rescue Groups are now competing for a slice of the pie. They work by adopting premium pets identified as pedigree quality and then arranging their fostering to applicants for a fee. However, their strict screening processes and restrictive guidelines on care for the animals are arousing concern. As millions of unwanted and abandoned pets are routinely euthanized across America annually, critics of the new private enterprise accuse them of ____.

(a) placing too much value on the life of an animal
(b) cashing in on a truly shameful state of affairs
(c) breaking the law by getting the pets for free
(d) not donating certain amount of money they earn

12. To coordinate your healthcare needs, the Health Maintenance Organization works by you first choosing a primary care physician. Its plan ensures that your primary care physician's responsibility is for not only treating you but also referring you to other physicians, hospitals and healthcare providers within the network for your specific healthcare needs. Under the Health Maintenance Organization plan, your primary care physician must ___________________________ that are necessary for you except in certain emergency situations.

(a) refund you for all charges
(b) provide or arrange all services
(c) arrange all accommodations
(d) focus fully on the needs of other patients

13. Black holes are regions of space-time _______________________________. If you throw a ball
hard enough gravity will not be able to pull it back down and it will escape from the earth.
The speed at which you have to throw the ball for it to leave the earth completely is known
as the escape velocity, which for earth is about 7 miles a second. If an object is crushed
into a smaller volume the gravitational attraction increases and the escape velocity gets
bigger. Eventually a point is reached when even light particles, traveling at 186 thousand
miles a second, are not traveling fast enough to escape. At this point, nothing can get out as
nothing known can travel faster than light – this is a black hole.

(a) to which the light is absorbed
(b) from which not even light can escape
(c) which makes matters travel faster than ever
(d) which is not trapped in the gravitational pull

14. A distinct feeling of déjà vu is present in the share market as investors swarm round
Internet startup companies long on hype and promises but short on actual customers and
all important dollar revenues. Reminders of the "dot-com bubble" can be seen in the
valuation of one popular social-networking site, Facebook, the current dollar value of
which analysts say is almost equal to half that of Internet behemoth Yahoo, based solely on
a future potential to draw an audience. The fuzzy math behind the last burst bubble should
be enough of a reminder at least for the individual investor and thus the advice is clear:

____.

(a) think carefully before you put your hard-earned salary into this round of dot-com startups
(b) invest now in the same way you did previously and the dividends could be yours to take
(c) dollar revenues are taking a back seat this time around so its time to jump into the market
(d) Yahoo is worth a lot more than Facebook because it started a long time beforehand

15. Smoking, the recreational activity is practiced by millions of people all over the world and has become an addiction. But as concerns on public health grow, smokers are losing their ground as researches show that smoking has detrimental effect not only on smokers themselves but also on others around them. _______________, in many parts of Canada, smoking indoors and outdoors around restaurants and workplaces have been banned and those that disobey the law can be fined up to and including two thousand Canadian dollars.

(a) On the whole
(b) In other words
(c) For example
(d) In addition

16. Along with anorexia nervosa, bulimia is an eating disorder in which patients consume a great amount of food and then only to relieve themselves of the extra weight almost right after through self-induced vomiting. Those that are bulimic enjoy eating but for reasons such as possessing low self-efficacy and a poor self-image; they feel guilty for devouring so much food. ___________, this eating disorder is more common in females at the adolescent age than it is for males, implying that there are more females than males that are unsatisfied with the image of their own bodies. This statistical finding is similar for those diagnosed with anorexia.

(a) After all
(b) Furthermore
(c) For example
(d) First of all

17. The work of some linguists focuses on the notion that languages evolve over time. Sometimes, even the complete meanings of words change. For example, the term "silly" had originally meant blessed. Over the years, that particular word's meaning has been altered several times to the point that today it means to be foolish. Additionally, other aspects that illustrate how language evolves include grammar changes, new slang conceived by younger generations, and the creation of new colloquial terms and idioms. Although this applies to all different cultures, certain linguists go as far as to argue that there is not such thing as official languages, merely diverse dialects. Ultimately, like any other facet in life, language is subject to constant change and will continue to evolve over time.

Q: What is the best title of the passage?

(a) The Changing Meanings of the Term "Silly"
(b) Standard Language and Dialects
(c) The Evolution of Languages
(d) The Creation of an Artificial Language

18. Recent studies have shown that getting divorced before the age of 30 has become so common that it has created a phenomenon called the 'starter divorce.' A 'starter divorce' is one that lasts only for a few years, and generally ends before the couple have children. Some young couples may even separate after being married in only a few months. Experts say one of the reasons for this is supposedly the immaturity of young people who get married in the caprice of the moment. The study also found that even though the divorce rate decreased in the 1990s, marriages that end within the first five years continue to be on the rise.

Q: What is the main point of the report?

(a) About half of all marriages are starter marriages.
(b) More and more people want to get married before they are 30.
(c) Starter divorces are becoming more common.
(d) Divorce rates after the 1990s have decreased.

19. There are appropriate manners of speaking according to the situation, more specifically, according to the ones listening. Suppose that you ran into a famous movie star on your way to work. Then you would probably want to tell everyone about your encounter. If you were to tell your story to your colleague, mother, or your boyfriend, would you describe your experience to each of these three people in the same way? Although the purpose might be the same, you will undoubtedly use a different approach to telling the story for each situation.

Q: What is the main point of the passage?

    (a) Amazing life experiences can change your views in communication.
    (b) It is preferable to confide in friends than in family.
    (c) It is important to talk about your experiences using a variety of approaches.
    (d) The audience of a story dictates how it is delivered.

20. Wing panels are the parts that provide heat shielding and prevent the space shuttle from burning up. In 2003, the shuttle Columbia's wing panels failed, leading to the loss of seven NASA astronauts and the stalling of America's entire space program for almost a decade. Regarding the safety risk of the recently approved launch of the Shuttle Discovery, Chief Engineer Wayne Hale expressed strong concern when wing panel flaws were detected with no clues to their origin. Flight managers, however, argue that the damage detected is microscopic in comparison to the destructive foot-wide hole in the panels of the ill-fated Columbia.

Q: What is the main idea of the passage?

    (a) Controversy surrounds the planned shuttle Discovery launch.
    (b) Damage to the wing panels has not aroused concern.
    (c) An engineer has advised NASA not to launch the shuttle Discovery.
    (d) America's space program is in limbo due to the shuttle Columbia disaster.

21. Authorities have reported many cases of outbreaks of Avian Influenza in a number of
Asian countries in the past few years. Most victims have acquired the disease through
contact with birds, but the Avian flu, or more commonly known as 'bird flu' has a high
potential to become the next human pandemic through human transmission. We have yet to
find a real cure for the virus, and with this in mind, prevention seems to be our best
defense against the deadly disease. The effects of an Avian Flu outbreak are quite fatal; it
could mean that millions of people could be killed within a matter of months if the disease
is not properly controlled.

Q: What is the main idea of the passage?

    (a) Avian flu is likely to spread in the next few months.
    (b) Without a cure for Avian flu, millions of people could die.
    (c) People tend to undermine the effects of a deadly disease outbreak.
    (d) Prevention is the aid for controlling the spread of Avian flu.

22. One of the most controversial theories that exist today is the notion regarding the process
of natural selection. Also referred to as the survival of the fittest, this idea revolves round
the basis that living beings that are best suited to their environment ultimately live longer
and breed more offspring than their weaker counterparts that are less suited to thrive in that
particular surrounding. Consequently, this results in the spreading of stronger genetic
characteristics over time since only those that are better suited to survive can successfully
pass on their genes. This concept of evolution applies to all forms of living beings
including human beings. Thus natural selection explains how the stronger and fitter beings
generally survive and pass on their desirable genetic traits while the weaker ones die out.

Q: What is the main idea of the passage?

    (a) Natural selection suggests that the strong survive while the weak die out.
    (b) The Western world has provided protection against disease thanks to evolution.
    (c) Evolution has ultimately created a superior living being: mankind.
    (d) In certain environments, certain types of animals live longer than others.

23. Dear Editor,

I am writing to disagree with your recent article regarding the negative effect of daytime television talk shows. Most people are often offended by these types of shows because of their explicit nature and the unhealthy influence it can have on viewers. However, as a high school teacher, I find that there is indeed some value and use for these "trashy" shows. Some of my students seem to respond to such shows and have impressed me by demonstrating that they have learned some important life lessons from watching this tabloid-like television programming. After watching them, we have often discussed important issues such as drug use, AIDS, school dropouts, and teenage pregnancy. Don't always assume the worst since teenagers can sometimes surprise and find ways to learn about life's lessons, even if it's from unlikely sources such as television talk shows.

Scott Logan, N.J

Q: What is the purpose of the letter?

   (a) To condemn those who blame TV talk shows for their sensational content
   (b) To tell the editor the importance of teaching teenagers about real life
   (c) To emphasize some benefits teenagers get from watching talk shows
   (d) To discuss the nature of day time television talk shows and their content

24. Eric Benhamou, CEO of the United States based $6 billion networking company 3Com, gave sobering remarks after a recent seminar about the future of our connected society. Ten million homes in the United States are expected to share a network connection for Web browsing, entertainment, and printing by 2009, according to analyst firm the YGK Group, which sponsored the home networking seminar. But Benhamou, warned that connecting millions of households is already unconsciously creating social changes, and challenged vendors to consider the ramifications of the changes.

Q: What would be the most likely topic of the following paragraph?

   (a) An industry trend toward greater profitability in hand-held devices
   (b) Informing the guest companies of the date of the next seminar
   (c) How a more connected world could fundamentally change society
   (d) The innovative nature of quick-adopters of new technology

25. Australia is mostly known for its natural wonders but recently, Australia has been branded by the cancer research council as the country with the highest rate of skin cancer in the world. A spokesperson for the council said that one out of two Australians get skin cancer and that three hundred thousand Australians seek surgery to remove cancerous lesions from their skin every year. The startling number of skin cancer patients in Australia may have a lot to do with global warming and the effect from the harmful sun rays. However, many also refer to the fact that most of the nation's twenty million people are descendents of immigrants from countries like Ireland and Britain, and their skins just can't withstand the Australian sun.

Q: Which is correct according to the passage?

    (a) In Australia, three hundred thousand people die from cancer each year.
    (b) Australia's rate of skin cancer is expected to increase.
    (c) Almost half of Australians are afflicted with skin cancer.
    (d) Australia is a country with twenty million Irish and British immigrants.

26. Chinese retailers' infatuation with Valentine's Day has been on display in nearly every store window and newspaper advertisement for weeks. As Valentine's Day draws near, Chinese singles with no dates tend to be reminded wherever they look around, that they will remain alone and miserable throughout their lives. If worse comes to worst, they can treat themselves to a chocolate or two as an instant 'love booster.' However, they should remember that Valentine's Day is, after all, an imported holiday and it should be treated as any other day.

Q: Which of the following is correct according to the passage?

    (a) Valentine's Day brings a lot of revenue from its advertisements.
    (b) Chinese couples celebrate Valentine's Day excessively.
    (c) One should not get caught in the tailspin of the Valentine's Day infatuation.
    (d) Chinese singles should condemn the extravagance associated with Valentine's Day.

27. With the increasing demand in geothermal energy as a source for electricity, it is true to say that the nuclear power industry is currently undergoing a depression period. High interest rates, a dramatic increase in construction costs and most of all, a low demand have reduced investors' enthusiasm. In 2001, twelve utilities had their bond ratings lowered and last year at least three more were close to undergoing a similar fate. Ruth Lynn, a nuclear industry analyst, says the poor financial health of the industry has generated many problems in the raising of long term capital.

Q: Which is correct according to the passage?

   (a) More demand for electricity has resulted in more investment.
   (b) Investors' enthusiasm for geothermal energy is increasing.
   (c) The bond ratings of utilities have worsened.
   (d) Construction costs have plummeted.

28. Since the beginning of history, people have gone through extreme measures to make themselves look younger. Many of today's aging baby boomers, those born between 1946 and 1964, are no exception to this stigma. An increasing number of them, now in their middle-ages, are beginning to seek operations and orthopedists' offices because of their desperation to stay young. From many years of obsessive exercise, they need knee and hip replacements, surgery for ligament damage, and treatment for stress fractures. The phenomenon even has a name in medical circles, boomeritis.

Q: What is correct about baby boomers according to the passage?

   (a) They are living longer and healthier lives than before.
   (b) They worry about getting injured during exercise.
   (c) They are exercising excessively to stay young.
   (d) They undergo plastic surgeries to look young.

29. There is more to yawning than just being tired. A scientific reason for yawning that is often depreciated is that there is a lack of oxygen in your body. If you are tired, bored, or sitting in a stuffy room, you tend to breathe more slowly and your body doesn't get all the oxygen it needs. Consequently, you let out less carbon-dioxide, and the rest will build up in your blood. Your brain then senses this and quickly sends a signal to your lungs to take an extra deep breath, or in other words, yawn.

Q: Which is correct according to the passage?

    (a) Exhaling more can cause yawning.
    (b) Yawning occurs more often among students.
    (c) A lack of oxygen in the body causes yawning.
    (d) Students tend to yawn less when they are sitting down.

30. In recent years, there has been an increasing focus on health in the workplace. Big businesses now strive to keep their employees healthy, with cleaner working environments as well as better insurance plans. Some view this as a way for big businesses to reduce the cost of future employee health problems. However, according to health economist, Timothy Bairnes, big businesses have other reasons to keep their employees healthy. He believes that businesses do not want to fall under greater government control and meet stricter guidelines for not having treated their employees well.

Q: Which is correct about big businesses according to passage?

    (a) Its employees are not being treated well enough.
    (b) It makes workers liable for their own health care.
    (c) Its objective is to avoid government interference.
    (d) Its motive lies in their willingness to keep their employees fit.

31. Are you sick and tired of typing your essay from your home computer? Have you been looking for decent student-priced laptops to take with you to school? Well, here is some good news for you! This week only, you can get a Tregg 2X laptop for a special student price of $699.00. The 2X comes with a super fast Intel-core duo processor, 2 GB of RAM, and a 300 GB hard drive. Included in the price is a 14.1 inch LCD flat panel monitor. Call 1-800-87344 to place your order now, while supplies last.

Q: Which is correct about the laptop being advertised?

    (a) An LCD monitor is also on sale.
    (b) All of the basic computer software is included.
    (c) A 14.1 inch LCD monitor is included.
    (d) It is twice the speed of a home computer.

32. For many years, members of the Malawian government have been trying to think of new ways to spur economic development in the large farms in the southern region. The southern commercial farms account for a large chunk of Malawi's export earnings, and many changes have been proposed to further increase in production. That's all very well for large scale farming operations, but what about independent, small scale farmers in Malawi? It's as if the Malawian government is only interested in increasing the land holdings of a few large commercial farm owners and is abandoning its independent, small scale farmers.

Q: What can be inferred from the passage?

    (a) Small scale farmers should sell out to larger commercial farm owners.
    (b) State economic development depends on the small scale farmers.
    (c) Industrial agriculture is on the rise in Malawi.
    (d) Small scale farmers need to receive more government support.

33. Experts warn that a flu pandemic is now eight times more likely to happen than twenty years ago. There is no way to predict when the next pandemic will hit, but researchers are certain that it is coming, and it's just a question of when. With underlying assumptions that there is going to be a flu outbreak, the government should take preventative measures and come up with a plan that is more affordable, workable and effective. Right now, the government seems to be just exacerbating people's fears by creating an unrealistic to-do list without any sort of implementation.

Q: What can be inferred about the government from the passage?

    (a) It has wasted a lot of money on recognizing the threat of the flu outbreak.
    (b) It has lessened the chances of a pandemic.
    (c) Its plans are viable but are going to be too expensive.
    (d) It is inefficient despite its efforts to control pandemics properly.

34. The exact emergence of the Renaissance is difficult to point out. In the past, historians used the term "Renaissance" for the period from the fourteenth to the sixteenth centuries, implying the rebirth of rational Roman and Greek civilization after the middle ages. Some historians regard Renaissance as the beginning of Modern age. Similarly, the term "Middle Ages," is defined as a primitive middle period between classical and modern civilizations. The Middle Ages, however, can be schematically divided into three 'ages' of European history, creating relatively a explicit divide in the time line.

Q: What can be inferred from the passage?

    (a) The concept of modern civilization does not really exist.
    (b) Renaissance and Medieval cultures differ significantly.
    (c) It has been difficult to determine a clear division for a specific era.
    (d) Classical civilization was largely forgotten until modern civilizations.

35. Today's seminar will focus on our common misbeliefs in daily exercise. Most of you may assume that daily exercise such as jogging can only benefit one's health. However, when your body is not conditioned for it, jogging and other daily workout can cause muscle cramps and serious joint injuries. The best way to prevent injury is by training to develop strong and flexible muscles that will act as your body's shock absorbers. Also, a healthy diet and regular life are the most important and essential two things and smoking and consuming excessive alcohol are the most detrimental and fatal two things for this.

Q: What can be inferred from the passage?

    (a) Women who are on a diet should also exercise regularly.
    (b) Overweight people are more prone to joint injury when they exercise.
    (c) Jogging injuries are due to inadequate stretching exercises.
    (d) Strengthening the leg muscles help prevent joint injuries when jogging.

36. Dear Ms. Kelly,

Social Science Monthly would like to congratulate you. We would like to publish your article about interpersonal attraction in our next issue. We found that your investigation of reward theory in relationships between male and female is very initiative and deserves much applause. However, several professionals in psychology field suggest that your article would be much more strengthened by having reviewers, who shall remain anonymous. Please note that the purpose of this process is solely to help you develop more complete and brilliant article and the reviews and feedbacks will be kept strictly confidential. Again, congratulations and feel free to contact me if you have any concerns.

Q: What can be inferred form the letter?

    (a) Ms. Kelly's article is the best article this journal hasever received.
    (b) The reviewers are renowned writers in the field of psychology.
    (c) Ms. Kelly is not to know the names of the reviewers.
    (d) The editor wants to hire Ms. Kelly as one of the reviewers of *Social Science Monthly*.

37. Unusually high winds are hampering firefighters in their efforts to contain a blaze spread over hundreds of square miles in California today. The blaze, apparently started by a discarded cigarette-end and exacerbated by hurricane force winds has so far destroyed several homes and now threatens the historic Pepperdine University, situated on the outskirts of Los Angeles. Traffic flows along roads and highways were blocked by billowing smoke and the fire has claimed one life so far, that of a homeowner trying to douse the flames on his property. Governor Arnold Schwartzenegger is considering declaring a state of emergency.

Q: What is the main idea of the passage?

(a) Smoke is causing firefighter's difficulty in reaching the fire.
(b) The historic Pepperdine University may be destroyed.
(c) The fire was started by a discarded cigarette.
(d) High winds are causing the blaze to spread beyond firefighter's control.

Part III　　**Question 38-40**

Read the passage. Then identify that does NOT belong.

38. Ireland's National Day, St. Patrick's Day, is celebrated on March 17th. (a) Although many cities and towns throughout Ireland hold parades on St. Patrick's Day, the main parade takes place in Dublin. (b) St. Patrick is considered the country's patron saint and is credited for ridding Ireland of snakes and for introducing Christianity to his people. (c) Most would assume that the first parade to celebrate this holiday would be held in Ireland; however, it was held in the United States. (d) This is because St. Patrick's Day is now celebrated by those of Irish and Non-Irish descendant all over the world.

39. FBI Director J. Edgar Hoover was ordered to investigate Martin Luther King Jr., who was speculated to be involved in communist activities. (a) These investigations were thoroughly acknowledged in FBI files. (b) Hoover trained FBI agents so scrupulously in modern investigation methods that it's not too much to say that FBI got one step ahead through him. (c) The FBI files exhibit the notion that Hoover had intentions of discrediting King and put him under superintendence. (d) He also sent anonymous letters to King suggesting that he commit suicide.

40. Those who are hearing-impaired at a young age may be incorrectly diagnosed as autistic children during the early stages of diagnosis. (a) To be diagnosed with autism depends on the patterns of social interactions from birth that last until after the age of three. (b) Children that develop normally but are hearing-impaired usually display social behaviors that are similar to autism and display an abnormal level of emotional and social contact with the world. (c) A pediatrician may be needed to conduct an audio-logical evaluation to determine whether the symptoms of autism are actually due to autism or to the fact that the child is unable to hear. (d) Other types of brain tests can also be conducted in order to determine if the cause of autistic behaviors is actually due to autism or if they exist as a result of the child being deaf.

정답: 249p

ANSWERS
정답과 해설

Answers
정답과 해설

Day 1

Build up 22p

1. (d)	2. (b)	3. (a)	4. (b)	5. (c)

1.

An overlooked yet essential aspect of human life is the intrinsic desire to create works of art. Arguably, a basic understanding and appreciation for art can help develop one's character and broaden the intellect. Many artists suggest that they engage in creating art not only to satisfy their creative dive but also as a means to learn about themselves. Thus, not only do these individuals create marvelous artwork for others to enjoy and marvel at, but they also __________________ __________________.

(a) gain material wealth and a comfortable senior life free from any financial worry
(b) develop an aesthetic sense to make them more mature
(c) make many friends across borders through works of art
(d) experience the euphoria of getting in touch with their inner selves

| 해석 |

인간의 삶에서 간과되고 있지만 본질적인 측면은 예술작품을 창조하려는 본질적인 욕망이다. 논의의 여지가 있지만, 이런 표현의 형태에 대한 기본적인 이해와 감상은 사람의 성격과 지성을 넓히는 데 도움을 줄 수 있다. 많은 예술가들은 그들이 예술 창작에 종사하는 것이 그들의 창조적인 탐구를 만족시키기 위해서 일뿐만 아니라 스스로에 대해서 배우기 위한 방법이라고 말한다. 그러므로 이러한 사람들은 다른 사람들이 즐기고 놀라워하는 예술작품을 창작하는 것일 뿐 아니라, 또한 자신 안의 자아와 조우하는 행복감을 경험하는 것이다.

| 해설 |

빈칸 바로 앞 문장에서 예술은 '스스로에 대해 배우기 위한 방법'이라고 하였으므로 정답 (d)에 대한 단서를 얻을 수 있다.

| 오답분석 |

(a) 물질적 부와 어떤 금전적 걱정도 없는 편안한 노년 생활을 얻는다 / 물질적 부에 대한 내용은 언급되지 않았다.
(b) 자신을 더욱 성숙하게 만들어주는 미적 감각을 발전시킨다 / 미적 감각에 대한 내용은 지문의 주제에서 벗어난다.
(c) 예술 작품을 통해 국경을 넘어 많은 친구를 만든다 / 지문에 나오지 않는 내용이다.

| 어휘 |

broaden 넓히다, 넓게 하다
engage 약속하다; 종사하다; 약혼시키다; 고용하다
dive 다이빙, 잠수; 몰두, 전념, 탐구
marvelous 놀라운, 믿기 어려운, 신기한
euphoria 행복감
inner 내적인, 안의

2.

Economies of scale occur when long term __________________ through specialization. Specialized inputs occurring during an increase in the scale of production of a company may allow it to utilize specialized labor and machines resulting in greater efficiency. This is because workers would be better qualified for a specific job; for example someone who only makes French fries, would not waste extra time training for tasks exterior to his specialization, such as tossing salads. Plant items, such as single-use deep fryers, would also enjoy a slower rate of depreciation because they would not be overused or used for a secondary purpose.

(a) average costs are increasing as output is falling
(b) average business costs fall whilst output increases
(c) costs remain static contrary to market fluctuations
(d) conditions and outlooks for the market sector deteriorate

| 해석 |

규모의 경제는 전문화를 통해 장기간 생산은 증대되고 평균 사업 비용은 떨어질 때 일어나게 된다. 어떤 회사의 생산 규모가 커지는 동안 전문화된 투입을 하는 것은 전문화된 노동력과 기계들을 이용하게끔 해주고, 그럼으로써 훨씬 더 큰 효율성을 거둘 수 있게 된다. 이것은 왜냐하면 직원들이 특정한 일에 더 잘 능력을 갖추게 되기 때문이다. 예를 들어, 프렌치프라이만을 만드는 사람이 자신의 전문 분야 외의 다른 일들—샐러드를 버무리는 일 등—을 위해 시간을 낭비하지 않게 될 것이다. 감자튀김 전용 기계와 같은 공장 물품들도 또한 과용되거나 원래의 목적 이외의 다른 목적을 위해 사용되지 않기 때문에 더 느리게 마모될 것이다.

| 해설 |

| 해설 |

지문에서 전문화된 노동력과 기계의 사용을 통해 더욱 효율성이 높아진다고 하였으므로 제일 첫 문장에는 평균적인 사업 비용은 낮아지고 생산성을 증대된다는 내용이 들어가야 함을 알 수 있다.

| 오답분석 |

(a) 생산품이 줄어들게 되면서 평균 가격이 높아지는 / 지문의 내용에서 생산율 증대에 대한 내용을 확인할 수 있으므로 정반대의 보기이다.

(c) 시장의 변동에 대조적으로 가격은 변화하지 않고 남아 있는 / 시장의 변동에 대한 내용은 지문에 언급되지 않았다.

(d) 시장 부문에 대한 상황과 전망이 나빠지는 / 규모의 경제와 상관없는 내용의 보기이다.

| 어휘 |

toss salad 샐러드를 버무리다

depreciation 가치 저하

static 정지하고 있는, 변화하지 않는

deteriorate ~을 악화시키다, (품질, 가치 등이) 떨어지다

outlook 전망, 예상

3.

The use of some words in the English language is highly regrettable, but a dictionary still has a duty to report and describe their existence. If we were to pretend that offensive words didn't exist, and then didn't include them, we'd be charged with dishonesty. Even if we did ignore such words they wouldn't stop being used and, in fact, may be used more without a proper conveyance of their exact meaning. People need accurate information about words in day to day use, including offensive words, and that is what we strive to provide.

Q. What is the main idea of the passage?

(a) Offensive words are a part and parcel of the English language.

(b) Offensive words have no place in the English language.

(c) English books are meant to include offensive words.

(d) If we don't use offensive words, they will eventually disappear from English.

| 해석 |

영어에서 어떤 단어들의 사용은 아주 유감스럽다. 그러나 사전은 여전히 그들의 존재를 알리고 묘사하는 의무를 가지고 있다. 만약 우리가 무례한 단어들이 존재하지 않는다고 가정하고 포함시키지 않는다면, 우리는 부정직하다는 책임을 지게 될 것이다. 만약 우리가 그들이 이런 단어들을 무시했더라도 그 단어들의 사용이 멈춰지지 않을 것이고, 사실상 정확한 의미가 전달되지 않은 채로 더욱 쓰일 것이다. 사람들은 무례한 단어들을 포함해 매일매일 쓰이는 단어에 대한 정확한 정보가 필요하고, 우리는 그것을 제공하려고 노력해야 한다.

| 해설 |

좋지 않은 의미를 가진 단어라 할지라도 영어의 한 부분이므로 그 정확한 의미와 쓰임을 알리기 위해서는 언어 안에 계속 포함시켜야 한다는 내용의 글이다. 따라서 이 글의 주제는 '(a) 무례한 단어들은 영어의 한 부분이다.'가 된다.

| 오답분석 |

(b) 무례한 단어들이 영어에서 차지할 위치는 없다. / 지문의 내용과 반대의 언급이다.

(c) 영어책들은 무례한 단어들을 포함한다. / 영어책들에 이러한 단어가 포함되어 있다는 것이 중점적 내용이 아니므로 정답이 될 수 없다.

(d) 만약 우리가 무례한 단어들을 사용하지 않는다면, 그것들은 궁극적으로 영어에서 사라질 것이다. / 사용하지 않는다 할지라도 사라지지 않고 부정확하게 더 많이 쓰일 수 있을 것이라고 하였으므로 정답이 될 수 없다.

| 어휘 |

regrettable 유감스러운, 후회되는

pretend ~인체 하다, 가장하다

conveyance 운반, 수송; 소리, 냄새, 의미 등의 전달

4.

It is wrong to assume that all university students are capable of self-directed learning. Self-directed learning is a lifelong endeavor because it requires not only high levels of thinking, but also motivation and persistence. But those who can identify their own strengths and weaknesses are able to make decisions about how to develop their skills through a devised program. In other words, people like this can select and carry out their own learning goals, objectives and methods, while also assessing their own progress to ensure that these goals are met.

Q. What can be inferred about self-directed learning?

(a) Its practice leads student to success in university.

(b) Its success depends on one's level of self discipline.

(c) It is mainly accomplished by those who seek higher level education.

(d) It should be pursued upon assessing one's own life goals.

| 해석 |

모든 대학교 학생들이 자발적인 학습을 할 수 있다는 것은 잘못된 가정이다. 자발적인 학습은 높은 단계의 사고를 요구할 뿐만 아니라 동기와 지속성도 요구되기 때문에 일생의 노력이다. 그러나 자신의 장점과 약점을 식별할 수 있는 사람들은 고안된 프로그램을 통해 어떻게 그들의 기술을 발전시킬 수 있는가에 대해 결정을 내릴 수 있다. 다시 말하면, 이와 같은 사람들은 자신의 배움의 목표와 목적, 수단을 선택하고 수행할 수 있으며, 동시에 목표가 달성되고 있다는 것을 확실히 하기 위한 과정을 평가할 수 있다.

| 해설 |

자발적 학습은 자신의 장점과 약점을 알고 있으며 배움의 과정을 스스로
통제할 수 있는 사람에게 있어 가능하다는 내용의 지문이므로 정답은
'(b) 그것의 성공은 자기 훈련 수준에 좌우된다.'가 된다.

| 오답분석 |

(a) 그것의 연습은 대학에서 학생들을 성공으로 이끈다. / 이 글은 어떤 사
    람이 자발적 학습에 성공적일 수 있는가를 말하고 있으므로 정답이 될
    수 없다.

(c) 그것은 주로 교육의 높은 수준을 추구하는 사람들에 의해 성취된다. /
    교육 수준과 관련되어 있다는 내용은 언급되지 않았다.

(d) 한 사람의 삶의 목표를 평가한 후 그것은 추구되어야 한다. / 삶의 목
    표를 평가한다는 내용은 언급되지 않았다.

| 어휘 |

endeavor 노력
persistence 지속성
assess 평가하다

5.

With the onset of Modernism, people began to
look at the world with a different view. (a) They
wished to reject tradition and convention by
stressing freedom of expression, experimentation,
and radicalism. (b) Along with culture and politics,
art was greatly affected by modernism. (c)
However, radical designers are often viewed with
the negative stereotype that they were actually
more interested in commerciality than art itself. (d)
Radical artists sought to support modernism by
applying new materials and technologies to their
artwork.

| 해석 |

모더니즘의 시작과 함께, 사람들은 다른 시각으로 세상을 보기 시작했다.
(a) 사람들은 표현의 자유와 실험성, 급진주의에 강조를 둠으로써 전통과
풍습을 거부하려 했다. (b) 문화와 정치학과 함께, 예술도 모더니즘에 엄
청난 영향을 받았다. (c) 그러나 사람들은 종종 급진주의 디자이너들이 사
실상 예술 그 자체보다 상업성에 더 관심을 가졌다는 부정적인 고정관념
을 가지고 그들을 보기도 한다. (d) 급진주의 예술가들은 새로운 재료와
기술을 예술작품에 도입함으로써 모더니즘에 대한 지지를 추구했다.

| 해설 |

모더니즘의 영향, 특히 예술에 있어서 모더니즘이 어떤 영향을 미쳤는가
에 대한 내용의 지문이다. (c)는 급진주의 디자이너들에 대한 부정적인 시
각을 말하고 있으므로 이 글의 주제에서 벗어난다.

| 오답 분석 |

(a)는 모더니즘의 특징, (b)는 모더니즘의 예술에 대한 영향, (d)는 그 중
급진주의 예술가들의 성향을 언급하고 있으므로 모두 소재와 주제가 잘
연결되어 있다.

| 어휘 |

stress 강조하다, 역설하다
radicalism 급진주의
commerciality 상업주의, 영리주의

Day 2

Build up   30p

1. (b)   **2.** (b)   **3.** (d)   **4.** (a)   **5.** (a)

1.

Dear Valued Customer,
We are writing to inform that our new
CompuServe branch has moved and is now
located at 1452 Bur Oak Avenue. Our brand new
location not only offers the standard sections and
services but also boasts an additional second
level service for computer hardware and spare
parts. To make your shopping experience more
efficient and enjoyable, customers are now also
able to browse through our catalogues and order
online. ___________________________, all you
have to do is contact us and we guarantee it will
be available the next day. Hopefully our new
location and shopping features will better meet
your computing needs.

(a) In the event that certain items are marked
    down
(b) If there is a particular product that is not
    available
(c) To ensure maximum efficiency in processing
    refunds
(d) Whenever you have any questions regarding
    computers

| 해석 |

소중한 고객님께

우리의 새로운 CompuServe 지점이 위치를 옮겨, 이제 1452 Bur Oak
가에 위치하게 되었다는 것을 알리기 위해 편지를 드립니다. 우리 새 지점
은 표준적인 부서들과 서비스를 제공할 뿐만 아니라 컴퓨터 하드웨어와
여분의 부품에 대한 추가적인 두 번째 단계를 제공해드림을 자랑스럽게
알리는 바입니다. 좀 더 효율적이고 즐거운 쇼핑 경험을 만들기 위해서,
고객님들은 이제 우리의 홍보책자들을 훑어보시고 온라인 주문도 하실 수
있습니다. 만약 특정 상품을 구할 수 없으시다면, 저희에게 연락만 해주시
면 다음날 이용하실 수 있도록 보장해드리겠습니다. 우리의 새 지점과 쇼
핑 특징들이 여러분의 컴퓨터 사용에 있어서의 필요를 더욱 잘 충족시켜
드리게 되길 희망합니다.

| 해설 |

빈칸 바로 앞의 내용은 카탈로그를 살펴보고 온라인으로 주문할 수 있다
는 것, 빈칸 뒤의 내용은 연락하면 바로 준비해드리겠다는 것이다. 따라서
빈칸에 알맞은 것은 원하는 상품을 구할 수 없을 때의 상황이라는 것을 유
추할 수 있다.

(a) 특정 품목이 할인되는 행사의 경우에 / 할인에 대한 내용은 언급되지
않았다.
(c) 환불 과정의 최대 효율성을 보장하기 위해 / 환불에 대한 내용은 언급
되지 않았다.
(d) 컴퓨터에 관한 어떤 질문들이 있다면 언제든 / 컴퓨터에 대한 질문도
지문에 언급되지 않은 내용이다.

| 어휘 |
boast 뽐내다, 자랑하다
spare 여분의
browse 검색하다, 둘러보다
hopefully 바라건대, 희망을 걸고

2.

In today's competitive market, advertisers will resort to any means in convincing consumers to buy certain products. One of the most effective, yet ruthless methods is to take advantage of people's insecurities by pointing out their shortcomings. In fact, many advertisements and commercials often place an onus on people's imperfections and the ideal that they should strive for. An example is the many different advertisements for toothpaste. Many of them depict people whose teeth are not very white or attractive thus they are not satisfied with their lives. However, once those individuals use the particular brand that is being advertised, the individuals not only have better looking teeth, but their lives instantly become perfect.

Q. Which of the following best summarizes the passage?
  (a) Toothpaste commercials are very silly and unrealistic.
  (b) Advertisements achieve their goals by making people feel insecure.
  (c) Advertisers help consumers feel good about themselves.
  (d) We should keep our teeth healthy and attractive using toothpaste.

| 해석 |
오늘날의 경쟁적인 시장에서, 광고업자들은 소비자들이 어떤 물품을 구매
하도록 설득하기 위해 어떤 방법에든 호소할 것이다. 가장 효율적이지만
무자비하기까지 한 방법 중의 하나는 소비자들의 약점을 지적해서 그들의
불안감을 이용하는 것이다. 사실상, 많은 광고들은 종종 사람들의 불완전
성과 그들이 얻고자 하는 이상적인 면에 짐을 지운다. 치약에 대한 수많은
광고로 예를 들어보자. 그 광고들은 대부분 치아가 하얗지 않거나 매력적
이지 않아서 삶에 만족하지 못하는 사람들을 묘사하고 있다. 그러나 어느
날 이 사람들이 광고하고 있는 특정 브랜드의 상품을 사용하면 그들은 더
예뻐 보이는 치아를 가지게 될 뿐만 아니라, 그들의 삶은 즉시 완벽하게

바뀐다.

| 해설 |
이 지문에서는, 광고에서 주입하는 메시지는 광고되는 상품을 사용하였을
때 삶이 더욱 풍요로워질 수 있다는 것과, 동시에 그 상품을 사용하지 않
았을 때 상대적으로 박탈당하는 것이 있을 것이라고 겁을 준다는 것임을
말하고 있다. 따라서 정답은 '(b) 광고는 사람들의 마음을 불안하게 만들
어서 그들의 목표를 성취한다.'이다.

| 오답 분석 |
(a) 치약 광고는 매우 바보 같고 비현실적이다. / 치약광고는 예시로 나왔
을 뿐이다.
(c) 광고주는 소비자들이 스스로에 대해 기분이 좋아지도록 돕는다. / 지
문의 내용과 반대 내용이다.
(d) 우리는 치약을 사용하여 건강하고 아름다운 치아를 지켜야 한다. / 치
약이 이 글의 소재가 아니다.

| 어휘 |
ruthless 무자비한, 가차 없는
onus 짐, 의무, 책임, 부담
strive for 노력하다, 분투하다, 얻으려 애쓰다

3.

A sedentary lifestyle, where people get little or no physical exercise, contributes directly to a deleterious effect on the physical construction of our bodies, hence an acceleration of the aging process. Everyday activities such as taking out the trash, washing the car or even tying our shoelaces do not necessarily have to be accompanied by aches and pains as we grow older. It is up to the individual to decide how best to employ steps to slow the aging process. By making wise choices you can make your perceived age more closely resemble your chronological age. Father Time can indeed be turned back.

Q. Which of the following best summarizes the passage?
  (a) The ability to tie our shoelaces is essential to the aging process.
  (b) As people get older their need for physical activity diminishes.
  (c) Aches and pains are a direct result of a sedentary lifestyle.
  (d) Aging should not necessarily prevent normal activities.

| 해석 |
육체적인 운동을 약간 하거나 안 하는 좌식 생활은 우리 몸의 육체적인 구
조에 직접적으로 해로운 영향을 미치고, 그럼으로써 노화를 가속화시킨
다. 우리가 나이를 먹어가면서, 매일 쓰레기를 버리거나 세차를 하거나 심
지어 구두끈을 묶는 이런 활동들이 반드시 아픔과 고통이 동반되어야 하
는 것은 아니다. 어떻게 노화를 느리게 하는 수단을 잘 선택할 수 있는가
를 결정하는 것은 개인에게 달려 있다. 현명한 선택에 의해 사람들이 당신

| 해설 |

을 보고 인식하는 나이를 당신의 원래 나이에 좀 더 가깝게 만들 수 있다. 시간은 실제로 되돌려질 수 있다.

| 해설 |

노화 때문에 일상적 활동에 제약을 받아서는 안 되며, 운동을 통해 신체 나이를 조절해야 한다는 내용의 글이다. 따라서 정답은 '(d) 노화가 반드시 정상적 활동을 방해하는 것은 아니다.

| 오답 분석 |

(a) 우리의 구두끈을 묶는 능력은 노화에 필수적이다. / 지문에서 언급되지 않은 내용이다.

(b) 사람들이 나이를 먹으면 먹을수록 육체적 활동에 대한 필요는 감소한다. / 이 글은 나이를 먹어가도 육체적 활동을 고통 없이 할 수 있어야 한다는 내용이므로 정답이 될 수 없다.

(c) 아픔과 고통은 좌식 생활의 직접적인 결과이다. / 좌식 생활은 운동 부족을 야기한다고 하였지, 아픔과 고통의 원인이라는 언급은 하지 않았다.

| 어휘 |

contribute 기여하다.
deleterious 심신에 해로운, 유독한
perceive 지각하다, 이해하다
resemble ~을 닮다, ~와 공통점이 있다
Father Time 시간을 의인화하여 나타낸 것

4.

In the rush to find those responsible for the September 11th destruction of the Twin Towers in New York and to determine the level of future vulnerability to such attacks, federal, state and local law enforcement officials began to target suspects of Middle Eastern appearance. This profiling exercise by the authorities led to an accusation that the detention and investigation of individuals were arbitrary and that it was based solely on their ethnicity. It has subsequently been proven that the foreign nationals of Middle Eastern origin who were of interest to the authorities often lacked any factors besides their appearance in warranting suspicion.

Q. Which of the following is correct about the passage?

(a) Post 9-11 racial profiling carried out by the federal authorities was somewhat absurd.

(b) Before 9-11 the FBI wasn't interested in people from the Middle East.

(c) The crime was carried out by American citizens whose cultural nationality was Middle Eastern.

(d) Federal, state and local law enforcement officials worked feverishly.

| 해석 |

뉴욕 쌍둥이 빌딩의 9월 11일 파괴에 대해 책임이 있는 사람을 찾고, 이런 공격들에 대한 앞날의 취약성 수준을 결정하기 위해 서둘러 조치를 취하면서, 연방, 주, 지역 법 집행 기관들은 중동인 외모의 용의자를 표적으로 삼기 시작했다. 당국의 이 인물 조사는 개인의 구금과 조사가 임의적이었고 단지 민족성에 기반을 둔 것이었기 때문에 비난을 받았다. 당국의 관심 대상인 중동 출신 국민들은 혐의를 보증하는 데에 있어 외모 이외에는 어떤 요인들도 없다는 것이 차후에 입증되었다.

| 해설 |

9.11 테러 용의자를 찾는 과정에서 민족성과 외모를 기준으로 조사를 진행한 것이 비난의 대상이 되었다는 내용의 글이다. 따라서 정답은 '(a) 9.11 이후 연방 당국에 의해 수행된 인종적 프로파일링은 좀 불합리하다.'이다.

| 오답 분석 |

(b) 9.11 전에 FBI는 중동 출신 사람들에게 관심이 없었다. / 지문에 언급되지 않았다.

(c) 그 범죄는 문화적 정체성이 중동인 미국 시민에 의해 수행되었다. / 지문에 언급되지 않았다.

(d) 연방, 주, 지방 법 집행기관은 열정적으로 일했다. / 지문에 언급되지 않았다.

| 어휘 |

vulnerability 상처받기 쉬움, 취약성
accusation 고발, 비난
detention 구금
arbitrary 임의의, 멋대로의, 독단적인
solely 혼자서, 단독으로, 단지, 다만
ethnicity 민족성
subsequently 그 후에, 다음에, 이어서
feverishly 열광적으로, 열정적으로

5.

The book *A Million Little Pieces* by James Frey has come under a considerable amount of criticism for stretching the truth in a memoir. (a) The book sold millions of copies worldwide, and was translated into over 20 different languages. (b) James Frey initially tried to publish his story as fiction, but was encouraged to present it as a true story instead. (c) So, *A Million Little Pieces* was sold as a memoir, as James Frey's personal account of overcoming addiction. (d) Many readers empathized with Frey's narrative, but were enraged at the later disclosure that some incidents were more fiction than fact.

| 해석 |

James Frey의 책 〈A Million Little Pieces〉는 회고록에서 사실을 과장한 것에 대해 상당한 비판에 처하게 되었다. (a) 이 책은 전 세계적으로 몇 백만 권이 팔렸으며, 20여 개의 언어로 번역되었다. (b) 처음에 James Frey는 자신의 이야기를 픽션으로 출판하려 하였으나, 실화라고 내세워보라는 부추김을 받았다. (c) 그래서 〈A Million Little Pieces〉는 James Frey가 약물중독을 극복한 개인적인 이야기인 회고록으로 팔리게 되었다. (d) 많은 독자들은 Frey의 이야기에 공감했지만, 이후에 어떤 사건들이 사실이 아니라 픽션이라는 폭로에 격분했다.

| 해설 |

첫 문장에서 Frey의 회고록에 대한 비판을 언급하였고, 그 원인과 진상에 대한 내용이 이어지고 있는 글이다. (a)는 이 책에 대한 비판과 관계없는 내용이므로 흐름상 어색한 문장이다.

| 오답 분석 |

첫 문장에서 사실을 과장한 것 때문에 비판을 받았다고 하였으므로, 그 내용에 바로 이어지는 것이 (b)이며, (b)의 결과가 (c), 그에 대한 독자들의 반응이 (d)이다.

| 어휘 |

criticism 비평, 비난, 혹평
memoir 자서전, 회고록
initially 처음에, 첫머리에
account 기사, 보도, 이야기, 설명서
addiction 중독, 탐닉
empathize 감정 이입하다, 공감하다
enrage 격분하게 하다, 화나게 하다
disclosure 발각, 탄로, 폭로, 적발

Day 3

Build up 38p

> **1.** (a) **2.** (b) **3.** (a) **4.** (c) **5.** (d)

1.

Besides sunglasses serving the traditional purpose of providing protection for your eyes from harmful ultraviolet (UV) rays, ________________ ________________. The shape of your face, the lens color, and the amount of UV protection you want are a few items you must consider when buying a pair to make you look good. You should check yourself out in a full-length mirror when you try them on because it is important to match your sunglasses with the look you wish to achieve. A critical point is to also match the pair you have chosen to the proportions of your body – not only your face.

(a) they can provide an aesthetic and style
(b) they offset harsh colored room decor
(c) they also control the ratio of direct sunlight
(d) they come with complete manufacturer's specifications

| 해석 |

선글라스는 해로운 자외선으로부터 눈을 보호해주는 원래의 목적을 제공하는 것에 더해서, 미적 감각과 스타일을 살리는 데에도 도움이 된다. 얼굴형과 렌즈의 색깔, 그리고 어느 정도의 자외선 차단을 원하는지 등이 당신을 보기 좋게 만들어줄 선글라스를 사려 할 때 고려해야 할 항목들이다. 당신이 원하는 모습과 선글라스가 잘 맞는지가 중요하기 때문에 전신 거울에서 스스로의 모습을 체크해 보아야 한다. 중요한 포인트는 당신이 고른 선글라스를 얼굴에 맞춰보는 것뿐 아니라 몸 전체의 비율에 맞춰보는 것이다.

| 해설 |

첫 문장에 빈칸이 있는, 주제문을 완성시키는 문제이다. 빈칸 뒷부분에서 선글라스를 어떻게 맞춰보아야 하는지를 계속해서 설명하고 있으므로 정답은 (a)가 된다.

| 오답 분석 |

(b) 조잡하게 꾸며진 방의 장식을 상쇄시키는 데 도움이 된다. / 선글라스를 방의 장식과 관련지어 생각할 수 있는 부분은 언급되지 않았다.
(c) 직접적인 태양빛의 비율을 통제하는 데 도움이 된다. / 자외선이나 태양빛을 막아주는 기능 외의 미적 기능에 대한 지문이므로 오답이다.
(d) 완전한 제조업자의 설명서가 따라온다. / 선글라스의 사용 설명서에 대한 설명은 이 글에서 언급되지 않았다.

| 어휘 |

aesthetic 미적인, 미의식, 미적 가치관
offset 상쇄하다
harsh 거친, 조잡한
specifications 사용 설명서

2.

Anti-quota petitioners before the Supreme Court in New Delhi argued that a law providing for 27 percent quota in Central Educational Institutions cannot last indefinitely and further demanded such special provisions be officially sanctioned. The Delhi Court was told by a group of private schools that an allocation of five more points to scheduled caste students for nursery classes would not be implemented at any time. The schools said it was an indirect way of introducing a discriminatory system for socially backward communities to gain access to private institutions. They added that ________________________, saying that they would not be put in place in the schools during the student admissions process.

(a) the decision has been made to recommend a scholastic cost waiver
(b) they will not implement a quota system
(c) it is unconstitutional to implement the quota system
(d) previously enrolled students will no longer be fully eligible

| 해석 |

뉴델리의 대법원에 정원 할당 제도에 반대하는 탄원을 올리는 사람들은
중앙 교육 기관에서 27퍼센트의 할당을 제공하는 것이 무한정 지속될 수
는 없다고 주장하면서, 더 나아가 이러한 특별 조항이 공식적으로 인가받
기를 요구했다. 한 그룹의 사립학교들은, 유아반의 최하층 천민 계급에게
5점을 더 할당하는 것이 시행되면 안 된다고 델리 법원에 말했다. 학교들
은 이것이 사회적으로 뒤쳐진 사람들이 사립 기관에 접근하도록 하는 차
별적 시스템을 도입하는 간접적인 방법이라고 말했다. 이들은 학교의 학
생 입학 허가 과정에서 받아들여지지 않을 것이라고 말하며 정원 할당제
를 이행하지 않을 것이라고 덧붙였다.

| 해설 |

지문의 앞부분에서 정원 할당제도에 반대하는 사립학교들에 대한 내용이
전개되고 있으므로 정답은 (b)가 된다.

| 오답 분석 |

(a) 이 결정은 학교 교육 비용을 포기하도록 하기 위해 만들어졌다 / 교육
　　비용에 대한 내용은 언급되지 않았다.
(c) 정원 할당제를 실시하는 것은 위험이다 / 법을 어기는 것이라는 내용
　　은 지문에서 확인할 수 없다.
(d) 이전에 등록한 학생들은 더 이상 완전히 적격이 아니다 / 이 글은 최하
　　층 천민에 속하는 학생들에 대한 내용이며, 이전에 등록한 학생들에
　　대한 언급은 없다.

| 어휘 |

scheduled castes 카스트 제도의 불가촉천민 계급, 최하층의 천민
scholastic 학교의, 학교 교육의
waiver (권리, 이익, 요구 등의) 포기
unconstitutional 헌법 위반의, 위헌의
eligible 적임의, 적격의, ~할 자격이 있는

3.

Tired of your old, boring look? Do you ever
wonder if you should give yourself a make-over
and inject some life into your dull sense of
fashion? If you have ever wished that you could
simply reinvent yourself and transform into a
stylish and bold goddess, look no further for
Beauty Magazine is the answer for you! This new
magazine offers everything an outgoing,
independent woman yearning for the freedom to
experiment with her sense of fashion needs. From
tips for avoiding fashion blunders to suggestions
on what the latest trends in clothing are, *Beauty
Magazine* is the ultimate source for the modern,
style conscious woman. Don't wait any longer,
pick it up at your local newsstands!

Q. What is the purpose of the passage?
(a) To advertise a magazine
(b) To help avoid fashion blunders
(c) To make a recruitment offer
(d) To offer a fashion design course

| 해석 |

오래되고 지루한 차림새에 싫증났습니까? 스스로의 외모에 변화를 주고
둔한 패션 감각에 어떤 생명력을 주입해야겠다는 생각을 하시나요? 만약
간단하게 자신을 일신하고 스타일을 변화시켜 스타일 좋은 숭배의 대상이
될 수 있기를 소망하신다면, 다른 것은 더 이상 보실 필요가 없습니다.
Beauty Magazine이 당신을 위한 정답이기 때문이죠! 이 새로운 잡지는
패션 만족에 대한 자신의 감각을 실험할 자유를 동경하는 외향적이고 독
립적인 여성에게 모든 것을 제공합니다. 패션에서 실수를 피하기 위한 조
언부터 최근 옷 경향에 대한 제안까지, Beauty Magazine은 도시적이고,
스타일에 민감한 여성들을 위한 궁극적인 정보처입니다. 더 이상 기다리
지 말고 가까운 신문 가판대에서 구입하십시오!

| 해설 |

전형적인 광고문의 형식을 띄고 있다. 더 이상 기다리지 말고 Beauty
Magazine을 사라고 하고 있으므로 정답은 '(a)잡지를 광고하기 위해'가
된다.

| 오답 분석 |

(b) 패션에서의 실수를 피하기 위해 / Beauty Magazine을 통해 패션에
　　서의 실수를 피할 수 있다고 했으므로 잡지광고이다.
(c) 채용 제안을 하기 위해 / 채용에 대한 내용은 언급되지 않았다.
(d) 패션 디자인 코스를 제의하기 위해 / 패션 디자인에 대한 내용은 언급
　　되지 않았다.

| 어휘 |

dull 무딘, 둔한, 활기 없는, 지루한
reinvent 개혁하다, 다시 고치다
goddess 여신, 절세미인
yearn 갈망하다, 간절히 바라다
blunder 큰 실수
newsstand 신문 가판대

4.

The skeleton of Ron the dinosaur is the largest
and most complete Velociraptor, or just simply
Raptor, ever found. It has provided scientists with
evidence that the smart, fast-running, bipedal
dinosaur is more closely related to the group
Theropods than Sauropodomorpha. Theropods
had a hip structure similar to that of today's lizards
– the pubis bone pointed downwards and
forwards that allowed dinosaurs like the Raptors
to have long back legs for speed. Ron's recent
discovery also provides support for the much
debated theory that birds evolved from meat
eating dinosaurs.

Q. What can be inferred from the passage?
(a) Raptors used to feed on various kinds of
　　 birds.
(b) Pubis bones were common in dinosaur
　　 species.
(c) Theropods were speedy carnivores.
(d) Ron's bones prove an evolutionary link to
　　 birds.

| 해석 |

공룡인 론의 해골은 발견된 벨로시랩터, 혹은 간단하게 말해 랩터 중 가장 크고 완벽하다. 그것은 과학자들에게 영리하고 빠르게 달리며 두 발을 쓰는 이 공룡이 사우로포도몰파보다 테로포드 그룹에 더 가깝다는 증거를 제공하고 있다. 테로포드는 엉덩이 구조가 오늘날의 도마뱀과 유사하여, 랩터와 같은 공룡에게 속도를 낼 수 있는 긴 뒷다리를 가질 수 있도록 치골뼈가 아래쪽과 앞쪽으로 향해 있다. 최근 론을 발견한 것은 많이 토론되어왔던 새가 육식 공룡으로부터 진화되었다는 이론에 대한 지지를 제공한다.

| 해설 |

지문에서 론의 뼈를 연구한 결과 긴 뒷다리로 빠르게 달렸다고 언급하였으며, 지문의 가장 마지막 문장에서 육식 공룡이라는 것을 알 수 있으므로 정답은 '(c) 테로포드는 속도가 빠른 육식 동물이다.'가 정답이 된다.

| 오답 분석 |

(a) 랩터는 다양한 종류의 새를 먹이로 삼곤 했다. / 지문에 언급되지 않았다.

(b) 치골뼈는 공룡에서 공통적이다. / 지문에서 언급되지 않았다.

(d) 론의 뼈는 새와의 진화적인 연결을 증명한다. / 이론을 지지한다는 것이 '증명'을 한다는 것과 동의어가 될 수 없으므로 정답이 될 수 없다.

| 어휘 |

bipedal 두 발 동물의
Sauropodomorpha 사우로포도몰파(목과 꼬리가 길고 머리가 작은 거대한 초식 공룡)
Theropod 테로포드, 수각아목(獸脚亞目)의 공룡(육식성이며 두 발로 보행)
pubis 치골

5.

Monopoly, one of the most popular board games around the world, is somewhat ironic in that the game's initial purpose was to tell us about the terribleness of monopoly. (a) The origin of Monopoly, 'The Landlord's game' was invented by Lizzie Maggie in 1904. (b) He created the game to explain the vicious cycle that the working poor cannot but remain in poverty as industrialization progressed. (c) Finally, Charles Darrow revised it to make Monopoly during the Great Depression, and it immediately monopolized the board game market. (d) Monopoly became so popular that most of the game's trademarks such as the community chest and the railroads are now copyrighted and legally protected.

| 해석 |

전 세계에서 가장 인기 있는 보드 게임 중 하나인 모노폴리는 게임의 원래 목적이 독점의 무서움을 말해주려는 것이었다는 점에서 좀 아이러니 하다. (a) 모노폴리의 기원이 되는 게임인 '건물주 게임'은 1904년에 리지 매기에 의해 발명되었다. (b) 그는 산업화가 진행되어도 노동자 계층의 빈민은 빈곤층에 머물 수밖에 없다는 악순환을 설명하기 위해 이 게임을 만들었다. (c) 마침내 찰스 대로우가 경제 대공황 때에 이 게임을 수정하여 모노폴리를 만들었고, 즉시 보드 게임 시장을 독점하였다. (d) 모노폴리는 너무나 유명해져서 이 게임의 공동 기금과 철도와 같은 게임의 트레이

드마크는 판권을 얻어 법적으로 보호받고 있다.

| 해설 |

모노폴리가 처음 만들어진 취지에 반대되게도 보드 게임 시장을 독점하고 있어 아이러니 하다는 내용의 글이다. 따라서 모노폴리의 유명세에 대한 내용인 (d)는 이 글의 주제에서 벗어난 문장이다.

| 오답 분석 |

첫 문장이 주제문이다. (a)와 (b)는 모노폴리의 기원이 되는 게임이 만들어진 배경과 목적을 설명하고, (c)는 모노폴리가 시장을 독점하게 되었다는 내용으로, 앞의 문장들과 이어져 주제문을 뒷받침하는 내용이므로 글의 흐름이 잘 이어지고 있다.

| 어휘 |

working poor 빈민 노동자 계층
vicious cycle 악순환
community chest 공동 모금에 의한 기금

Day 4

Build up   46p

| 1. (d) | 2. (d) | 3. (c) | 4. (d) | 5. (c) |

1.

Far from being in a state of crisis and with its current standard of living among the world's highest, Japan is one of the wealthiest countries in the world. For example, the sales of luxurious brands on the high-end spectrum such as Burberry, Louis Vuitton and Gucci continue to remain very high. At one point in the late 20th Century, the economy of this Asian country was recorded as possessing the highest annual growth rate out of all the developed countries. _________, the speculation of this economic miracle has been the chief subject matter of many debates around the world.

(a) Nevertheless
(b) Instead
(c) After all
(d) Hence

| 해석 |

현재 세계에서 가장 높은 삶의 기준을 갖고 있으며 위기의 상태와 거리가 먼 일본은 세계의 부국 중의 하나이다. 예를 들어, 최고급 영역인 버버리, 루이비통, 구찌 같은 사치스러운 브랜드 이름의 판매가 끊임없이 유지되고 있다. 20세기 후반에 이 아시아 국가의 경제는 모든 선진국을 능가하는 높은 경제 성장률을 이룩한 것으로 기록되었다. 따라서 이 경제적인 기

적에 대한 숙고는 전 세계의 많은 토론의 주요 주제가 되어왔다.

| 해설 |
빈칸 앞의 내용은 일본의 높은 경제 성장이 전 세계의 다른 선진국들을 능가하였다는 것이고 빈칸 뒤의 내용은 전 세계에서 이러한 일본의 경제 성장이 토론의 주제가 되고 있다는 것이므로 빈칸에는 '(d) 따라서'가 들어가는 것이 알맞다.

| 오답 분석 |
(a) 그럼에도 불구하고 / 역접의 접속사이다.
(b) 대신에 / 앞에 언급된 것의 대안이나 다른 방안을 말할 때 쓴다.
(c) 결국 / 앞에서 모든 과정이 언급된 뒤 그 결과를 말할 때 쓴다.

| 어휘 |
high end 최고급의
possess 소유하다, 지니다
speculation 사색; 추론, 추측
miracle 기적

2.

Many consider businesses to be the biggest contributors to environmental degradation. While businesses are known to play a significant role, we also need to understand that individual homeowners should play their parts as well in reducing their impact on Earth. In order for them to take part in energy reduction on a larger scale, local governments should give more incentives, such as easing the current restrictions on integrated solar panels and wind turbines to encourage homeowners to generate their own power.

Q. What is the main idea of this passage?
(a) It is the local government's responsibility to reduce energy waste.
(b) Minimizing climate change requires help from businesses.
(c) Businesses should be encouraged to generate their own alternative energy resources.
(d) The government should promote energy reduction in homes as well as in businesses.

| 해석 |
많은 사람들은 기업체들이 환경 퇴보에 가장 큰 원인이라고 생각하고 있다. 기업체들이 큰 영향을 미친다고 알려져 있지만, 우리는 또한 집을 소유한 개인들도 지구에 대한 충격을 감소시키기 위해 필요한 역할을 해야 한다는 점을 알아야 한다. 그들이 대규모의 에너지 절약에 참여하려면 통합 태양 전지판과 풍력 터빈에 대한 현행 규제를 완화하여 스스로 전력을 생산하도록 격려하는 등, 지방 정부들이 좀 더 많은 동기를 부여해야 한다.

| 해설 |
정부에서 개인이 직접 전력을 생산하도록 장려해야 한다는 내용이므로 정답은 '(d) 정부는 사업체는 물론 가정에서의 에너지 절약을 독려해야 한다.'가 된다.

| 오답 분석 |
(a) 에너지 낭비를 감소시키는 것은 지방 정부의 책임이다. / 지방 정부에서 책임을 모두 져야 한다는 내용은 언급되지 않았다.
(b) 기후 변화를 최소화시키기 위해서는 재계의 도움이 필요하다. / 기후 변화에 대한 내용은 언급되지 않았다.
(c) 기업체들은 그들 자신의 대체 에너지 자원을 생산하기 위해 장려되어야 한다. / 가정들에서 대체 에너지를 생산하도록 장려해야 한다고 하였으므로 틀린 내용이다.

| 어휘 |
degradation 퇴보, 타락
incentive 자극, 동기
restriction 제한, 한정, 규제
solar panel 태양 전지판
wind turbine 풍력 발전용 터빈

3.

Married life seems to have more benefits than we might have thought. The National Center for Health Research released a new study that proved the co-relationship between married life and longevity. The report, based on health examinations of 132,000 single and married adults, shows married people are less likely to smoke, drink heavily, or be physically inactive. They're also more likely than single adults to keep mentally and physically fit and to have less stress symptoms.

Q. Which is correct about married people?
(a) They tend to take up smoking after marriage.
(b) They are more likely to stress out over work.
(c) They are more motivated to stay fit than single people.
(d) They have fewer opportunities to drink than singles.

| 해석 |
결혼한 삶은 우리가 알고 있는 것보다 더 많은 이점을 가지고 있다. 건강 연구에 대한 국가 연구소는 결혼한 삶과 장수 사이의 연관성을 입증하는 새로운 연구를 발표하였다. 13만 2천 명의 미혼, 기혼 성인의 건강 조사를 기반으로 한 그 리포트는 결혼한 사람이 담배를 피우거나 술을 굉장히 많이 마시거나 육체적으로 수동적인 성향이 덜하다는 것을 보여주었다. 그들은 또한 미혼 성인보다 정신적, 육체적 건강을 잘 유지하고, 스트레스 증상을 덜 가지는 경향을 보인다.

| 해설 |
지문의 마지막 부분에서 결혼한 사람들이 미혼인 사람들보다 건강을 더잘 유지한다고 하였으므로 정답은 '(c) 그들은 미혼인 사람들보다 건강 유지에 대한 동기 부여가 크다.'이다.

| 오답 분석 |
| 오답 분석 |
(a) 결혼 후에 그들은 담배를 피우는 경향이 있다. / 지문에서 결혼한 사람
들은 담배를 덜 피운다고 하였으므로 틀린 내용이다.
(b) 그들은 일에서 좀 더 스트레스를 받는다. / 지문에서 결혼한 사람들은
스트레스를 덜 받는다고 했다.
(d) 그들은 미혼인 사람들보다 음주 기회를 덜 가지고 있다. / 음주에 대한
기회를 덜 가지는 것이 아니라, 술을 많이 마시는 경향이 덜하다고 하
였다.

| 어휘 |
longevity 장수
symptom 징후, 징조

4.

A new study suggests that liposuction may also
help to treat chronic depression. The study is still
undergoing final stages of scientific tests, but
researchers believe they have good reasons to be
confident. So far, the research has found that 9
out of 10 participants of liposuction treatment for
reducing body fat experienced a lift in mood after
the therapy. Conversely, skeptics disagree, stating
that liposuction may temporarily trigger positive
self image but it does not account for the overall
happiness of the patient.

Q. What can be inferred about liposuction from
the passage?
(a) It blurs one's body image and level of self
confidence.
(b) It contains a chemical that triggers brain
activity.
(c) Its ability to cure depression makes it
popular.
(d) Its influence on emotions has not been fully
validated.

| 해석 |
새로운 연구는 지방 제거가 아마도 만성적인 우울증을 고치는 데 도움이
될 것이라고 제시한다. 그 연구는 아직 과학적 테스트의 마지막 단계를 거
치고 있는 중이지만 연구자들은 자신들의 견해가 충분히 옳다고 믿고 있
다. 지금까지, 이 연구에서는 체지방의 감소를 위해 지방 제거 치료를 한
10명의 환자 중 9명이 치료 후에 기분이 좋아진 것을 알아냈다. 반대로 회
의론자들은, 지방 제거는 일시적으로는 긍정적인 자기 이미지를 유발할
수는 있지만 그것이 환자의 전체적인 행복을 책임져 주지는 않는다고 말
하며 동의하지 않고 있다.

| 해설 |
두 번째 문장에서 마지막 단계의 과학적 테스트를 거치고 있다고 하였으
므로 정답은 '(d) 감정에 대한 그것의 영향은 완전히 밝혀진 것이 아니
다.'라는 것을 알 수 있다.

| 오답 분석 |
(a) 그것은 한 사람의 신체 이미지와 자신감의 정도를 흐려지게 만든다. /
이 지문에서 연구자들은 좋은 쪽으로 작용한다는 의견을 가지므로 정

답이 될 수 없다.
(b) 그것은 뇌 활동을 일으키는 화학물질을 담고 있다. / 뇌의 활동에 관련
된 내용은 언급되지 않았다.
(c) 우울증을 치료하는 그것의 능력은 그것을 인기 있게 만들었다. / 인기
에 대한 내용은 언급되지 않았다.

| 어휘 |
liposuction (지방 제거의) 미용 수술의 한 기법
skeptics 회의론자
trigger (방아쇠를) 당겨서 쏘다; (일을) 일으키다, 유발하다
blur 흐리게 하다
validate 정당함을 확인하다, 유효하게 하다

5.

Stephen William Hawking was born on January
8th, 1942 in Oxford, England. (a) He possessed
one of the brightest minds in his time and his
principal fields of research were theoretical
cosmology and quantum gravity. (b) He was able
to greatly contribute to the world of science
through his research despite being diagnosed with
Lou Gehrig's disease at the age of 21. (c) There is
no particular medication or remedy for Lou
Gehrig's disease, which became well-known to
the public as the disease Hawking is suffering. (d)
Stephen Hawking's works include *A Brief History
of Time*; *The Universe of a Nutshell*, and *Black
Holes and Baby Universes: and Other Essays*.

| 해석 |
스티븐 윌리엄 호킹은 1942년 1월 8일, 영국 옥스포드에서 태어났다. (a)
그는 당대의 가장 영리한 사람이었으며, 그의 대표적인 연구 영역은 이론
우주학과 양자 중력 이론이었다. (b) 그는 21세의 나이에 루게릭병으로
진단되었음에도 불구하고 연구를 통해 과학 분야에 지대한 공헌을 하였
다. (c) 호킹이 앓고 있는 병으로 대중에게 잘 알려진 루게릭병에는 특별
한 약물 치료나 치료법이 없다. (d) 스티븐 호킹의 저서는 〈시간의 역사〉,
〈호두 껍질 속의 우주〉, 그리고 〈블랙홀과 아기 우주; 그리고 그 밖의 이야
기들〉 등이다.

| 해설 |
스티븐 호킹의 업적에 대한 내용의 글이다. (c)는 루게릭병에 대한 내용이
므로 이 글의 흐름에서 벗어나 있다.

| 오답 분석 |
(a)는 호킹의 연구 영역, (b) 질병에도 불구하고 과학에 공헌하였다는 점,
(d)는 저서에 대해 말하고 있으므로 이 글의 주제에 잘 맞는 문장들이다.

| 어휘 |
theoretical cosmology 이론 우주 철학
quantum gravity 양자 중력 (이론)
Lou Gehrig's disease 루게릭 병, 근위축성 측삭 경화증

Day 5

Build up

54p

> **1.** (d) **2.** (d) **3.** (c) **4.** (c) **5.** (b)

1.

The International Dyslexia Association (IDA) is a non-profit organization dedicated to helping individuals with dyslexia and their families. IDA was founded in 1949 in memory of Dr. Samuel T. Orton. Its goal has been the sharing of knowledge, methods and experience, and providing the most comprehensive forum on the issue. Thanks to IDA's endeavor to let the public know about Dyslexia, many of us now understand the nature of this disorder; it is characterized by __________ _________________. Commonly sufferers may read and understand a given topic, however, upon transcribing details they will display a transposition of letters or words.

(a) brutality and mercilessness toward foreigners
(b) repetitive loss of memory related to everyday life
(c) a speech impediment under some particular conditions
(d) interference in the acquisition and processing of language

| 해석 |

국제 난독증 협회(IDA)는 비영리재단으로, 난독증에 걸린 사람들과 그들의 가족들을 돕는 데 헌신한다. IDA는 1949년 유명한 신경과 의사인 사무엘 T. 오튼 박사를 기리며 설립되었다. 이 단체의 목적은 가장 종합적인 포럼을 제공하며 지식, 방법, 경험을 나누는 것이다. 대중에게 난독증에 대해 알리려는 IDA의 노력에 힘입어, 우리는 이제 난독증이라는 질환의 성질에 대해 알게 되었다. 난독증은 언어의 획득과 처리 중의 간섭에 의해 특징 지워진다. 일반적으로 환자는 아마도 주어진 주제를 읽고 이해할 수 있을 것이지만, 세부사항을 옮기는 데 있어 문자 또는 단어를 바꾸어 놓는 증상을 나타낼 것이다

| 해설 |

이 지문의 앞부분은 국제 난독증 협회에 대한 설명이며, 뒷부분은 난독증의 증상에 대한 설명이다. 빈칸 뒤의 문장을 통해 정답 (d)를 유추할 수 있다.

| 오답 분석 |

(a) 외국인들을 향한 야만성과 무자비함 / 외국인에 대한 태도는 지문에 언급되지 않았다.
(b) 매일매일의 생활에 관련된 기억의 반복적 상실 / 지문에 언급되지 않은 내용이다.
(c) 어떤 특정한 상황들 하에서의 언어 장애 / 언어의 획득과 처리에 있어

서의 장애를 언급하고 있는 지문으로, speech(말하기)에 대한 장애를 언급하고 있지 않다.

| 어휘 |

dyslexia 난독증
distinguished 저명한, 유명한
interference 간섭, 방해
acquisition 획득
sufferer 환자
transcribe 다른 글자로 옮겨 쓰다, 문자화하다, 음성으로 나타내다

2.

"Urban sprawl" is a relatively new phenomenon in which it describes the process of cities spreading out and rural land being developed to sustain further expansion. From an urban planner's standpoint, the growth factor is very important. However, there are also those that are concerned about the effects of urban sprawl on the natural environment and agricultural resources, that don't regard development as a factor of importance. For them, what matters is the amount of land being used for development. Both sides have equally valid goals, although not necessarily mutually exclusive.

Q. What is the main topic of the passage?
(a) Urban sprawl is often the result of poor city planning.
(b) Plans for sustainable development are accelerating urban sprawl.
(c) Urban sprawl is bad for agriculture and the natural environment.
(d) There are two different perspectives on urban sprawl.

| 해석 |

'스프롤' 현상은 도시가 확장해나가는 과정과 더 나아간 확장을 유지하기 위해 개발된 교외지역을 묘사하는, 상대적으로 새로운 현상이다. 도시 계획자의 관점에서 생각해볼 때, 성장 요소는 매우 중요하다. 그러나 스프롤 현상이 자연 환경과 농경 자원에 미치는 영향에 대해 염려하고 개발을 중요한 요소로 여기지 않는 사람들도 있다. 그들에게 있어 중요한 것은 개발에 사용되는 땅의 양이다. 양측의 입장은 꼭 상호 배타적인 것은 아니지만, 똑같이 타당한 목적들을 가지고 있다.

| 해설 |

스프롤 현상에 대한 설명과 함께, 그것에 대한 각기 다른 두 관점을 나타내고 있는 글이다. 따라서 이 글의 주제는 '(d) 스프롤 현상에 대한 두 가지 관점이 존재한다.'가 된다.

| 오답 분석 |

(a) 스프롤 현상은 종종 조잡한 도시 계획의 결과물이다. / 도시 계획을 잘 못하였기 때문에 스프롤 현상이 일어난다는 내용은 지문에 언급되지 않았다.
(b) 지속 가능한 발달에 대한 계획은 스프롤 현상을 가속화시키고 있다. /

지속 가능한 발달에 대한 내용은 지문에 언급되지 않았다.
(c) 스프롤 현상은 농업과 자연환경에 나쁘다. / 스프롤 현상이 농업과 자
연환경에 미치는 영향에 대해 염려하는 사람들에 대한 언급이 있으나,
반드시 '나쁘다' 라고 언급된 것은 아니며 이 글의 주제로 보기에는 너
무 범주가 좁다.

| 어휘 |

urban sprawl 스프롤 현상(도시의 불규칙하고 무계획한 교외 발전)
standpoint 관점, 견지, 입장
mutually 서로, 상호간에
exclusive 배타적인, 모순되는

3.

In examining your daily life, perhaps you have a job
that is no longer interesting and you work just for
the money. Yet, your bills are difficult to pay and
you spend your leisure time stressed about your
finances. Or, perhaps you are at home every day,
and bored with nothing to look forward to except
cooking the next dinner and redecorating the spare
room. The number of stressful scenarios can be
endless for all of us, whether we are blue collar
workers, high-powered executives, housewives or
the unemployed. We should use some of our time
to enjoy more stress-free hobbies and pastimes as
we're all vulnerable to the lock-ins that stress our
mental and physical health.

Q. Which of the following is correct according to
the passage?
   (a) Many people now regard the main goal of
   relaxation to be self-taught.
   (b) The body and the mind are to be
   emphasized over our life situation.
   (c) People should consider relaxation as
   integral to their lifestyle.
   (d) Relaxation is deemed to be more important
   in modern times than in times past.

| 해석 |

일상을 점검해보면, 어쩌면 당신은 더 이상 흥미가 없지만 단지 돈 때문에
일을 하고 있을 수 있다. 그런데도 청구서에 돈을 지불하기가 어렵고, 여
가 시간도 금전적인 문제에 대해 스트레스를 받으며 보낼 것이다. 혹은,
아마도 당신은 매일 집안에서 보내며 다음 저녁을 요리하거나 남는 방을
다시 꾸미는 것을 제외하고는 기대하는 것 없이 지루해할 것이다. 우리가
육체 노동자이든지, 큰 권력을 갖고 있는 경영간부이든지, 주부이든지, 백
수이든지 간에 스트레스를 주는 시나리오들은 수없이 많다. 우리는 모두
정신적, 육체적 건강에 압박을 가하는 속박에 취약하므로, 스트레스와 무
관한 취미와 소일거리를 즐기는 데에 시간을 좀 보내야 한다.

| 해설 |

별로 흥미도 없는 일을 하고 일을 하지 않을 때에도 삶에 대해 스트레스를
받거나 지루하게지내는 경우가 많으므로 스트레스를 피해야 한다는 내용
의 글이다. 마지막 문장이 정답 '(c) 사람들은 긴장을 푸는 것을 생활양식

에 필수적인 것으로 생각해야 한다.' 를 고를 수 있는 직접적인 단서이다.

| 오답 분석 |

(a) 많은 사람들은 지금 휴식의 주요한 목적을 독학하는 것으로 여긴다. /
독학에 대한 내용은 언급되지 않았다.
(b) 생활의 상황보다 몸과 마음이 강조되어야 한다. / 지문에서 언급되지
않았다.
(d) 휴식은 과거보다 현재에 더 중요하게 생각된다. / 과거와 현재를 비교
하지 않았으므로 정답이 될 수 없다.

| 어휘 |

blue collar 육체 노동자의
executive 기업의 임원, 관리직원
lock-in 감금, 속박, 제약
vulnerable 상처 입기 쉬운, 공격받기 쉬운

4.

Social mobility is the degree to which, in a
given society, an individual or a family or a
group's social status can change throughout
their life within a system of social hierarchy.
There are two types of social mobility:
structural mobility and exchange mobility.
Structural mobility is the movement up or down
the social scale from a change in distribution of
statuses in a society, as when an individual
from a blue-collar background becomes a
professional. Exchange mobility is when
someone else must step up or down when a
position is dropped. Although social mobility is
common in places where achievement is the
basis for one's position in society, most people
remain close to the social level from which they
started from.

Q. What can be inferred from the passage?
   (a) Higher education is a prerequisite for a
   person's social mobility.
   (b) Structural mobility occurs more often in
   white collar professions.
   (c) Structural mobility and exchange mobility
   are rare these days.
   (d) Social mobility occurs when there is a
   demand of a particular occupation.

| 해석 |

사회 이동성은 주어진 사회에서 일생 동안 개인, 가족, 혹은 그룹의 사회
적 지위가 사회계층 시스템을 통해 바뀔 수 있는 범위이다. 사회 이동에는
두 가지 유형이 있다. 구조상의 이동과 교환 이동이다. 육체 노동자인 한
개인이 교수가 되는 경우와 같이, 구조상의 이동은 사회에서 지위의 분포
변화로부터 사회적인 계급이 올라가거나 내려가는 움직임이다. 교환 이동
은 어떤 지위가 떨어졌을 때, 다른 어떤 사람이 반드시 상승하거나 하강해
야만 한다. 사회에서의 지위에 있어 성취가 기본이 되는 곳에서는 사회적

인 이동이 흔한 일이지만, 대부분의 사람들은 그들이 시작했던 사회적인
단계와 비슷하게 남아 있는다.

I 해설 I
사회 이동에 대해 설명하고 있는 글이다. 지문의 마지막 문장에서 정답
'(c) 구조적인 이동과 교환 이동은 오늘날 드물다.'를 유추할 수 있다.

I 오답 분석 I
(a) 고등교육은 한 사람의 사회적인 이동에서 필요조건이다. / 교육에 대
　한 내용은 지문에서 언급되지 않았다.
(b) 구조적인 이동은 화이트칼라 직업에서 종종 더 발생한다. / 직업의 종
　류에 따라 비교하지 않았으므로 정답이 될 수 없다.
(d) 특정한 직업에 대한 수요가 있을 때, 사회 이동은 발생한다. / 지문에
　언급되지 않은 내용이다.

I 어휘 I
hierarchy 계급 제도
scale 눈금, 저울, 규모, 계급, 등급

5.
The first adult figured toy available to children in
the United States was the Barbie doll. (a) It was
created by Ruth Handler, the wife of a co-founder
of the Mattel toy company, inspired by their
daughter Barbara. (b) For the age of 3 to 7, playing
role games with dolls is very helpful for kids to
develop sociability. (c) As we all know, the Barbie
doll became a great success, however, it always
has been the source of a series of controversies.
(d) For example, many people blame that the
shape of the doll created an unrealistic body
image that young adolescent girls have tried to
emulate by losing weight.

I 해석 I
미국의 어린이들이 가질 수 있었던 어른 형상의 첫 번째 장난감은 바비 인
형이었다. (a) 바비는 매텔 장난감 회사의 공동 설립자의 부인인 루스 핸
들러가 딸인 바바라에 의해 영감을 받아 만들어졌다. (b) 3세에서 7세 사
이의 아이들에게 있어, 인형을 가지고 역할 놀이를 하는 것은 사회성을 개
발하는 데에 매우 도움이 된다. (c) 우리가 모두 알다시피, 바비 인형은 엄
청난 성공을 거두었지만, 바비는 항상 끊이지 않는 논란의 대상이었다.
(d) 예를 들어, 바비의 형상은 십대 소녀들이 살을 빼서 흉내 내려 하는 실
제적이지 않은 신체상을 만들었다고 많은 사람들이 비난한다.

I 해설 I
(b) 문장은 인형을 통한 역할 놀이가 아이들의 사회성 발달에 도움이 된다
는 내용이므로, 바비 인형과 관계가 없는 문장이다.

I 오답 분석 I
제일 첫 문장과 (a) 문장에서는 바비 인형이 처음 만들어진 배경을 말하고
있으며, (c)문장에서는 바비가 성공을 거두었으나 논란의 대상이라는 내
용이 언급되고 있다. (d) 문장은 (c)에 대한 예시이므로 유기적으로 연결
되고 있다.

I 어휘 I
inspire 영감을 주다, 고무하다
sociability 사회성, 사교성
controversy 논쟁, 말다툼
adolescent 청년, 젊은이

emulate 겨루다, 열심히 배우다, 흉내 내다

Day 6
Build up 62p

> **1.** (a) **2.** (c) **3.** (c) **4.** (c) **5.** (d)

1.
Many massage therapists are lobbying the
government and strongly urging it to intervene in
their industry. Various scandals and the increasing
number of malpractice lawsuits have forced
thousands of massage therapists to close their
businesses. The concerned individuals are seeking
for government assistance under the argument
that their means for a livelihood has been taken
away. As politicians at all levels agree that these
massage therapists are in dire need of assistance,
new legislation is expected to ________________

________________.

(a) provide financial aid and other grants
(b) close down any remaining businesses
(c) suggest some massage therapy for relief
(d) reform the universal health care system

I 해석 I
많은 마사지 치료사들은 정부에 로비하면서 정부가 마사지 치료 산업에
개입해야 한다고 강력하게 촉구하고 있다. 다양한 스캔들과 잘못된 치료
에 대한 소송이 늘어나고 있어 수천의 마사지 치료사들이 문을 닫고 있다.
관련된 사람들은 자신의 생계 수단이 사라져버렸다는 주장을 내세워 정부
의 도움을 구하고 있다. 모든 정치인들은 마사지 치료사들에게 긴박한 도
움이 필요한 상태라는 것에 동의하고 있어, 새로운 법안이 재정적인 도움
과 다른 보조금을 제공해줄 것으로 예상된다.

I 해설 I
마사지 치료사들이 정부의 개입을 촉구한다는 내용의 지문이므로 정답은
(a)가 된다.

I 오답 분석 I
(b) 살아남은 어떤 사업도 문을 닫을 것으로 / 새로운 법안은 마사지 치료
　사들을 돕기 위한 의도이므로 정답과 반대의 내용이다.
(c) 고통을 덜기 위해 어떤 마시지 치료를 제안할 것으로 / 마사지 치료사
　들의 사업적 내용을 다루고 있으므로 정답이 될 수 없다.
(d) 전반적인 건강 관리 시스템을 개혁할 것으로 / 마사지 치료사들에 대
　한 내용이므로 이 보기는 다루고 있는 범주가 너무 넓다.

I 어휘 I
intervene 사이에 들다, 사이에 일어나다; 방해하다; 중재하다, 개입하다

malpractice (의사의) 부정 치료; 배임 행위
livelihood 생계, 살림, 호구지책
dire 무서운, 비참한, 끔찍한, 급박한
legislation 법률 제정, 입법 행위; (집합적) 법률, 법령

2.

A problem that usually affects colleges and universities is the issue of academic dishonesty. Numerous surveys indicate that approximately 50% of students have cheated in some manner during their stint at a post-secondary institution. Furthermore, results also suggested that the most common forms of academic dishonesty were plagiarism on written assignments, cheating during exams, and falsifying information. To discourage such practices, colleges and universities will often resort to severe, disciplinary actions. In fact, if a student is found guilty of academic dishonesty, the individual ___________________________.

(a) can be sentenced to a term in prison
(b) has his parents notified of the incident
(c) will be often suspended or even expelled
(d) required to attend counseling sessions

| 해석 |

대학들에 영향을 주고 있는 문제는 학문에 있어서의 부정직이라는 이슈이다. 다수의 설문은 약 50%의 학생이 중등교육 이후의 교육기관에 있는 동안 어떤 방법으로든 부정행위를 해왔다는 것을 나타내준다. 더 나아가, 이 조사 결과는 가장 흔한 형태의 부정행위는 쓰기 과제에서의 표절과 시험 때의 베끼기, 정보의 위조 등이라는 것을 제시하였다. 이런 행동들을 단념시키기 위해, 대학들은 엄한 징계를 내리는 조치에 호소할 것이다. 사실상, 만약 학생이 학문적 부정행위를 저질렀다는 것이 발견된다면, 그 학생은 정학이나 퇴학을 당하게 될 것이다.

| 해설 |

빈칸 바로 앞 문장에서 징계를 내릴 것이라고 하였으므로 정답 (c)에 대한 단서를 얻을 수 있다.

| 오답 분석 |

(a) 감옥에서 기한을 선고 받을 수 있다. / 학교 내의 규율에 따른 징계이므로 감옥에 가는 것은 내용상 부적절하다.
(b) 학생의 부모에게 그 사건을 알린다. / '징계'에 어울리지 않는 조치이다.
(d) 상담 수업을 받는 것이 요구된다. / '징계'에 어울리지 않는 조치이다.

| 어휘 |

dishonesty 부정직, 불성실, 부정행위
stint 할당된 기간, 할당된 일(의 양)
plagiarism 표절 행위, 도용
cheat 기만하다, 속이다, (시험) 베끼다
falsify (서류 등을) 위조하다, (사실을) 속이다, 왜곡하다
disciplinary 훈련의, 훈육의, 규율상의, 징계의
suspend 매달다, 중지하다
expel 내쫓다, 쫓아버리다

3.

The advertising industry's conduct, especially with respect to the targeting of children with junk food commercials, was thrown into sharp focus today by a report commissioned by congress which said that current food company marketing techniques were leading to a dramatic increase in childhood obesity and diabetes. The report was prepared by the Institute of Medicine, which also called on food manufacturers directly to produce and promote more healthy food than they do at present. They further pressed for congress to mandate a 2 year period during which food producing companies would be forced to comply or be barred from advertising via the media, particularly broadcast and cable TV.

Q. What is the passage about?
(a) Children's habit of watching too much television
(b) The frequency of food advertisements on children's television
(c) The detrimental effect of junk food advertising on children
(d) Food advertisers taking steps toward self-regulation

| 해석 |

광고업계의 행위, 특히 정크 푸드 상업 광고로 아이들을 표적으로 삼는 것이 의회가 의뢰한 보고서에 의해 날카로운 집중 조명에 들어갔다. 의회는 요즘의 식품 회사 마케팅 기술이 아동 비만과 당뇨를 엄청나게 증가시켰다고 밝힌 바 있다. 의학 연구소에 의해 준비된 그 리포트는 음식 제조업자들에게 직접적으로 그들이 현재 생산하는 것보다 더 건강한 음식을 생산하고, 장려하는 것을 요청했다. 의학 연구소는 식품 생산회사들이 이러한 조치에 따르거나, 그렇지 않으면 2년간 미디어를 통한, 특히 케이블 TV와 방송 미디어를 통한 광고에 규제를 받도록 하라고 의회에 더욱 압력을 넣었다.

| 해설 |

정크 푸드 광고가 아이들에게 좋지 않은 영향을 미치므로 규제를 받아야 한다는 압력이 진행되고 있다는 내용의 글이다. 따라서 이 글은 '(c) 정크 푸드 광고가 아이들에게 미치는 해로운 영향'에 대한 내용이다.

| 오답 분석 |

(a) 너무 많이 텔레비전을 보는 아이들의 습관 / 이 지문은 아이들의 TV 시청을 문제 삼고 있지 않다.
(b) 아이들의 TV에서 음식 광고의 빈번함 / 음식 광고의 빈도가 문제시 되고 있지는 않다.
(d) 자가 규제를 하기 위해 조치를 취하고 있는 음식 광고주들 / 의학 연구소에서 의회에 규제 조치를 제안하고 있으므로 정답이 될 수 없다.

| 어휘 |

conduct 행위, 지도, 안내
commission 위임하다, ~에게 권한을 주다
mandate 명령, 요구하다

comply 응하다, 따르다
bar 빗장을 지르다, 방해하다, 금하다

4.

Clement Marot is one of the most important figures in French poetry in the sixteenth century. He published intimate poetry, often in the forms of the ballade and the rondeau about his own mind, feelings, and habits. During the Renaissance, he mostly wrote about his love for Marguerite d'Angouleme, the king's sister, while later on in his life, he wrote about the horrors of war. In Flanders, he expressed his disgust for man's pursuit of power and his own attempt to detach himself from worldly things. However, the true genius of Marot is that in describing himself, he described all people.

Q. What can be inferred about Marot according to the passage?
(a) His emotional detachment kept him from pursuing power in the literary court.
(b) His personal writings accurately portrayed the sentiment of war at the time.
(c) He used self criticism as a means of critiquing humanity.
(d) He ingeniously detailed common people's everyday lives during the Renaissance.

| 해석 |
Clement Marot는 16세기 프랑스 시에서 가장 중요한 인물 중의 하나이다. 그는 사적인 감정에 대한 시집을 출판했는데, 자신의 마음, 느낌, 그리고 습관 등에 대한 론도체와 발라드의 형식이었다. 르네상스 시대에, 그는 주로 왕의 누이인 Marguerite d'Angouleme에 대한 자신의 사랑에 관해 썼고, 인생의 후반부에는 전쟁의 공포에 관해 썼다. Flanders에서 그는 사람들의 권력에 대한 추종에 대한 혐오감을 표현했고, 세속적인 것들로부터 자신을 분리하려는 시도를 표현했다. 그러나 Marot의 진짜 천재적인 면은 그 자신의 묘사 속에서 모든 사람들을 묘사했다는 것이다.

| 해설 |
제일 마지막 문장에서 자신에 대한 묘사를 통해 모든 사람들을 묘사하였다고 하였으므로, 다른 사람에 대한 혐오나 비판도 자신의 모습을 통해 하였다는 것을 유추할 수 있다. 따라서 정답은 '(c) 그는 인간성을 비평하는 방법으로 자가 비평을 사용했다.' 가 된다.

| 오답 분석 |
(a) 그의 감정적인 분리는 문학에서 그가 권력을 추종하는 것을 막았다. / Marot이 문학에 있어 권력을 추종하였다는 내용은 언급되지 않았다.
(b) 그의 개인적인 글쓰기는 그 시대 전쟁에 관한 감정을 정확하게 묘사했다. / intimate(사적인 감정에 관한, 내밀한)를 personal(개인적인)과 동의어로 볼 수 없다.
(d) 그는 르네상스 시대에 대중의 일상을 독창적으로 묘사했다. / 대중의 일상을 묘사했다는 내용은 언급되지 않았다.

| 어휘 |
intimate 친밀한, 친숙한; 마음속의, 개인적인, 사사로운
ballaede 발라드
rondeau 론도체; 시의 최초의 단어가 두 번 후렴으로 쓰임
disgust 싫음, 메스꺼움, 혐오감
detach 떼다, 떼어내다, 분리하다

5.

Fermented drinks, also known as alcoholic beverages, are popular all over the world. (a) Most cultures have different methods of producing such drinks. (b) Chinese people make fermented drinks by mixing rice, honey and fruits, while those in the Middle East mix barley beer and grape wine. (c) These types of alcoholic beverages are not only fragrant but also nutritious for the body, but can be detrimental to the health if consumed in large amounts. (d) Storing alcohol drinks in bottles has always been the very best way to keep them from degenerating in quality.

| 해석 |
술이라고도 알려져 있는 발효된 음료는 전 세계에 걸쳐 유명하다. (a) 대부분의 문화권에는 이러한 발효 음료를 생산하는 각기 다른 방법이 있다. (b) 중동에서는 보리로 만든 맥주와 포도주를 섞는 반면, 중국 사람들은 쌀과 꿀, 과일을 섞어서 술을 만든다. (c) 이러한 종류의 술은 향기로울 뿐 아니라 우리 몸에 영양분을 주기도 하지만, 다량을 섭취할 경우 건강에 해로울 수도 있다. (d) 술이 변질되지 않게 지키기 위해 가장 좋은 방법은 항상 유리병에 보관하는 것이었다.

| 해설 |
(d) 문장은 술의 보관에 대한 내용인데, 지문의 앞부분에서 전혀 언급되지 않았기 때문에 문맥상 어색한 문장이다.

| 오답 분석 |
(a)와 (b)에서는 발효된 음료인 술을 생산하는 방법을, (c) 문장에서는 이러한 술의 긍정적, 부정적 영향을 설명하고 있으므로 유기적으로 연결되고 있다.

| 어휘 |
ferment 발효하다
fragrant 향기 좋은
nutritious 영양분이 있는
detrimental 유해한, 해로운
degenerate 나빠지다, 퇴보하다, 변질하다

Day 7

Build up 70p

1. (b)	2. (d)	3. (c)	4. (c)	5. (c)

1.

The first branch of the Ku Klux Klan was established in Pulaski, Tennessee, in May, 1866. A year later a general organization of local Klans was established in Nashville in April, 1867. Most of the leaders were former members of the Confederate Army and the first Grand Wizard was Nathan Forrest, an outstanding general during the American Civil War. During the next two years Klansmen wearing masks, white cardboard hats and draped in white sheets, tortured and killed black Americans and sympathetic whites. Immigrants, who they blamed for the election of radical republicans, were also targets of their hatred. Between 1868 and 1870 the Ku Klux Klan ____ in North Carolina, Tennessee and Georgia.

(a) assisted in federal efforts toward desegregation
(b) played an important role in restoring white rule
(c) encouraged members of the public toward pragmatism
(d) helped senior black citizens file for federal aid packages

| 해석 |

Ku Klux Klan의 첫 번째 지부는 1866년 5월, 테네시 주의 Pulaski에서 처음으로 설립되었다. 1년 뒤, 1867년 4월에 네슈빌에서 각 지역의 Ku Klux Klan 지부들의 총체적 조직이 세워졌다. 이들의 리더들 중 대부분이 전직 남부 동맹군 멤버들이었으며, 미국 남북전쟁 동안에 뛰어난 장군이었던 Nathan Forrest가 초대 대마법사가 되었다. 다음 2년 동안, 가면과 하얀색 마분지 모자를 쓰고 흰 천을 우아하게 두른 멤버들은 흑인들과 흑인을 동정하는 백인들을 고문하고 죽였다. 급진파 공화당이 선출된 것에 대한 비난의 개상이 되었던 이민자들도 역시 Ku Klux Klan의 분노의 표적이었다. 1868년과 1870년 사이에 Ku Klux Klan은 노스 캐롤라이나와 테네시, 조지아 주에서 백인들의 통치를 회복하는 데 중요한 역할을 했다.

| 해설 |

Ku Klux Klan의 조직과 성향에 대한 글이다. 흑인과 이민자들을 배척한Ku Klux Klan이 백인 우월주의 집단임을 알 수 있으므로 정답은 (b)가 된다.

| 오답 분석 |

(a) 인종차별 폐지를 향한 국가의 노력을 도왔다. / Ku Klux Klan의 성질과 정반대의 내용이다.
(c) 대중이 실용주의를 채택하도록 장려했다. / 지문에 실용주의에 대한 언급은 없다.
(d) 노년층의 흑인 시민들이 국가의 일괄적 보조를 요청하도록 도왔다. / Ku Klux Klan의 성질과 정반대의 내용이다.

| 어휘 |

confederate 동맹한, 연합한, 남부 동맹의
drape 옷 등을 두르다, 낙낙하게 덮다, 주름 잡다
desegregation 차별 폐지
pragmatism 실용주의

2.

Since the development of guns, a weapon which could deliver a continuous stream of fire was a highly attractive concept to gun manufacturers. Early designs basically copied the stationary gun, so a single trigger would provide the flash to ignite several barrels of a weapon at once. Whilst effective, the obvious drawback of the early devices was the prolonged loading and reloading, so alternatives were actively pursued. The first true machine-gun was invented by a dentist from North Carolina named Richard Gatling. His "Gatling Gun" revolutionized killing efficiency by delivering up to six hundred shots in two minutes. The key to his invention was the rotating 6-barrel cylinder.

Q. What is the main idea of the passage?
(a) Modern weapons are based on Richard Gatling's machine gun designs.
(b) Early attempts at machine guns were ineffective.
(c) Continuous fire is the key to killing efficiency.
(d) The evolution of the machine gun hinged on Gatling's rotating barrel.

| 해석 |

총의 개발 이래, 끊임없이 발사할 수 있는 무기는 총기 생산자들에게 아주 매력적인 개념이었다. 초기 디자인은 기본적으로 고정된 총을 베껴 만들어서, 하나의 방아쇠가 한 번에 여러 개의 총신들을 발화시키도록 하였다. 효율적이긴 했지만, 초기 장치의 명백한 결점은 장전과 재장전에 시간이 오래 걸린다는 것이었다. 그래서 대안들이 활발하게 추구되었다. 첫 번째 진짜 기계총은 리차드 개틀링이란 이름의 노스캐롤라이나 출신 치과의사에 의해 발명되었다. 그의 '개틀링 기관총'은 2분 동안 600발까지를 발사할 수 있었기 때문에 살인 효율성에 혁명을 일으켰다. 그의 발명에 있어 가장 중요한 요소는 회전하는 6총신 실린더였다.

| 해설 |

개틀링 기관총이 총기류의 발달에 미친 영향에 대한 글이다. 따라서 정답은 '(d) 기계총의 진화는 개틀링의 회전하는 총신에 따라 결정되었다.'가 된다.

| 오답 분석 |

(a) 현대 무기들은 리차드 개틀링의 기계 총 디자인에 기반을 두었다. / 개틀링 기관총은 디자인 때문에 의미가 있는 것이 아니라 회전하는 6총신 실린더이기 때문이다.
(b) 기계 총들의 초기 시도는 비효율적이다. / 초기 시도의 효율성에 대해서는 지문에서 언급하지 않았다.
(c) 끊임없는 불꽃은 살인 효율에 중요한 요소이다. / 지문에 등장한 단어를 이용한 오답이다.

| 어휘 |

stream 흐름, 유출
stationary 고정된, 움직이지 않는

flash 번쩍임, 섬광
ignite 불을 붙이다, 발화시키다.
barrel 총열, 포신, 총신
Gatling gun 개틀링 기관총(여러 개의 총신을 가진 초기의 기관총)
hinge on ~에 따라 결정되다

3.

A trend that could be harmful to personal relationships and American society has been identified in a comprehensive new study by psychologists that showed that self-centeredness among today's students is on the rise. Researchers at San Diego State University assert that kids are already selfish enough, and to avoid having them grow into self-obsessed adults we need to stop endlessly telling children 'You're special' and having them repeat it back. The study measured people's level of narcissism and cited the responses of 16,475 college students nationwide. The results spanned the period from 1982 to 2006 and showed a distinct rise in narcissistic tendencies among the participants.

Q. Which of the following is correct according to the passage?
(a) The author is fully satisfied with parents' attitudes to their children.
(b) Parents have become better informed than in the past.
(c) Children should not exclusively receive positive reinforcement.
(d) The author defines the relationship between the self-centered parents and child.

| 해석 |
인간 관계와 미국 사회에 해로운 영향을 미칠 수 있는 한 경향이 심리학자들에 의한 포괄적인 새로운 연구에서 확인되었다. 그 연구는 오늘날의 학생들에게 자기중심적 성향이 상승하고 있다는 것을 보여주었다. 샌디에이고 주립대학의 연구자들은 아이들은 이미 충분히 이기적이며, 아이들이 자아도취적인 어른으로 자라나는 것을 피하기 위해서 우리는 아이들에게 '너는 특별해' 라는 말을 끊임없이 하면서 아이들이 그것을 반복하게 하는 것을 멈추어야 한다고 단언했다. 그 연구는 사람들의 자아도취증의 수준을 측정했고, 16,475명의 전국 대학생의 반응을 언급했다. 그 결과는 1982년부터 2006년까지의 기간에 걸친 것으로, 참여자들 사이에서 자아도취적인 성향의 두드러진 상승을 보여주었다.

| 해설 |
사람들이 점점 더 자기중심적이고 자아도취적이 되어가고 있다는 내용의 글이다. 아이들에게 '너는 특별하다'는 말을 끊임없이 하는 것을 멈춰야 한다고 했으므로 정답은 '(c) 아이들은 독점적으로 긍정적 강화를 받으면 안 된다'가 된다.

| 오답 분석 |
(a) 화자는 아이들에 대한 부모들의 태도에 완전히 만족하고 있다. / 이 글의 화자는 이와 반대의 입장이다.
(b) 부모들은 과거보다 더 많은 정보를 얻고 있다. / 지문에 언급되지 않았다.
(d) 저자는 자기중심적인 부모와 아이들 사이의 관계를 정의했다. / 이 글은 자기중심적, 자아도취적 성향에 대한 것으로, 부모와 자식간의 관계를 정의한 것은 찾아볼 수 없다.

| 어휘 |
assert 단언하다, 역설하다; 주장하다
narcissism 자아도취증
nationwide 전국적인
span 기간; (세월이) 걸치다

4.

Welcome to PLAN 101- Introduction to Urban Planning. In this course, we'll examine the history of urban planning by looking at early theories and practices since Rome. We will discuss planning theories that have stood the test of time and those that haven't, including the ones that failed to recognize the human need of 'sense of place.' We will also delve into pioneering architectural designs so as to have a complete understanding of how urban planning has developed into what it is today.

Q. What can be inferred from the notice?
(a) The professor disagrees with modern planning practice.
(b) Most of the lecture will focus on examples of bad planning.
(c) The objective of the class is to have an all-rounded understanding about urban planning.
(d) None of the theory that will be studied in the class is fit for today's circumstances.

| 해석 |
PLAN 101– 도시 계획 입문 수업에 온 것을 환영합니다. 이 수업에서 우리는 로마 시대부터의 초기 이론들과 관례를 봄으로써 도시 계획의 역사를 조사할 것입니다. 우리는 '장소 감각'의 필요를 인식하는 데 실패한 것들을 포함해서, 시간에 의한 테스트를 견딘 계획 이론들과 그렇지 못한 계획 이론들을 토의할 것입니다. 우리는 또한 어떻게 도시 계획이 오늘날처럼 발전해 왔는지 완벽하게 이해할 수 있도록 건축학의 디자인을 개척하는 데 깊이 파고 들 것입니다.

| 해설 |
도시 계획 수업에 대한 안내글이다. 로마시대부터의 성공적이었던 것들 뿐 아니라 실패했던 도시 계획 이론에 대해서도 살펴본다고 하였으므로 정답은 '(c) 강의의 주제는 도시 계획에 관한 전반적인 이해이다.' 가 된다.

(a) 교수님은 현대 계획의 실제에 동의하지 않는다. / 교수님의 성향에 대해서는 언급하지 않고 있다.
(b) 강의의 대부분은 나쁜 계획의 예들에 초점이 맞추어질 것이다. / 성공적인 사례도 다룰 것이라고 했으므로 정답이 될 수 없다.
(d) 이 수업에서 공부할 어떤 이론도 오늘날의 상황에 들어맞지 않는다. / 시간의 테스트를 견딘 계획 이론에 대해 토의할 것이라고 하였으므로 정답이 될 수 없다.

l 어휘 l
delve 탐구하다, 깊이 파고들다
pioneer 개척하다; 지도하다

5.

If you're tired of the old dusty air, give your home the mountain fresh, clean air. (a) Air filters are a great addition to any household as they are able to cleanse the air of any bacteria, dust, pollen or mold. (b) Air conditioners and heaters also consist of air filters and help to keep the air fresh while dispensing that much needed cool or warm air. (c) Air fresheners are often used by people to hide foul odors in enclosed spaces. (d) Keeping air filters clean is a key to avoiding expensive maintenance bills and get clear air at the same time.

l 해석 l
오래된 먼지 나는 공기에 지치셨다면, 당신의 집에 산의 신선하고 깨끗한 공기를 주세요. (a) 에어 필터는 박테리아, 먼지, 꽃가루, 곰팡이 등을 정화해주기 때문에 어떤 가정에나 훌륭한 추가물입니다. (b) 에어컨과 히터도 역시 에어 필터로 구성되어 있으므로 필요한 시원하거나 따뜻한 공기를 내보내주면서도 공기를 신선하게 지킬 수 있습니다. (c) 공기 청정기는 밀폐된 공간의 악취를 숨기려고 사용됩니다. (d) 에어 필터를 깨끗하게 유지하는 것은 비싼 유지비를 피하면서 동시에 깨끗한 공기를 얻기 위해 중요합니다.

l 해설 l
에어 필터의 장점과 관리 요령 등에 대한 글이다. (c)는 공기 청정기의 사용 목적을 나타내고 있으므로 이 글의 소재에서 벗어나 있다.

l 오답 분석 l
첫 문장은 에어 필터를 소개하기 위한 일반적 도입문장이고, (a)는 에어 필터의 기능, (b)는 에어 필터를 에어컨이나 히터와 함께 사용할 수 있다는 점, (d)는 에어 필터의 관리 방식을 언급하고 있으므로 하나의 소재를 잘 다루고 있다.

l 어휘 l
cleanse 깨끗이 하다, 정화하다
dispense 분배하다, 나누어주다
maintenance 유지, 간수

Build up
78p

1. (b) **2.** (c) **3.** (b) **4.** (a) **5.** (b)

1.

The Australian Prime Minister, John Howard, has repelled pressure to apologize to aborigines for the dispossession of their land or to agree to reparations for the "stolen generations" of black children removed from their families in the 1940s and 1950s. Last year, more than 150,000 people marched across Sydney Harbor Bridge calling for reconciliation. The march was followed by a National Sorry Day during which white people signed books of atonement. Though Mr. Howard didn't participate in these movements, he

_________________________.

(a) looked closely at apologizing process
(b) apologized for the "hurt" of not apologizing
(c) began to take a keen interest in the Sydney Harbor Bridge
(d) apologized for previously having made an apology

l 해석 l
호주의 총리 존 하워드는 원주민의 땅을 강탈한 것에 대해 사과하거나, 1940년대와 1950년대 그들의 가족으로부터 강제로 떨어지도록 하였던 '강탈당한 세대'인 흑인 아이들에 대한 보상에 동의하라는 압력을 물리치고 있다. 지난해, 15만 명이 넘는 사람들이 화해를 외치며 시드니 하버 브리지를 행진했다. 백인들이 속죄의 책에 서명했던 국가적 속죄의 날에 시위가 뒤따랐다. 비록 하워드는 이러한 움직임에 동참하지 않았지만 사과하지 않은 것으로 인한 상처에 대해서는 사과하고 있다.

l 해설 l
총리인 하워드는 대중의 화해와 사과를 향한 움직임에 동참하지 않았다고 하였다. 따라서 정답 (b)에 대한 단서를 얻을 수 있다.

l 오답 분석 l
(a) 사과 과정을 면밀히 살펴보았다. / 절차에 대해서 지문에 언급되지 않았다.
(b) 시드니 하버 브리지에 큰 흥미를 갖기 시작했다. / 지문의 소재에서 벗어났다.
(d) 이전에 사과를 한 것에 대해 사과했다. / 이전에 사과했다는 내용은 언급되지 않았다.

l 어휘 l
repel 쫓아버리다; 물리치다
aborigine 호주의 원주민
dispossession 몰아내기; 강탈
reparation 배상

curiously 이상하게도, 호기심에서, 진기한 듯이
reconciliation 화해
atonement 보상, 속죄

2.

In today's day and age, far too many adolescents
seem to take things for granted. Many of these
young adults have no appreciation or even an idea
of the work that is required to provide basic needs
such as food and shelter. Since many of them
have never had to grow crops or raise their own
livestock for sustenance, this notion can be an
unfamiliar one to them. Due to an utter and total
dependence on technology in today's modern
world, few adolescents can make the connection
between production and consumption. Taking
these facts into consideration, it would be wise to
encourage students to participate in work
seminars that examine the importance of work in
their lives. Doing so would undoubtedly give them
a better appreciation for all the products and
services that are easily available to them.

Q. What is the main idea of this passage?
  (a) The attitudes of today's young people are
     satisfactory.
  (b) Teenagers are better informed today than
     they were in the past.
  (c) Teenagers today should be more aware of
     the nature of work.
  (d) The relationship between production and
     technology should be taught at school.

| 해석 |
오늘날, 수많은 청소년들은 많은 것들을 당연한 일로 생각하는 듯하다. 이
어린 성인들의 대다수는 감사하지도 않고, 심지어 피신처(집)와 음식 같
은 기본적인 필요를 제공하기 위해 일이 필요한 것이라는 생각도 하지 않
았다. 그들의 대다수는 생계를 위한 작물을 키워본 적이 없고 자신의 가축
을 돌보아본 적이 없기 때문에, 이 개념은 그들에게 친숙하지 않은 것이
다. 오늘날의 현대 세상에서는 전적으로 기술에 의존하기 때문에, 생산과
소비의 연결을 만들 수 있는 청소년들은 거의 없다. 이런 사실들을 고려해
볼 때, 학생들의 삶에서 일의 중요성을 알려주는 세미나에 참석하도록 독
려하는 것이 좋을 것이다. 이것은 확실히 그들이 쉽게 이용할 수 있는 물
품과 서비스에 대해 더욱 감사하는 마음을 가지게 해줄 것이다.

| 해설 |
오늘날의 청소년들은 많은 것들을 당연시하며 생산과 소비에 대한 개념이
약하다고 하였기 때문에 정답은 '(c) 오늘날 청소년들은 일의 본질에 대
해 좀 더 알아야 한다'이다.

| 오답 분석 |
(a) 오늘날 젊은 사람들의 태도는 만족스럽다. / 이 글의 화자는 젊은이들
  에 대해 만족스럽지 않다는 견해를 가진 쪽이다.

(b) 청소년들은 과거보다 많은 정보를 얻고 있다. / 청소년들이 얻는 정보
  의 양에 대한 지문이 아니다.
(d) 기술과 생산의 관계가 학교에서 가르쳐져야 한다. / 지문에서 언급되
  지 않았다.

| 어휘 |
take ~ for granted 당연시하다
utter 전적인, 단전한, 철저한

3.

The assumption that birds are the descendants of
dinosaurs runs into a roadblock in the form of
blood. Whilst it is widely believed that dinosaurs
belonged to the reptile species and so were cold-
blooded, therein lies the problem; birds are
without dispute warm-blooded. This has led to a
rethinking of whether dinosaurs were indeed cold-
blooded or not. It has been suggested that they
may have retained body heat, and therefore
controlled their blood temperature because most
dinosaurs had a distinctly upright posture, unlike
modern reptiles like the crocodile which sprawl on
the ground in order to absorb heat.

Q. Which of the following is correct about the
  passage?
  (a) Dinosaurs' blood temperatures change very
     quickly.
  (b) Most people believe dinosaurs were cold-
     blooded reptiles.
  (c) Dinosaurs and birds share the same blood
     type.
  (d) Crocodiles don't share any traits with
     upright dinosaurs.

| 해석 |
새들이 공룡의 후손이라는 추측은 피의 형태에 있어 장애물을 만나게 되
었다. 공룡이 파충류에 속하고 따라서 냉혈동물이라고 널리 믿어지고 있
는데, 바로 그 점에 문제가 있다. 새는 논쟁의 여지없이 온혈동물이다. 이
것은 공룡이 실제로 냉혈동물인지 아닌지를 다시 생각하도록 이끌었다.
열을 흡수하기 위해 땅을 엎드려 기어가는 악어 같은 현대 파충류와는 뚜
렷이 다르게 대부분의 공룡들은 직립 자세를 갖기 때문에, 공룡은 체온을
유지하고 스스로의 피 온도를 조절했다고 제시된다.

| 해설 |
두 번째 문장에서 공룡이 파충류이므로 냉혈동물이라고 생각된다고 하였
으므로 정답은 '(b) 대부분의 사람들은 공룡이 냉혈 파충류였다고 믿는
다.'이다.

| 오답 분석 |
(a) 공룡의 피 온도는 급격하게 변화한다. / 동물의 크기에 따른 피 온도
  변화는 언급되지 않았다.
(c) 공룡과 새들은 혈액형이 같다. / 혈액형에 대한 내용은 이 지문에서 언
  급되지 않았다.
(d) 악어들은 직립 공룡들과 어떤 특징도 공유하고 있지 않다. / 공룡과 악

어는 둘 다 파충류라는 공통점을 갖는다.

| 어휘 |

assumption 가정, 가설, 추측
descendant 자손, 후예
roadblock 장애물
therein 그점에, 그속에, 거기에
retain 계속 유지하다, 간직하다, 보유하다
reptile 파충류동물
sprawl 기어 다니다
warm-blooded 온혈의
cold-blooded 냉혈의

4.

Faust: A Tragedy is the title given for the masterpiece by Johann Wolfgang Von Goethe. Yet, many consider the play a musical comedy, in that it features many comic passages, songs, and lacks a tragic ending. The play's hero, Faust, is not a classic tragic figure either. The fact that he gains spiritual salvation after death has made it difficult for some people to regard it as tragic. In fact, his characteristic yearning for "divine knowledge" created a type for the romantic age still known as the Faustian hero.

Q. What can be inferred from the passage?

(a) We may think Goethe's Faust is somewhat contradictory.

(b) Faust concludes that one should strive to attain divine knowledge.

(c) We can explore the intellect of Goethe through Faust.

(d) Goethe's Faust emphasizes that life is tragic.

| 해석 |

요한 볼프강 괴테의 명작에 대해 주어진 제목은 〈Faust: A tragedy(파우스트: 비극)〉이다. 그러나 많은 사람들은 코믹한 구절들과 노래를 많이 보여주며 비극적으로 끝나지 않는다는 점에서 그 연극을 뮤지컬 희극이라고 생각한다. 이 연극의 주인공인 파우스트도 전통적인 의미의 비극적 인물이 아니다. 죽은 뒤에 영적인 구제를 얻었다는 사실은 어떤 사람들이 이 연극을 비극으로 생각하기 힘들게 만든다. 사실상, 그의 특징이라 할 수 있는 '신성한 지식'에 대한 동경은 파우스트적인 영웅으로 여전히 알려져 있는 로맨틱 시대의 하나의 유형을 창조했다.

| 해설 |

파우스트가 전통적인 의미의 비극은 아니라는 점에서 이 작품을 읽는 사람들은 혼란을 느낄 여지가 있다고 하였으므로 정답은 '(a) 우리는 괴테의 파우스트가 다소 모순적이라고 생각할 수도 있다.'가 된다.

| 오답 분석 |

(b) 파우스트는 사람이 신성한 지식을 얻기 위해 노력해야 한다고 결론지었다. / 이 지문에서 파우스트의 결론은 언급되지 않았다.

(c) 우리는 파우스트를 통해 괴테의 지적 능력을 살펴볼 수 있다. / 이 지

문에 언급되지 않은 내용이다.

(d) 괴테의 파우스트는 삶이 비극이라는 것을 강조한다. / 작품인 파우스트가 비극이라고 언급된 것이다.

| 어휘 |

masterpiece 걸작, 명작
salvation 구제
yearning 동경, 열망
divine 신성한

5.

If you are interested in experiencing foreign culture and want to earn money needed to finance your sojourn at the same time, then perhaps imparting your knowledge of the English language overseas would be apt for you. (a) Copious English-teaching positions are available all around the world, especially in China, Korea, Japan and Taiwan. (b) In order to take advantage of this once in a lifetime opportunity, all you need is parental permission and a high school diploma. (c) Couples that embark on a journey to work in a foreign country together more easily adapt to the chosen country than people who arrive at their destination alone. (d) Also, they are less prone to the severity of culture shock as the relationship itself acts partially as a "shock absorber."

| 해석 |

외국 문화를 경험하는 데 관심이 있고 동시에 체류하는 데 필요한 돈을 벌고 싶다면, 영어에 대한 지식을 해외에서 가르치는 것이 당신에게 적절할 것이다. (a) 전 세계적으로 영어를 가르치는 일은 많으며, 특히 중국, 한국, 일본, 타이완에서 많이 찾아볼 수 있다. (b) 일생에 한 번뿐인 이 기회를 이용하기 위해서 당신은 부모님의 허가와 고등학교 졸업장만 있으면 된다. (c) 외국에서 일하는 여행을 함께 떠나는 커플들은 혼자 목적지에 도착한 사람들보다 선택한 나라에 더 잘 적응하고 익숙해진다. (d) 또한, 그들은 관계 자체가 '충격 흡수제'로서 일부분 작용하기 때문에 심한 문화 충격을 겪을 확률이 더 적다.

| 해설 |

외국에서 일하며 여행하기 위해 영어를 가르치는 일을 가질 수 있으며, 커플이 함께 떠나면 더 잘 적응할 수 있다는 내용의 글이다. (b)는 이러한 주제에서 벗어나 있다.

| 오답 분석 |

첫 문장과 (a)는 영어를 가르치는 일에 대한 설명, (c)와 (d)는 커플이 함께 떠날 때 더 좋은 점을 설명하고 있으므로 서로 연결되어 있다.

| 어휘 |

sojourn 묵다, 체류하다
impart 정보를 알리다

Day 9

Build up

1. (a)	2. (c)	3. (d)	4. (b)	5. (c)

1.

Ultrasound scanners consist of a computer and electronics control console, a video display screen and ________________________________.
This is a small hand-held device that resembles a microphone attached to the scanner by a cord. A returning sound wave or "echo" is picked up by the transducer after it sends out a high frequency sound wave. The ultrasound image is visible real-time on a nearby screen that looks a lot like a small television or computer monitor. The image is created based on the amplitude, frequency and time it takes for the sound signal to return from the patient to the transducer.

(a) a transducer that is used to scan the body
(b) foot, ankle and knee restraint made from spandex
(c) large piece of digital electronic medical equipment
(d) comprehensive set of instructions written underneath

| 해석 |

초음파 스캐너는 컴퓨터와 전자공학 조절 콘솔, 비디오 디스플레이 스크린, 몸을 스캔할 때 사용되는 변환기로 구성되어 있다. 이것은 마이크로폰을 닮은 작은 휴대용 장치인데, 코드로 스캐너에 부착되어 있다. 고주파의 음파를 보낸 뒤, 반향되는 음파 또는 '메아리'는 변환기에 의해 수집된다. 초음파 이미지는 가까이에 있는 스크린에 실시간으로 보여지는데, 그 스크린은 작은 텔레비전이나 컴퓨터 모니터처럼 보인다. 그 이미지는 진폭, 진동수, 그리고 음파 신호가 환자에게서 변환기로 돌아오는 데 걸리는 시간에 기반해서 생성된다.

| 해설 |

빈칸 뒤의 지문 내용을 통해 이 글에서 소개하고 있는 것이 무엇인지 그려 보면 정답을 고를 수 있다. 환자에게서 되돌아오는 음파를 이미지화하는 장치이므로 정답은 (a)임을 유추할 수 있다.

| 오답 분석 |

(b) 스판텍스로부터의 발, 발목, 무릎의 속박 / 지문에 언급되지 않은 내용이다.
(c) 커다란 디지털 전자 의료기기 / 다음 문장에서 손으로 들고 쓰는 장치라 하였으므로 정답이 될 수 없다.
(d) 아래에 쓰여진 포괄적 지시사항들 / 지문에 언급 되지 않은 내용이다.

| 어휘 |
ultrasound 초음파
electronics 전자공학
hand-held 휴대용의
device 장치
resembles ~을 닮다
transducer 변환기
nearby 가까이에
amplitude 진폭
frequency 진동수

2.

Parents often tend to focus too much on how well their children do in school. Giving too much praise to students for getting good grades may mislead students into thinking that results are all that really matters in life. Instead, we should nurture students to develop practical life skills such as cooperation and independent thinking. To reinforce these characteristics, positive feedback should be given when they collaborate well in a group setting and are seen dividing up the work evenly among themselves.

Q. What is the topic of the passage?
(a) Continuing to praise students who excel in school
(b) Constructive criticism and positive reinforcement regarding classroom behavior
(c) Complimenting on students' cooperative behavior in order to foster life skills
(d) Encouraging students to achieve goals through discipline

| 해석 |

부모들은 종종 그들의 아이들이 학교에서 얼마나 잘하는가에 대해 너무 많이 집중하는 경향이 있다. 좋은 점수를 획득하는 것에 대해서 아이들에게 너무 많은 칭찬을 주는 것은 아마도 학생들을 삶에서 결과가 모든 것이라는 잘못된 생각으로 이끌 것이다. 대신, 우리는 협동과 독립적인 생각이라는 실용적인 삶의 기술을 발전시키도록 학생들을 양육해야 한다. 이런 특성들을 강화시키기 위해, 그들이 그룹 환경에서 협동을 잘하고 공평하게 일을 나눈다는 것이 보여졌을 때 긍정적인 피드백이 주어져야 한다.

| 해설 |

학교에서 아이들이 얼마나 공부를 잘하는가에 집중하기보다, 그룹 활동 등에 대해 긍정적인 피드백을 주어야 한다는 내용이므로 정답은 '(c) 삶의 기술을 강화하기 위해 학생들의 협동 행동을 칭찬하는 것'이다.

| 오답 분석 |

(a) 학교에서 뛰어난 학생들을 끊임없이 칭찬하기 / 지문의 제일 앞쪽에서 이러한 것은 바람직하지 않다고 하였다.
(b) 교실 행동에 관한 건설적인 비판과 긍정적인 강화 / 비판에 대한 내용은 등장하지 않는다.
(d) 훈련을 통해서 학생들이 목표를 성취하도록 장려하기 / 훈련에 대한

내용은 등장하지 않는다.

| 어휘 |
mislead 잘못 인도하다, 현혹시키다
reinforce 강화하다
collaborate 협력하다, 협동하다, 합작하다
excel 능가하다, ~보다 낫다, 뛰어나다
compliment 칭찬, 찬사(하다)

3.

New computer monitor displays employ an integral-type imaging system that reproduces light beams similar to those produced by a real object and not its visual representation. This overcomes the main problem with a flatbed display: distance. The difference in the distance from the eye to the center of a display and to the display's edges and corners is greater for a flatbed than for a standard upright display. To solve this problem, flatbeds produce 3-D images with a wide viewing angle by using multiple live-action or CG images.

Q. Which of the following is correct according to the passage?
  (a) The development of a true 3D image application for monitors has yet to occur.
  (b) 3D viewing on a flatbed monitor will not be available commercially for 10 to 20 years.
  (c) The technology used to create a 3D image is unrelated to that used for a flatbed display.
  (d) 3D technology is reproducing similar light beams to those produced by a real object.

| 해석 |
새로운 컴퓨터 모니터 디스플레이는 완전한 타입의 이미지를 그려 보여주는 시스템을 사용하는데 그것은 시각적인 묘사가 아니라 실제 물체에 의해 생산되는 것과 비슷한 빛 광선을 재생산하는 것이다. 이것은 평반형 디스플레이가 가지고 있는 주요한 문제인 거리를 극복한다. 눈에서부터 디스플레이 중심까지의 거리와, 눈에서 디스플레이의 가장자리와 모서리까지의 거리의 차이는 표준 직립 디스플레이보다 평반형 디스플레이가 더 크다. 이런 문제점을 해결하기 위해, 평반형 디스플레이는 다중의 생생한 액션이나 CG이미지들을 사용함으로써 넓은 감상 각도를 제공하는 3-D 이미지들을 생산한다.

| 해설 |
첫 번째 문장에서 시각적 묘사가 아니라 실제 물체에 의해 생산되는 것과 비슷한 빛 광선을 재생산한다고 하였으며, 이 평반형 디스플레이는 3D 이미지를 생산한다고 하였으므로 정답은 '(d) 3D 기술은 실제 물체에 의해 생산되는 것과 비슷한 빛 광선을 재생산한다.'가 됨을 알 수 있다.

| 오답 분석 |
(a) 모니터에 대한 진정한 3-D 이미지 응용의 발전은 아직 일어나지 않고 있다. / 이 지문은 현재 개발된 모니터에 대한 내용이다.
(b) 평반형 모니터로 3D를 보는 것은 10~20년 사이에 상업적으로 이용

가능하지 않을 것이다. / 평반형 모니터는 현재 개발되어 있다.
(c) 3D 이미지를 창조하는 데 사용되는 기술은 평반형 디스플레이에 사용되는 기술과 관계가 없다. / 평반형 디스플레이가 3D 이미지를 생산해 내므로 관계가 있다.

| 어휘 |
employ 쓰다, 고용하다; 사용하다
integral 완전한, 없어서는 안 될
overcome 이기다, 극복하다
flatbed 평상 꼴의, 평반형인

4.

At the moment online banking has attracted around 23 million users, a figure which is projected to rise by nearly 300% by the year 2012. The main barrier to achieving this growth is not the reluctance of consumers to adopt non-traditional approaches to banking but existing financial institutions themselves. For instance, most still do not offer simple account opening procedures or real-time account credit and debit facilities both stumbling blocks toward their future growth. The whole situation is expected to change as the world's major banks enhance their investment in online product development in an effort to boost business efficiency.

Q. What can be inferred from the passage?
  (a) Explosive growth is predicted in the retail banking sector.
  (b) Increased investment in online banking will lead to greater product availability.
  (c) Current online banking services are expected to continue to dominate the market.
  (d) By 2012 few customers are expected not to be using banks.

| 해석 |
현재 온라인 뱅킹은 대략 2천3백만 명의 사용자를 끌어들이고 있고, 이 수치는 2012년이 되면 거의 300% 상승할 것으로 보인다. 이러한 성장을 성취하는 데 있어 주된 장벽은 은행에 전통적이지 않은 방식으로 접근하는 것을 선택하기 꺼려하는 소비자들이 아니라, 현존하고 있는 금융기관 그 자체이다. 이를테면, 이들 대부분은 여전히 계좌를 여는 간단한 절차나 실시간 계좌 조회와 직불 시설을 제공하지 않고 있는데, 이런 것들은 차후 성장의 장애물로 마주치고 있다. 세계의 주요 은행들이 사업의 효율성을 높이려는 노력으로써 온라인 상품 발전에 대한 투자를 강화시키고 있기 때문에 전체적인 상황이 변화할 것이라고 예측된다.

| 해설 |
지문의 마지막 문장에서 사업 효율성을 높이려는 노력에서 온라인 상품을 개발하고 있다고 하였으므로 정답은 '(b) 온라인 뱅킹에 있어서의 상승된 투자는 큰 상품 유용성을 이끌 것이다.'가 된다.

(a) 소매 은행 부분에서 폭발적인 성장이 예측된다. / 이 지문은 은행의 유
    형에 따라 성장 가능성을 예측하지는 않았다.
(c) 현재 온라인 뱅킹 서비스는 시장을 끊임없이 지배할 것이라고 예측되
    고 있다. / 시장에 대한 지배력은 지문에 언급되지 않았다.
(d) 2012년에는 소비자들이 거의 은행을 이용하지 않을 것이라고 예측된
    다. / 이 글에서는 2012년에 온라인 뱅킹을 이용하는 소비자들의 수
    가 늘어날 것이라고 했다.

| 어휘 |
reluctance 싫음, 마지못해 함
stumbling 우연히 마주치다
enhance 강화하다

5.

There exists a certain type of flower suitable to
every holiday, event and special occasion. (a) For
example, soldiers that took part during World War
II are commemorated by showy, red flowers called
poppies. (b) Another type of red flower commonly
used during the Christmas season is the
poinsettia, while irises and lilies act as symbols of
resurrection and life at burial sites. (c) An
abundance of people proclaim roses to be the
queen of all flowers due to its prickly thorns
coupled with a strong heady scent. (d) During
romantic occasions such as Valentine's Day,
engagements, weddings and the like, roses are
used as presents as a token of love.

| 해석 |
모든 휴일과 행사와 특별한 일에는 알맞은 종류의 꽃이 있다. (a) 예를 들
어, 세계 2차 대전에 참여했던 군인들을 기리기 위해서는 양귀비라는 화
려하고 붉은 꽃이 쓰인다. (b) 묘지에서는 아이리스와 백합이 소생과 삶을
나타내는 역할을 하는 반면, 크리스마스 시즌 동안에 흔히 쓰이는 다른 빨
간 꽃은 포인세티아이다. (c) 많은 사람들이 장미가 머리를 멍하게 하는
향기와 따끔하게 찌르는 가시가 짝을 이루어 모든 꽃의 여왕이라고 주장
한다. (d) 밸런타인데이, 약혼식, 결혼식 등의 로맨틱한 날에는 장미가 사
랑을 표현하는 선물로 쓰인다.

| 해설 |
여러 가지 행사에 쓰이는 꽃들에 대한 내용이다. (c)는 장미에 대한 일반적
인 사람들의 생각을 나타내는 문장이므로 이 글의 논지에서 벗어나 있다.

| 오답 분석 |
첫 문장이 주제문으로, (a), (b), (d)는 모두 그에 대한 예시들이다.

| 어휘 |
poppy 양귀비
resurrection 소생, 부활
prickly 가시가 많은, 바늘 투성이의, 따끔하게 아프고 쑤시는
heady 완고한; 무한한; 두통이 나는; (술이) 빨리 취하는
token 표; 징후, 상징

Day 10
Build up   94p

1. (d)　　**2.** (a)　　**3.** (c)　　**4.** (c)　　**5.** (b)

1.

Though it has had various nicknames over time,
the United States has often been referred to as a
"Melting Pot." This particular term is derived from
the fact that although the demographic make-up
of the country entails a diverse variety of races
and cultures, they often end up blending in with
American culture. In fact, it can be argued that a
form of cultural assimilation takes place as
immigrants will eventually ________________
and adopt the ways of their new host country.

(a) make many new friends and acquaintances
(b) experience severe culture shock and
    homesickness
(c) totally forget all about their country of birth
(d) abandon their original customs and cultures

| 해석 |
시간이 흐르면서 다양한 별명을 가지게 되었지만, 미국은 종종 용광로라
고 불려지고 있다. 이 용어는, 비록 그 나라의 인구통계학의 구성이 다양
한 인종과 문화를 수반하지만, 그들은 결국 미국 문화에 녹아들게 된다는
사실로부터 유래되었다. 사실상, 이민자가 궁극적으로 그들 고유의 관습
과 문화들을 포기하고 새로운 나라의 방법을 채택할 때 문화적인 동화가
발생한다고 할 수 있을 것이다.

| 해설 |
미국을 용광로에 비유하는 근거에 대한 내용의 지문이다. 빈칸 바로 앞 문
장에서 이민자들이 결국 미국의 역사에 동화된다고 하였으므로 빈칸에 적
절한 것은 (d)이다.

| 오답 분석 |
(a) 많은 친구들과 아는 사람들을 만든다. / 친구가 늘어난다고 해서 미국
    문화에 동화되는 것은 아니다.
(b) 심한 문화 충격과 향수병을 경험한다. / 미국 문화에 동화되는 것에 대
    한 내용이므로 알맞지 않다.
(d) 자신이 태어난 나라에 대해 완전히 잊는다. / 미국의 문화를 따르게 된
    다고 하였지, 고국을 잊는다고 하지 않았으므로 지문에 언급되지 않은
    내용이다.

| 어휘 |
demographic 인구(통계)학의
entail (필연적 결과로서) 수반하다, 일으키다
assimilation 동화, 동화작용
adopt 채용하다, 채택하다, 고르다

2.

Gallstones develop in the gallbladder, a small pear-shaped organ located beneath the liver on the right side of the abdomen. The gallbladder is about 3 inches long and 1 inch wide at its thickest part. Gallstones can form when people who are obese produce bile containing a higher level of cholesterol than can be dissolved. When this happens, they may also develop swollen gallbladders that do not empty normally or completely. Some studies have shown that men and women who carry fat around their midsections may be at a greater risk for developing gallstones than those who carry fat around their hips and thighs.

Q. What can be inferred from this passage?
(a) A prevalence of gallstones has been found to exist in the obese.
(b) The anatomical position of the gallbladder affects obesity.
(c) Reducing ones body weight causes a consequent reduction in gallstones.
(d) Appetite control is an effective treatment for gallstones.

| 해석 |
담석은 복부의 오른쪽, 간 아래에 위치해 있는 작은 배처럼 생긴 기관인 쓸개에서 생긴다. 쓸개는 3인치 정도의 길이이고, 가장 두꺼운 부분의 넓이가 1인치 정도 된다. 담석은 비만인 사람들이 용해될 수 있는 수치 이상의 콜레스테롤이 함유된 담즙을 만들어낼 때 생성된다. 이러한 현상이 일어날 때, 이들은 정상적으로, 즉 완전하게 비워지지 않는 부풀어오른 쓸개를 가진다. 몇몇 연구들은 복부 주변에 지방이 많은 사람들이 허벅지나 엉덩이 주변에 지방이 많은 사람들보다 담석이 생길 위험이 더 높다는 것을 보여준다.

| 해설 |
담석이 무엇인지 정의 내린 뒤, 세 번째 문장부터 마지막 문장까지 담석과 비만 간의 상관관계를 말하고 있으므로 추론할 수 있는 바는 '(a) 담석은 비만인 사람들에게서 흔히 발견된다.' 이다.

| 오답 분석 |
(b) 쓸개의 해부학적 위치가 비만에 영향을 미친다. / 쓸개의 위치와 비만 간의 상간관계는 지문에 언급되지 않았다.
(c) 체중을 줄이는 것은 담석을 줄이는 결과를 야기한다. / 비만인 사람이 체중을 줄이는 것이 담석에 어떤 영향을 미치는가는 지문에 언급되지 않았다.
(d) 식욕 통제는 담석의 효과적인 치료 방법이다. / 치료에 대한 것은 지문에 언급되지 않았다.

| 어휘 |
gallstone 담석
gallbladder 쓸개, 담낭
bile 담즙
midsection 중간부

anatomical 해부의, 해부(학)상의

3.

Globalization has produced migrations of people domestically and internationally. For example, as a matter of economic survival, rural dwellers, through the loss of their traditional forms of income and opportunities, have been forced to leave their villages and join a rural drift to urban centers. Global agri-business corporations have used advances in technology to reduce the need for a large manual workforce. One of the most dramatic changes is in Asia where the rapid adoption of technology has further displaced rural workers.

Q. Which of the following is correct according to the passage?
(a) Global agri-business has replaced rural dwellers' lost incomes.
(b) A great number of jobs in the rural sector have been recently created.
(c) A major cause of rural drift has been the mechanization of farms.
(d) Human migration from urban areas is mainly caused by advanced technology.

| 해석 |
세계화는 국내적, 국제적으로 사람들이 이동하게끔 하고 있다. 예를 들어 경제적인 생존의 문제로 시골 거주자들은 전통적 형태의 수입이나 기회를 잃게 됨으로써 자신의 마을을 떠나 도심으로 향하는 흐름에 가담하도록 강요당하고 있다. 다국적 농업회사는 많은 인력의 필요를 감소시키기 위해 진보된 기술을 사용하는 중이다. 가장 극적인 변화 중의 하나는 아시아에서 일어나는데, 아시아에서는 기술의 급속한 채택이 더 나아가 시골의 노동자들을 대체하고 있다.

| 해설 |
대규모 농업회사들에 의해 기계화가 진행됨에 따라 시골 거주자들이 도심으로 향할 수밖에 없다는 내용의 지문이다. 따라서 정답은 '(c) 시골 인구 이동의 가장 큰 이유는 농장의 기계화이다.' 가 된다.

| 오답 분석 |
(a) 다국적 농업회사는 시골 거주자들의 없어진 수입을 대체해주고 있다. / 지문에서 언급되지 않은 내용이다.
(b) 시골에서 많은 일자리들이 최근에 생겨나고 있다. / 시골에서는 직업이 창출되는 것이 아니라 일자리를 잃고 있다고 하였다.
(d) 도시 지역에서 사람들의 이동은 주로 진보된 기술에 의해 유발된다. / 도시 지역의 인구 이동은 지문에 언급된 바가 없다.

| 어휘 |
migration 이주, 이동
domestic 가정의 , 국내의
adoption 채택
displace 바꾸어 놓다, 대신 들어서다

4.

Many of us have great interest in astronomy and more often, an irresistible worship for astrology. While some of us are more fascinated than others by the wonders of the night scene, most of us have trouble if we were asked to locate our favorite stars in the sky. In the northern hemisphere, the star most commonly recognized is Polaris, which is about 15 light years from the Earth, and is located on the edge of the constellation, Ursa Minor. Interestingly enough, although its scientific name is Polaris, most people know it as the Northern Star.

Q. Which of the following would follow this passage?
(a) Group of stars of the Ursa Minor constellation
(b) Wrongly recognized names of stars in the northern hemisphere
(c) Why people are more familiar with 'Northern star' than 'Polaris'
(d) Scientific names and common names of stars

| 해석 |

사람들은 천문학에 큰 관심을 가지고 있고, 종종 점성학에 저항할 수 없는 존경심을 가지고 있다. 어떤 사람들은 다른 사람들보다 더욱 밤하늘의 놀라움에 매혹되어 있기도 하지만, 밤하늘에서 가장 좋아하는 별의 위치가 어디냐는 질문을 받으면 그들 중 대부분은 곤란해할 것이다. 북반구에서 일반적으로 인지되는 별은 북극성으로, 지구에서 15광년 떨어져 있으며 작은곰자리의 가장자리에 위치해 있다. 흥미롭게도 이 별의 학명은 '폴라리스'이지만, 대부분의 사람들은 그것을 '북극성'이라고 알고 있다.

| 해설 |

사람들이 가장 많이 알고 있는 별이 북극성임에도 불구하고, 그 정확한 이름을 잘 알지 못한다는 내용의 지문이다. 따라서 이 지문 뒤에는 왜 이러한 현상이 일어나게 되었는가에 대한 이유가 이어질 것이므로 정답은 "(c) 왜 사람들은 '폴라리스'보다 '북극성'에 더 친숙한가" 이다.

| 오답 분석 |

(a) 작은곰자리의 별 무리 / 작은곰자리에 어떤 별이 있는가는 언급되지 않았다.
(b) 잘못 알려져 있는 북반구 별들의 이름 / 북극성 외에 다른 별들의 이름이 잘못 알려져 있다는 내용은 지문에 언급되지 않았다.
(d) 별의 학명과 일반적인 이름 / 이 글은 북극성의 이름에 관련된 내용이지, 전반적인 별에 대한 내용이 아니다.

| 어휘 |

irresistible 저항할 수 없는, 이겨낼 수 없는
worship 숭배, 존경, 예찬
fascinate ~을 황홀하게 하다, 매혹하다
wonder 놀랄만한 것, 경이, 불가사의 기이한 광경
constellation 별자리, 성좌
northern hemisphere 북반구

5.

World War I and World War II had an immense influence on the traditional representation of female figures and their roles in society. (a) Prior to the wars, women were often viewed as being inferior to men although female characters still managed to play crucial roles that affected the lives of the people around them. (b) It is undoubtedly certain that men are superior to women in terms of physical strength. (c) During the war periods, while the men were serving, the women were in charge of 'bringing home the bacon' as well as fulfilling their domestic roles. (d) During the post war years, even though come still viewed females as second-rate citizens, their social status had become equal to that of men.

| 해석 |

1차 세계 대전과 2차 세계 대전은 여성과 여성의 사회적 역할에 대한 전통적인 묘사에 엄청난 영향을 끼쳤다. (a) 전쟁 전에는, 여성들이 주변 사람들의 삶에 영향을 미치는 중대한 역할을 하고 있음에도 불구하고 남성보다 열등하다고 여겨졌다. (b) 남성들이 물리적인 힘에서 여성보다 우월하다는 것은 의심할 여지 없이 사실이다. (c) 남성들이 군복무를 했던 전쟁 기간 동안, 여성들은 집안의 역할을 다하는 것은 물론 '집에 먹을 것을 가져오는' 것도 책임을 졌다. (d) 전쟁 뒤에, 일부 사람들은 여전히 여성을 더 낮은 등급의 시민으로 보긴 했지만, 여성들의 지위가 남성들의 지위와 동등해졌다.

| 해설 |

1차, 2차 세계 대전 전과 전쟁 중, 전쟁 후의 여성의 사회적 지위의 변화에 대한 내용의 글이다. (b)는 남성들에 대한 내용이므로 소재에서 벗어난 문장이다.

| 오답 분석 |

첫 문장이 주제문이며, (a)는 1, 2차 세계 대전 이전의 여성들의 상황, (c)는 전쟁 중의 상황, (d)는 전쟁 후의 상황을 설명하고 있으므로 시간 순서에 따라 잘 전개되고 있다.

| 어휘 |

immense 막대한, 거대한
representation 표현, 묘사, 표시, 설명
inferior 열등한, 하위의 (↔ superior 보다 높은, 우수한)
crucial 결정적인, 중대한
serve 군대에 복무하다
fulfill 이행하다, 완수하다
domestic 가정의, 집안의
status 사회적 지위, 신분

Day 11

Build up

---

1. (c)   **2.** (a)   **3.** (d)   **4.** (d)   **5.** (d)

1.

The "Third World" is a commonly used term that has been the subject of much controversy and discussion since ___________________________.
During the period of the Cold War, the "Third World" was defined as those countries that were not ideologically aligned with either the "First World" or "Second World" which comprised of the United States and the Soviet Union respectively. Today, the more common interpretation of the term is that it consists of the developing and underdeveloped countries of Asia, Latin America, and Africa.

(a) it represented the ideological conflicts during the Cold War
(b) it has been employed to mark a geographic territory
(c) it has been interpreted in different ways
(d) it presented a highly disputable scientific theory

| 해석 |
제3세계는 공공연히 사용되는 용어로, 여러 가지 방식들로 해석되어 왔기 때문에 많은 논쟁과 토론의 주제가 되어오고 있다. 냉전시대 동안 제3세계는, 각각 미국과 소련으로 이루어진 제1세계 또는 제2세계와 이념적으로 같은 태도를 취하지 않는 나라들로 정의되었다. 오늘날 이 용어는 아시아, 라틴 아메리카, 아프리카의 개발도상국과 저개발국으로 구성되어 있는 것으로 흔히 해석된다.

| 해설 |
'Third World'라는 용어는 냉전시대 동안과 오늘날 나타내는 바가 각각 다르다는 내용이므로 정답은 (c)가 된다.

| 오답 분석 |
(a) 냉전시대 동안의 이데올로기적 충돌을 나타내기 때문에 / 오늘날 의미하는 바가 포함되지 않는 보기이므로 정답이 될 수 없다.
(b) 지리적 영역을 표시하는 데에 사용되어왔기 때문에 / 영역에 대한 내용은 지문에서 언급되지 않았다.
(d) 매우 확실치 않은 과학 이론을 나타내기 때문에 / 과학적 이론 역시 지문에서 언급되지 않았다.

| 어휘 |
align 일직선으로 하다; 정렬시키다
ideologically 이념적으로
comprise 함유하다, 포함하다, ~로 이루어져 있다

2.

Though there have been many major battles in Roman history, the Battle of the Teutoberg Forest is certainly one of the most famous ones. This battle had many ramifications for Rome and also played a big factor in changing the course of European history. From a historian's point of view, the Battle of the Teutoberg Forest was a fascinating event and still continues to be the topic of much study and research. Aside from military knowledge, much can also be learned about Roman society from this conflict. Clearly, this battle is a valuable resource because of the significant insights and understanding it provides pertaining to ____________ in Roman history.

(a) the roles of war and society
(b) the sway and influence of scholars
(c) the lavish lifestyles of Caesars
(d) the appeal of gladiators

| 해석 |
비록 로마 역사에서 많은 중요한 전투들이 있었지만, Teutoberg Forest 전투는 확실히 가장 유명한 전투 중 하나이다. 이 전투는 로마에 많은 파장을 가져왔으며, 유럽 역사의 방향을 변화시키는 데에도 중요한 요소로 작용했다. 역사가의 관점에서 볼 때, Teutoberg Forest의 전투는 매혹적인 사건이었으며 여전히 많은 연구의 주제가 되고 있다. 군사적인 관점을 제쳐두고도 이 전투로부터 로마 사회에 대한 많은 것들을 배울 수 있다. 명백히 이 전투는 로마 역사의 전쟁과 사회의 역할에 관한 중요한 통찰력과 이해를 제시해주기 때문에 가치 있는 원천이 된다.

| 해설 |
빈칸 바로 앞 문장에서 로마 사회에 대한 많은 것을 배울 수 있다고 하였으므로 정답은 (a)가 된다.

| 오답 분석 |
(b) 학자들의 동요와 영향 / 지문에 나오지 않았다.
(c) 카이사르의 사치스러운 생활양식 / 지문에 나오지 않았다.
(d) 검투사들의 매력 / 지문에 나오지 않았다.

| 어휘 |
ramification 파장
conflict 전투, 투쟁
insight 통찰력, 간파
pertaining to ~ 관련된

3.

If you know you are being bullied, ask a potential counselor you are considering if he or she knows what psychological violence or bullying in the workplace is, and don't hesitate to ask them questions to ascertain their expertise. A good counselor will know that many commonly held facets about personality conflicts are tough to handle, and that his or her solutions may not apply to your situation. If your counselor does not have the skills to identify the differences, then the bully may spot further vulnerability which could lead to his discovering other ways to impair your health and employment.

Q. Which of the following is correct according to the passage?
(a) Sometimes you should change a counselor for the sake of your job.
(b) You should never sympathize with an employer who yells at employees.
(c) If you confront the workplace bully, you will probably back down.
(d) A counselor's experience is one key to understanding your situation.

| 해석 |
만약 당신이 왕따를 당하고 있다는 것을 알게 되면, 당신은 염두에 두고 있는 잠재적인 상담자에게 직장에서의 정신적인 폭력이나 왕따가 무엇인지 아는지를 물어보고, 주저하지 말고 그들의 전문적 지식을 확인하기 위한 질문을 해야 한다. 좋은 상담자는 성격 충돌과 거친 관리에 관한 많은 일반적인 현상들과 그것들에 대한 해결책들이 당신의 상황에 적용되지 못한다는 것을 알고 있을 것이다. 그리고 바로 이러한 점이 당신이 머지 않아 회복되는 데 도움이 될 것이다. 만약 상담자가 각기 다른 점들을 식별하지 못한다면, 당신을 괴롭히는 사람이 당신의 건강과 고용 상태를 해치기 위한 다른 방법을 발견할 수 있도록 하는 약점들을 더 발견할 수도 있다.

| 해설 |
이 글은 직장에서의 왕따에 대한 대처 방안을 말해주고 있다. 그 중에서도 좋은 상담자의 역할에 대해 언급하였으므로 정답은 '(d) 상담자의 경험이 당신의 상황을 이해하는 데 있어 중요하다.'이다.
| 오답 분석 |
(a) 때때로 당신은 직업을 위하여 상담자를 바꿔야 한다. / 상담자를 바꾼다는 것은 지문에 언급되지 않았다.
(b) 당신은 고용인에게 소리치는 고용주를 동정하지 말아야 한다. / 고용주에 대한 내용은 언급되지 않았다.
(c) 만약 당신이 직장 왕따에 직면한다면, 아마도 물러서게 될 것이다. / 왕따를 당했을 때의 반응은 언급되지 않았다.

| 어휘 |
bully 약자를 괴롭히다, 괴롭히다
ascertain 확인하다
facet 면, 국면
vulnerability 취약성

4.
The 16th "Annual Reading for the Love of It Conference" will be held this year in Toronto, Canada from April 25th to 29th. Some of the most renowned authors and guest lecturers will be in

attendance. Please note that the conference does not offer discounted conference rates. However, register before March 31st, and you will get a free conference package that includes Gabbi Mann's latest research on dyslexia and other learning disabilities, as well as a full description of the attending speakers.

Q. What could be inferred from the conference notice?
(a) Medical experts will attend for a tutorial in learning disabilities.
(b) Attendees who register early will get a discount.
(c) The conference is a national event held in Canada every year.
(d) The conference will deal with those who have trouble in learning.

| 해석 |
제16회 '독서에 대한 사랑을 위한 컨퍼런스'가 이번 해에는 4월 25~29일 캐나다 토론토에서 행해질 것입니다. 유명한 작가 몇 분과 객원 강사들이 참석할 것입니다. 이 컨퍼런스에서는 요금 할인을 제공하지 않는다는 것을 알아주시기 바랍니다. 그러나 3월 31일 이전에 등록하면, 난독증과 다른 학습 장애에 관한 Gabbi Mann의 최신 연구뿐 아니라 연설자의 완전한 설명도 포함되어 있는 무료 컨퍼런스 패키지를 받게 될 것입니다.

| 해설 |
마지막 문장에서 학습장애에 대한 내용도 다룬다고 하였으므로 '(d) 이 컨퍼런스는 학습에 어려움을 겪는 사람들에 대해 다룰 것이다.'가 정답이 된다.

| 오답 분석 |
(a) 학습 장애에 대한 강의를 위해 의학 전문가들이 참석할 것이다. / 의료계 전문가들의 참석은 지문에 언급되지 않았다.
(b) 일찍 등록하는 출석자들은 할인을 받을 것이다. / 할인은 제공되지 않는다고 하였다.
(c) 이 컨퍼런스는 매년 캐나다에서 열리는 국가적 행사이다. / 첫 문장에서 이번 해에 캐나다에서 열린다고 하였으며, 캐나다의 국가적 행사라는 내용은 언급되지 않았다.

| 어휘 |
renowned 유명한, 명성 있는
dyslexia 난독증
learning disabilities 학습 장애
description 묘사, 서술

5.
The study of women's history in East Asia is a complex yet fascinating topic that is quite relevant in the academic field of gender studies. (a) Molly Beaulac, a university professor, is considered one of the leading scholars in the field of gender studies in the history of pre-modern China. (b) Her

book, *The Lives of Chinese Women in the Sung Period*, explores the lives of Chinese women during the period of the Sung Dynasty. (c) Beaulac's work is undoubtedly a valuable resource for scholars interested in the study of women in China. (d) To this day, many women in China still enjoy reading historical journals about Sung Dynasty.

| 해석 |

동아시아 여성의 역사에 대한 연구는 성(性) 연구에 대한 학술 분야에 관련되어 있는 복잡하지만 매력적인 주제이다. (a) 대학 교수인 Molly Beaulac은 근대 이전의 중국 역사에서의 성(性) 연구 분야를 이끌어가는 학자들 중 한 명으로 여겨진다. (b) '송 시대의 중국 여성들의 삶'이라는 그녀의 책은 송 왕조 시대의 중국 여성들의 삶에 대해 드러내준다. (c) Beaulac의 업적은 확실히 중국의 여성 연구에 흥미가 있는 학자들에게 가치 있는 자원이다. (d) 오늘날까지, 중국의 많은 여성들은 송 왕조에 대한 역사 저널을 즐겨 읽는다.

| 해설 |

Molly Beaulac이라는 학자의 송 왕조의 성 연구에 대한 글이다. (d)는 오늘날 중국 여성들의 독서에 대한 내용이므로 이 글의 소재에서 벗어난 문장이다.

| 오답 분석 |

첫 문장은 이 글의 소재를 소개하고 있고, (a)는 더욱 구체적으로 Molly Beaulac이라는 학자를 소개하고 있다. (b)는 Molly Beaulac의 업적인 책을, (c)는 그 책의 가치에 대한 것을 언급하고 있으므로 유기적으로 연결되어 있다.

| 어휘 |

fascinating 매혹적인
gender 성(性), 성별
undoubtedly 틀림없이, 확실히, 의심의 여지없이

Day 12

Build up　　　　　　　　　110p

> **1.** (d)　**2.** (b)　**3.** (d)　**4.** (a)　**5.** (a)

1.

In 1995 the U.S. Department of Agriculture and a pharmaceutical research firm received a patent on a technique to extract an anti-fungal agent from the Neem tree, or Azadirachta indica, which grows throughout India; Indian villagers have long understood the tree's medicinal value. Although the patent had been granted on an extraction technique, the Indian press described it as a patent on the Neem tree itself and the result was widespread public outcry, which was echoed throughout the developing world. ________________________, with the patent eventually being overturned in 2005.

(a) Legal action by the American government followed
(b) The Indian government assented to the US rights
(c) The anti-fungal agent proved to be wholly ineffectual
(d) Legal action by the Indian government followed

| 해석 |

1995년, 미국 농림부와 약학 연구 회사는 인도 전역에서 자라는 님 나무, 즉 Azadirachta indica로부터 균의 번식을 막는 성분을 추출하는 것에 대한 특허를 획득했다. 인도 사람들은 오랫동안 이 나무의 의학적 가치를 알고 있었다. 이 특허는 추출 기술에 대해 주어진 것임에도 불구하고, 인도 언론은 님 나무 자체에 대한 특허로 묘사했다. 이것이 대중의 강한 항의를 불러일으켰으며, 개발도상국 전반에 퍼지게 되었다. 인도 정부에 의한 법적 조치가 뒤따르게 되었고, 이 특허는 마침내 2005년에 무효화되었다.

| 해설 |

인도 대중의 항의 때문에 특허권이 뒤집어지려면(overturn) 인도 정부에 의한 법적 조치가 있었다는 내용이 알맞다. 따라서 정답은 (d)가 된다.

| 오답 분석 |

(a) 미국 정부에 의한 법적 조치가 뒤따랐다. / 미국 정부라고 했으므로 틀렸다.
(b) 인도 정부가 미국의 권리에 대해 승인했다. / 특허권이 취소된 것으로 보아 승인했다는 내용은 맞지 않다.
(c) 균의 번식을 막는 성분이 완전히 효과가 없는 것으로 입증되었다. / 균의 번식을 막는 성분의 효과는 예전부터 인도 사람들에 의해 알려져 있다고 하였으므로 틀린 내용이다.

| 어휘 |

pharmaceutical 제약(학)의
outcry 부르짖음, 항변, 강한 항의
overturn 뒤집어엎다, 전복시키다

2.

In Georgetown, a group of young men broke into a local discount clothing store. Only minutes after, an anonymous person made a phone call to the Georgetown police notifying them of the situation and officers rushed off to the reported area. Upon their arrival at the scene, the group of allegedly armed young men tried to flee in a car they had stolen a couple of days ago in Carbon City and reportedly fired several times at the police cars chasing behind them. __________, the police were eventually able to arrest all the members of the group without any injuries on either party.

(a) Accordingly
(b) Nevertheless
(c) Although
(d) In addition

| 해석 |

조지타운에서, 한 무리의 젊은 남자들이 지역 옷 할인 매장에 침입했다. 몇 분 후, 익명의 한 사람이 그 상황을 알리기 위해 조지타운 경찰에 전화를 했고, 책임자는 그 보고된 지역으로 서둘러 출발했다. 그들이 그 현장에 도착했을 때, 무장된 것으로 여겨지는 한 무리의 젊은 남자들이 2일 전 카본 시에서 훔친 차를 타고 도망가려 했고, 보고된 바에 의하면 그들을 뒤쫓는 경찰차에 수차례나 총을 쏘았다고 한다. 그럼에도 불구하고, 경찰은 마침내 양측에 어떤 부상도 없이 그 무리를 모두 잡을 수 있었다.

| 해설 |

빈칸 앞 문장에서 무장한 젊은이늘이 발포하였다고 하였고, 빈칸이 있는 문장에서는 부상이 없었다고 하였으므로 정답은 '(b) 그럼에도 불구하고'가 된다.

| 오답 분석 |

(a) 그에 따라 / 앞에 언급된 것으로 인해 뒤의 내용이 수반되는 의미 관계일 때 쓰인다.
(c) 비록 ~ 일지라도 / 양보의 의미이다.
(d) 게다가 / 다른 내용을 추가할 때 쓰인다.

| 어휘 |

anonymous 작자불명의, 익명의
notify ~에게 통지하다, 알리다, 신고하다
allegedly (진위는 모르나) 주장하는 바에 따르면, 들리는 바에 의하면
flee (위험, 추격자 따위로부터) 달아나다, 벗어나다, 피난하다

3.

Dispute resolution laws in Australia provide mechanisms at both State and Federal levels covering relationship breakups or periods of crisis. Heterosexual and de facto relationships have been recognized by these laws yet relationships between same sex couples have not, even though such relationships have been deemed lawful. To address this anomaly, an amendment was passed by the New South Wales parliament in 1999 extending the definition of a de facto couple to include same sex and other domestic partnerships. Other acts have to be amended to ensure a dovetailing of current laws, particularly in the areas of inheritance, compensation and guardianship.

Q. Which of the following is correct according to the passage?
   (a) Heterosexual married couples do not receive legal recognition.

(b) De facto couples are defined as those facing crises or a break up.
(c) Divorced couples did not receive legal protection in Australia before 1999.
(d) Gay and lesbian relationships have been legally recognized since 1999.

| 해석 |

호주에서 분쟁 해결법은 주 차원과 연방 차원에서 관계 불화 또는 위기의 시기를 다루는 메커니즘들을 제공한다. 이성애 관계나 사실혼의 관계들은 이런 법들에 의해 인식되고 있지만, 같은 성별 간의 커플의 관계는 합법적이 되었음에도 불구하고 아직 인정되지 않고 있다. 이런 예외를 처리하기 위해 1999년에 뉴사우스웨일즈 의회에 의해 수정안이 통과되었는데, 그 수정안은 사실혼 관계 부부의 정의를 동성 부부와 다른 가정적 파트너십을 포함한 것으로 확장시켰다. 현행법과의 긴밀한 연계를 확보하기 위해 특히 상속, 배상, 후견인에 관힌 분아의 다른 법녕늘도 수정될 필요가 있다.

| 해설 |

지문의 세 번째 문장에서 정답 '(d) 게이와 레즈비언 관계는 1999년부터 법적으로 인정되었다.'에 대한 단서를 찾을 수 있다.

| 오답 분석 |

(a) 결혼한 이성애 커플은 법적인 승인을 받지 않는다. / 이러한 부부 관계는 이 지문에서 다루고 있지 않다.
(b) 사실혼 상태의 부부들은 위기나 헤어짐에 직면한 사람들로 정의된다. / 사실혼 관계의 부부를 정의 내리지 않았다.
(c) 이혼한 커플들은 1999년 전까지 호주에서 법적인 보호를 받지 못했다. / 이혼한 부부는 이 지문에서 다루고 있는 대상이 아니다.

| 어휘 |

heterosexual 이성애의
de facto 사실상 존재하는, 현존의
anomaly 변칙, 이례
extend 넓히다, 연장하다
dovetail 긴밀하게 서로 연계하다
inheritance 상속
guardianship 후견인의 임무, 보호

4.

The Lord David Cecil's essay, *Fits of Despair*, examined in many college courses is the biographical study of the lawyer and poet William Cowper. The essay praises Cowper as a precursor of the English Romantic Movement represented by Wordsworth. The essay certainly gives us a great introduction to his wonderful, though tragic work. Also, there are many life lessons to be learned from Cowper's lifelong struggle with depression in this essay. But Cecil adjudicates others' commentary on Cowper rather than initiates in much of it. Indeed, his essay often reads as a critique of other critics.

Q. What could be inferred from the passage?

(a) Cecil drew criticism of other critics for his study of Cowper.

(b) Cowper is not as gifted as scholars once assumed.

(c) Cecil's work on Cowper has received undue criticisms from many.

(d) *Fits of Despair* fails to portray the real Cowper as a poet.

| 해석 |

많은 대학 과정에서 고찰되는 Lord David Cecil의 에세이 〈분노의 격발〉은 법률가이자 시인인 William Cowper의 전기 연구이다. 그 에세이는 Cowper를 워즈워스로 대표되는 영국 낭만주의 운동의 선구자로 칭찬한다. 그 에세이가 비극적인 작품이긴 하지만 틀림없이 경이로운 그의 작품에 대한 탁월한 소개이다. 또한 이 에세이에는 우울증에 대한 Cowper의 일생의 싸움에서 배울 수 있는 많은 삶의 교훈들도 있다. 그러나 Cecil은 이 에세이의 많은 부분에서 Cowper에 대한 새로운 시각을 보여주기보다는 다른 사람들의 논평에 대한 판단을 더 많이 내렸다. 실제로, 그의 에세이는 종종 다른 비평가들에 대한 비평으로 읽힌다.

| 해설 |

지문의 가장 마지막 부분에서 Cecil의 에세이에 다른 비평가들에 대한 비평이 들어 있다는 것을 유추할 수 있으므로 정답은 '(a) Cecil은 그의 Cowper 연구를 위해 다른 비평가들의 비평을 끌어왔다.'이다.

| 오답 분석 |

(b) Cowper는 한때 학자들이 여겼던 것만큼 재능 있는 것은 아니다. / 지문에 언급되지 않은 내용이다.

(c) Cowper에 대한 Ceil의 작품은 많은 사람들로부터 부당한 비평을 받고 있다. / 지문에 언급되지 않았다.

(d) 〈분노의 격발〉은 시인으로서 실제 Cowper를 묘사하는 데 실패했다. / 지문에 언급되지 않았다.

| 어휘 |

fit 발작, 격발,
despair 절망
precursor 선구자
lifelong 일생의, 필생의
adjudicate 판결을 내리다
initiate 시작하다, 창시하다
critics 비평가
critique 비평, 평론, 비평법

5.

Anxiety disorders that are the result of a traumatic experience are referred to as a post-traumatic stress disorder. (a) STD is the abbreviation for sexually transmitted diseases; thus, the abbreviation for post-traumatic stress disorder is PPSD. (b) Post-traumatic disorders can result from warfare, the death of someone close or other dire events that can lead to severe psychological traumas. (c) Symptoms consist of insomnia, flashbacks, emotional detachment, loss and many others. (d) During World War II, many soldiers were diagnosed with this anxiety disorder due to the constant exposure to violent warfare and may still be trying to recover from it as of today.

| 해석 |

정신적 외상을 일으키는 경험의 결과인 불안 장애는 외상 후의 스트레스 질환으로 일컬어진다. (a) STD는 성적으로 전염되는 질병의 약자이다. 따라서 외상 후 스트레스 질환의 약자는 PPSD이다. (b) 외상 후 스트레스 질환은 심한 정신적 외상으로 이어지는 전쟁, 가까운 사람의 죽음, 혹은 다른 끔찍한 일들의 결과로 일어날 수 있다. (c) 불면증, 과거의 일을 반복적으로 보는 것, 감정적 분리, 상실감 등의 많은 것들이 그 증상이다. (d) 세계 2차 대전 동안, 폭력적인 전쟁에 대한 계속적인 노출 때문에 많은 군인들이 불안 장애로 진단되었고, 오늘날에도 여전히 회복하기 위해 노력 중일 것이다.

| 해설 |

불안 장애의 원인과 증상에 대한 글이다. (a)는 약자를 만드는 예시를 보여주고 있으므로 이 글의 주제에서 벗어난다.

| 오답 분석 |

첫 문장은 불안 장애에 대한 정의, (b)는 원인, (c)는 증상, (d)는 불안 장애를 겪는 사람에 대한 예라고 볼 수 있다. 따라서 모두 하나의 주제로 연결된다.

| 어휘 |

abbreviation 생략, 단축, 약자
anxiety disorder 불안 장애
dire 무서운, 비참한, 끔찍한
insomnia 불면증
flashback 환각의 재발, 과거를 봄

Day 13

Build up 118p

1. (d)	**2.** (b)	**3.** (d)	**4.** (d)	**5.** (c)

1.

Choosing a web host is one of the most important decisions facing every person who wishes to have their own web site for personal or business use. You need to look at price and dependability, keeping in mind the web host is someone you pay a fee to and in return he or she provides you with much space on their server in which to reliably store the files that make up your web site.

____________________ because you want to make sure you go with a web host that provides enough server space for you to grow your business at the rate you want.

(a) Stability is the most essential
(b) 3-dimensional graphics technology is a
    requisite
(c) Business expansion can be achieved
(d) Speed and support are also important

| 해석 |

웹 호스트를 선택하는 것은 개인적으로나 사업상 사용을 위하여 그들 자신의 웹 사이트를 갖기를 소망하는 모든 사람들이 직면하는 가장 중요한 결정 중의 하나이다. 웹 호스트는 당신이 돈을 지불하면 그 대가로 당신의 웹사이트를 구성하는 파일들은 확실하게 저장할 수 있도록 서버의 많은 공간을 제공하는 사람이라는 것을 기억하면서 가격과 신뢰성을 살펴보아야 한다. 바라는 속도로 사업이 성장하기 위한 충분한 서버 공간을 제공해 주는 웹 호스트와 함께 하기를 바랄 것이므로 속도와 지원 또한 중요하다.

| 해설 |

빈칸이 있는 문장에서 빈칸에 들어갈 말의 단서를 얻을 수 있다. 사업의 성장과 함께 빠른 웹사이트의 확장을 가능케 해주어야 한다는 내용이 이어지므로 정답은 (d)가 된다.

| 오답 분석 |

(a) 안정성이 가장 중요하다. / 지문에서 안정성에 대한 내용은 언급되지 않았다.
(b) 3차원 그래픽 기술은 필수적이다. / 그래픽 기술에 대한 내용은 언급되지 않았다.
(c) 사업 확장이 이루어질 수 있다. / 웹 호스트를 통해 사업이 확장되는 것이 아니라, 사업 확장의 속도에 맞추어 웹 사이트를 키우는 것이므로 정답이 될 수 없다.

| 어휘 |

dependability 의존할 수 있음, 믿을 수 있음
reliably 믿을 수 있는, 의지가 되는
in advance 미리, 전방에, 앞에
accumulate 모으다, 축적하다

2.

Getting an important promotion may hinge more on your ability to avoid the gossip trap than your qualifications and job skills. A positive atmosphere at work is generated by the staff and how well they get along together, so employees who make more of an effort to get along and be friendly will usually lead to their climbing the corporate ladder faster. Conversely, employees who engage in gossip risk damage not only to their reputation at work, but are also more unlikely to get ahead. Good advice to avoid the gossip trap includes searching for subjects other than co-workers to talk about and setting a time limit on conversations with colleagues.

Q. What is the main idea of the passage?
   (a) You're less likely to be promoted at work if
       you eschew gossip.
   (b) You're more likely to be promoted at work if
       you eschew gossip.
   (c) Creating a positive atmosphere in the
       workplace leads to promotion.
   (d) Talking about colleagues will enhance your
       prospects of promotion.

| 해석 |

중요한 승진을 하는 방법은 아마도 당신의 자격이나 직업에 대한 기술보다 가십을 피하는 능력에 좀 더 달려 있을 수 있다. 직장 내의 긍정적인 분위기는 직원들과 직원들이 함께 어울려 잘 지내는 방식에 의해 만들어진다. 따라서 잘 어울리고 친근하게 행동하는 직원들은 보통 승진 단계를 빠르게 올라가게끔 이끌어줄 것이다. 반대로, 가십 위험에 관여된 직원들은 일에서의 그들의 명성에 손상을 입을 뿐만 아니라 출세하지 못하는 경향이 있다. 가십의 덫을 피하는 좋은 충고는 동료에 대해 이야기하는 것보다 다른 주제를 찾는 것, 그리고 동료와의 대화 시간을 정해 놓는 것이다.

| 해설 |

직장에서 승진을 하는 데에는 가십을 피하는 것이 중요한 역할을 한다는 내용의 지문이다. 따라서 정답은 '(b) 만약 당신이 가십을 피한다면 당신은 좀 더 직장에서 승진할 것이다.'가 된다.

| 오답 분석 |

(a) 만약 당신이 가십을 피한다면 당신은 승진을 못할 것이다. / 지문의 내용과 반대이다.
(c) 일터에서 긍정적인 분위기를 생산하는 것은 승진을 이끈다. / 지문의 소재에서 벗어나 있다.
(d) 동료에 대해 말하는 것은 당신의 승진에 대한 전망을 강화시킨다. / 지문의 내용과 반대이다.

| 어휘 |

hinge on ~에 의해 정해지다, ~여하에 달려 있다
corporate ladder 기업의 승진 단계
eschew 피하다, 삼가다

3.

Modern day technology allows several methods to safeguard aircrafts from lightning. One of the most commonly employed methods is to combine aluminum with other materials containing layers of conductive fibers designed to carry lightning currents. In the case that lightning strikes, the currents travel along the exterior as these aircrafts are designed to have no gaps in conductive paths, and the tail would act as an outlet for the current to flow out.

Q. Which is correct according to the passage?
   (a) Conductive paths are engineered without
       gaps.
   (b) Aircraft skins are designed to withstand
       electric currents.
   (c) Very few aircrafts are constructed with
       aluminum exteriors.
   (d) Lightning currents cannot reach the

interiors of the aircraft.

| 해석 |
현대 기술은 번개로부터 비행기를 보호하기 위한 몇 가지 방법을 마련했다. 가장 흔히 채택되는 방법 중의 하나는 번개의 전류를 옮기기 위해 디자인된 전도성의 섬유들을 함유한 다른 물질들과 알루미늄을 결합하는 것이다. 번개가 강타했을 때, 전류는 바깥쪽을 타고 이동한다. 왜냐하면 이 비행기들은 전도성의 통로에 갈라진 틈이 없게끔 설계되었기 때문이다. 그리고 후부는 흘러나오는 전류에 대한 배출구의 역할을 할 것이다.

| 해설 |
번개의 전류는 바깥쪽을 타고 흐르며 전도성 물질이 없다고 했으므로 정답은 '(d) 번개의 전류는 비행기의 내부에 들어갈 수 없다.'가 된다.

| 오답 분석 |
(a) 전도성 통로는 갈라진 틈 없이 만들어진다. / 지문에 나온 단어들을 이용한 오답이다.
(b) 비행기의 외부는 전류를 견디도록 만들어진다. / 전류를 견디는 것이 아니라 전도력이 없도록 만들어진다.
(c) 극소수의 비행기들만이 알루미늄 외장으로 만들어진다. / 알루미늄을 사용하는 것이 가장 흔한 방법이라고 하였다.

| 어휘 |
conductive 전도성의, 전도력 있는
path 통로

4.

The National Sleep Foundation says sleeping habits are a key factor in weight loss. People who get a recommended 7-9 hours of sleep daily weigh less on average than those who do not. The majority of obese people falls into the category of sleep deprived. It is estimated that only 25% of Americans currently get enough sleep, causing the majority to suffer at least some endocrine system problems leading to fluctuations in insulin production. This causes a breakdown of the body's ability to metabolize sugar and can lead to diabetes. Sleep apnea is another condition caused largely by obesity, and although most sufferers show lighter symptoms such as interrupted breathing patterns, it can be fatal.

Q. What can be inferred from the passage?
  (a) Getting enough sleep daily is the key to becoming obese.
  (b) Diabetes is caused directly by sleep deprivation.
  (c) A link between obesity and sleeping habits is unproven.
  (d) Getting 7-9 hours of sleep each day can control weight.

| 해석 |
국가 수면 재단은 수면 습관이 체중 감소에서 중요한 요소라고 말한다. 추천되는 7~9시간의 수면을 매일 취한 사람들은 그렇지 않은 사람보다 평균적으로 체중이 덜 나갔다. 비만인 사람들의 대다수가 수면 박탈의 범주에 들어가 있었다. 현재 미국 사람들의 단지 25%만이 충분한 수면을 취하는데, 따라서 대다수의 사람들이 적어도 인슐린 생산에 있어 변동을 일으키는 어떤 내분비 시스템의 문제를 겪고 있다. 이것은 당을 물질대사 시키는 신체의 능력에 고장을 일으키고, 당뇨병을 일으킬 수 있다. 수면 시의 무호흡증은 비만에 의해 주로 유발되는 또 다른 증상이며, 대부분의 환자들이 호흡 장애와 같은 가벼운 증상을 보여주는데, 그것은 치명적일 수 있다.

| 해설 |
첫 문장에 (d)와 관련된 내용이 제시되어 있으며, 충분한 수면을 취한 사람들이 체중이 덜 나가며 당뇨나 비만 등을 피할 수 있다고 하였으므로 정답은 '(d) 매일 7~9시간 수면을 취하는 것은 몸무게를 조절할 수 있다.'이다.

| 오답 분석 |
(a) 매일 충분한 수면을 취하는 것은 지나치게 살이 찌게 되는 요소이다. / 지문의 내용과 반대이다.
(b) 수면 박탈이 직접적으로 당뇨병을 발생시킨다. / 지문에서 비만이 생기는 원인이라고 하였으며, 내분비 시스템의 문제를 일으킨다고 하였으므로 당뇨의 직접적인 원인이라고 할 수 없다.
(c) 비만과 수면 습관 사이의 관계는 입증되지 않았다. / 지문에서 비만과 수면 습관 사이의 관계를 설명하고 있다.

| 어휘 |
obese 지나치게 살찐
deprive 빼앗다
endocrine 내분비물
fluctuation 변동, 오르내림
metabolize 물질대사로 변화시키다, 신진대사를 시키다
apnea 일시 호흡 정지
fatal 치명적인, 운명의

5.

Football, more commonly referred to as soccer, is a sport copious amounts of people all over the world are enthused with. (a) In every continent, there are people that spend their waking moments thinking about soccer, watching soccer and playing soccer. (b) For many soccer fans, this renowned sport is not just a favorite pastime, but a passion; a way of life. (c) Although many people are enthusiastic about soccer, they frown at the astronomical figures of money star players acquire. (d) To further attest to the popularity soccer, many individuals take great pleasure in watching soccer games on the "tube" and are overexcited when the time comes for the World Cup to occur.

| 해석 |
축구로 더욱 잘 알려져 있는 풋볼은 전 세계의 엄청나게 많은 사람들의 관심을 받고 있는 스포츠이다. (a) 모든 대륙에는 잠에서 깨는 순간에 축구에 대해 생각하고, 축구를 보고 축구를 하는 것에 대해 생각하는 사람들이 있다. (b) 많은 축구 팬들에게 있어, 이 잘 알려진 스포츠는 단지 가장 좋

아하는 취미가 아니라 하나의 열정, 삶의 방식이다. (c) 많은 사람들이 축구에 대해 열정적이기는 하지만, 스타 선수들이 받는 천문학적인 숫자의 돈에 눈살을 찌푸리기도 한다. (d) 많은 사람들이 TV에서 축구 경기를 보며 큰 즐거움을 느끼며 월드컵이 열리는 시기가 되면 매우 들뜨게 된다는 것이 축구의 인기를 더욱 증명해준다.

| 해설 |

축구의 엄청난 인기에 대한 지문이다. (c)는 축구 스타들이 받는 몸값에 대한 내용이므로 이 글의 소재에서 벗어나 있다.

| 오답 분석 |

첫 문장이 주제문이며 (a)와 (b), (d) 문장은 주제문을 뒷받침해주는 부연 설명문들이다.

| 어휘 |

enthuse ~에 열중하다, 열광하다
copious 매우 많은, 풍부한
passion 열정, 열망하는 것, 매우 좋아하는 것
frown 눈살을 찌푸리다, 불쾌감을 표시하다
astronomical figure 천문학적 숫자
attest 증명하다, 입증하다
tube (구어) 텔레비전

Day 14

Build up

1. (d) **2.** (c) **3.** (c) **4.** (d) **5.** (c)

1.

In exploring morality in context one starting point may be the change in the socio-structural and socio-cultural conditions of modern societies. This involves change in the social demand on morality and in the empirical conditions of moral action. New perspectives emerge and problems are observed as these changes are accounted for and analyzed in the social sciences. Philosophers and social scientists can cooperate to solve these problems; the 'placeholder' function of philosophy is served by data from social scientists, and ________________________ is provided by the philosopher.

(a) essential philosophical and theological directions
(b) social changes asked for by the social activist
(c) political, law enforcement and welfare roles
(d) conceptual clarity required by the social scientist

| 해석 |

문맥 안에서 도덕을 탐구하는 데 있어 하나의 시작 지점은 아마도 현대 사회의 사회구조적, 사회문화적 상태에서의 변화가 될 것이다. 이것은 도덕성에 대한 사회적 요구와 도덕적인 행동의 경험적 상황에 있어서의 변화에 관련된 것이다. 이러한 변화들이 사회과학에서 설명되고 분석될 때 새로운 관점들이 나타나고, 문제점들이 관찰된다. 철학자들과 사회과학자들은 이런 문제들을 해결하는 데 협력할 수 있다. 즉, 철학의 현상 유지 기능은 사회과학자들로부터의 데이터의 도움을 받고, 사회과학자가 요구하는 개념적인 명쾌함은 철학자에 의해 제공된다.

| 해설 |

빈칸 바로 앞 문장에서 철학자들과 사회과학자들이 협동할 수 있다고 하였으므로 정답은 (d)가 된다.

| 오답 분석 |

(a) 기본적인 철학적, 신학적 지침들 / 지문에서 신학에 관련된 내용은 언급되지 않았다.
(b) 사회 행동가들이 요청하는 사회적 변화들 / 철학자들에 의해 사회적 변화가 제공되는 것은 아니다.
(c) 정치적, 법적 시행과 복지의 역할 / 정치, 법에 대한 내용은 지문과 관련이 없다.

| 어휘 |

morality 도덕
context 문맥, 정황, 배경
empirical 경험적인
perspective 견해, 관점

2.

How can one distinguish between a regular person and a criminal? Certainly, one cannot determine this based on an individual's appearance or other physical characteristics. Unfortunately, there is no foolproof way to determine whether a particular person is susceptible to engaging in violent, criminal activities. However, some methods to identify individuals with potential criminal characteristics exist. For example, a common technique used to identify serial killers and terrorists is profiling. Due to its effectiveness, it has even begun to be commonly used by most law enforcement agencies. Some schools also try using this method as a form of early detection to identify any troubled children whose aggressive traits might result in future criminal behavior.

Q. What is the main idea of the passage?
  (a) Criminal behavior is seldom predictable.
  (b) Serial killers and terrorists often fit into certain profiles.
  (c) Methods such as profiling exist that are used to try and identify the criminal mind.
  (d) Criminals do not possess any different

physical characteristics.

| 해석 |

평범한 사람과 범죄자를 어떻게 구분할 수 있을까? 확실히, 이것은 개인의 겉모습이나 다른 육체적인 특징에 기반을 두고 결정할 수 없다. 불행히도 어떤 특정한 사람이 폭력과 범죄 행동을 쉽게 하는지 안 하는지를 결정할 수 있는 쉬운 방법은 없다. 그러나 개인의 잠재적인 범죄 특성을 식별하는 방법들이 존재한다. 예를 들어, 연쇄 살인범들과 테러리스트들을 식별하는 데 사용되는 흔한 기술은 인물 특징에 대한 통계이다. 그 효율성 덕분에, 이것은 대부분의 법 집행기관에서 공공연하게 사용되기 시작하였다. 몇몇 학교들은 공격적인 특성을 가지고 있어 미래 범죄 행동의 결과를 낳을 것 같은 문제아를 식별하는 초기 탐색의 형태로서 이 방법을 사용하려 하고 있다.

| 해설 |

범죄자를 식별할 수 있는 쉬운 방법은 없지만, 그래도 profiling을 통해 범죄 성향을 많이 가진 사람들을 구별할 수 있다고 하였으므로 정답은 '(c) 프로파일링처럼 범죄적 인간을 식별하는 데 쓰이는 방법이 존재한다.' 가 된다.

| 오답 분석 |

(a) 범죄 행동은 거의 예측되지 않는다. / 이 글의 소재는 범죄 행동의 예측이 아니므로 주제가 될 수 없다.

(b) 연쇄 살인범과 테러리스트들은 종종 특정 데이터 통계에 들어맞는다. / 이 글의 주제가 아니라 세부적 사항이다.

(d) 범죄자는 어떤 다른 육체적인 특성을 가지고 있지 않다. / 세부적 사항이므로 주제가 될 수 없다.

| 어휘 |

distinguish 구별하다, 식별하다
foolproof 아주 간단한
susceptible ~의 여지가 있는, ~을 받아들이는; ~의 영향을 받기 쉬운
effectiveness 유효성, 효과적임
enforcement 시행, 집행
aggressive 공격적인

3.

Welcome to New Zealand's Whakairo Visitor's Center. The Whakairo Center offers many attractions from lush tropical rainforests to waterfalls to white sandy beaches, but nothing is as spectacular as the Maori cultural demonstrations. Five times each afternoon, the villagers will put on a demonstration that explains the symbolic significance of their unique carvings, as well as their Haka dance. Kids will enjoy learning to play a traditional Maori stick game, called the Tititorea, as well as getting facial tattoos at the front porch.

Q. Which is correct according to the passage?
  (a) Whakairo's main attraction is its white sandy beaches.
  (b) Whakairo is the world's largest tropical rainforest region.
  (c) Whakairo offers evidence of Maori settlement and cultivation.
  (d) Whakairo's Visitor's Center is as popular as the waterfalls.

| 해석 |

뉴질랜드의 와카이로 방문 센터에 온 걸 환영합니다. 와카이로 센터는 무성한 열대우림부터 폭포수, 백사장까지 많은 관광지를 제공해줍니다. 그러나 마오리 문화를 실제로 보여주는 것이 가장 뛰어난 볼거리라고 할 수 있죠. 매일 오후에 5번씩, 마을 사람들은 그들의 Haka 춤뿐만 아니라 그들의 독특한 조각물들의 상징적인 중요성을 설명하는 시연회를 엽니다. 아이들은 입구에서 얼굴에 문신을 그리고, Tititorea로 불리우는 전통적인 마오리 막대기 게임을 배우며 즐거운 시간을 보낼 수 있습니다.

| 해설 |

지문에서 와카이로에서 가장 뛰어난 볼거리는 마오리 문화를 실제로 보여주는 것이라 하였으므로 정답은 '(c) 와카이로는 마오리의 정착과 경작의 증거를 제공한다.' 이다.

| 오답 분석 |

(a) 와카이로의 주된 관광지는 백사장이다. / 여러가지 볼거리를 나열하고 있으므로 백사장을 주된 매력이라고 볼 수 없다.

(b) 와카이로는 세계에서 가장 큰 열대우림 지역이다. / 가장 큰 열대 우림 지역이라는 언급은 찾아볼 수 없다.

(d) 와카이로의 방문 센터는 폭포만큼 인기가 있다. / 방문 센터의 인기를 언급하지 않았다.

| 어휘 |

lush 푸르게 우거진, 무성한
demonstration 논증, 실연
porch 현관, 차 대는 곳, 입구
unearthly 초자연적인, 터무니없는, 불가사의한

4.

Auto-plagiarism is defined as an author republishing or reusing the same piece of writing without citing the initial publication. The practice is prohibited by colleges and universities because the refereed journals they produce require that material had not been published elsewhere. Even a student who hands in the same essay paper in two different classes without permission is guilty of auto-plagiarism. Unethical faculty members have been paid for submitting the same literature to multiple organizations and therefore, defraud journals, publishers and universities.

Q. What can be inferred from the passage?
  (a) Some professors and students claim unpublished work as originally their own.
  (b) Corrupt faculty members take student's work and publish it as their own.
  (c) Corrupt students take faculty members' work and publish it as their own.

(d) Some students and professors claim work as original that has been previously published.

| 해석 |

자동 표절은 저자가 원래의 출판물을 언급하지 않고 글의 같은 부분들을 재발행하거나 재사용하는 것으로 정의된다. 이런 행동은 단과대학과 종합대학에 의해 금지되었다. 왜냐하면 그들이 만드는 심사를 통과한 논문들은 어딘가 다른 곳에서 발행된 적이 없었을 것을 요구하기 때문이다. 심지어 허락 없이 두 개의 서로 다른 수업에서 같은 에세이 보고서를 제출한 학생은 자동 표절의 죄가 있다. 비윤리적인 교수들은 다수의 단체들에게 같은 저술을 제출하여 이익을 보고 있고, 그렇게 해서 저널들과 출판업자들과 대학들을 기만한다.

| 해설 |

자신이 쓴 것이라도 이미 다른 데에 제출했거나 출판한 적이 있는 것을 다시 제출하는 것은 표절에 해당된다는 내용의 지문이다. 따라서 정답은 '(d) 어떤 학생들과 교수들은 이전에 출판되었던 것을 새로운 것이라고 주장한다.'가 된다.

| 오답 분석 |

(a) 어떤 교수들과 학생들은 출판되지 않은 작품이 원래 자신의 것이라고 주장한다. / 지문에서 다루고 있는 내용이 아니다.

(b) 부패한 교수진은 학생들의 저작물을 취해서 그것을 자신의 것으로 출판한다. / 다른 사람의 저작물을 취하는 것은 지문에서 언급되지 않은 내용이다.

(c) 부패한 학생들은 교수들의 저작물을 취해서 그것을 자신의 것으로 출판한다. / 다른 사람의 저작물을 취하는 것은 지문에서 언급되지 않은 내용이다.

| 어휘 |

plagiarism 표절
referee 중재하다, 심판하다
defraud 속이다, 사취하다

5.

In many households, pets are cherished and even considered as part of the family. (a) Thus, it's not too much to say that starting a pet grooming business may be the best way to "reel in the dough." (b) One thing to know before starting the business is that it may be necessary to tend to those pets in the comfort of their own homes. (c) Pet owners don't like animals that are too big since they will be quite heavy to carry around. (d) This will allow pet owners to have more free time to complete other tasks as care-giving responsibility for their pets is very time consuming.

| 해석 |

많은 가정에서 애완동물들은 소중히 여겨지고 가족의 일부로 여겨지기도 한다. (a) 그러므로 애완동물을 가꾸어주는 사업을 시작하는 것은 '현금을 끌어모으는' 가장 좋은 방법이라고 말하는 것도 과언이 아니다. (b) 이 사업을 시작하기 전에 알아야 할 한 가지는, 애완동물들이 제 집에 있는 것과 같이 편안하게 돌보는 것이 필요할 것이라는 점이다. (c) 애완동물 주인들은 데리고 다니기 좀 무겁기 때문에 너무 큰 동물들은 좋아하지 않는다. (d) 애완동물을 돌보는 책임에는 매우 시간이 많이 들기 때문에 이것은 애완동물 주인들이 다른 일을 할 수 있는 더 많은 자유 시간을 갖게 해줄 것이다.

| 해설 |

애완동물을 가꾸는 사업의 유망성과 그 이유를 말해주고 있는 글이다. 따라서 (c)는 이 글의 주제에서 벗어난 문장이다.

| 오답 분석 |

첫 문장은 도입 문장으로 소재를 소개하고 있다. (a)는 애완동물을 가꾸어주는 사업의 유망성, (b)는 이 사업을 시작할 때 유념해야 할 점, (d)는 (b)문장에 이어진 내용이므로 서로 잘 연결되어 있다.

| 어휘 |

cherish 소중히 하다, 아끼다
groom 손질하다, 돌보다
reel in 끌어당기다, 낚다
dough 밀가루 반죽; 돈, 현금
tend 돌보다, 배려하다

Day 15

Build up

134p

1. (b) **2.** (c) **3.** (b) **4.** (c) **5.** (b)

1.

Mary Shelley's *Frankenstein* is arguably one of the most popular and influential novels of the early 20th Century. Infused with elements from Romanticism as well as Gothic Horror, the novel has had _______________ in contemporary popular culture. At a first glance, Shelley's work appears to be a straightforward gothic horror novel based on the premise of a monster. However, the many themes and messages in the novel hint at the actual complexity of the story. In fact, part of the novel's appeal has been the fact that the story is so rich with metaphors and allegories that can be interpreted in many ways.

(a) its fair share of critics
(b) a significant influence
(c) a negative response
(d) no impact whatsoever

| 해석 |

Mary Shelley의 〈프랑켄슈타인〉은 20세기 초의 인기 있고 영향력 있는 소설 중의 하나임에 틀림없다. 고딕풍의 공포뿐 아니라 로맨티시즘의 요소가 주입된 이 소설은 당대의 대중문화에 큰 영향력을 끼쳐왔다. 얼핏보면 Shelley의 작품은 괴물을 전제로 하여 직접적인 고딕풍 소설을 나타낸다. 그러나 소설에서의 많은 주제들과 메시지들이 그 이야기의 실질적인 복잡성을 암시한다. 사실상, 소설의 매력 중의 하나는 그 이야기가 다양한 방법으로 해석될 수 있는 은유와 상징이 풍부하다는 것이다.

| 해석 |

첫 문장에서 〈프랑켄슈타인〉이 20세기 초의 중요한 작품임을 알 수 있다. 또, 빈칸 뒤에 이어지는 내용은 이 작품이 단순한 고딕풍 소설이 아니라 복잡하고 다양한 의미를 가진다는 것이다. 따라서 정답은 (b)임을 알 수 있다.

| 오답 분석 |

(a) 비평가들의 공정한 몫 / 비평가에 대한 내용은 지문에 언급되지 않았다.

(c) 부정적인 반응 / 〈프랑켄슈타인〉이라는 작품의 특징을 다루고 있으며, 부정적인 면은 언급되지 않았다.

(d) 어떤 영향도 없는 / 첫 문장에서 20세기 초의 영향력 있는 소설이라 하였다.

| 어휘 |

arguably 이론의 여지는 있지만; 거의 틀림없이
contemporary 같은 시대의; 현대의; 동시의
straightforward 똑바른; 정직한, 솔직한; 직접의
premise 전제
complexity 복잡성
metaphors 은유
allegory 풍유; 우화; 비유한 이야기; 상징

2.

Ratings juggernaut *CSI: Crime Scene Investigation* has invited Rolling Stones' lead guitarist Ron Wood to appear as a guest star as a safecracker. But he, after being warned by Daltrey that producers were extremely demanding, turned down the opportunity to be in *CSI*. Roger Daltrey, another famed musician of *The Who*, coincidentally the band who recorded the *CSI* main theme, made an appearance as a back-from-the-dead gangster. But after that, he was required to act as five different characters; the roles apparently stretching his talents to their limit.

Q. What is the main idea of the passage?
  (a) Roger Daltrey is shortly to appear in a cameo role on CSI.
  (b) Ron Wood advised his old friend Roger not to appear on CSI.
  (c) A rock musician has refused an offer to appear on CSI.
  (d) The Rolling Stones will soon record a new CSI theme tune.

| 해석 |

엄청난 시청률을 올리고 있는 〈CSI: 범죄 현장 조사〉는 롤링 스톤즈의 리드 기타리스트 Ron Wood를 게스트 스타로서 금고털이범으로 출연하도록 초대했다. 그러나 프로듀서들이 많은 것을 요구했다는 Daltrey의 경고

를 들은 뒤에, Wood는 CSI에 출연하는 기회를 거절했었다. CSI 메인 테마를 녹음하기도한 밴드 The Who의 다른 유명한 음악가인 Roger Daltrey는 거의 죽을 뻔 하는 갱스터로 출연하였다. 그러나 그 후, 그는 다섯 가지 캐릭터를 연기하도록 요구되었고, 명백히 그 역할들은 그의 재능의 한계에 이르게 하는 것이었다.

| 해설 |

롤링 스톤즈의 리드 기타리스트는 Daltrey의 경고를 듣고 CSI에 출연할 기회를 거절했다고 하였으므로 정답은 '(c) 락 음악가는 CSI에 출연하라는 제안을 거절하고 있다.'가 된다.

| 오답 분석 |

(a) Roger Daltrey는 CSI에서 곧 카메오 역으로 나올 것이다. / 다섯 개의 역할을 맡겼다고 했으므로 정답이 될 수 없다.

(b) Ron Wood는 그의 오랜 친구인 Roger에게 CSI에 출연하지 말라고 충고했다. / 지문에 두 사람이 오랜 친구라는 언급은 없다.

(d) Rolling Stones는 새로운 CSI 주제곡을 곧 녹음할 것이다. / Daltrey가 이미 주제곡을 녹음했다.

| 어휘 |

juggernaut 거대한 파괴력, 불가항력, 위압적인 거대한 것
safecracker 금고털이
back-from-the-dead 죽음에서 되돌아온, 거의 죽을뻔 했던

3.

We owe to our students, interns, and trainees, nondiscriminatory access to education and training. We shall provide education and training that is relevant, informed and accurate with respect to the needs of our student body. We recognize the need to responsibly mentor our students in their professional and academic development. We are committed to continuing education in order to improve and expand our skills and knowledge, and our onus to inform students of their ethical responsibilities. Students can be assured that their contributions to our professional activities, including research and publication, will be appropriately recognized.

Q. According to the passage, which of the following statements is NOT true?
  (a) Careful monitoring of student progress is a key area of responsibility.
  (b) The needs of students engaged in continuing education take precedence.
  (c) It is important that student's research be properly acknowledged.
  (d) One key goal is to utilize unbiased criteria for entry to education.

| 해석 |

학생, 인턴, 견습생들에게 우리는 교육과 훈련에 대한 차별적이지 않은 접근을 보장할 의무가 있다. 우리는 전 학생의 필요에 관해 정보가 확실하며

정확한 교육과 훈련을 제공할 것이다. 우리는 학생들의 전문적이고 학문적인 발전을 위해 그들에게 책임감을 가지고 지도할 필요성을 인식하고 있다. 우리는 기술과 지식, 학생들에게 윤리적 책임감을 알려줄 의무를 향상하고 확장시키기 위한 계속적인 교육에 헌신하고 있다. 학생들은 연구와 출판을 포함한 우리의 전문적인 활동에 대한 그들의 기여가 적절하게 인정될 것이라고 확신해도 좋다.

| 해설 |
이 글은 학생들을 교육하는 데 있어 어떠한 원칙을 가지고 있는지를 설명하고 있다. 그러나 '(b) 계속되는 교육에 관여되어 있는 학생들의 필요성들이 우선시된다.'는 내용은 찾아볼 수 없으므로 정답이 된다.

| 오답 분석 |
(a) 학생의 진전을 조심스럽게 관찰하는 것은 책임의 중요 영역이다. / 세 번째 문장에서 알 수 있다.
(c) 학생들의 연구가 적절히 인정받는 것이 중요하다. / 마지막 문장에서 알 수 있다.
(d) 하나의 중요 목표는 교육에서 입학에 대한 편견 없는 기준을 사용하는 것이다. / 첫 번째 문장에서 교육과 훈련에 대한 차별적이지 않은 접근을 보장할 의무가 있다고 하였다.

| 어휘 |
owe 빚지고 있다, ~을 다할 의무를 지고 있다.
nondiscriminatory 차별 없는
mentor 스승, 은사, 지도하다
onus 부담, 의무, 책임

4.

There used to be the world's largest and most successful tuna fishing fleet in San Diego until the 1980's. However, in more recent years, tuna fishing has been proven to be harder as migratory tuna have deviated from their usual migratory route. Representatives of San Diego's tuna fishing industry announced that tuna used to only follow warm currents but accelerating global warming is causing the melting of northern glaciers, producing cold water currents and driving the fish deeper and farther offshore, making them much more difficult to catch.

Q. What can be inferred from the news report?
(a) San Diego's tuna fishing industry will not last long.
(b) The temperature of San Diego's coastal waters has risen.
(c) The recent pattern in tuna migration is bound to continue in the next few years.
(d) Tuna migration has not been effected by sea level rise.

| 해석 |
샌디에이고는 1980년대까지 세계에서 가장 크고 성공적인 참치잡이 선단이 있었다. 그러나 최근에, 이동해 다니는 참치가 원래의 이동 경로로부터 이탈하고 있어 참치잡이가 어려워지고 있다고 증명되고 있다. 샌디에

이고 참치잡이 산업의 대표자들은 참치들이 과거에는 단지 난류를 따라갔지만, 가속되고 있는 지구 온난화가 북극 빙하를 녹여 한류를 생성시키고 참치를 해안에서 더 멀고 더 깊은 곳으로 향하게 하며, 따라서 참치를 잡는 것을 더 어렵게 하고 있다고 발표했다.

| 해설 |
가속화되고 있는 지구 온난화로 인해 한류가 생기고, 그로 인해 참치의 이동 경로가 바뀌게 되어 참치잡이가 어려워졌다고 하였다. 따라서 정답은 '(c) 참치 이동의 최근 패턴은 다음 몇 해 동안 계속될 것이다.'가 된다.

| 오답 분석 |
(a) 샌디에이고의 참치잡이 산업은 길게 지속되지 못할 것이다. / 이 지문에서는 참치 산업의 미래를 예측하고 있지 않다.
(b) 샌디에이고의 해변 수온은 점차 상승하고 있다. / 한류 때문에 해안에서 더 먼 곳으로 참치들이 이동한다고 했으므로 이 지문의 내용과 반대가 된다.
(d) 참치 이동은 해수면 상승에 영향을 받지 않고 있다. / 해수면 상승에 대한 내용은 언급되지 않았다.

| 어휘 |
fleet 함대, 선단
migratory 이주하는, 이주성의
deviate 빗나가게 하다, 일탈시키다

5.

Pilates is a form of physical exercise developed by Joseph Pilates in the early 20th century. (a) It is a form of fitness that teaches accurate methods of breathing and aligning the spine in order to promote a healthy lifestyle while avoiding severe back pains. (b) Pilates and yoga are two different names for the same form of fitness. (c) Extreme concentration is needed to help keep the body balanced and to pay attention to the body while continuing to perform controlled breathing. (d) Precision is also heavily emphasized as each Pilate form requires precise and perfected movement which, when practiced enough, eventually becomes second nature to our everyday lives.

| 해석 |
필라테스는 조셉 필라테스에 의해 20세기 초에 만들어진 일종의 신체적 운동이다. (a) 필라테스는 심한 요통을 피하는 동시에 건강한 라이프스타일을 권장하기 위해 정확한 숨쉬기 방법과 척추를 맞추는 방법을 교육시켜주는 신체적 운동의 일종이다. (b) 필라테스와 요가는 같은 형태의 운동을 부르는 두 개의 다른 이름이다. (c) 통제된 호흡을 계속해서 수행하면서 신체의 균형을 지키고 신체에 신경을 쓰기 위해서는 극도의 집중력이 필요하다. (d) 각각의 필라테스 동작이 정확하고 완벽해진 움직임을 요구하기 때문에 정확함 또한 매우 강조되며, 이러한 동작이 충분히 연습되면 마침내는 우리의 생활에 있어 제2의 천성이 된다.

| 해설 |
이 글은 필라테스라는 운동에 대한 내용을 다루고 있다. 다른 문장들에서는 요가에 대한 언급이 전혀 없기 때문에 정답은 (b)가 된다.

| 오답 분석 |
(a)에서는 필라테스의 목적과 어떤 것을 수련하는가를 말해주고 있으며,

(c)는 이에 이어지는 문장으로 필라테스 수련에 집중력이 필요하다는 것,
(d)는 필라테스를 충분히 연습하였을 때 습관처럼 굳어질 수 있다는 것을
말하고 있으므로 모두 유기적으로 연결되어 있음을 알 수 있다.

| 어휘 |

accurate 정확한, 정밀한
align 한 줄로 하다, 일직선으로 맞추다
spine 등뼈, 척추
back pain 요통
extreme 극단의, 극적인
precise 정확한, 정밀한

Day 16

Build up
142p

1. (a)　**2.** (d)　**3.** (c)　**4.** (c)　**5.** (c)

1.

In terms of cancer and nutrition, it is said that there are some foods geared towards cancer prevention but others detrimental to our health. To defend against our health from cancer, it is important to reduce the intake of dietary saturated and unsaturated fat by approximately 30 to 40 percent. Many experts have undergone experiments with the hopes to prove that fiber can lead the fight for the prevention of cancer. They hypothesized that fiber may reduce the risk of cancer by slowing down and inactivating the effect of carcinogens. ___________, even though many believe in this theory, studies of the fiber-cancer connection have been inconsistent and controversial.

(a) However
(b) Moreover
(c) Otherwise
(d) Indeed

| 해석 |

암과 영양에 관해서, 어떤 음식은 암 예방에 잘 맞지만 어떤 음식은 우리 건강에 나쁘다고 한다. 암으로부터 우리의 건강을 지키기 위해, 포화지방과 불포화지방의 섭취를 거의 30~40% 정도 감소시키는 것이 중요하다. 많은 전문가들은 섬유소가 암의 예방을 위해 싸워준다는 것을 입증하려는 희망을 가지고 실험을 해왔다. 그들은 섬유소가 발암 물질의 효과를 느려지게 하고 불활성화시킴으로써 암의 위험을 아마도 감소시킬 것이라고 가정했다. 그러나 많은 사람들이 이 이론을 믿었음에도 불구하고 섬유소와 암과의 관계에 대한 연구는 일관성이 없었고 논쟁의 여지가 있었다.

| 해설 |

암과 관련하여 우리의 건강에 좋거나 나쁜 음식들이 있고, 그 중 섬유소가 암의 예방에 좋은 영향을 끼친다는 가설에 대한 내용이다. 제일 마지막 문장에서는 앞에 소개된 가설이 논쟁의 여지가 있다고 하였으므로 정답은 '(a) 그러나'가 된다.

| 오답 분석 |

(b) 게다가 / 다른 내용을 덧붙일 때 쓴다.
(c) 그렇지 않다면 / '~와 만약 달랐다면'의 뜻이므로 정답이 될 수 없다.
(d) 실로, 참으로, 정말로 / 앞의 내용과 같은 논지를 이어갈 때 쓴다.

| 어휘 |

intake 흡입, 섭취
undergo ~ 겪다, 경험하다
hypothesize 가설을 세우다, 가정하다
carcinogens 발암 물질

2.

The history of today's simple mechanical devices goes back in time to ancient Greece. For example, Archimedes, a Greek mathematician, physicist and engineer, who lived some two thousand years ago, was one of the leading scientists in mechanics. Archimedes is known to us today for his innovative machines and simple devices such as the lever. While Archimedes did not invent the lever, he was the first to understand the principle involved. To explain the principle of levers, he once designed pulley systems that allowed sailors enabled to move a large ship by themselves.

Q. What is the topic of the passage?
　(a) The history and science of mechanical devices
　(b) The beginnings of Greek mathematics
　(c) The various uses of levers in ancient Greece
　(d) The influence of Greek mathematicians on physics

| 해석 |

오늘날 간단한 기계 장치들의 역사는 고대 그리스 시대로 거슬러 올라간다. 예를 들어, 2천년 전에 살았던 그리스 수학자이자 물리학자이며 기술자였던 아르키메데스는 기계학에서 선도적인 과학자 중의 한 명이었다. 아르키메데스는 우리에게 레버와 같은 간단한 기구와 혁신적인 기계 장치로 알려져 있다. 아르키메데스는 레버를 발명하지는 않았지만, 그는 레버에 관련된 원리를 처음으로 이해한 사람이었다. 레버의 원리를 설명하기 위해서, 그는 선원들이 거대한 배를 움직일 수 있게 하는 도르래 시스템을 디자인했다.

| 해설 |

첫 문장이 주제문, 그것을 뒷받침해주는 내용이 그 뒤의 아르키메데스에 대한 내용이므로 정답은 '(d) 그리스 수학자들의 물리학에 끼친 영향'이 된다.

| 오답 분석 |
(a) 기계 장치들의 과학과 역사 / 기계장치의 역사가 어떤 과정을 거쳤는
가를 설명하는 글이 아니다.
(b) 그리스 수학의 시작 / 이 글은 수학에 대한 내용이 언급되지 않았다.
(c) 고대 그리스에서 레버의 다양한 사용 / 그리스 시대에 레버를 사용하
였다는 내용은 언급되지 않았다.

| 어휘 |
innovative 혁신적인
pulley 도르래

3.

The latest step toward greater realism in virtual
reality comes in the form of a unique pressure
vest, which allows the wearer to experience the
physical sensation caused by a blow from being
struck by a fist or weapon, a crashing vehicle or
falling down. The 3rd Space Vest, as it has been
named, was developed from a medical device
designed to allow doctors to more accurately
remote-diagnose patient illnesses. While still
currently pending approval from the US Food and
Drug Administration the vest is expected to
complement existing sensor gloves and virtual
headsets in the lucrative first-person shooter
computer game market.

Q. Which is correct about the passage?
   (a) The market for first-person shooter
       computer games is expanding.
   (b) The FDA will approve the vest if it is found
       to be safe.
   (c) The computer game market is about to get
       another exciting accessory.
   (d) Doctors can now diagnose patient illnesses
       without being there.

| 해석 |
가상 현실에서 더욱 진보된 현실감을 향한 최근의 발걸음은 독특한 압박
조끼의 형태에 이르렀는데, 그것은 착용자에게 주먹이나 무기에 의해 얻
어맞거나, 차량의 충돌이나 또는 낙하로부터 오는 타격에 의한 육체적인
감각을 경험하도록 해준다. 그것은 3차원 조끼라고 명명되었는데, 의사들
이 좀 더 정확하게 원거리 환자의 질병을 진단해주기 위해 고안된 의료기
기로부터 발전되었다. 현재 여전히 미국 식품의약청으로부터 승인을 기다
리고 있지만, 그 조끼는 수익성이 있는 1인 사수 컴퓨터 게임 시장에서 현
재의 센서글러브와 가상 헤드셋을 보완해줄 것으로 기대된다.

| 해설 |
원래 의학적 목적으로 고안된 조끼가 컴퓨터 게임 시장에서 쓰일 것으로
예상된다고 하였으므로 정답은 '(c) 컴퓨터 게임 시장은 다른 흥미로운
액세서리를 취하려고 한다.'이다.

| 오답 분석 |
(a) 1인 사수 컴퓨터 게임에 대한 시장은 확장되고 있다. / 시장 전반에 대
   한 전망은 언급되지 않았다.

(b) 만약 그것이 안전하다는 것을 알게 되면, FDA는 그 조끼를 승인할 것
   이다. / 이 지문을 통해 승인 가능성은 알 수 없다.
(d) 의사는 이제 거기에 없는 환자의 질병도 진단할 수 있다. / 이 지문에
   언급된 3차원 조끼가 이러한 기능을 위해 발명된 것으로부터 발전된
   것이기는 하지만, 이러한 기능이 실현되었는지 여부는 언급되지 않
   았다.

| 어휘 |
virtual reality 가상 현실
vest 조끼
pending 미결정의, 계류중인
approval 승인

4.

The word subculture suggests that there is a
separate entity within a larger society with which
the larger society must contend. In other words, a
subculture is a socio-cultural formation that exists
as a sort of enclave or island within the larger
society. Subcultures constitute meaningful
systems and modes of expression or life styles
developed by subordinately positioned groups in
response to the dominant systems. They reflect
the attempt to solve structural contradictions
arising from the wider societal context.

Q. What can be inferred from the passage?
   (a) Cultures and subcultures exist for one and
       the same purpose.
   (b) A subculture helps to provide an important
       public service.
   (c) Subcultures exist to counterpoint a larger
       society's contradictions.
   (d) Subcultures are necessary to maintain a
       well-functioning wider society.

| 해석 |
하위 문화라는 말은, 더 큰 사회 안에 그 사회가 경쟁해야 하는 하나의 분
리된 실체가 있다는 것을 제시한다. 다른 말로, 하위 문화는 일종의 큰 사
회에 있는 소수의 이문화 단체, 또는 섬처럼 동떨어져 존재하는 사회문화
적인 구조이다. 하위 문화들은 지배적인 시스템에 반응하여 그 하위에 위
치해 있는 그룹에 의해 발전된 의미 있는 시스템과 표현 양식, 혹은 삶의
방식으로 구성된다. 그들은 사회의 넓은 문맥에서 떠오른 구조적인 모순
을 해결하려는 시도를 반영한다.

| 해설 |
하위 문화가 무엇인지를 설명하고 있는 글이다. 마지막 문장에서 정답
'(c) 하위 문화는 큰 사회의 모순을 강조하기 위해 존재한다.'에 대한 단
서를 찾을 수 있다.

| 오답 분석 |
(a) 문화와 하위 문화는 하나의 같은 목적을 위해 존재한다. / 지문에서 하
   위 문화는 동떨어져 있는 있는 문화이므로, 같은 목적을 가진다고 볼
   수 없다.
(b) 하위 문화는 중요한 공공 서비스를 제공하는 것을 도와준다. / 하위 문

화의 기능에 공공 서비스의 기능은 언급되지 않았다.
(d) 하위 문화는 잘 기능하고 있는 폭넓은 사회를 유지하는데 필요하다. / 하위 문화는 사회의 구조적 모순을 해결하는 데 필요하므로 틀린 언급이다.

| 어휘 |
subculture 하위 문화
entity 실재, 존재
separate 분리된
enclave 소수의 이문화 집단 주거지
constitute 구성하다
contradiction 모순
counterpoint 강조하다, 두드러지게 하다

5.

As pollution is one of key concerns of the people all over the world, it's important to search for ways to help the environment. (a) Using tactful techniques to remove carbons from the atmosphere is one way of reaching this goal. (b) Also, replanting trees and ceasing or at least reducing deforestation can be another way to save our environment. (c) Increasing the usage of toxic products containing chlorofluorocarbons or CFCs, which exist in common household items such as hair sprays, is the culprit for the destruction of the ozone layer. (d) Recycling and using environmentally-friendly materials can also give mother earth a helping hand.

| 해석 |
오염이 전 세계 사람들의 주요 관심사들 중 하나이기 때문에 환경을 돕기 위한 방법들을 찾는 것이 중요하다. (a) 대기로부터 탄소를 제거하기 위한 재치 있는 방법들을 사용하는 것도 이러한 목표에 도달하기 위한 한 방법이 된다. (b) 또한, 나무를 다시 심고 산림 벌채를 멈추거나 적어도 줄이는 것이 우리의 환경을 구하기 위한 또 다른 방법이 될 수 있다. (c) 헤어스프레이 등의 흔한 가정용품에 존재하는 클로로플루오로카본, 즉 CFC를 포함하고 있는 유독성 상품들의 사용이 증가하는 것은 오존층의 파괴의 주범이다. (d) 재활용과 친환경적인 재료를 사용하는 것도 또한 지구에 도움을 줄 수 있는 방법들이다.

| 해설 |
환경 오염을 막기 위한 방안들에 대한 글이다. (c)는 오존층 파괴의 주범에 대한 문장이기 때문에 이 글의 주제에서 벗어나 있다.

| 오답 분석 |
첫 문장에서 환경을 돕기 위한 방법들을 찾는 것의 중요성을 언급하고, (a), (b), (d) 문장에서 어떤 방법들이 있는지를 구체적으로 밝혔으므로 유기적으로 연결되어 있는 지문이다.

| 어휘 |
tactful 재치 있는, 기지가 넘치는
cease 그만두다, 멈추다
deforestation 산림 벌채, 남벌
chlorofluorocarbon 순환성 냉매 오존 파괴를 일으킴
ozone layer 오존층
environmentally-friendly 친환경적인

Day 17
Build up
150p

1. (b)　**2.** (d)　**3.** (c)　**4.** (b)　**5.** (b)

1.

Dear Sir,
I'm writing this letter of appreciation on behalf of the entire crew of flight attendants working with XYZ International Airlines for providing us with newly designed uniforms. We are very grateful to be working at such a wonderful company that consists of team-oriented people and are now in high spirits at how befitting and spectacular the new uniforms turned out to be. We all agree that this innovative design is more comfortable, allowing for more movement. __________, on behalf of all of the flight attendants, I would like to tell you that we cannot thank enough for making such an incredibly great design!

(a) In fact
(b) Therefore
(c) However
(d) Similarly

| 해석 |
XYZ 국제항공에서 근무하는 비행기 승무원을 대표하여 우리에게 새롭게 디자인된 유니폼을 제공해준 것에 대한 감사 편지를 씁니다. 우리는 팀 지향적인 사람들로 구성되어 있는 이런 좋은 회사에서 근무하고 있는 것을 매우 기쁘게 생각합니다. 그리고 우리는 새로운 유니폼이 얼마나 잘 맞고 멋진가에 들떠 있습니다. 우리 모두는 이 혁신적인 디자인이 더 많은 활동량을 허용하고 편안하다는 것에 동의합니다. 그러므로 모든 비행기 승무원을 대신하여, 이런 놀라운 디자인을 해주신 것에 대해 다시 한번 감사를 드립니다!

| 해설 |
마지막 문장에서 지문의 내용을 한 번 더 종합, 정리하여 마무리하고 있으므로 정답은 (b)가 된다.

| 오답 분석 |
(a) 사실상 / 진상을 밝힐 때 쓴다.
(c) 그러나 / 역접 관계에 쓴다.
(d) 비슷하게 / 앞 뒤 문맥에 비슷한 내용이 이어질 때 쓴다.

| 어휘 |
crew 승무원
befitting 적당한; 어울리는; 알맞은
spectacular 구경거리의, 장관의

2.

Lara Croft: Tomb Raider is a film highly recommended by many who consider it a great achievement to make a live action film look like a video game. However, I don't see anything remarkable in this, nor as any reason to celebrate. Live action that is indistinguishable from animation, does not make films more real for us; rather, it makes it hyper illusive. Furthermore, director Simon West's overuse of visual effects in *Lara Croft: Tomb Raider* diverts the viewers' attention from the storyline. What many of us should realize is that what he gives us is an over-fantasized world of violence to improve the heroine's aggression skills.

Q. Which best summarizes the writer's opinion of the film *Lara Croft: Tomb Raider*?
  (a) It distorts the legend of the video game for the purpose of film making.
  (b) It fails in using live action in a contemporary setting.
  (c) It misrepresents the main character with underlying sarcasm.
  (d) It compounds live action film inaccuracies with excessive visual effects.

| 해석 |

〈라라 크로프트: 툼 레이더〉는 비디오 게임과 비슷한 생생한 액션을 만드는 데 큰 획을 그었다고 생각하는 사람들이 많이 추천해주는 영화이다. 그러나 나는 이 작품에서 주목할 만한 어떤 것도 보지 못했고, 칭찬할 어떤 이유도 찾지 못했다. 애니메이션과 구별할 수 없는 생생한 액션은 우리에게 영화가 더욱 실제적으로 보이도록 만들어주지 못하며 오히려 영화를 매우 현혹적이게 만들었다. 게다가, 〈툼 레이더〉의 감독인 시몬 웨스트의 과도한 시각효과의 사용은 관객의 관심을 스토리 라인으로부터 다른 곳으로 돌리게 했다. 우리가 깨달아야 할 것은, 감독이 우리에게 주는 것이 이 영화의 여주인공의 공격 기술을 향상시키는 과도하게 몽환적인 폭력 세계라는 것이다.

| 해설 |

'라라 크로프트: 툼 레이더'라는 영화에 대한 글로, 화자는 이 영화에 대해 비판적인 시각을 가지고 있으므로 정답은 '(d) 그것은 생생한 액션영화의 부정확함과 과도한 시각효과가 혼합되어 있다.'가 된다.

| 오답 분석 |

(a) 그것은 영화 제작의 목적 때문에 비디오 게임의 전설을 왜곡시켰다. / 비디오 게임을 왜곡시켰다는 내용은 언급되지 않았다.
(b) 동시대의 환경에서 그것은 생생한 액션을 사용하는 데 실패했다. / 화자는 생생한 액션이 사용되었다는 것은 인정하지만, 그것에 대해 부정적 시각을 가지고 있는 것이므로 '실패했다'고 할 수 없다.
(c) 그것은 모호한 풍자로 주요 캐릭터를 잘못 나타내었다. / 이 글에서 풍자에 대한 내용은 언급되지 않았다.

| 어휘 |

indistinguishable 구별할 수 없는, 분간할 수 없는; 알아볼 수 없는
illusive 착각을 일으키게 하는, 현혹시키는, 속이는; 실체가 없는, 가공의
divert ~을 딴 데로 돌리다, 전환하다.
aggression 공격, 침략
fantasize 공상하다, 꿈에 그리다

3.

Malaria is a parasitic disease which affects over 300 million people globally and is fatal to between 1 and 1.5 million people annually. Though malaria was once spread wherever mosquitoes existed, recently it has been confined to Africa, South America and Southeast Asia. It is carried by only the female mosquito, whilst the male only feeds on plant juices and so presents no threat of disease transmission to humans. As the infected insect bites it injects the contents of its guts, thereby transporting the parasite to a new victim. The parasite then makes its way to the liver of its new host where it destroys red blood cells causing anemia. If untreated, the parasite spreads to other organs leading to death.

Q. Which is correct about the passage?
  (a) The gut contents of the female mosquito contain the malaria parasite.
  (b) Malaria, despite its containment, continues to be a fatal problem.
  (c) Male mosquitoes are not part of the malaria problem.
  (d) Malaria spreads to wherever mosquitoes live.

| 해석 |

말라리아는 전 세계적으로 3억 명의 사람들에게 영향을 주고, 연간 1백만에서 1백 50만 사이의 사람들에게 치명적인 기생충 질병이다. 말라리아는 한 때 모기가 존재하는 모든 지역에 퍼졌었지만, 최근에는 아프리카와 남미, 동남아시아 지역에 제한되고 있다. 수컷 모기는 단지 식물 수액을 먹고 살기 때문에 사람들에게 질병을 옮기는 위협을 나타내지 않으므로, 말라리아는 암컷 모기에 의해서만 옮겨진다. 감염된 곤충이 물 때 그것은 자신의 내장의 내용물을 주입함으로써 새로운 희생자에게 기생충을 옮긴다. 그러면 기생충은 새로운 숙주의 간으로 가서 적혈구 세포를 파괴하여 빈혈을 일으킨다. 그리고 만약에 치료되지 않으면 다른 장기로 퍼져나가 죽음에 이르게 한다.

| 해설 |

지문에서 수컷 모기들은 식물 수액을 먹고 살 뿐이라고 하였으므로 정답은 '(c) 수컷 모기들은 말라리아 문제의 한 부분이 아니다.'이다.

| 오답 분석 |

(a) 암컷 모기의 내장 내용물은 말라리아 기생충을 갖고 있다. / 모든 암컷 모기가 말라리아 기생충을 가진 것은 아니므로 정답이 될 수 없다.
(b) 억제에도 불구하고, 말라리아는 계속해서 치명적인 문제이다. / 치료되지 않으면 죽음에 이를 수도 있지만, 그 자체로 치명적인 질병이라고는 하지 않았다.

(d) 말라리아는 모기가 사는 곳 어디서나 퍼진다. / 과거 한 때는 그랬다고
   하였으므로 정답이 될 수 없다.

| 어휘 |
parasitic 기생적의, 기생물의
confine 한정하다, 제한하다, 가두다
gut 소화기관, 장
anemia 빈혈증

4.

Rudeness is not usually considered a crime, but
"flames" – angry or heated messages exchanged
online – may be considered out of bounds by law.
For psychologists, the phenomenon individuals
anonymously post insulting messages on the
Internet is a new area of interest. "Flaming" is not
simply because of individual personality traits, but
is largely due to the way the human brain is
shaped. In face to face encounters, people
experience an array of stimuli such as vocal tone
and facial expressions. With online text-only
communications, these stimuli are luxury items.

Q. What could be inferred from the lecture?
   (a) Poor communication skills lead to flaming.
   (b) Sensory input may work to inhibit flaming.
   (c) Impulsive behavior is not innate but learned.
   (d) Internet flamers are typically jealous of
       others.

| 해석 |
무례함은 보통 범죄로 간주되지 않는다. 그러나 flames, 즉 온라인상에서
교환되는 화가 났거나 과열된 메시지들은 아마도 법 규정의 한계를 넘은
것이라고 간주될 것이다. 심리학자들에게 있어, 인터넷에 개인들이 익명
으로 모욕적인 메시지를 올리는 이런 현상들은 새로운 관심 영역이다.
flaming은 단순히 개개인의 성격적 특징 때문뿐 아니라, 인간의 두뇌가 형
성된 방식에도 크게 관련되어 있다. 직접 얼굴을 맞대고 만난 사람들은 목
소리 톤과 얼굴 표정과 같은 일련의 자극을 경험한다. 문자로만 하는 의사
소통에서 이런 자극들은 호사스러운 항목들이다.

| 해설 |
인터넷 상에서 상대를 모욕하는 메시지를 보내는 것은 얼굴과 얼굴을 맞대
고 하는 의사소통에서는 거의 일어나지 않으며, 그 이유가 얼굴 표정이나
목소리 톤 등의 경험적 자극 때문이라고 하였다. 따라서 정답은 '(b) 지각
적 입력이 모욕적인 flaming(메시지 발송)을 억제하는 데 효과가 있을 것
이다'가 된다.

| 오답 분석 |
(a) 빈약한 의사소통 기술은 flaming을 유도한다. / flaming은 개인적 성
   격과 인간의 타고난 두뇌의 성격에 관련되어 있는 것이라고 하였다.
(c) 충동적인 행동은 타고난 것이 아니고 습득되는 것이다. / 인간의 뇌가
   형성된 방식에 관련이 있으므로 습득되는 것으로 볼 수 없다.
(d) 인터넷 flamers는 전형적으로 다른 사람을 질투한다. / 지문에 언급되
   지 않은 내용이다.

| 어휘 |
rudeness 버릇없는
flame 전자 우편의 성난 메시지
be out of bounds by law 법에 어긋나다
anonymously 익명으로
insult 모욕하다
encounter 우연히 만나다
sensory 감각의, 지각의

5.

Halloween is a popular holiday that is celebrated
by North Americans every year on October 31. (a)
Though its origin stems from religious roots, it has
become the most commercialized holidays in the
present day. (b) The jack-o-lantern, a carved
pumpkin, is often synonymous with this particular
tradition. (c) Children dress up in costumes of their
favorite heroes or comic book characters and go
from door to door 'trick or treating.' (d) This
tradition is fun for children, but in terms of
industry, the costumes and sweets are actually a
good means to make people spend extra money.

| 해석 |
할로윈은 북미에서 매년 10월 31일에 기념되는 인기 있는 명절이다. (a)
할로윈은 종교적 뿌리로부터 기원하나, 현재에는 가장 상화된 명절이
되었다. (b) 호박에 조각을 한 호박등은 때때로 이 특이한 전통과 동의어
로 여겨진다. (c) 아이들은 가장 좋아하는 영웅이나 만화책의 캐릭터 의상
을 차려 입고 집집마다 '사탕을 안 주면 장난칠 테야'를 외치러 다닌다.
(d) 이러한 전통은 아이들에게는 즐거운 경험이지만, 산업적인 관점에서
보면 의상과 사탕은 사람들이 여분의 돈을 쓰게끔 하는 좋은 수단이다.

| 해설 |
할로윈이 가장 상업화된 명절이라는 내용의 지문이다. (b)는 호박에 얼굴
모양을 새겨넣은 등에 대한 내용이므로 상업화와 관계가 없는 문장이다.

| 오답 분석 |
첫 문장은 할로윈이라는 소재를 소개하는 도입 문장이며, (a)는 할로윈의
상업성에 대한 내용을 언급하는 주제문이다. (c)와 (d)에서는 (a)에서 말
한 상업성을 뒷받침하는 내용이므로 잘 연결되어 있음을 알 수 있다.

| 어휘 |
stem 유래하다, 일어나다, 생기다
jack-o-lantern 도깨비불, 할로윈의 호박에 얼굴 모양을 새겨 등으로
만든 것
synonymous 동의어의, 같은 뜻의
trick or treat 할로윈날 밤, 어린이들이 이웃집에 찾아가 '사탕을 안주
면 장난칠 거야!'라고 외치는 말, 또는 그 행동을 나타내는 말.

Day 18

Build up

> **1.** (c) **2.** (c) **3.** (a) **4.** (a) **5.** (c)

1.

A "fringe benefit" is a payment to an employee, but _____________________________. Both the terms benefit and fringe benefit have broad meanings for Fringe Benefit Taxation purposes. Benefits wholly include rights, privileges or services associated with a company and the employees' position within it, including fringe benefits. Examples of fringe benefits may include allowing an employee to use a work car for private purposes, reimbursing an expense incurred by an employee, such as school fees, or providing entertainment by way of free tickets to concerts.

(a) not everyone can take it
(b) allows two weeks of unpaid leave
(c) in a different form to salary or wages
(d) in a restricted form of bonus

| 해석 |

'부가급부'는 고용인에 대한 봉급 또는 임금과는 다른 형태의 보수이다. 급부와 부가급부 두 가지 용어는 모두 부가급부 과세 목적들에 대해 넓은 뜻들을 가진다. 급부는 부가급부를 포함하여, 전적으로 회사와 관련된 권리, 특권 또는 서비스들과 회사 안에서의 고용인의 위치를 모두 포함한다. 부가급부의 예들은 아마도 고용인이 사적인 목적으로 회사차를 사용하는 것을 허용하는 것, 학비와 같이 고용인에 의해 초래된 비용을 상환해주는 것, 또는 콘서트 무료 티켓과 같은 방식으로 오락을 제공해주는 것 등이 포함될 것이다.

| 해설 |

제일 첫 문장에 빈칸이 있으므로 주제와 관련된 빈칸 채우기 문제이다. 이 글의 소재인 부가급부에 대한 설명이 들어가야 하는데, 지문의 전체적인 내용으로 볼 때, 특히 제일 마지막 문장의 예들을 통해 정답이 (c)가 됨을 확인할 수 있다.

| 오답 분석 |

(a) 모두가 얻을 수 있는 것은 아니다. / 부가급부를 얻을 수 있는 대상이 누구인지 언급되지 않았다.
(b) 2주간의 무급 휴가를 허락한다. / 지문에서 휴가에 대한 내용은 언급되지 않았다.
(d) 보너스의 제한된 형태로 / 지문의 마지막 문장에서 나열된 부가급부의 예시와 맞지 않는다.

| 어휘 |

fringe benefit 부가급부
salary 봉급
wage 임금

privilege 특권
reimburse 상환하다, 변상하다
incur 초래하다

2.

In today's modern society, leisure is defined as free time that is used for recreational purposes and fun. However, that was not always the case, as perceptions of this word have had different meanings and interpretations over time. This often depended on specific groups of people from particular periods in time. One notable example is that of the ancient Greek philosophers who considered leisure to be a form of mental work. In fact, they believed that this notion encompassed studying and focusing on academia in order to develop their intellect through an exertion of the mind. As a result, philosophy and the concept of debates originated from the Greek's use of leisurely time.

Q. What is the main idea of this passage?
(a) Many people today regard the main goal of leisure as educating themselves.
(b) The body as well as the mind was emphasized by many Greek philosophers.
(c) The concept and interpretation of leisure has varied depending on different time periods.
(d) Leisure is more important in the present day than it was during ancient Greece.

| 해석 |

오늘날의 현대 사회에서, 레저는 오락적인 목적과 재미에 사용되는 자유 시간으로 정의된다. 그러나 이 단어는 시간이 흐르면서 다른 뜻과 다른 해석을 가졌기 때문에 항상 이와 같은 뜻으로 쓰이는 것은 아니다. 이것은 종종 특정 시기에 특정 그룹의 사람들에 의해 좌우되었다. 한 가지 주목할 만한 예는 고대 그리스 철학자가 레저를 정신적인 일의 형태라고 생각한 것이다. 사실, 그들은 이 개념이 정신적 노력을 통해 그들의 지성을 발전시키기 위한 학구적 생활에 초점을 맞추는 것과 연구하는 것을 포함한다고 믿었다. 그 결과, 철학과 토론의 개념은 그리스인의 레저 시간의 사용으로부터 생겨나게 되었다.

| 해설 |

레저라는 단어가 각기 다른 시대에 각기 다른 뜻을 가졌다는 것을 설명하며, 그 예로 고대 그리스 시대를 들고 있는 글이다. 따라서 이 글의 주제는 '(c) 레저의 해석과 개념은 시대에 따라 다양했다.'가 된다.

| 오답 분석 |

(a) 오늘날 많은 사람들은 레저의 주요 목표를 그들 자신을 교육하는 것으로 생각한다. / 지문에 언급되지 않은 내용이다.
(b) 마음만큼 몸도 많은 그리스 철학자에 의해 강조되었다. / 그리스 철학자가 이 글의 소재가 아니다.

(d) 레저는 고대 그리스 시대에서보다 현재 더 중요하다. / 지문에서 고대 그리스 시대와 현재를 비교하지 않았다.

| 어휘 |

perception 지각, 인지; 견해
interpretation 해석, 설명
encompass 둘러싸다, 포위하다; ~을 포함하다, 싸다
exertion 노력, 진력, 분발
perspective 전망, 전도; 견해, 관점

3.

The issue of language in schools is a key issue for many political groups in Malaysia. Although private schools using the Tamil and Chinese languages are allowed, the United Malays National Organization has championed the cause of Malay language usage in schools. As a reflection of this movement, there are now two groups of schools; the private schools are referred to only as national-type schools, whereas public schools that use Malay language receive the title of a national school. English-medium schools, which no longer exist in Malaysia, would have been refered to as national-type schools.

Q. Which of the following is correct according to the passage?
(a) Schools in Malaysia adopting Malay language can be entitled as national schools.
(b) Tamil, Malay and English-medium schools coexist with official recognition in Malaysia.
(c) English-medium schools comprise international and returnee students.
(d) Students who do not speak Chinese must attend a Malay or English-medium school.

| 해석 |

학교에서의 언어 문제는 말레이시아의 많은 정치 그룹에 있어서 중요한 사안이다. 비록 사립학교에서 타밀어와 중국어를 사용하는 것은 허용되어 있지만, 말레이 연방 조직은 학교에서 말레이 언어의 사용에 대한 명분을 지지하고 있다. 이러한 움직임을 반영하는 것으로, 현재 학교에는 두 그룹이 있다. 사립학교들은 단지 국가 타입 학교라고 불려지는 반면, 말레이어를 사용하는 공립학교들은 국가학교의 명칭을 받는다. 더 이상 말레이시아에 존재하지 않는 영어 사용 학교들은 국가 타입 학교로 언급되었을 것이다.

| 해설 |

말레이지아에서 외국어를 쓰는 학교는 '국가 타입 학교'로, 말레이어를 사용하는 학교만을 '국가학교'로 부른다고 하였으므로 정답은 '(a) 말레이어를 채택하는 말레이의 학교들만 국가학교로 명칭을 받을 수 있다.'가 된다.

| 오답 분석 |

(b) 말레이시아에서 타밀어, 말레이시아, 영어가 전달 수단인 학교들은 공식적인 승인과 함께 공존한다. / 영어가 전달 수단인 학교들은 더 이상 존재하지 않는다고 하였다.
(c) 영어를 사용하는 학교들은 외국 학생과 복학생들로 구성된다. / 복학생에 대한 언급은 없다.
(d) 중국어를 말하지 않는 학생들은 말레이어 또는 영어 사용 학교에 입학해야 한다. / 중국어를 쓰지 않는 학생들에 대한 언급은 없다.

| 어휘 |

champion 옹호하다
whereas ~에 반해서
returnee 복학생

4.

If you're doing web work you should have a website, because without a website you are invisible to your core audience. A website serves two main purposes. First, a page should display your skills with a few clear and simple examples of your work. This isn't for the accidental visitor to your site who might just hire you, but to increase your network of valuable contacts. The second key purpose of a website is to keep you visible by updating your network on your interests, completed works, and works-in-progress.

Q. What can be inferred from the passage?
(a) The target of this passage is a web-freelancer.
(b) The writer is a web page designer.
(c) Web related job opportunities are scarce.
(d) Maintaining a web site is a very demanding job.

| 해석 |

만약 당신이 웹에 관련된 일을 하고 있다면, 웹사이트가 없이는 주요 관객에게 당신이 드러나지 않기 때문에 웹사이트를 가져야 한다. 웹사이트는 두 가지 주된 목적을 수행한다. 첫 번째로, 하나의 페이지는 당신의 업적에 있어 몇 가지 깔끔하고 간단한 예들로 당신의 기술을 나타내 보여주어야 한다. 이것은 당신을 고용할지도 모르는, 사이트의 우연한 방문객을 위한 것이 아니라, 가치 있는 접촉에 대한 당신의 네트워크를 늘리기 위한 것이다. 웹사이트의 두 번째 중요 목적은, 당신의 관심과 완성된 일들 그리고 진행 중인 일에 대한 네트워크를 업데이트함으로써 당신을 눈에 띄게 유지하는 것이다.

| 해설 |

웹에 관련된 일을 한다면 스스로를 노출시키기 위해 웹사이트를 가지라는 내용의 글이다. 고객에게 스스로를 눈에 띄게 만들어야 하는 사람을 대상으로 쓰여진 글이므로 정답은 '(a) 이 글의 대상은 웹 프리랜서이다.'가 된다.

| 오답 분석 |

(b) 화자는 웹 페이지 디자이너이다. / 웹에 관련된 일을 하는 사람들에게 충고를 하고 있으므로 이 글을 통해 확인할 수 없다.
(c) 웹 관련된 직업 기회가 매우 드물다. / 지문에 언급되지 않았다.

(d) 웹 사이트를 관리하는 것은 매우 힘든 일이다. / 지문에 언급되지 않았다.

| 어휘 |
invisible 눈에 안 보이는
scarce 부족한; 드문, 희귀한

5.

For over 30 years, Greenpeace has committed themselves to the protection and conservation of the earth while using non-violent methods to promote peace. (a) The organization is geared towards solving problems "from the gecko"; where they start. (b) Among other things, they demote the usage of chemicals hazardous to our environment by promoting products that are environmentally safer. (c) Hairspray causes the ozone layer to thin out, plastic bags remain in the soil without degrading for several decades, and many foods we take in everyday contain chemicals that eventually do harm to our health. (d) They also seek to cease climate change, to protect and defend oceans and forests as well as the animals in danger of extinction.

| 해석 |
그린피스는 30여년 동안 평화를 장려하기 위한 비폭력적 수단들을 사용하고, 지구를 보호하고 보존하는 데에 전념해왔다. (a) 이 단체는 문제가 시작된 곳에서부터 문제를 해결하는 데 주력한다. (b) 다른 것들 중에서도, 그린피스는 환경적으로 더 안전한 물건들을 장려함으로써 우리 환경에 해로운 화학물질들의 사용을 막으려 한다. (c) 헤어스프레이는 오존층이 얇아지도록 하며, 비닐봉투는 몇 십 년 동안이나 분해되지 않고 토양에 남아 있는다. 또한 우리가 매일 섭취하는 많은 음식들은 결국 우리의 건강에 해를 끼치게 되는 화학물질들을 포함하고 있다. (d) 그들은 또한 멸종 위기에 처한 동물들뿐 아니라 바다와 숲을 보호하기 위해 기후의 변화를 멈추려고 노력한다.

| 해설 |
그린피스라는 기관의 역할을 설명하고 있는 글이다. (c)는 우리의 환경과 건강에 해를 끼치는 요소들을 나열하고 있으므로 이 글의 주제에서 벗어난 문장이다.

| 오답 분석 |
첫 문장이 주제문의 역할을 하고 있다. (a)는 첫 문장에 대한 부연 설명, (b)와 (d)는 구체적인 활동을 언급하고 있으므로 주제에 맞게 전개되고 있음을 알 수 있다.

| 어휘 |
commit oneself to ~에 전념하다, 전력을 기울이다, 헌신하다
from the gecko 위험한
hazardous 위험한
degrade 지위를 낮추다, 강등시키다, 퇴화하다, 분해되다
extinction 멸종, 소멸

Day 19

Build up 166p

| **1.** (b)   **2.** (b)   **3.** (c)   **4.** (a)   **5.** (d) |

1.

Canada is one of the few countries that provide free heath care to its citizens. However, the nation's universal health care system has been _________________ in recent years. Arguably, big factors in all the upheaval and change have been the cost of funding this service and the decrease in federal transfers. Is it feasible to continue providing free health care for everyone? Have recent reforms affected the quality of health care that is provided? Many issues have been raised over whether such cutbacks and decreases in federal funding will affect the accessibility of health care to the Canadian public.

(a) a privately funded public campaign
(b) the subject to various reforms
(c) gaining more popularity and support
(d) modeled after by less liberal countries

| 해석 |
캐나다는 국민에게 무상 의료를 제공하는 몇 안 되는 나라 중의 하나이다. 그러나 최근 그 나라의 전반적인 의료 시스템은 다양한 개혁의 대상이 되고 있다. 이론의 여지는 있지만 거의 틀림없이, 모든 변화와 큰 변동에 있어서의 커다란 원인은 이런 서비스에 대한 비용과 연방에서 내려오는 자금의 감소이다. 모든 사람에게 무상 의료를 계속해서 제공하는 것이 가능한 것일까? 최근의 개혁들은 제공되는 의료의 질에 영향을 주고 있을까? 연방 자금의 감소와 삭감이 캐나다 대중의 의료 접근성에 영향을 미치는지 아닌지 많은 쟁점들이 떠오르고 있다.

| 해설 |
빈칸 뒤에 이어지는 내용에서 큰 변동이 일어나고 있으며 그에 따라 많은 쟁점이 생기고 있다고 하였다. 따라서 답은 (b)가 된다.

| 오답 분석 |
(a) 사적으로 자금을 댄 공공 캠페인 / 사적 자금에 대한 내용이 지문에 나오지 않았다.
(c) 더 많은 인기와 지지를 얻고 있는 / 지문에 언급된 바 없다.
(d) 덜 자유스러운 국가들이 모델로 따라하는 / 캐나다 외의 다른 국가들은 언급되지 않았다.

| 어휘 |
arguably 이론의 여지는 있지만 거의 틀림없이
upheaval 밀어올림; 대변동
feasible 실행할 수 있는; 가능한; 그럴싸한, 있음직한
cuttback 삭감

2.

Each child develops in a unique way, and some develop language more quickly than others. Typically, during the infancy period of up to 12 months of age, the child is getting ready to talk, responding to noises and babbling. At 18 months of age, you can expect a significant increase in language development, as toddlers reach the third stage of language development. During this period, babies are able to communicate using telegraphic sentences comprised primarily of nouns. For example, a baby might say, "Mommy, no sleep" rather than "Mommy, I don't want to sleep yet." Children in this stage of language development will often repeat the same words of a phrase, because their vocabulary is still developing.

Q. What is the main topic of the lecture?
  (a) Typical problems with telegraphic communication for children
  (b) Aspects of the third stage of childhood language development
  (c) Communication with mothers and its relationship with children's language development
  (d) The importance of repetition in increasing children's vocabulary

| 해석 |

아이들은 각각의 방식으로 발달하며, 어떤 아이들은 다른 아이들보다 언어가 더 빨리 발달한다. 전형적으로, 12개월까지의 유아기에, 아이는 소음과 옹알이에 반응하며 말을 할 준비가 된다. 아장아장 걷는 아기가 언어 발달의 세 번째 단계에 도달하는 18개월 때에는 아기의 언어 발달에서 중요한 발전을 기대할 수 있을 것이다. 이 시기 동안에, 아기들은 주로 명사들로 구성된 간결한 문장을 사용해서 의사소통을 할 수 있다. 예를 들어, 아기는 "엄마, 저 잠자기를 원치 않아요."라고 하는 것이 아니라 "엄마, 잠 싫어." 라고 말 할 것이다. 언어 발달의 이런 단계에서 아이들은 어휘력이 여전히 발전 중이기 때문에 같은 단어로 이루어진 말을 반복할 것이다.

| 해설 |

아이들의.언어 발달에 대한 내용의 지문으로, 그 중에서도 특히 언어 발달의 세 번째 단계에 대해 자세히 설명하고 있다. 따라서 이 글의 주제는 '(b) 유아기 언어 발달에 있어서 세 번째 단계의 측면'임을 알 수 있다.

| 오답 분석 |

(a) 아이들에 대해 간결한 의사소통이 가지고 있는 전형적인 문제점 / 간결한 의사소통의 문제점에 대해서는 언급되지 않았다.

(c) 엄마와의 의사소통과, 그것의 아이들의 언어 발달에 대한 관계 / 엄마와의 의사소통이 아이들의 언어 발달에 어떤 영향을 미치는가는 언급되지 않았다.

(d) 어린이들의 어휘력 향상에 있어 반복의 중요성 / 반복의 중요성은 언급되지 않았다.

| 어휘 |

babbling 수다, 옹알이, 재잘거림
telegraphic 간결한

3.

There's nothing more spectacular than a sunrise or sunset over the mountainous Caribbean forest, surrounded by the crystal-clear waters of the sea. However, in order to experience the true panoramic splendor of the Caribbean, you need to see the drenching slopes of the forests when it rains. Over 200 inches of rain fall on the forest each year amounting to an astounding 100 billion gallons of water. Mild temperatures combined with this abundant moisture from the rain create ideal tropical conditions for the forest's various exotic flora and fauna including the nearly extinct Puerto Rican parrot.

Q. Which is correct about the Caribbean natural forest?
  (a) It rains for more than 200 days a year.
  (b) It has numerous species of endangered animals.
  (c) It has mild temperatures.
  (d) It has 200 different kinds of tropical plants.

| 해석 |

수정같이 맑은 바닷물로 둘러싸인 거대한 캐리비언 숲의 일출과 일몰보다 더 경이로운 것은 없다. 그러나 캐리비언의 파노라마와 같은 진정한 탁월함을 경험하려면 비가 내릴 때 숲의 흠뻑 젖은 경사지를 보아야 한다. 매년 숲에 200인치가 넘는 비가 내리는데, 합산해보면 놀랍게도 1조 갤런의 물이다. 비로부터의 풍부한 습기와 결합하여, 온화한 기온은 거의 멸종된 푸에르토리코 앵무새를 포함하여 숲의 다양한 이국적인 식물군과 동물군에 대한 이상적인 열대성 환경을 창조했다.

| 해설 |

캐리비언 숲의 탁월한 자연 경관과 기후에 대한 내용의 글이다. 지문에서 온화한 기온을 가진다고 하였으므로 정답은 '(c) 온화한 기온을 가진다.'이다.

| 오답 분석 |

(a) 1년에 200일이 넘게 비가 내린다. / 언급되지 않은 내용이다.

(b) 그것은 수많은 종의 멸종 위기 동물을 가지고 있다. / 푸에르토리코 앵무새가 예로 등장하였지만, '수많은 종류'라고 언급하지는 않았으므로 정답이 될 수 없다.

(d) 그것은 200가지의 다른 열대식물을 가지고 있다. / 지문에 언급되지 않은 내용이다.

| 어휘 |

splendor 훌륭함; 탁월, 현저; 빛남, 광채
drenching 흠뻑 젖음
slope 경사, 비탈
amount 총계가 ~에 이르다
astound 몹시 놀라게 하다

exotic 이국적인
flora 식물상
fauna 동물군

4.

The best satire seeks to administer a shock to the audience when they recognize a joke that deals with a vice. It doesn't necessarily exist to harm or ridicule, but it does seek to damage the structure of the vice. A satire's job is to expose the vice in all its repulsiveness with the aim to eradicate it from a person or society. Bitter medicine followed by candy is a time-honored formula for relief from sickness, and so does satire work by sweetening the barb of wit with laughter. Satirists are often portrayed as constructive critics; far from being destructive, they often depict themselves as redeemers of society from its ills.

Q. What can be inferred from the passage?
- (a) Satire plays a role in making people recognize bad practices.
- (b) Satire should not be taken seriously because it's only for fun.
- (c) Satirists have proven to be very efficient in spreading vices.
- (d) Most satire tends to ignore issues related to everyday life.

| 해석 |
최고의 풍자는 관중들이 악덕에 대한 농담을 인지할 때 충격을 주는 것을 추구한다. 그것은 반드시 해로움과 조소를 창조하기 위해 존재하는 것은 아니며, 악덕의 구조에 손상을 입히는 것을 추구한다. 풍자의 역할은 사람이나 사회로부터 악덕을 없애려는 목표를 가지고 악덕을 불쾌감과 함께 노출시키는 것이다. 달콤한 사탕 뒤에 오는 쓴 약은 병으로부터 오는 위안에 대한 전통적인 방식이며, 웃음과 함께 위트의 가시를 달콤하게 함으로써 풍자도 그렇게 작용한다. 풍자하는 사람은 종종 건설적인 비평가로 묘사된다. 그들은 해로운 것과는 거리가 멀고, 폐단으로부터 사회를 구하는 사람으로 스스로를 묘사한다.

| 해설 |
풍자의 역할에 대해 설명하고 있는 글이다. 풍자는 악덕을 노출하여 그것을 없애려는 목적을 가진다고 하였으므로 정답은 '(a) 풍자는 사람들이 나쁜 행위를 인식하게 하는 데 중요한 역할을 한다.'가 된다.

| 오답 분석 |
(b) 풍자는 단지 웃긴 것이기 때문에 심각하게 받아들여서는 안 된다. / 조소를 창조하려는 것이 풍자의 목적이 아니라고 하였으므로 정답이 될 수 없다.
(c) 풍자하는 사람들은 악이 퍼지는 것을 매우 효율적으로 입증하고 있다. / 풍자를 통해 악이 퍼지는 것이 아니므로 정답이 될 수 없다.
(d) 대부분의 풍자는 일상과 관련된 사안들을 무시하는 경향이 있다. / 지문에 언급되지 않았다.

| 어휘 |
satire 풍자
administer 주다, 베풀다, 공급하다
vice 악, 악덕
repulsive 불쾌한, 혐오감을 일으키는; 물리치는, 쫓아버리는
eradicate 박멸하다, 근절하다
barb 가시, 바늘, 가시 돋친 말
redeem 되찾다, 회복하다, 구하다

5.

Popeye, the Sailor, first starred in the cartoon strip *Thimble Theatre* in 1929. (a) Popeye was created by a man named Elzie Crisler Segar and eventually became a popular animated cartoon series. (b) The title of the comic strip officially modified to being called Popeye, after the death of Segar, by those that continued his work on the cartoon. (c) In the series, in order to defeat villains, Popeye, the Sailor, had to consume spinach and gain physical power. (d) This boosted the sales of spinach by 50 percent, but it didn't last long because kids' interest moved to other cartoon heroes.

| 해석 |
항해사 뽀빠이는 1929년 연재만화 〈Thimble Theatre〉에 처음 주인공으로 나타났다. (a) 뽀빠이는 Elzie Crisler Segar라는 이름을 가진 사람에 의해 만들어졌고, 마침내 인기 있는 만화영화 시리즈가 되었다. (b) Segar가 죽은 뒤, 이 만화를 계속한 사람들에 의해 이 연재만화의 제목이 공식적으로 '뽀빠이'라고 불리도록 수정되었다. (c) 이 시리즈에서, 항해사 뽀빠이는 악당을 물리치기 위해 시금치를 먹고 물리적인 힘을 얻는다. (d) 이것은 시금치의 판매를 50퍼센트 증가시켰지만, 아이들의 관심이 다른 만화의 영웅들로 옮겨갔기 때문에 그리 오래 지속되지 않았다.

| 해설 |
이 글은 만화 뽀빠이에 대한 대략적 설명이다. (d)는 시금치의 판매량에 대한 내용이므로 이 글의 주제에서 벗어나 있다.

| 오답 분석 |
첫 문장과 (a)는 뽀빠이가 탄생한 배경을, (b)는 원작자가 죽은 뒤 만화 시리즈의 제목이 '뽀빠이'로 바뀌게 된 것을, (c)는 뽀빠이의 캐릭터를 설명하고 있으므로 모두 뽀빠이와 직접적으로 관련된 내용을 다루고 있는 문장들이다.

| 어휘 |
star 주연하다
comic strip 1회 4컷의 연재만화
villain 악한, 악역
spinach 시금치

Day 20

Build up

174p

> **1.** (c) **2.** (c) **3.** (b) **4.** (c) **5.** (c)

1.

One of the most important events in China's history was the Chinese May Fourth Movement in 1919. It was the first mass movement in modern Chinese history as it occurred during the early 20th Century. Basically, the intellectuals and students of the nation rallied together in an anti-foreign movement and protest of the Treaty of Versailles. However, the magnitude of this event went far beyond that of a mere mass. The Chinese May Fourth Movement was an epic event in modern Chinese history _________________ as evidenced by the changes in the nation's social, political, and cultural way of life.

(a) as the nation adopted some capitalist principles

(b) as popular leaders appeared to change the nation's practices

(c) **as it began the shift away from classical tradition**

(d) as people realized the importance of participation

| 해석 |

중국의 역사에서 가장 중요한 사건 중의 하나는 1919년 5월 4일에 일어난 문화혁명이다. 이것은 20세기 초에 일어났기 때문에 현대 중국 역사에 있어 첫 번째 대중운동이다. 기본적으로, 중국의 학생들과 지식인들은 반외세 운동에 함께 집합했고, 베르사유 조약에 항의했다. 그러나 이 사건의 중대성은 단순한 대중 항의를 넘어섰다. 문화혁명은 현대 중국 역사에 있어서 대규모 사건이다. 왜냐하면 국가의 사회적, 정치적, 그리고 삶의 문화적인 방법에 있어서 변화가 증명해 주듯이, 고전적인 전통으로부터 멀어지는 쪽으로 변화해가기 시작했기 때문이다.

| 해설 |

현대 중국 역사에 있어 아주 큰 사건인 문화혁명을 통해 중국의 여러 삶의 방식이 바뀌게 되었다는 내용의 지문이다. 특히 빈칸 뒤에서 사회적, 문화적 삶의 방식이 바뀌게 되었다고 하였으므로 정답은 (c)가 된다.

| 오답 분석 |

(a) 이 국가가 자본주의 원리를 채택했으므로 / 자본주의에 대한 내용은 언급되지 않았다.

(b) 인기있는 지도자들이 이 국가의 관행들을 바꾸기 위해 등장했기 때문에 / 지문에 언급되지 않은 내용이다.

(d) 사람들이 참여의 중요성을 깨달았으므로 / 빈칸 뒤에 나온 사회적, 정치적, 문화적 방식의 변화는 참여와 관련이 없다.

| 어휘 |

rally 다시 모이다; 집합하다
epic 서사시의, 웅장한, 장중한
shift away 방향을 바꾸어놓다
ideology 이데올로기, 관념형태

2.

Heisenberg argued that it's impossible to measure a system without interfering with that system. That is, the method of observation we use essentially changes the system's dimensions. If you wish to look at a subatomic particle, you have to bounce another particle off it for it to appear; thus its motion will be altered during the process of observation. In measuring the position of an electron, for example, its speed will be changed. However, as a consequence of this change in speed its position is no longer certain. This explains the basis for Heisenberg's Uncertainty Principle.

Q. What is the best title for the passage?

(a) How to Measure Particle Velocity Successfully

(b) Heisenberg and the Nobel Prize

(c) **The Uncertainty of the Velocity of a Particle**

(d) The Heisenberg Experiment: Changing the Speed of Particles

| 해석 |

하이젠베르크는 어떤 체계에 방해를 주지 않고 그 체계를 측정할 수는 없다고 주장했다. 즉, 우리가 사용하는 관찰 방법이 그 체계의 특징들을 바꾸어놓는다는 것이다. 만약 미립자를 관찰하려 한다면, 그 미립자가 보이게 하기 위해 다른 미립자가 충돌했다가 되튀어 나오게 해야 하고, 그럼으로써 그 미립자의 움직임은 관찰의 과정에서 바뀌게 된다. 예를 들어, 전자의 위치를 측정하기 위해서는 전자의 속도가 바뀌어야 한다. 그러나 속도에 있어서의 변화의 결과로 전자의 위치는 더 이상 확실하지 않다. 이것이 하이젠베르크의 불확정 이론의 기본을 설명해주는 것이다.

| 해설 |

하이젠베르크의 이론을 설명하기 위해 미립자나 전자의 속도, 위치를 알기 위한 관찰 방식을 설명하고 있는 글이다. 관찰 방식이 체계 자체에 영향을 미칠 수 밖에 없어서 속력과 위치에 대해 확실히 알 수 없게 된다고 했으므로 정답은 '(c) 미립자 속력의 불확실성'이 된다.

| 오답 분석 |

(a) 미립자의 속력을 성공적으로 측정하는 방법 / 이 글은 어떻게 하면 속력을 정확히 측정할 수 있는가라는 방법론에 대한 내용이 아니라, 하이젠베르크 법칙을 설명하고 있는 글이다. 관련이 있는 것 같지만 지문의 주제에서 초점이 빗나갔다.

(b) 하이젠베르크와 노벨상 / 노벨상에 관련된 내용은 지문에서 언급되지 않았다.

(d) 하이젠베르크의 실험: 미립자의 속도 바꾸기 / 미립자의 속도를 바꾸는 것은 하이젠베르크의 실험 그 자체가 아니라, 관찰의 방법에서 파

생된 결과일 뿐이다.

| 어휘 |
interfere (with) 간섭하다, 방해하다
dimension 치수, 차원, 특징, 특질
subatomic 원자보다 작은 입자의
bounce 되튀다, 튀어오르다
alter 바꾸다, 변하다, 바뀌다

3.

The World Wildlife Fund's job is to safeguard hundreds of species around the world and pay special attention to flagship species such as pandas, tigers and whales. Flagship species commonly serve as umbrella species, helping other species that live in the same habitats, and thus require extra protection. In addition to these flagship species, the fund works to protect other species in peril that live within priority eco-regions. Animals that live in these eco-regions, such as grizzly bears and songbirds, depend on the fund's conservation efforts to ensure their future.

Q. Which of the following is correct according to the article?
  (a) Less effort is going to the protection of flagship species than umbrella species.
  (b) The World Wildlife Fund thinks seriously about the future of its priority eco-regions.
  (c) Grizzly bears are highly protected and their numbers are increasing rapidly.
  (d) There used to be many more forms of protection in priority eco-regions than at present.

| 해석 |
세계 야생 동물 기금의 일은 전 세계의 수백 종을 지키고 팬더, 호랑이, 고래와 같은 깃대종에 특별한 주의를 기울이는 것이다. 깃대종은 일반적으로 같은 서식지에 사는 다른 종들을 도와주는 우산종의 역할을 하므로 특별한 보호가 필요하다. 이러한 깃대종 동물들에 더하여, 그 기금은 우선 생태 지역에 살고 있는 위험에 처한 다른 종들을 보호하는 일을 한다. 이 생태 지역에 살고 있는 그리즐리 곰이나 노래 새와 같은 동물들은 그들의 미래를 보호하는 기금의 보전 노력에 의존하고 있다.

| 해설 |
세계 야생동물 기금이라는 단체에서 동물을 보호하기 위한 노력을 기울이고 있다는 내용의 지문이다. 따라서 정답은 '(b) 세계 야생동물 기금은 우선 생태 지역의 미래에 관해 심각하게 생각한다.'가 된다.

| 오답 분석 |
(a) 우산종보다 깃대종을 보호하는 데 노력을 덜 들일 것이다. / 우산종과 깃대종을 비교하는 내용은 등장하지 않는다.
(c) 그리즐리 곰은 매우 보호를 받고 있으며 개체 수가 급속하게 늘어나고 있다. / 그리즐리 곰의 개체 수에 대한 언급은 없다.
(d) 과거에는 현재보다 우선 생태 지역에 대한 많은 보호 형태들이 있었다.

/ 과거와 현재의 보호 형태에 대한 비교의 내용은 언급되지 않았다.

| 어휘 |
flagship species 깃대종(한 지역의 생태계를 대표하는 중요하고 특징적인 동·식물을 일컫는 말)
habitat 동·식물의 서식지
umbrella species 우산종(생물보전학적으로 먹이사슬의 가장 꼭대기에 있는 종)
peril 위험

4.

Freedom of the press is a tenet central to most nations claiming adherence to democracy. However, the following example shows how that very freedom may be abused. In 1993, The Sunday Sport paid substantial amount of money out of court damages to a police officer who had been acquitted of assault. Although exonerated, the officers' reputation remained besmirched because the paper failed to mention the alleged victims' weak testimony. The Sunday Sport should have reported a fair and balanced account of the event.

Q. Which of the following is correct according to the passage?
  (a) Freedom of the press in the U.S.A has been a declared civil right since the 20th century.
  (b) A free press has been taken for granted in most European countries since the late 1700s.
  (c) Freedom of the press, however vital, does not constitute license to misreport.
  (d) The Sunday Sport, notwithstanding the judgment against them, reported the case fairly.

| 해석 |
언론의 자유는 민주주의의 충실함을 외치는 대부분의 나라에서 중심이 되는 신조이다. 그러나 다음의 예는 바로 그 자유가 어떻게 남용되었는지를 보여준다. 1993년에 Sunday Sport는 폭행에 대해 무죄를 선고 받았던 경찰관에게 법정 배상금으로 상당한 돈을 지불했다. 비록 혐의는 풀렸지만, 그 신문이 희생자일 것으로 추정되는 사람의 증언이 취약하다는 것을 언급하지 않았기 때문에 그 공무원의 명예는 손상된 채로 남아 있었다. Sunday Sport는 그 사건의 공정하고 균형적인 설명을 보도했었어야만 했다.

| 해설 |
이 지문에서는 언론의 자유가 있다 할지라도 오보는 명백히 잘못된 것이라는 내용을 예를 들어 보여주고 있다. 따라서 정답은 '(c) 언론의 자유가 기본적인 것이긴 하지만, 오보를 할 수 있는 권리가 있는 것은 아니다.'이다.

| 오답 분석 |
(a) 미국에서 언론의 자유는 20세기부터 명시된 시민의 권리였다. / 지문

에 언급되지 않았다.

(c) 1700년대 후반 이후로 대부분의 유럽 국가에서는 무료 신문이 당연
시 되었다. / 지문에 언급되지 않았다.

(d) Sundy Sport는 그들에게 반대되는 판결에도 불구하고 그 사건을 공정
하게 보도했다. / 마지막 문장에서 이 글의 내용과 반대임을 알 수 있다.

| 어휘 |

tenet (특히 집단이 신봉하는) 주의, 교의, 신조
adherence 고수, 집착
acquit 무죄로 하다, 무죄를 선고하다
exonerate 결백을 증명하다, 혐의를 벗겨 주다
besmirch (명예, 인격을) 손상시키다; 더럽히다
alleged (근거 없이) 주장된, 추정된
constitute 합법화하다
underreport 너무 적게 보고하다
notwithstanding ~에도 불구하고, ~을 무릅쓰고

5.

Through various studies, it has been observed that the sense of smell is of great importance in attracting the opposite sex. (a) For example, in an experiment by a research team from the University of Toronto, some men and women were put in a single room to mingle. (b) After choosing an individual they felt most attracted to, the women were blindfolded and asked to smell the clothing of various men in order to find the one they felt had the "preferred" scent. (c) Before the experiment, women felt that they were attracted to handsome men who possess musky scents. (d) Putting their sense of smell to good, each woman was able to choose the same man selected during the mingling time, by olfactory skills alone.

| 해석 |

다양한 연구를 통해, 냄새를 맡는 감각은 이성을 유혹하는 데 있어 굉장히
중요하다는 것이 관찰되었다. (a) 예를 들어, 토론토 대학의 연구 팀에 의
한 한 실험에서, 몇몇 여성과 남성들이 교제하도록 하나의 방에 넣어졌다.
(b) 자신이 가장 끌리는 사람을 고른 뒤, 연구원들은 여성들은 눈을 가리
고 다양한 남성들의 옷을 냄새 맡아보고 선호하는 냄새라고 느끼는 것을
찾도록 하였다. (c) 이 실험 전에, 여성들은 자신이 사향 냄새를 지닌 잘생
긴 남성에게 끌린다고 느꼈다. (d) 냄새에 대한 감각을 활용하여, 각각의
여성은 오로지 후각만을 이용해서 짝짓는 시간에 고른 남성과 같은 남성
을 찾을 수 있었다.

| 해설 |

(c)는 이 실험 이전에 여성들이 가졌던 성향이므로 이 지문에서 벗어난 문
장이다.

| 오답 분석 |

냄새를 통해 이성에 끌리며, 냄새가 그 이성을 식별하는 기준이 될 수 있
다는 내용의 글이다. (a), (b), (d),에서는 이 글에 소개된 실험의 과정을
순서대로 설명하고 있다.

| 어휘 |

blindfold 눈가리개를 하다, 눈을 속이다
mingle 섞다, 사귀다, 교제하다

musky 사향의, 사향 냄새 나는
olfactory 후각의, 냄새의

Final Check

178p

1. (a)	2. (a)	3. (c)	4. (c)	5. (b)	6. (c)
7. (b)	8. (b)	9. (d)	10. (c)	11. (b)	12. (b)
13. (b)	14. (a)	15. (c)	16. (b)	17. (c)	18. (c)
19. (d)	20. (a)	21. (d)	22. (a)	23. (c)	24. (c)
25. (c)	26. (c)	27. (c)	28. (c)	29. (c)	30. (c)
31. (c)	32. (d)	33. (d)	34. (c)	35. (d)	36. (c)
37. (d)	38. (a)	39. (b)	40. (a)		

1.

The radio is one of the oldest, yet most widely distributed inventions of all time. Its versatility stems not only from its availability all around the world but also from its useful application in many areas. The radio can be turned on to catch "up to the minute" newscasts, listen to music and even to check the weather or traffic reports. History demonstrates how valuable access to a radio has been over the years. Even with the growing popularity of the Internet along with other forms of communication and entertainment; the radio will most likely ___________________.

(a) continue to have a place in society
(b) become banned from households
(c) become utterly obsolete and fogotten
(d) cater to an exclusive, niche audience

| 해석 |

라디오는 가장 오래되었지만, 전대미문의 가장 널리 퍼진 발명품 중 하나
이다. 그것의 다재다능함은 세계 도처에서의 유용성과 많은 영역에 있어서
의 유용한 적용에서 발생한다. 가장 참신한 뉴스 방송을 듣고, 음악을 듣
고, 교통정보와 날씨를 확인하기 위해서도 라디오를 켠다. 역사는 시간의
흐름에 걸쳐 라디오의 접속이 얼마나 가치 있었는가를 증명해주고 있다.
다른 형태의 의사소통과 오락거리들과 함께 인터넷의 인기가 상승함에도
불구하고, 라디오는 끊임없이 사회에서 하나의 위치를 차지하고 있다.

| 해설 |

지금까지 라디오가 많은 기능을 하고 있으며 많이 이용되고 있다는 내용
의 지문이다. 따라서 이 글의 가장 마지막 부분은 '(a) 끊임없이 사회에서
하나의 위치를 차지하고 있다.'가 들어가는 것이 알맞다.

| 어휘 |
versatility 다재다능
demonstrate 논증하다, 설명하다

2.

Anaheim, California has been synonymous with Walt Disney World since its opening in 1955 and spectacular success. Its sibling, however, has not fared so well. California Adventure, founded in 2001 as a younger, more street-hip alternative to the stayed family image of its elder brother is about ________________________.
The retooling and expansion plans include a complete revamp of the amusement areas and rides, as well as a major hotel and condominium construction project to encourage more long-term guests.

(a) to undergo a transformation to counter falling gate revenues

(b) to receive a federal grant to stave off impending insolvency

(c) 20 miles by road across the county from Walt Disney World

(d) to get a name-change to Walt Disney World II

| 해석 |
캘리포니아 애너하임은 1955년 월트디즈니 월드가 개장하여 엄청난 성공을 거둔 이후, 그것과 동의어가 되었다. 그러나 그 형제는 그리 잘 대접받지 못했다. 월트디즈니 월드의 지속적인 가족 이미지보다 더 젊고 유행에 민감한 대안으로써 2001년에 세워진 캘리포니아 어드벤처는, **떨어져 가는 입장 수익을 높이기 위해 변화를 겪게 될 것이다.** 이러한 개조와 확장 계획은 장기간 머무르는 손님들을 더욱 유치하기 위한 호텔과 콘도미니엄의 건설뿐 아니라, 놀이동산과 놀이기구의 완전한 개조도 포함한다.

| 해설 |
월트디즈니 월드와 달리 같은 지역에 더 늦게 생긴 캘리포니아 어드벤처는 수입이 낮아, 큰 개조를 할 계획이라는 내용의 지문이다. 따라서 빈칸에는 (a)가 알맞다.

| 어휘 |
fare 대접받다, 대우 받다, 살아가다, 지내다
street-hip 유행에 민감한
retool 설비를 일신하다, 개조하다
revamp 수선, 개혁, 개조
counter 반대하다, 거스르다
revenue 소득, 수입
stave off 피하다, 간신히 모면하다
impending 절박한, 임박한
insolvency 파산 (상태)

3.

France's national transport network has been paralyzed by a major strike involving most of the country's rail federations. Officials said routes in and around most major cities have been ________ ________________________, showing a worry for this weekend's soccer fans hoping to get to Paris for the World Cup Final. France's President, Nikolas Sarkozy is, however, resolute in his determination to restructure the nation's transport sector, citing general waste, overstaffing and unaffordable retirement benefits as key issues to be addressed. Public concern is also mounting with some calling the union's demands infuriating, unrealistic and greedy.

(a) renovated recently in the hopes of more users

(b) dilapidated and are not expected to be fixed

(c) closed or are running at minimum capacity

(d) cleared and are running at full capacity

| 해석 |
대부분의 철도 연합이 연루된 대규모의 파업에 의해 프랑스의 국가 운송 네트워크가 마비되었다. 관료들은 이번 주말에 월드컵 결선 경기를 보러 파리에 오기를 바라는 축구 팬들에 대해 걱정을 나타내며, 주요 도시 안과 도시 주변으로 통하는 길이 **폐쇄되었거나 최소한으로 운행되고** 있다고 말했다. 그러나 프랑스 대통령인 Nikolas Sarkozy는 전반적 낭비, 필요 이상의 직원, 그리고 감당하기 힘든 퇴직 연금 등을 고쳐야 할 주요 사안들로 언급하며, 프랑스의 운송 부분의 구조를 다시 잡겠다는 굳은 결심을 보이고 있다. 노동조합의 요구가 사람들을 화나게 하고 비현실적이며 탐욕스러운 것이라는 대중의 염려도 높아지고 있다.

| 해설 |
철도 연합의 파업에 대한 지문이므로, 주요 도시로 연결되거나 도시 안의 교통이 매우 제한되었음을 알 수 있다. 따라서 빈칸에는 (c)가 알맞다.

| 어휘 |
strike 파업
federation 동맹, 연합
overstaff 필요 이상의 직원을 두다
mount 오르다
infuriate 매우 화나게 하다
dilapidate 못쓰게 만들다, 황폐화하다

4.

Too often twins are defined only by their being a part of a whole, rather than by their own identity. This can be especially damaging during the time children are struggling to establish their own self worth and place in the world. One of the most important things that parents of twins should do when their children are still young is to foster independence. As parents, they will find their children heavily dependent on each other. While it is important for the twins to draw on each other's support throughout their early stages of

development, parents should also make sure that
they are fostering a comfortable atmosphere to

_______________.

(a) be separated from each other at an early age
(b) be together in their early years
(c) encourage the development of their own
    interests
(d) amend each other's differences through strict
    discipline

| 해석 |
쌍둥이들은 너무나 자주 자신의 정체성에 의해서보다는 전체의 일부라고
정의된다. 이것은 특히나 아이들이 세상에서 자신만의 가치와 자리를 확
립하려 할 때 해롭다. 쌍둥이들이 아직 어릴 때 부모들이 해야 할 가장 중
요한 것들 중 하나는, 자립심을 키워주는 것이다. 부모로서, 아이들이 서
로에게 굉장히 많이 의존한다는 것을 알 수 있다. 쌍둥이들이 발달 초기
단계를 지내면서 서로의 도움을 받는 것이 중요하긴 하지만, 부모들은 아
이들이 자신만의 흥미를 발전시키도록 장려하는 편안한 분위기를 육성해
주도록 해야 한다.

| 해설 |
쌍둥이들이 상호 의존적이거나 전체 중 일부로 보이는 경우, 자립심이나
스스로의 가치를 잘 발전시키지 못할 수도 있으므로 부모의 역할이 중요
하다는 내용의 지문이다. 따라서 빈칸에는 '(c) 아이들이 자신만의 흥미
를 발전시키도록 장려하는 것'이 적절하다.

| 어휘 |
identity 주체성, 정체성
struggle 노력하다, 분투하다
foster 기르다, 양육하다, 육성하다
atmosphere 대기, 분위기, 상황
amend 개정하다, 고치다, 바로잡다
discipline 훈련, 규율

5.
Women are freezing their eggs _______________
_______________ in greater and greater
numbers. Controversy surrounds the practice
because many clinics, even though they are
government approved and licensed, do not fully
inform their clients of the risks associated with the
procedure. Not only are the chances of becoming
pregnant after 40 much smaller than those in their
20s, but also the chances of retaining the
structure of eggs in a long-term frozen state are
minimal. Despite these factors contributing to a
high failure rate for in-vitro procedures, previously
popular for women suffering an illness or perhaps
undergoing a course of chemotherapy, some
clinics have begun to market their services to
otherwise healthy women.

(a) because later they will produce them
(b) in the hope of using them later in life
(c) expecting to have healthy babies
(d) in competition with other women

| 해석 |
점점 더 많은 여성들이 나중에 사용하려는 희망을 가지고 자신의 난자를
냉동시키고 있다. 정부에 의해 승인을 받고 면허를 얻었다 할지라도, 많은
병원들은 고객들에게 이 과정에 수반되는 위험에 대해 제대로 알려주지
않고 있기 때문에 논쟁이 따르고 있다. 20대보다 40세가 넘어서 임신을
하게 되는 가능성도 훨씬 더 적을 뿐만 아니라, 난자의 구조를 오랜 기간
냉동된 상태로 유지하는 가능성도 매우 적다. 시험관 임신 과정에서의 높
은 실패율에 기여하는 이러한 요소들에도 불구하고, 일부 병원들에서는
예전에는 질병으로 고통을 받았거나 화학 요법을 받았던 여성들에게 인기
있었던 이러한 시험관 임신을 건강한 여성들에게도 시행하고 있다.

| 해설 |
냉동한 난자를 이용한 임신을 건강한 여성들에게도 시행하는 병원들이 있
다는 내용의 지문이다. 지문의 앞쪽에 빈칸이 있으므로 이 글의 주제에 관
련된 보기를 찾아야 한다. 따라서 정답은 (b)이다.

| 어휘 |
egg 난자
in-vitro 시험관 내에
chemotherapy 화학 요법

6.
Former Pakistani President Benazir Bhutto
returned home today after years in exile and the
whole of Karachi ground to a halt as she made her
way from the airport to her residence on the
outskirts of the city that was once her power base.
Cheering spectators lined the streets and flags
waved in honor of Bhutto, unseated by Pervez
Musharraf in a military coup almost a decade ago.
Returning to Pakistan in political turmoil, she is
expected to seek some form of power-sharing
agreement with Musharraf, yet no definite plans
have been drawn up. At the moment in Pakistani
politics, _______________.

(a) Benazir Bhutto will definitely regain her former
    power
(b) the settled situation looks sure to continue
(c) the only certain thing seems to be the
    uncertainty
(d) Pervez Musharraf will win his court case
    conclusively

| 해석 |
파키스탄 전 대통령인 Benazir Bhutto가 몇 년간의 망명 끝에 오늘 집으
로 돌아왔다. 그녀가 공항으로부터 한때 그녀의 권력의 베이스였던
Karachi 시 외곽의 집으로 돌아오면서 시 전체는 정지 상태가 되었다. 환
호를 보내는 구경꾼들이 길에 늘어섰고, 거의 10년 전 군사 쿠데타에서

Pervez Musharraf에 의해 대통령 자리를 빼앗긴 Bhutto에게 경의를 표하는 깃발이 흔들렸다. 그녀가 정치적 혼란기에 파키스탄으로 돌아오면서, Musharraf와 일종의 권력을 나누는 협의를 볼 것으로 기대되지만 아직 어떤 뚜렷한 계획도 입안되지 않았다. 현재로서는 파키스탄 정치에서 유일하게 확실한 한 가지는 불확실성인 것으로 보인다.

| 해설 |
전 대통령 Bhutto가 돌아오면서 Musharraf와 권력을 나누게 될지도 모른다는 전망이 나타나지만, 아직 구체적으로 정해진 것은 없다고 하였다. 따라서 정답은 (c)가 된다.

| 어휘 |
exile 망명, 추방, 유배
grind to a halt 멈추다, 정지되다
coup 쿠데타
turmoil 소란, 혼란
definite 뚜렷한, 명확한

7.

Do you need another reason to switch to green tea? Aside from fighting Alzheimer's and Parkinson's disease, researchers have found that drinking green tea may also ________________. The findings built on evidence from lab experiments show that certain compounds in green tea, called catechins help burn calories and lower LDL cholesterol, therefore mildly reducing body fat. The results also suggest that catechins in green tea contribute to the prevention of and improvement in various lifestyle-related diseases, particularly obesity.

(a) allow you to look more youthful and well-rested
(b) help you have a slender figure
(c) help you live longer than others
(d) have a lesser risk of mental diseases such as dementia

| 해석 |
녹차로 바꿔야 할 다른 이유가 필요하세요? 연구원들은 녹차를 마시는 것이 치매나 파킨슨 병과 싸워주는 것 외에도 날씬한 몸매를 지켜준다는 것을 발견했습니다. 실험실에서의 증거를 기반으로 한 이 발견은 녹차에 들어있는 카테킨이라는 요소가 칼로리를 연소시키고 LDL 콜레스테롤을 낮추도록 하여 서서히 체지방을 줄여준다는 것을 보여줍니다. 이러한 결과는 또한, 녹차의 카테킨이 특히 비만과 같은 다양한 생활 습관에 관련된 질병의 예방과 개선에 기여한다는 것도 보여줍니다.

| 해설 |
녹차의 건강상의 여러 가지 장점에 대해 설명하고 있는 글이다. 빈칸 뒤의 문장들에서 체지방을 줄여준다는 것과 비만에 효과가 있다는 내용이 이어지고 있으므로 정답은 (b)이다.

| 어휘 |
Alzheimer's disease 노인성 치매
compound 혼합물
obesity 비만

slender 날씬한, 호리호리한
dementia 치매

8.

Toyota has lost its aura of invincibility in the North American market, with the release this week of the 2007 automobile reliability and safety rankings. In the list, compiled by the magazine Consumer Report, since 1996 this year is the first that Toyota has not been included in the recommended vehicle listing. So long the pretender to the perennially top-ranked Ford's throne, the Japan-based Toyota Motor finally took top spot this year to become the world's largest automaker. But a rash of recalls on its vehicles has tarnished its new crown and ________________________. Reaction in Tokyo to the news was swift; the chief executive reportedly demanded the immediate resignation of a number of senior executives.

(a) had them take the responsibility of accidents
(b) subsequently caused a sharp slide in sales
(c) was forced to apologize for the recalls
(d) prompted the withdrawal from the North American market

| 해석 |
도요타는 이번 주 발표된 2007 자동차의 확실성과 안전성 순위에서, 북미 시장에서의 '무적'이라는 아우라를 잃었다. 〈소비자 리포트〉라는 잡지에 의해 집계된 이 리스트는 1996년에 시작되었는데, 올해가 도요타가 추천 차량 리스트에 포함되지 않았던 첫 해이다. 지금까지 항상 최고의 순위였던 포드의 왕좌를 넘보던 일본에 본사를 둔 도요타 모터는 마침내 올해 세계에서 가장 큰 자동차 회사의 최고 자리를 차지했다. 그러나 차량 리콜이 쇄도하면서 새로운 왕관이 빛을 잃게 되었고 그에 따라 판매가 저하되었다. 이 뉴스에 대한 도쿄의 반응은 신속했다. 들리는 바에 의하면 회장은 많은 이사들의 즉각적인 사임을 요구했다고 한다.

| 해설 |
리콜이 쇄도하여 도요타 자동차의 명성이 떨어지게 되었다는 내용의 지문이다. 빈칸 앞에서는 도요타의 명성이 빛이 바랬다는 내용이, 뒤에서는 이사들의 사임이 요구되었다는 내용이 이어지고 있으므로 빈칸에는 실질적 판매량이 줄었다는 내용이 들어가는 것이 알맞다. 따라서 (b)가 정답이 된다.

| 어휘 |
invincibility 무적, 불패
compile 편집하다, 집계하다, 수집하다
pretender 요구자, 왕위 요구자
throne 왕좌, 옥좌
rash 빈발, 돌연한 다발
tarnish 흐리게 하다, 손상시키다
swift 빠른, 신속한
reportedly 들리는 바에 의하면

9.

Now you can prepare and register your last will
and testament online at a far lower cost than that
of the usual route of signatories and attorney
witnesses, all of whom charge a substantial fee for
their services. A last will prepared for you by a
lawyer could, for an average-size estate, cost up
to $1,000. Now experience the online service
running at around $70 and you will also find
________________________. Just last year
the downloadable DIY form of one web-will
provider registered a massive 33% increase yet
seems to represent only the tip of a very large
iceberg.

(a) a heavily discounted product being offered by
the legal community
(b) it difficult to imagine how an attorney could
match such a good price
(c) the usual fee calculated by dividing by ten, then
less another thirty dollars
(d) it easy to see why consumers prefer their
testament with their computer mouse

| 해석 |
이제 당신은 상당한 수수료를 청구하는 서명인과 변호사 증언의 일반적
방법보다 훨씬 더 낮은 비용으로 마지막 유언과 유언장을 온라인으로 준
비하고 등록할 수 있다. 일반적인 재산에 대해 변호사가 준비해주는 유언
장은 천 달러까지의 금액이 든다. 이제 70달러 정도면 되는 온라인 서비
스를 경험해보면 왜 소비자들이 컴퓨터 마우스를 가지고 유언장을 준비하
는지 쉽게 알 수 있을 것이다. 지난해에 다운로드를 받을 수 있는 DIY형식
의 웹 유언장 제공자는 33퍼센트의 엄청난 증가를 기록했지만, 이것은 매
우 큰 빙산의 일각만을 보여주고 있는 것 같다.

| 해설 |
웹상으로 유언장을 작성할 때에 비용을 많이 절감할 수 있다는 내용의 지
문이다. 따라서 빈칸에는 마우스를 가지고 유언장을 작성한다는 내용이
들어가는 (d)가 알맞은 보기이다.

| 어휘 |
testament 유언장, 유서
signatory 서명인
attorney 변호사, 법조인

10.

There has never been a greater need to stay alert
and informed, as our fast-paced and technological
society requires us to make quick and smart
decisions everyday. The celebrated speaker
Matthias Large is famous for saying that it is in
your short moments of decisions that your life is
shaped. Trivial or profound, our everyday
decisions tweak our pathway in lives in a positive
or negative direction. While our brain cells crackle
to deal with the many choices in life that we have
to make, we need to act shrewdly to
________________.

(a) succeed in forming our pathway in life
(b) debate about our lives' decisions with others
(c) keep up with the smart decisions being made
(d) get rid of the stress with your poor decision-
making skills

| 해석 |
빠르게 진행되는 기술적 사회가 매일 빠르고 똑똑한 결정을 내리도록 요
구하고 있기 때문에, 오늘날 긴장하고 정보를 얻으며 살아야 할 필요가 가
장 커졌다. 잘 알려진 연설가인 Matthias Large는 당신의 인생이 형성되
는 것은 결정을 내리는 짧은 순간이라고 말한 것으로 유명하다. 사소하든
심오하든 간에, 매일 매일의 결정들은 인생의 진로를 긍정적이거나 부정
적인 방향으로 바꾸어 준다. 우리의 뇌세포가 인생의 많은 선택들을 내리
기 위해 부지런히 움직이는 동안, 우리는 현명한 선택에 맞춰 행동하기 위
해 빠르게 행동해야 한다.

| 해설 |
삶을 결정하고 삶의 방향을 바꾸는 것은 짧은 순간의 결정들이므로 항상
현명한 결정을 내리고 그에 맞춰 기민하게 움직여야 한다는 내용의 지문
이므로 정답은 (c)가 된다.

| 어휘 |
celebrated 유명한, 저명한, 잘 알려진
trivial 사소한
profound 심오한, 난해한
tweak 잡아당기다, 조정하다
crackle 바지직 소리 내다
shrewdly 빈틈없이, 빠르게

11.

Municipal shelters have traditionally provided a
service to lost pet owners in reuniting them with
their lost dog, cat or other treasured family pet but
so-called Private Rescue Groups are now
competing for a slice of the pie. They work by
adopting premium pets identified as pedigree
quality and then arranging their fostering to
applicants for a fee. However, their strict
screening processes and restrictive guidelines on
care for the animals are arousing concern. As
millions of unwanted and abandoned pets are
routinely euthanized across America annually,
critics of the new private enterprise accuse them
of ________________________.

(a) placing too much value on the life of an animal
(b) cashing in on a truly shameful state of affairs
(c) breaking the law by getting the pets for free
(d) not donating certain amount of money they earn

시에서 운영하는 보호소는 전통적으로 잃어버린 개나 고양이, 다른 아끼
는 가족과 같은 애완동물과 그 주인이 다시 만나게 해주는 서비스를 제공
해왔다. 그러나 사립 구조 단체라고 하는 곳이 이제 이러한 영역의 파이
조각을 두고 다투고 있다. 그들은 혈통이 분명한 품종이라고 확인된 고급
애완동물을 데려다가 지원자들에게 일정한 금액을 받고 키우도록 연결해
주는 일을 한다. 그러나 그들의 선발 과정과 동물을 돌보는 것에 대한 제
한적인 가이드라인이 염려를 불러일으키고 있다. 매년 미국 전역에서 몇
백만 마리의 버려진 애완동물들이 안락사를 당하고 있기 때문에 이 새로
운 사립 기업에 대해 비평하는 사람들은 정말로 파렴치한 일로 돈을 벌고
있다고 비난한다.

| 해설 |

잃어버린 애완동물을 되찾아주는 시의 사업의 좋은 의도와 대조되게도,
혈통 좋은 애완동물을 돈을 받고 새 주인과 연결시켜주는 서비스에 대한
비난이 일고 있다는 내용의 글이다. 빈칸 앞에서 '비평가들'의 비난이라
는 것이 나타나 있으므로 정답은 (b)이다.

| 어휘 |

municipal 시(市)의, 도시의
pedigree 혈통이 분명한
screen 선발하다, 심사하다
arouse 깨우다, 자극하다
euthanize 안락사 시키다
cash in 돈을 벌다

12.

To coordinate your healthcare needs, the Health
Maintenance Organization works by you first
choosing a primary care physician. Its plan
ensures that your primary care physician's
responsibility is for not only treating you but also
referring you to other physicians, hospitals and
healthcare providers within the network for your
specific healthcare needs. Under the Health
Maintenance Organization plan, your primary care
physician must _______________________ that
are necessary for you except in certain emergency
situations.

(a) refund you for all charges
(b) provide or arrange all services
(c) arrange all accommodations
(d) focus fully on the needs of other patients

| 해석 |

건강 관리에 있어서의 필요를 조절하기 위해, 건강 관리 공단은 우선 주치
의를 선택하는 것으로 당신을 위한 일을 시작하게 된다. 건강 관리 공단의
계획은 당신의 주치의의 책임이 당신을 치료하는 것에 있는 것뿐만 아니
라, 당신을 다른 내과 의사들이나, 병원, 그리고 당신의 구체적인 건강 관
리 요구에 있어서의 네트워크 안에 있는 건강 관리 공급자들에게 위탁하
는 책임도 있다는 것을 보증한다. 건강 관리 공단의 계획 하에서, 당신의
주치의는 특정한 긴급 상황을 제외하고, 당신에게 필요한 모든 서비스를
제공하거나 조정해야 한다.

| 해설 |

건강 관리 공단의 주치의 제도에 대한 내용의 글이다. 빈칸이 있는 문장의
앞 문장에서 주치의는 치료뿐 아니라 다른 의료인이나 의료 기관에 환자
를 위탁하는 일도 책임진다고 하였으므로 정답은 (b)가 된다.

| 어휘 |

coordinate 조절하다, 조정하다, 조화시키다
maintenance 유지, 관리, 보수
primary care 1차 진료
physician 내과의사
ensure 안전하게 하다, 보증하다

13.

Black holes are regions of space-time
_______________________. If you throw a ball
hard enough gravity will not be able to pull it back
down and it will escape from the earth. The speed
at which you have to throw the ball for it to leave
the earth completely is known as the escape
velocity, which for earth is about 7 miles a second.
If an object is crushed into a smaller volume the
gravitational attraction increases and the escape
velocity gets bigger. Eventually a point is reached
when even light particles, traveling at 186
thousand miles a second, are not traveling fast
enough to escape. At this point, nothing can get
out as nothing known can travel faster than light –
this is a black hole.

(a) to which the light is absorbed
(b) from which not even light can escape
(c) which makes matters travel faster than ever
(d) which is not trapped in the gravitational pull

| 해석 |

블랙홀은 빛조차 도망갈 수 없는 시공간의 지역이다. 만약 당신이 중력이
공을 아래로 잡아당길 수 없을 정도로 충분히 세게 던진다면, 공은 지구로
부터 달아날 것이다. 공이 지구를 완벽하게 떠나기 위해 당신이 던져야 할
속도는 탈출속도라고 알려져 있는데, 그것은 지구에 있어 초당 7마일의
속도이다. 만약 물체가 더 작은 부피로 쪼개진다면, 중력의 끌어당김은 상
승하고 탈출 속도는 커지게 된다. 궁극적으로, 초당 18만 6천 마일의 속
도로 이동하는 빛의 입자조차도 탈출하기에 충분한 속도로 이동하지 않는
지점에 도달하게 된다. 이런 지점에서, 빛의 속도보다 빠르게 이동할 수
있다고 알려진 것은 없으므로 아무것도 빠져나가지 못하게 되고, 이것이
바로 블랙홀이다.

| 해설 |

블랙홀의 원리에 대해 설명하고 있는 글이다. 제일 첫 문장에 빈칸이 있으
므로 정답은 주제와 관련된 것을 찾으면 된다. 지문에서 빛 입자도 탈출할
수 없는 지점에 이르면 빛보다 빠르게 이동하는 것은 아무것도 없으므로
어떤 물체도 빠져나갈 수 없게 되며, 이것이 바로 블랙홀이라고 하였으므
로 정답은 (b)이다.

| 어휘 |

gravity 중력

escape velocity 탈출 속도
particle 미립자, 작은 조각

14.

A distinct feeling of déjà vu is present in the share market as investors swarm round Internet startup companies long on hype and promises but short on actual customers and all important dollar revenues. Reminders of the "dot-com bubble" can be seen in the valuation of one popular social-networking site, Facebook, the current dollar value of which analysts say is almost equal to half that of Internet behemoth Yahoo, based solely on a future potential to draw an audience. The fuzzy math behind the last burst bubble should be enough of a reminder at least for the individual investor and thus the advice is clear: ___________
____.

(a) **think carefully before you put your hard-earned salary into this round of dot-com startups**
(b) invest now in the same way you did previously and the dividends could be yours to take
(c) dollar revenues are taking a back seat this time around so its time to jump into the market
(d) Yahoo is worth a lot more than Facebook because it started a long time beforehand

| 해석 |

투자자들이 과대 광고와 가망성에는 길게 그러나 실제적 고객과 중요한 달러 수입에는 짧게 인터넷 신생 회사들에 모여들면서 주식 시장에 뚜렷한 데자뷰의 느낌이 들고 있다. 인기 있는 사회 조직망 사이트인 페이스북에 대한 평가에서 '닷컴 거품'을 떠오르게 하는 요소가 보인다. 전문가들은, 관중을 끌어들이는 것에 있어서의 미래의 가능성에만 기반을 두면 페이스북의 최근 달러 가치는 거의 인터넷의 거인인 야후의 절반이라고 한다. 이러한 최근의 거품 사태 뒤에 있는 확실치 않은 숫자 놀음은 적어도 개인 투자자들이 과거를 떠올리는 데 충분할 것이다. 따라서 명백한 조언이 나온다. 열심히 번 월급을 신생 인터넷 회사에 투자하기 전에 신중하게 생각해라.

| 해설 |

제일 첫 문장에서, 인터넷 신생 회사들에 투자자들이 과대 광고에는 길게 모여들지만 실제적 수입에는 짧게 모여들고 있다고 하였으므로, 거품이나 과대 광고에 속지 않도록 조심해야 한다는 것이 조언의 내용이 될 것임을 알 수 있다. 따라서 정답은 (a)이다.

| 어휘 |

distinct 뚜렷한, 별개의, 독특한
swarm around 떼를 짓다, 모여들다
startup 개시(의), 이제 막 활동을 시작한
hype 과대 광고
behemoth 거인, 강력한 것
fuzzy 희미한, 분명치 않은

15.

Smoking, the recreational activity is practiced by

millions of people all over the world and has become an addiction. But as concerns on public health grow, smokers are losing their ground as researches show that smoking has detrimental effect not only on smokers themselves but also on others around them. ________________, in many parts of Canada, smoking indoors and outdoors around restaurants and workplaces have been banned and those that disobey the law can be fined up to and including two thousand Canadian dollars.

(a) On the whole
(b) In other words
(c) **For example**
(d) In addition

| 해석 |

오락적인 행동인 흡연은, 전 세계의 많은 사람들이 하고 있으며 중독이 되었다. 그러나 대중의 건강에 대한 관심이 커지면서 연구들이 흡연이 흡연자들 자신뿐 아니라 주변의 사람들에게도 유해한 영향을 끼친다는 것을 보여주고 있어, 흡연자들은 설 자리를 잃게 되었다. 예를 들어 캐나다의 많은 지역에서는 식당과 직장 근처에서 실내와 실외 흡연은 금지되고 있으며, 이 법을 따르지 않는 사람들에게는 최대한 캐나다 달러로 2천 달러까지 벌금을 물릴 수 있다.

| 해설 |

흡연자들이 점점 설 자리를 잃고 있다는 내용 뒤에 캐나다에서의 흡연 규제와 벌금 시행에 대한 내용이 이어지고 있으므로, 앞 문장에 대한 예를 보여주고 있음을 알 수 있다. 따라서 정답은 (c)가 된다.

| 어휘 |

addiction 중독
detrimental 유해한, 손해되는
ban ~을 금지하다
disobey (사람, 규율, 명령 따위)에 따르지 않다, ~을 어기다

16.

Along with anorexia nervosa, bulimia is an eating disorder in which patients consume a great amount of food and then only to relieve themselves of the extra weight almost right after through self-induced vomiting. Those that are bulimic enjoy eating but for reasons such as possessing low self-efficacy and a poor self-image; they feel guilty for devouring so much food. __________, this eating disorder is more common in females at the adolescent age than it is for males, implying that there are more females than males that are unsatisfied with the image of their own bodies. This statistical finding is similar for those diagnosed with anorexia.

(a) After all
(b) Furthermore
(c) For example
(d) First of all

| 해석 |

신경성 거식증과 함께 과식증은 섭식 장애로, 환자가 엄청나게 많은 양의 음식을 섭취한 뒤 여분의 체중에 대해 자신을 안심시키기 위해 바로 스스로 구토를 하는 것이다. 과식증인 사람들은 먹는 것을 즐기지만, 낮은 자아 효능감과 형편없는 자아상을 소유하는 것과 같은 이유로 인해 많은 음식을 게걸스럽게 먹는 것에 대해 가책을 느낀다. 나아가, 이런 섭식 장애는 남성보다 사춘기의 여성에서 좀 더 흔히 나타나는데, 남성보다 여성이 그들 자신의 몸에 대한 이미지에 덜 만족한다는 것을 의미한다. 이런 통계학적인 발견은 거식증으로 진단된 사람들의 통계와 유사하다.

| 해설 |

과식증에 대한 전반적인 설명을 하고 있는 글이다. 빈칸 앞에서는 과식증의 증상, 뒤에서는 어떤 사람들에게서 더 많이 발견되는가를 설명하고 있다. 설명이 덧붙여지고 있으므로 정답은 (b)가 된다.

| 어휘 |

anorexia nervosa 신경성 거식증
bulimia 과식증
eating disorder 섭식장애
vomit 토하다, 게우다
self-efficacy 자아 효능감
self-image 자아상
devour 게걸스럽게 먹다, 탐식하다

17.

The work of some linguists focuses on the notion that languages evolve over time. Sometimes, even the complete meanings of words change. For example, the term "silly" had originally meant blessed. Over the years, that particular word's meaning has been altered several times to the point that today it means to be foolish. Additionally, other aspects that illustrate how language evolves include grammar changes, new slang conceived by younger generations, and the creation of new colloquial terms and idioms. Although this applies to all different cultures, certain linguists go as far as to argue that there is not such thing as official languages, merely diverse dialects. Ultimately, like any other facet in life, language is subject to constant change and will continue to evolve over time.

Q. What is the best title of the passage?
  (a) The Changing Meanings of the Term "Silly"
  (b) Standard Language and Dialects
  (c) The Evolution of Languages
  (d) The Creation of an Artificial Language

| 해석 |

몇몇 언어학자들의 연구는 언어는 시간이 흐를수록 진화한다는 개념에 초점이 맞추어져 있다. 때때로 단어의 뜻이 완전히 변화되기도 한다. 예를 들어, 'silly'라는 단어는 원래 축복을 받았다는 의미였다. 세월이 흐르자, 그 단어 특유의 뜻은 여러 번 변화되어 그것은 오늘날 어리석다는 것을 뜻한다. 또한, 어떻게 언어가 진화하는지를 보여주는 다른 측면들은 문법의 변화와 어린 세대에 의해 인식된 새로운 속어, 그리고 새로운 구어체와 숙어의 생성을 포함한다. 비록 이것은 모든 다른 문화에도 적용되지만, 어떤 언어학자들은 이것들이 단지 다양한 파생 언어일 뿐 공식적인 언어가 아니라고 주장하기도 한다. 궁극적으로, 삶의 다른 면들과 같이 언어는 끊임없이 변하려는 경향을 띠고, 시간이 흐르면서 끊임없이 진화할 것이다.

| 해설 |

시간의 흐름에 따른 언어의 변화에 대한 글이다. 지문의 마지막 부분에서 언어는 끊임없이 변화하며 진화하는 것이라고 하였으므로 정답은 '(c) 언어의 진화'가 된다.

| 어휘 |

linguist 언어학자
colloquial 구어체의
go as far as ~까지도 하다, ~할 정도로 극단에 흐르다
merely 단지, 다만
dialect 방언, 사투리, 파생 언어

18.

Recent studies have shown that getting divorced before the age of 30 has become so common that it has created a phenomenon called the 'starter divorce.' A 'starter divorce' is one that lasts only for a few years, and generally ends before the couple have children. Some young couples may even separate after being married in only a few months. Experts say one of the reasons in this is supposedly the immaturity of young people who get married in the caprice of the moment. The study also found that even though the divorce rate decreased in the 1990s, marriages that end within the first five years continue to be on the rise.

Q. What is the main point of the report?
  (a) About half of all marriages are starter marriages.
  (b) More and more people want to get married before they are 30.
  (c) Starter divorces are becoming more common.
  (d) Divorce rates after the 1990s have decreased.

| 해석 |

최근의 연구들은 서른 살 이전에 이혼하는 것이 너무나 흔해지고 있어, '신혼 이혼'이라고 불리는 현상을 만들어내고 있다는 것을 보여준다. '신혼 이혼'은 단지 몇 년만 지속되고, 일반적으로 커플이 아이를 갖기 전에 끝난다. 몇몇의 나이 어린 커플들은 결혼한 지 몇 달 되지 않아 갈라서기도

한다. 전문가들은 일시적 변덕으로 결혼을 하는 젊은 사람들의 미성숙함
이 이러한 현상의 이유 중 하나일 것이라고 말한다. 이 연구는 또한, 1990
년대에 이혼율이 감소했음에도 불구하고, 처음 5년 사이에 이혼으로 끝나
는 결혼은 계속해서 증가했다는 사실을 발견했다.

| 해설 |

서른 살 이전의 이혼이 증가하는 현상과 그 원인, 추세에 대한 글이다. 따
라서 이 글의 주제는 '(c) 신혼 이혼은 점점 흔해지고 있다.'가 된다.

| 어휘 |

divorce 이혼
phenomenon 현상
supposedly 아마도
immaturity 미성숙함
caprice 변덕
separate 분리하다, 떼어놓다, 갈라지다

19.

There are appropriate manners of speaking
according to the situation, more specifically,
according to the ones listening. Suppose that you
ran into a famous movie star on your way to work.
Then you would probably want to tell everyone
about your encounter. If you were to tell your story
to your colleague, mother, or your boyfriend,
would you describe your experience to each of
these three people in the same way? Although the
purpose might be the same, you will undoubtedly
use a different approach to telling the story for
each situation.

Q. What is the main point of the passage?
  (a) Amazing life experiences can change your
      views in communication.
  (b) It is preferable to confide in friends than in
      family.
  (c) It is important to talk about your
      experiences using a variety of approaches.
  (d) The audience of a story dictates how it is
      delivered.

| 해석 |

상황에 따라, 더 구체적으로 말하자면 듣고 있는 사람들에 따라 적절한
말하기 방식이 있는 것이다. 직장에 가다가 유명한 영화 스타를 우연히
만났다고 가정해보자. 그러면 당신은 아마도 이 우연한 마주침에 대해서
모든 사람들에게 말하고 싶을 것이다. 만약 당신이 당신의 이야기를 직장
동료, 어머니, 혹은 남자친구에게 말한다면, 당신은 그 경험을 각각의 세
사람에게 똑같은 방식으로 묘사하게 될까? 목적이 같다 할지라도, 당신
은 각각의 상황에서 그 이야기를 하는 것에 대해 다른 접근을 사용하게
될 것이다.

| 해설 |

상황에 따라, 특히나 듣는 사람에 따라 이야기를 하는 방식이 달라진다는
내용의 지문이다. 따라서 이 글의 주제는 '(d) 청자가 이야기 전달 방식을
결정한다.'가 된다.

| 어휘 |

manner 방식
specifically 구체적으로, 명확하게
encounter ~과 우연히 만나다, 조우하다, 마주치다
undoubtedly 확실히, 의심할 여지없이, 틀림없이

20.

Wing panels are the parts that provide heat
shielding and prevent the space shuttle from
burning up. In 2003, the shuttle Columbia's wing
panels failed, leading to the loss of seven NASA
astronauts and the stalling of America's entire
space program for almost a decade. Regarding
the safety risk of the recently approved launch of
the Shuttle Discovery, Chief Engineer Wayne Hale
expressed strong concern when wing panel flaws
were detected with no clues to their origin. Flight
managers, however, argue that the damage
detected is microscopic in comparison to the
destructive foot-wide hole in the panels of the ill-
fated Columbia.

Q. What is the main idea of the passage?
  (a) Controversy surrounds the planned shuttle
      Discovery launch.
  (b) Damage to the wing panels has not
      aroused concern.
  (c) An engineer has advised NASA not to
      launch the shuttle Discovery.
  (d) America's space program is in limbo due to
      the shuttle Columbia disaster.

| 해석 |

날개의 패널들은 열기로부터의 보호를 제공하고 불타는 것으로부터 우주
선을 보호하는 부속들이다. 2003년 우주선 콜롬비아의 날개 패널이 기능
을 하지 못하여, 7명의 NASA 우주인의 목숨을 앗아갔고, 거의 10년간 미
국 전체의 우주 프로그램을 멈추게 했다. 최근 승인된 디스커버리호를 발
사하는 것의 안전 위험에 관련하여, 발견된 날개 패널의 결점들이 무엇으
로부터 유래했는지 단서가 없어 수석 엔지니어 Wayne Hale는 강한 우려
를 표현했다. 그러나 비행 매니저들은 탐지된 손상이 불운한 콜롬비아의
패널에 있었던 파괴적인 발 크기의 넓은 구멍과 비교해서 미세하다고 주
장했다.

| 해설 |

이 지문은 우주선 날개의 패널들의 기능을 설명하고, 그것이 디스커버리
호의 안전에 어느 정도 영향을 미칠지 의견이 엇갈리고 있다는 내용을 말
해주고 있다. 따라서 이 글의 주제는 (a) '디스커버리호 발사 계획을 둘러
싼 논쟁'이 된다.

| 어휘 |

panel 작은 조각, 네모꼴의 판자
stall 멎게 하다, 움직이지 않게 하다
flaw 결점, 결함
ill-fated 불운한, 불길한

21.

Authorities have reported many cases of outbreaks of Avian Influenza in a number of Asian countries in the past few years. Most victims have acquired the disease through contact with birds, but the Avian flu, or more commonly known as 'bird flu' has a high potential to become the next human pandemic through human transmission. We have yet to find a real cure for the virus, and with this in mind, prevention seems to be our best defense against the deadly disease. The effects of an Avian Flu outbreak are quite fatal; it could mean that millions of people could be killed within a matter of months if the disease is not properly controlled.

Q. What is the main idea of the passage?
- (a) Avian flu is likely to spread in the next few months.
- (b) Without a cure for Avian flu, millions of people could die
- (c) People tend to undermine the effects of a deadly disease outbreak.
- **(d) Prevention is the aid for controlling the spread of Avian flu.**

| 해석 |

과거 몇 년 간 수많은 아시아 국가에서 발생한 조류독감의 많은 사례들을 당국이 보고해 왔다. 대부분의 희생자는 새와의 접촉을 통해서 그 병을 얻고 있다. 그러나 bird flu라고 좀 더 일반적으로 알려진 조류독감은 인간을 통해 전염되는 전 세계적 전염병이 될 높은 잠재력을 가지고 있다. 우리는 아직 그 바이러스에 대한 실제적인 치료 방법을 찾지 못했고, 이 사실을 염두에 두면 예방이 이 치명적인 질병의 방어에 가장 최선의 방어처럼 보인다. 조류독감 발생의 영향은 아주 치명적이어서, 만약 이 질병이 적당하게 통제되지 않는다면 수백만의 사람들이 몇 달 안에 죽을 수 있다는 것을 의미할 수도 있다.

| 해설 |

치료 방법이 아직 없으며 사람을 통해 전염될 수도 있는 조류독감이 치명적일 수 있다는 사실을 밝히며, 예방이 조류 독감에 대한 최선의 방어임을 말하고 있다. 따라서 정답은 (d)가 된다.

| 어휘 |

outbreak (전쟁, 질병 등의) 발생, 발발
Avian Influenza 조류 독감 (= bird flu)
pandemic 널리 퍼져 유행하는 병
transmission 전송, 전염
fatal 치명적인

22.

One of the most controversial theories that exist today is the notion regarding the process of natural selection. Also referred to as the survival of the fittest, this idea revolves round the basis that living beings that are best suited to their environment ultimately live longer and breed more offspring than their weaker counterparts that are less suited to thrive in that particular surrounding. Consequently, this results in the spreading of stronger genetic characteristics over time since only those that are better suited to survive can successfully pass on their genes. This concept of evolution applies to all forms of living beings including human beings. Thus natural selection explains how the stronger and fitter beings generally survive and pass on their desirable genetic traits while the weaker ones die out.

Q. What is the main idea of the passage?
- **(a) Natural selection suggests that the strong survive while the weak die out.**
- (b) The Western world has provided protection against disease thanks to evolution.
- (c) Evolution has ultimately created a superior living being: mankind.
- (d) In certain environments, certain types of animals live longer than others.

| 해석 |

오늘날 존재하는 가장 논쟁적인 이론들 중 하나는 자연 선택의 과정에 대한 개념이다. 적자생존이라고도 불리는 이 개념은, 환경에 적합한 생명체는 그 환경에 덜 적합한 생명체보다 더 오래 살고, 좀 더 많은 자손을 남긴다는 원칙을 중심으로 한다. 따라서 생존에 더욱 적합한 것들이 성공적으로 유전자를 물려주게 되기 때문에 시간이 흐를수록 살아남기 적합한 강한 유전자가 퍼지게 되는 결과를 낳게 된다. 진화의 이런 개념은 인간을 포함한 모든 살아있는 것에 적용된다. 그러므로 자연 선택은 약한 것들은 죽는 반면, 어떻게 더 강하고 더 적합한 생명체들이 살아남아 바람직한 유전적 특징들을 물려주는가에 대해서 설명해준다.

| 해설 |

적자생존의 원칙에 맞게, 환경에 더 적합하고 강한 개체들이 살아남게 되는 과정인 자연 선택을 설명하고 있는 글이다. 따라서 정답은 (a)가 된다.

| 어휘 |

controversial 논쟁의, 논쟁의 여지가 있는
regarding ~에 관하여
natural selection 자연선택
revolve 회전하다, 공전하다, ~ 주위를 돌다
offspring 자식, 새끼; 자손
counterpart 상대자, 대응물
consequently 따라서, 그 결과로
pass on 넘겨주다, 전하다

23.

Dear Editor,
I am writing to disagree with your recent article regarding the negative effect of daytime television

talk shows. Most people are often offended by these types of shows because of their explicit nature and the unhealthy influence it can have on viewers. However, as a high school teacher, I find that there is indeed some value and use for these "trashy" shows. Some of my students seem to respond to such shows and have impressed me by demonstrating that they have learned some important life lessons from watching this tabloid-like television programming. After watching them, we have often discussed important issues such as drug use, AIDS, school dropouts, and teenage pregnancy. Don't always assume the worst since teenagers can sometimes surprise and find ways to learn about life's lessons, even if it's from unlikely sources such as television talk shows.

Scott Logan, N.J.

Q. What is the purpose of the letter?
 (a) To condemn those who blame TV talk shows for their sensational content
 (b) To tell the editor the importance of teaching teenagers about real life
 (c) To emphasize some benefits teenagers get from watching talk shows
 (d) To discuss the nature of day time television talk shows and their content

| 해석 |
편집장님에게
낮 시간 텔레비전 토크쇼의 부정적인 효과를 말하고 있는 당신의 최근 기사에 반대하기 위해 이 편지를 씁니다. 대부분의 사람들은 시청자들에게 끼치는 노골적인 성향과 건전하지 못한 영향 때문에 이러한 종류의 쇼에 불쾌감을 가집니다. 그러나 고등학교 선생님으로서, 저는 이런 저질 쇼에 실제로 어떤 가치와 용도가 있다는 것을 발견했습니다. 저의 학생들 중 몇몇은 이런 쇼에 반응을 보이는 듯하며, 그들은 타블로이드판 신문 같은 이러한 선정적인 텔레비전 프로그램을 보면서 몇 가지 삶의 중요한 교훈을 배웠다고 설명하여 저에게 깊은 인상을 주었습니다. 그것들을 보고, 우리는 종종 마약, 에이즈, 학교 중퇴, 청소년 임신 같은 중요한 이슈를 토론합니다. 원천이 텔레비전 토크쇼와 같은 비호감적인 것이라고 하더라도, 청소년들은 때때로 놀라면서 삶의 교훈을 배우는 방법을 찾을 수 있으니, 항상 너무 나쁘게만 가정하지는 마시기 바랍니다.

| 해설 |
TV 토크쇼 프로그램의 선정성이 부정적인 영향을 끼친다는 편집장의 주장에 반대하여, 오히려 십대들이 그러한 프로그램을 봄으로써 삶에 대한 중요한 교훈들을 배울 수도 있다는 내용으로 편지를 쓰고 있는 글이다. 따라서 이 글의 목적은 (c)가 된다.

| 어휘 |
explicit 명백한, 뚜렷한, 노골적인
trashy 쓰레기의, 쓸모없는
tabloid 그림을 넣은 소형 신문; 선정적인
demonstrate 증명하다, 논증하다, 설명하다

dropout 중퇴자, 탈락자

24.
Eric Benhamou, CEO of the United States based $6 billion networking company 3Com, gave sobering remarks after a recent seminar about the future of our connected society. Ten million homes in the United States are expected to share a network connection for Web browsing, entertainment, and printing by 2009, according to analyst firm the YGK Group, which sponsored the home networking seminar. But Benhamou, warned that connecting millions of households is already unconsciously creating social changes, and challenged vendors to consider the ramifications of the changes.

Q. What would be the most likely topic of the following paragraph?
 (a) An industry trend toward greater profitability in hand-held devices
 (b) Informing the guest companies of the date of the next seminar
 (c) How a more connected world could fundamentally change society
 (d) The innovative nature of quick-adopters of new technology

| 해석 |
미국에 본사를 둔 60억원 규모의 네트워킹 회사 3Com의 회장인 Eric Benhamou는 우리의 연결된 사회의 미래에 대한 최근의 세미나 후에 진지한 언급을 하였다. 홈 네트워킹 세미나를 후원한 분석 회사인 YGK Group에 따르면, 미국의 천만 가구가 2009년에 웹 브라우징, 오락, 프린팅을 위한 네트워크 연결을 공유하게 될 것이라 예측된다. 그러나 Benhamou는 몇백만 가구들을 연결하는 것은 이미 의식하지 못하는 사이에 사회를 변화시키고 있고, 매각자들로 하여금 이러한 변화의 파급 효과를 고려해야 한다는 당면과제를 주었다고 경고하였다.

| 해설 |
이 지문 다음에 나올 지문의 주제를 묻고 있다. 지문의 마지막 부분에서, 사회가 이미 변화해 가고 있으며 그 변화를 고려해야 한다고 했으므로 정답은 '(c) 서로 더욱 연결된 세상이 어떻게 근본적으로 사회를 변화시킬 것인가.'이다.

| 어휘 |
sobering 진지하게 하는, 정신이 들게 하는
analyst 분석가
vendor 매각자
ramification 파생한 결과, 효과
profitability 이익률, 수익성

25.
Australia is mostly known for its natural wonders

but recently, Australia has been branded by the cancer research council as the country with the highest rate of skin cancer in the world. A spokesperson for the council said that one out of two Australians get skin cancer and that three hundred thousand Australians seek surgery to remove cancerous lesions from their skin every year. The startling number of skin cancer patients in Australia may have a lot to do with global warming and the effect from the harmful sun rays. However, many also refer to the fact that most of the nation's twenty million people are descendents of immigrants from countries like Ireland and Britain, and their skins just can't withstand the Australian sun.

Q. Which is correct according to the passage?
  (a) In Australia, three hundred thousand people die from cancer each year.
  (b) Australia's rate of skin cancer is expected to increase.
  (c) Almost half of Australians are afflicted with skin cancer.
  (d) Australia is a country with twenty million Irish and British immigrants.

| 해석 |

호주는 그것의 경이로운 자연으로 대부분 알려져 있다. 그러나 최근에 호주는 암 연구 회의에서 세계에서 가장 높은 피부암 비율을 가지고 있는 나라라는 낙인이 찍혔다. 회의 대변인은 호주 사람 두명 중 한 명은 피부암에 걸리고, 3십만 명의 호주인들이 매년 그들의 피부에서 암 성질의 손상들을 제거하기 위해 외과의사를 찾고 있다고 말했다. 이러한 호주의 깜짝 놀랄만한 피부암 환자 수는 아마도 지구 온난화와 해로운 태양 광선의 영향과 많은 관련을 가지고 있는 것 같다. 그러나 또한 많은 사람들은 국가의 2천만 명의 사람들 중 대부분이 아일랜드와 영국과 같은 나라에서 온 이민자의 후손이라는 사실을 제기하면서, 그들의 피부가 단지 호주의 햇빛에 견디어낼 수 없는 것이라고 언급한다.

| 해설 |

지문의 두 번째 문장에서 두 명 중 한 명이 피부암에 걸린다고 하였으므로 정답은 '(c) 거의 절반의 호주인들이 피부암으로 괴로움을 겪는다' 가 된다.

| 어휘 |

brand 상표를 붙이다, 낙인을 찍다
council 회의, 협의
spokesperson 대표자, 대변인
cancerous 암의
lesion (조직기능의) 장애, 손상
withstand 저항하다, 견디어 내다
afflict 괴롭히다

26.

Chinese retailers' infatuation with Valentine's Day has been on display in nearly every store window and newspaper advertisement for weeks. As Valentine's Day draws near, Chinese singles with no dates tend to be reminded wherever they look around, that they will remain alone and miserable throughout their lives. If worse comes to worst, they can treat themselves to a chocolate or two as an instant 'love booster.' However, they should remember that Valentine's Day is, after all, an imported holiday and it should be treated as any other day.

Q. Which of the following is correct according to the passage?
  (a) Valentine's Day brings a lot of revenue from its advertisements.
  (b) Chinese couples celebrate Valentine's Day excessively.
  (c) One should not get caught in the tailspin of the Valentine's Day infatuation.
  (d) Chinese singles should condemn the extravagance associated with Valentine's Day.

| 해석 |

중국 소매상들의 밸런타인데이에 대한 열중은 모든 가게의 쇼윈도와 신문 광고들에서 몇 주 동안이나 보여지고 있다. 밸런타인데이가 가까이 오면서, 데이트 약속이 없는 중국의 싱글들은 어디를 보든 자신이 혼자 남아있고 사는 동안 계속해서 비참한 상태일 것이라는 생각을 하게 된다. 만약 안 좋은 상태가 최악의 상태가 된다면 그들은 초콜릿 한두 개를 먹으며 잠깐이라도 기분이 좋아지게끔 할지도 모른다. 그러나 그들은 밸런타인데이는 어쨌든 수입된 명절일 뿐이고 다른 날과 똑같이 취급해야 한다는 것을 알아야 한다.

| 해설 |

밸런타인데이의 분위기에 휩쓸려 싱글들이 비참한 기분에 빠지는 경우가 있는데, 밸런타인데이는 외국에서 들어온 명절일 뿐이라는 것을 기억해야 한다는 내용의 지문이다. 따라서 정답은 밸런타인데이의 열중된 분위기의 허탈감에 빠지면 안 된다는 (c)가 된다.

| 어휘 |

infatuation 열중, 심취
miserable 불쌍한, 비참한, 가련한
tailspin 당황, 허탈, 의기소침

27.

With the increasing demand in geothermal energy as a source for electricity, it is true to say that the nuclear power industry is currently undergoing a depression period. High interest rates, a dramatic increase in construction costs and most of all, a low demand have reduced investors' enthusiasm. In 2001, twelve utilities had their bond ratings lowered and last year at least three more were close to undergoing a similar fate. Ruth Lynn, a nuclear industry analyst, says the poor financial health of the industry has generated many problems in the raising of long term capital.

Q. Which is correct according to the passage?
   (a) More demand for electricity has resulted in more investment.
   (b) Investors' enthusiasm for geothermal energy is increasing.
   (c) The bond ratings of utilities have worsened.
   (d) Construction costs have plummeted.

| 해석 |

전기에 대한 원천으로 지열 에너지의 수요가 증가하게 되면서, 핵에너지 산업이 현재 침체기를 겪고 있다는 것은 사실이다. 높은 이자율, 건설 비용의 엄청난 상승, 그리고 무엇보다도 낮은 수요는 투자자들의 열정을 감소시키고 있다. 2001년에 12개의 공공 사업체의 채권 등급 평가가 낮아졌으며, 작년에는 적어도 세 개 이상의 회사가 비슷한 운명을 겪을 위기에 있었다. 핵 산업 전문가인 루스 린은 산업의 형편없는 재정 상태가 장기간 자본의 마련에 많은 문제를 발생시키고 있다고 말한다.

| 해설 |

세 번째 문장에서 공공 사업체들의 채권 등급 평가가 낮아졌다고 하였으므로 정답은 (c)가 된다.

| 어휘 |

geothermal 지열의
undergo 겪다, 경험하다
most of all 무엇보다도
enthusiasm 열광, 감격; 열중; 열의
bond rating 채권 등급 평가
utilities (가스, 수도, 전기 등의) 공익사업체, 공공시설
plummet 떨어지다, 급락하다

28.

Since the beginning of history, people have gone through extreme measures to make themselves look younger. Many of today's aging baby boomers, those born between 1946 and 1964, are no exception to this stigma. An increasing number of them, now in their middle-ages, are beginning to seek operations and orthopedists' offices because of their desperation to stay young. From many years of obsessive exercise, they need knee and hip replacements, surgery for ligament damage, and treatment for stress fractures. The phenomenon even has a name in medical circles, boomeritis.

Q. What is correct about baby boomers according to the passage?

   (a) They are living longer and healthier lives than before.
   (b) They worry about getting injured during exercise.
   (c) They are exercising excessively to stay young.
   (d) They undergo plastic surgeries to look young.

| 해석 |

역사가 시작된 이래로, 사람들은 자신을 더 젊어 보이게 만들기 위해 극단의 조치들을 써 왔다. 오늘날 나이가 들어가고 있는 1946년과 1964년 사이의 베이비 붐 시대에 태어난 많은 사람들도 이러한 점에서 예외가 아니다. 이제 중년의 나이인 그들의 많은 수가 젊음을 유지하려는 절실함 때문에 수술과 정형외과 병원을 찾기 시작하고 있다. 수년간의 강박적인 운동으로 인해 그들은 무릎과 엉덩이 교체, 인대 손상에 대한 수술, 피로 골절에 대한 치료가 필요하다. 의학계에서는 이런 현상에 대해 boomeritis라는 이름까지 있다.

| 해설 |

베이비 붐 시대에 태어난 사람들이 젊어 보이기 위한 노력으로 과도할 만큼 운동을 하고 그 결과 신체의 일부가 손상되어 병원을 찾기도 한다는 내용의 지문이다. 따라서 정답은 (c)가 된다.

| 어휘 |

go through 경험하다, 겪다.
stigma 오명, 치욕, 오점
orthopedist 정형외과 의사
desperation 절망, 자포자기
obsessive 강박적인, 집착하는
ligament 인대
stress fracture 피로 골절 (다리뼈에 금이 간 것)

29.

There is more to yawning than just being tired. A scientific reason for yawning that is often depreciated is that there is a lack of oxygen in your body. If you are tired, bored, or sitting in a stuffy room, you tend to breathe more slowly and your body doesn't get all the oxygen it needs. Consequently, you let out less carbon-dioxide, and the rest will build up in your blood. Your brain then senses this and quickly sends a signal to your lungs to take an extra deep breath, or in other words, yawn.

Q. Which is correct according to the passage?
   (a) Exhaling more can cause yawning.
   (b) Yawning occurs more often among students.
   (c) A lack of oxygen in the body causes yawning.
   (d) Students tend to yawn less when they are sitting down.

하품하는 것에는 단지 피곤한 것보다 더 많은 무엇인가가 있다. 종종 경시되는 하품에 대한 과학적인 이유는 당신의 몸에 산소가 부족하다는 것이다. 만약 당신이 피곤하고 지루하거나 또는 통풍이 잘 안 되는 방에 앉아 있다면, 당신은 좀 더 천천히 숨을 쉬게 되고 당신의 몸은 필요한 모든 산소를 얻지 못한다. 결과적으로 이산화탄소를 덜 배출하게 되고, 나머지는 당신의 혈액에 쌓이게 될 것이다. 그리고 나서 당신의 두뇌가 이러한 상황을 감지하고, 폐가 특히 깊은 숨을 쉬도록, 즉 하품을 하게끔 재빨리 신호를 보낸다.

| 해설 |

체내에 산소가 부족할 때 하품을 하게 되는 과정을 설명하고 있는 글이다. 따라서 정답은 (c)가 된다.

| 어휘 |

yawn 하품하다
depreciate 가치를 저하시키다; 얕보다, 경시하다
stuffy 통풍이 잘 안 되는, 숨 막히는
consequently 결과적으로
exhale 숨을 내쉬다

30.

In recent years, there has been an increasing focus on health in the workplace. Big businesses now strive to keep their employees healthy, with cleaner working environments as well as better insurance plans. Some view this as a way for big businesses to reduce the cost of future employee health problems. However, according to health economist, Timothy Bairnes, big businesses have other reasons to keep their employees healthy. He believes that businesses do not want to fall under greater government control and meet stricter guidelines for not having treated their employees well.

Q. Which is correct about big businesses according to passage?
   (a) Its employees are not being treated well enough.
   (b) It makes workers liable for their own health care.
   (c) Its objective is to avoid government interference.
   (d) Its motive lies in their willingness to keep their employees fit.

| 해석 |

최근에 직장에서의 건강에 초점을 맞추는 일이 증가하고 있다. 사업체들은 지금 더 나은 보험 계획뿐 아니라 청소부가 일하고 있는 환경 등으로 직원들이 건강을 유지하도록 노력하고 있다. 일부 사람들은 이것이 사업체에서 미래의 고용인 건강 문제 비용을 감소시키기 위한 방법이라고 보고 있다. 그러나 건강 경제학자인 Timothy Bairnes에 의하면 사업체들은 그들의 직원들을 건강하게 유지시켜야 하는 다른 이유들을 가지고 있다.

그는 사업이 큰 정부의 규제 하에 처하게 되기를 원하지 않으며, 직원들을 잘 대우해주지 못한 것에 대해 더 엄격한 지침을 지키게 되기를 원하지 않는다.

| 해설 |

직장에서 직원들의 건강에 더욱 신경을 쓰고 있는 추세에 대한 이유는 더욱 엄격한 정부의 규제와 지침에 직면하기를 원치 않기 때문이라고 밝히고 있다. 따라서 정답은 (c)이다.

| 어휘 |

strive to 노력하다, 힘쓰다, 얻으려고 애쓰다

31.

Are you sick and tired of typing your essay from your home computer? Have you been looking for decent student-priced laptops to take with you to school? Well, here is some good news for you! This week only, you can get a Tregg 2X laptop for a special student price of $699.00. The 2X comes with a super fast Intel-core duo processor, 2 GB of RAM, and a 300 GB hard drive. Included in the price is a 14.1 inch LCD flat panel monitor. Call 1-800-87344 to place your order now, while supplies last.

Q. Which is correct about the laptop being advertised?
   (a) An LCD monitor is also on sale.
   (b) All of the basic computer software is included.
   (c) A 14.1 inch LCD monitor is included.
   (d) It is twice the speed of a home computer.

| 해석 |

당신의 집 컴퓨터로 당신의 에세이를 작성하기가 짜증나고 지치십니까? 학교에 가져갈 괜찮은 학생 가격대의 노트북 컴퓨터를 찾고 계신가요? 자, 여기에 당신을 위한 뉴스가 있습니다. 단 이번 주에만, Tregg 2X 노트북을 699달러라는 특별 학생 가격으로 살 수 있습니다. 이 2X는 아주 빠른 인텔 코어 듀오 프로세서, 2GB의 RAM, 그리고 300GB의 하드디스크가 장착되어 있습니다. 14.1인치 LCD 평면패널 모니터도 가격에 포함되어 있습니다. 물건이 남아 있을 때, 1-800-87344로 전화하셔서 당장 주문하세요.

| 해설 |

699달러의 특별 학생가격으로 Tregg 2X노트북을 살 수 있으며, 끝에서 두 번째 문장에서 그 가격에는 LCD 모니터도 포함되어 있다고 밝히고 있다. 따라서 정답은 (c)이다.

| 어휘 |

sick and tired 아주 싫어진
decent 남부럽잖은, 점잖은, 상당한
look for 찾다

32.

For many years, members of the Malawian

government have been trying to think of new ways to spur economic development in the large farms in the southern region. The southern commercial farms account for a large chunk of Malawi's export earnings, and many changes have been proposed to further increase in production. That's all very well for large scale farming operations, but what about independent, small scale farmers in Malawi? It's as if the Malawian government is only interested in increasing the land holdings of a few large commercial farm owners and is abandoning its independent, small scale farmers.

Q. What can be inferred from the passage?
- (a) Small scale farmers should sell out to larger commercial farm owners.
- (b) State economic development depends on the small scale farmers.
- (c) Industrial agriculture is on the rise in Malawi.
- (d) Small scale farmers need to receive more government support.

| 해석 |
수년간 말라위 정부의 일원들은 남쪽 지역 거대 농장에서 경제적인 발전에 박차를 가하기 위한 새로운 방법을 생각해내려 하고 있다. 남쪽 상업 농장은 말라위 수출 소득의 상당한 양을 차지하며, 생산량을 더욱 늘리기 위해 많은 변화들이 제안되고 있다. 이러한 현상은 큰 규모의 농장 가동에는 매우 좋지만, 말라위의 소규모, 독립적인 농부들에 대해서는 어떨까? 그것은 마치 말라위 정부가 단지 소수의 큰 상업 농장 주인의 토지 소유를 상승시키는 것에만 관심이 있고, 독립적이고 소규모인 농부들을 저버리는 것처럼 보인다.

| 해설 |
말라위 정부가 규모가 큰 상업 농장에 좋게 작용하는 정책들을 시행함으로써, 상대적으로 소규모 농장들이 정부의 도움을 받지 못하고 있다는 내용의 지문이다. 따라서 이 글에서 추론할 수 있는 것은 소규모 농장들이 정부의 지원을 더 받아야 한다는 (d)가 된다.

| 어휘 |
spur 박차를 가하다, 격려하다, 고무하다
account for 차지하다
chunk 상당한 양, 대강, 큰 덩어리
earning 소득, 벌이
abandon 포기하다, 저버리다

33.

Experts warn that a flu pandemic is now eight times more likely to happen, than twenty years ago. There is no way to predict when the next pandemic will hit, but researchers are certain that it is coming, and it's just a question of when. With underlying assumptions that there is going to be a flu outbreak, the government should take preventative measures and come up with a plan that is more affordable, workable and effective. Right now, the government seems to be just exacerbating people's fears by creating an unrealistic to-do list without any sort of implementation.

Q. What can be inferred about the government from the passage?
- (a) It has wasted a lot of money on recognizing the threat of the flu outbreak.
- (b) It has lessened the chances of a pandemic.
- (c) Its plans are viable but are going to be too expensive.
- (d) It is inefficient despite its efforts to control pandemics properly.

| 해석 |
전문가들이 전 세계적으로 퍼지는 독감은 20년 전보다 지금 8배 정도 더 발생하고 있다고 경고했다. 언제 다음의 전국적인 유행병이 나타날지를 예측할 수 있는 방법은 없지만, 연구자들은 전국적 유행병이 다가오고 있다는 것을 확신하며 다만 언제 발생할지의 문제일 뿐이라고 한다. 감기 발생이 곧 있을 것이라는 가정이 아래에 깔려 있기 때문에 정부는 예방법을 취해야 하며 비용상 더 알맞고 실행 가능하며 효율적인 계획들을 생각해 내야 한다. 지금으로서는, 정부가 어떤 종류의 실천도 없이 비현실적인 방안들을 생성해냄으로써 사람들의 공포를 가중시키는 것으로 보인다.

| 해설 |
지문 후반부에서, 유행성 독감 등의 질병에 대한 정부의 대응이 현실적이지 않고 비효율적인 방안들만을 만들어내고 있다고 하였으므로 정답은 '(d) 유행병을 적절히 통제하려는 노력에도 불구하고 비효율적이다.'가 된다.

| 어휘 |
pandemic 전염병이 전국적으로 퍼지는
assumption 사실이라고 생각함; 가정
outbreak (전쟁, 질병 등의)발발, 돌발
come up with 생각해내다, 떠올리다
affordable (값이) 알맞은
exacerbate (고통, 병, 원한 등을) 더욱 심하게 하다, 악화시키다
implementation 이행, 실행; 완성, 성취; 충족
viable 실행 가능한, 실용적인

34.

The exact emergence of the Renaissance is difficult to point out. In the past, historians used the term "Renaissance" for the period from the fourteenth to the sixteenth centuries, implying the rebirth of rational Roman and Greek civilization after the middle ages. Some historians regard Renaissance as the beginning of Modern age. Similarly, the term "Middle Ages," is defined as a primitive middle period between classical and modern civilizations. The Middle Ages, however, can be schematically divided into three 'ages' of European history, creating relatively a explicit divide in the time line.

Q. What can be inferred from the passage?
   (a) The concept of modern civilization does not really exist.
   (b) Renaissance and Medieval cultures differ significantly.
   (c) It has been difficult to determine a clear division for a specific era.
   (d) Classical civilization was largely forgotten until modern civilizations.

| 해석 |
르네상스의 정확한 출현을 지적하기는 어렵다. 과거에 역사가들은 14세기부터 16세기에 대해 르네상스라는 용어를 사용했는데, 중세 이후의 이성적인 로마와 그리스 문명의 재탄생을 의미했다. 어떤 역사학자들은 르네상스를 근대의 시작으로 여긴다. 이와 비슷하게, 중세라는 용어는 고전적 문명과 현대적 문명 사이의 원시적 중간 시대로 정의 되었다. 그러나 중세시대는 시간의 흐름상 상대적으로 명백한 경계선을 그리며 유럽역사에서 개략적으로 3개의 시대로 나누어 질 수 있다.

| 해설 |
르네상스와 중세의 시대적 구분이 명확하지 않거나 잘못 알려져 있어왔다는 내용의 지문이다. 따라서 이 지문으로부터 유추할 수 있는 것은 '(c) 구체적 시대에 대해 명확한 경계선을 결정하는 것은 어려운 일이다.'가 된다.

| 어휘 |
emergence 출현, 발생
primitive 초기의, 원시의
schematically 개략적으로

35.

Today's seminar will focus on our common misbeliefs in daily exercise. Most of you may assume that daily exercise such as jogging can only benefit one's health. However, when your body is not conditioned for it, jogging and other daily workout can cause muscle cramps and serious joint injuries. The best way to prevent injury is by training to develop strong and flexible muscles that will act as your body's shock absorbers. Also, a healthy diet and regular life are the most important and essential two things and smoking and consuming excessive alcohol are the most detrimental and fatal two things for this.

Q. What can be inferred from the passage?
   (a) Women who are on a diet should also exercise regularly.
   (b) Overweight people are more prone to joint injury when they exercise.
   (c) Jogging injuries are due to inadequate stretching exercises.
   (d) Strengthening the leg muscles help prevent joint injuries when jogging.

| 해석 |
오늘의 세미나는 매일 하는 운동에 대한 우리의 흔한 잘못된 믿음에 대해 초점이 맞추어 질 것이다. 대부분의 사람들은 아마도 조깅과 같이 매일 하는 운동이 단지 우리의 건강에만 도움이 될 것이라고 생각한다. 그러나 당신의 몸이 조깅에 맞는 상태가 아닐 때, 조깅과 다른 날마다 하는 운동은 근육경련과 심각한 관절부상을 일으킬 수 있다. 부상을 막을 수 있는 최고의 방법은 당신의 몸에 대한 충격을 흡수하는 역할을 하는 강하고 유연한 근육을 발달시키는 훈련을 하는 것이다. 또한, 이를 위해 건강한 식사와 규칙적인 생활이 가장 중요하고 기본적인 두 가지이고, 흡연과 과도한 음주가 가장 해롭고 치명적인 두 가지이다.

| 해설 |
조깅으로 인한 관절 부상을 피하기 위해서 강하고 유연한 근육을 발달시켜야 한다고 하였으므로 정답은 '(d) 다리 근육을 강화시키는 것이 조깅할 때에 근육 부상을 예방하는 데 도움이 된다.'가 된다.

| 어휘 |
misbelief 잘못된 생각
cramp 근육의 경련, 쥐
joint 관절
detrimental 유해한, 이롭지 못한

36.

Dear Ms. Kelly,
Social Science Monthly would like to congratulate you. We would like to publish your article about interpersonal attraction in our next issue. We found that your investigation of reward theory in relationships between male and female is very initiative and deserves much applause. However, several professionals in psychology field suggest that your article would be much more strengthened by having reviewers, who shall remain anonymous. Please note that the purpose of this process is solely to help you develop more complete and brilliant article and the reviews and feedbacks will be kept strictly confidential. Again, congratulations and feel free to contact me if you have any concerns.

Q. What can be inferred form the letter?
   (a) Ms. Kelly's article is the best article this journal hasever received.
   (b) The reviewers are renowned writers in the field of psychology.
   (c) Ms. Kelly is not to know the names of the reviewers.

(d) The editor wants to hire Ms. Kelly as one of the reviewers of *Social Science Monthly*.

| 해석 |

친애하는 켈리 씨께.

〈Social Science Monthly〉가 축하를 드립니다. 우리는 당신의 개인 간의 매력에 대한 논설을 다음달 호에 싣고 싶습니다. 우리는 여성과 남성의 관계에 있어서의 보상이론에 대한 당신의 연구가 매우 독창적이며 많은 찬사를 받을 만하다는 것을 알게 되었습니다. 그렇지만, 심리학 분야의 몇몇 전문가들은 익명으로 남을 비평가들을 통해 당신의 논설이 훨씬 더 강화될 것이라고 제시합니다. 이러한 과정은 단지 당신의 논설을 더욱 완성도 높고 훌륭하게 만들 목적이며, 비평과 피드백은 기밀로 지켜질 것입니다. 다시 한번 축하드리며, 궁금한 점이 있으시면 언제든 연락주시기 바랍니다.

| 해설 |

Social Science Monthly지에서 논설을 높이 사며, 리뷰를 거쳐 더욱 완성된 형태로 싣기를 원한다는 내용의 편지글이다. 네 번째 문장에서 비평가들은 익명으로 남을 것이라고 하였으므로 정답은 '(c) 켈리 씨는 비평가들의 이름을 알지 못할 것이다.'가 된다.

| 오답 분석 |

(a) 켈리 씨의 논설은 이 저널이 받아본 가장 뛰어난 것이다. / 이러한 내용은 지문에 언급되지 않았다.

(b) 비평가들은 심리학 분야에서 저명한 저자들이다. / 비평가들이 누구인가는 밝히지 않고 있다.

(d) 편집장은 켈리 씨를 〈Social Science Monthly〉의 비평가로 고용하기를 원한다. / 이 잡지사에서 켈리 씨에게 연락을 취한 이유는 논설을 싣기 위해서이다.

| 어휘 |

investigation 조사, 연구
initiative 진취적인, 독창적인
applause 칭찬, 박수 갈채
anonymous 익명의
brilliant 찬란히 빛나는, 훌륭한
confidential 비밀의, 기밀의

37.

Unusually high winds are hampering firefighters in their efforts to contain a blaze spread over hundreds of square miles in California today. The blaze, apparently started by a discarded cigarette-end and exacerbated by hurricane force winds has so far destroyed several homes and now threatens the historic Pepperdine University, situated on the outskirts of Los Angeles. Traffic flows along roads and highways were blocked by billowing smoke and the fire has claimed one life so far, that of a homeowner trying to douse the flames on his property. Governor Arnold Schwartzenegger is considering declaring a state of emergency.

Q. What is the main idea of the passage?
(a) Smoke is causing firefighter's difficulty in reaching the fire.
(b) The historic Pepperdine University may be destroyed.
(c) The fire was started by a discarded cigarette.
(d) High winds are causing the blaze to spread beyond firefighter's control.

| 해석 |

몹시 모진 바람이 오늘 캘리포니아에서 수백 제곱 마일이 넘게 퍼진 화염을 억제하려는 소방관들의 노력에 훼방을 놓고 있다. 확실히 버려진 담배꽁초에 의해 시작되고 허리케인의 힘을 가진 바람에 의해 악화된 그 화염은 지금까지 몇 채의 집을 파괴했고, 이제 로스엔젤레스의 외곽에 위치한 역사 깊은 페퍼다인 대학을 위협하고 있다. 도로와 고속도로의 교통 흐름은 소용돌이치는 연기에 의해 막혔으며, 지금까지 한 명의 목숨을 앗아갔다. 죽은 사람은 자신의 집의 불길에 물을 끼얹으려던 집주인이었다. 주지사인 아놀드 슈왈제네거는 비상사태 선포를 고려중이다.

| 해설 |

캘리포니아의 화재에 관한 글의 주제문은 첫 번째 문장에 잘 나타나 있다. 따라서 답은 '(d) 세찬 바람은 소방관의 억제를 넘어가는 화염의 퍼짐을 유발시키는 중이다.'가 된다.

| 어휘 |

hamper 방해하다
contain 포함하다, 함유하다, 억제하다
blaze 불꽃, 화염
exacerbate (고통, 병, 원한 등을) 더욱 심하게 하다, 악화시키다
outskirt 변두리, 교외
billow 큰 물결; 소용돌이치는 것
douse 물을 끼얹다, 흠뻑 젖음, 억수

38.

Ireland's National Day, St. Patrick's Day, is celebrated on March 17th. (a) Although many cities and towns throughout Ireland hold parades on St. Patrick's Day, the main parade takes place in Dublin. (b) St. Patrick is considered the country's patron saint and is credited for ridding Ireland of snakes and for introducing Christianity to his people. (c) Most would assume that the first parade to celebrate this holiday would be held in Ireland; however, it was held in the United States. (d) This is because St. Patrick's Day is now celebrated by those of Irish and Non-Irish descendant all over the world.

| 해석 |

아일랜드의 국경일인 성 패트릭 축일은 5월 17일에 경축된다. (a) 비록 아일랜드에 있는 많은 도시들과 마을들이 성 패트릭 축일에 퍼레이드를 벌이지만, 그 주요 퍼레이드는 더블린에서 열린다. (b) 성 패트릭은 이 나라의 수호성인으로 생각되며, 아일랜드를 악의가 있는 사람들에게서 구하고 사람들에게 기독교를 소개했다고 믿어지고 있다. (c) 사람들은 이 명절을 축하하기 위한 첫 번째 퍼레이드가 아일랜드에서 열릴 것이라고 추정했지만, 첫 번째 퍼레이드는 미국에서 열렸다. (d) 이것은 왜냐하면 성 패

트릭 축일이 이제 전 세계적으로 아일랜드인의 후손과 아일랜드인의 후손이 아닌 사람들 모두에 의해 경축되고 있기 때문이다.

| 해설 |

성 패트릭 축일이 어떤 의미를 가지는 명절인지를 설명하고, 이 명절이 아일랜드의 축제에서 전 세계적인 축제가 되었다는 내용을 언급하고 있는 지문이다. (a)는 아일랜드에서의 성 패트릭 축일 퍼레이드만을 언급하고 있기 때문에 뒤에 이어지는 내용들과 연결되지 않는다.

| 어휘 |

patron 보호자, 후원자, 지지자, 은인; 단골손님
rid ~에게서 없애다, 제거하다, 자유롭게 하다; 면하다, 벗어나다
snake 뱀; 음흉한 사람, 악의가 있는 사람
descendant 후손, 자손

39.

FBI Director J. Edgar Hoover was ordered to investigate Martin Luther King Jr., who was speculated to be involved in communist activities. (a) These investigations were thoroughly acknowledged in FBI files. (b) Hoover trained FBI agents so scrupulously in modern investigation methods that it's not too much to say that FBI got one step ahead through him. (c) The FBI files exhibit the notion that Hoover had intentions of discrediting King and put him under superintendence. (d) He also sent anonymous letters to King suggesting that he commit suicide.

| 해석 |

FBI 국장 후버는 공산주의 운동에 연루되었다고 추정되는 마틴 루터 킹 주니어를 조사하라는 지시를 받았다. (a) 이 조사는 FBI 파일에 철저하게 쓰여져 있다. (b) 후버는 FBI 요원들을 현대적인 수사기법에 있어 세심하게 훈련시켰기 때문에 FBI가 후버를 통해서 한 단계 진보했다고 하여도 과언이 아니다. (c) 후버가 킹의 명성을 해치려는 의도를 가지고 그를 감독하에 두었다는 것을 FBI 파일들이 드러내 준다. (d) 그는 또한 킹에게 자살할 것을 제안하는 익명의 편지를 보냈다.

| 해설 |

후버가 킹의 명성을 해치기 위해 특별 감시하에 두고 조사하였다는 내용의 지문이다. (b)는 후버가 FBI 요원들을 훈련시켰다는 내용이므로 이 글의 전체적 주제에서 벗어나 있다.

| 어휘 |

speculate 추측하다
communist 공산주의의
scrupulously 세심한, 꼼꼼한
discredit 의심하다, 신용을 해치다, 평판을 나쁘게 하다
superintendence 감독, 관리
anonymous 익명의
suicide 자살

40.

Those who are hearing-impaired at a young age may be incorrectly diagnosed as autistic children during the early stages of diagnosis. (a) To be diagnosed with autism depends on the patterns of social interactions from birth that last until after the age of three. (b) Children that develop normally but are hearing-impaired usually display social behaviors that are similar to autism and display an abnormal level of emotional and social contact with the world. (c) A pediatrician may be needed to conduct an audio-logical evaluation to determine whether the symptoms of autism are actually due to autism or to the fact that the child is unable to hear. (d) Other types of brain tests can also be conducted in order to determine if the cause of autistic behaviors is actually due to autism or if they exist as a result of the child being deaf.

| 해석 |

어린 시절에 청각이 손상된 사람들은 진단 초기단계에서 아마도 자폐증 아이로 부정확하게 진단받을 지도 모른다. (a) 태어나서 3살 이후까지의 사회적인 상호작용 패턴이 자폐증으로 진단되는 것을 좌우한다. (b) 정상적으로 자라고 있지만 청각이 손상된 아이들은, 보통 자폐증 아이와 비슷한 사회적인 행동을 나타내고, 비정상적 수준의 세상에 대한 감정적, 사회적 접촉을 보인다. (c) 소아과 의사는 자폐증 증세가 실제로 자폐 때문인지 아니면 사실 그 아이가 들을 수 없기 때문인지를 결정하기 위해 음성 논리 평가를 할 필요가 있다. (d) 자폐 행동의 원인이 실제로 자폐증인지 아니면 아이가 귀머거리이기 때문인지를 결정하기 위한 두뇌 측정의 다른 방법들 또한 수행될 수 있다.

| 해설 |

귀가 안 들리는 아이가 자폐증과 비슷한 행동을 보이기 때문에 자폐증으로 잘못 진단될 수도 있으므로 자폐 행동을 보이는 아이에게 청력 테스트와 다른 두뇌 검사를 해보아야 한다는 내용의 글이다. (a)는 귀가 안 들리는 아이에 대한 내용이 아니라 자폐증에 대한 내용이므로 이 글의 소재에서 벗어난 내용의 문장이다.

| 어휘 |

impair 해치다, 손상하다
diagnose 진단하다
autism 자폐증
abnormal 비정상의, 이상한
pediatrician 소아과 의사

Test of English Proficiency
Seoul National University

앞면

수험번호	
성	한글
명	한자

좌 석 번 호

Ⓐ Ⓑ Ⓒ Ⓓ Ⓔ
① ② ③ ④ ⑤ ⑥ ⑦

청 해 Listening Comprehension	문 법 Grammar	어 휘 Vocabulary	독 해 Reading Comprehension

고사실란
감독관 만족도

100 / 90 / 80 / 70 / 60 / 50 / 40 / 30 / 20 / 10

문제지번호

답안수정개수

감독관확인란

〈답안작성시 유의사항〉

1. 답안지 작성은 반드시 **컴퓨터용 싸인펜**만을 사용하셔야 합니다.

2. 답안을 정정할 경우 수정테이프(수정액불가)를 사용하셔야 합니다.

3. 본 답안지는 컴퓨터로 처리되므로 훼손하시면 안되며, 답안지 하단의 타이밍마크(▮▮▮)를 찢거나, 낙서 등을 하시면 본인에게 불이익이 발생할 수 있습니다.

4. 답안은 문항당 정답을 1개만 골라 ● 와 같이 정확히 기재하여야 하며, 필기구 오류나 본인의 부주의로 잘못 표기한 경우에는 당 관리위위회의 OMR판독기의 판독결과에 따르며, 그 결과는 본인이 책임집니다.

Good ●   Bad ◖ ◔ ◖ Ⓧ Ⓥ

5. 감독관의 확인이 없는 답안지는 무효처리됩니다.

〈부정행위 처리규정〉

1. 모든 부정행위 적발 및 이에 대한 조치는 TEPS 관리위원회의 처리규정에 따라 이루어집니다.

2. 부정행위 현장적발 뿐만 아니라 사후에도 적발될 수 있으며 모두 동일한 조치가 취해집니다.

3. 부정행위 적발 시 당해 성적은 무효화되며 사안에 따라 최대 5년까지 TEPS 관리위원회에서 주관하는 모든 시험의 응시자격이 제한됩니다.

4. 문제지 이외에 메모를 하는 행위와 시험문제의 일부 또는 전부를 유출하거나 공개하는 경우 부정행위로 처리됩니다.

5. 각 파트별 시간을 준수하지 않거나, 시험 종료 후 답안 작성을 계속할 경우 부정행위로 처리됩니다.

서 약	본인은 필기구 및 기재오류와 답안지 훼손으로 인한 책임을 지고, 부정행위 처리규정을 준수할 것을 서약합니다.

TEPS

뒷면

성 / 영문
명 / 서명

응시일자 : 20   년   월   일

수 험 번 호 | PASSWORD

성 명 (성·이름순으로 기재)

EX HONG GIL DONG

주 민 등 록 번 호

단 체 구 분

학생   일반

질 문 란

1. 귀하의 TEPS 응시목적은?
ⓐ 입사지원   ⓑ 인사정책
ⓒ 개인실력측정   ⓓ 입시
ⓔ 국가고시지원   ⓕ 기타

2. 귀하의 영어권 체류 경험은?
ⓐ 없다   ⓑ 6개월미만
ⓒ 6개월이상1년미만   ⓓ 1년이상3년미만
ⓔ 3년이상5년미단   ⓕ 5년이상

3. 귀하께서 응세하고 계신 고사장에 대한 만족도는?
ⓐ 0점   ⓑ 1점
ⓒ 2점   ⓓ 3점
ⓔ 4점   ⓕ 5점

4. 최근 2년내 TEPS 응시횟수는?
ⓐ 없다   ⓑ 1회
ⓒ 2회   ⓓ 3회
ⓔ 4회   ⓕ 5회이상

학 력

	재학	졸업
초등학교	◯	◯
중 학 교	◯	◯
고등학교	◯	◯
전문대학	◯	◯
대 학 교	◯	◯
대 학 원	◯	◯

계 열

인 문 학 ◯
사회과학 · 법학 ◯
경제학 · 경영학 ◯
자 연 과 학 ◯
의학 · 약학 · 간호학 ◯
공 학 ◯
교 육 학 ◯
음악 · 미술 · 체육 ◯
기 타 ◯

직 업

공 무 원 ◯
고시준비 ◯
교 사 ◯
군 인 ◯
의 료 인 ◯
자 영 업 ◯
학 생 ◯
회 사 원 ◯
무 직 ◯
기 타 ◯

직 종

고 위 임 직 원 ◯
전 문 직(과학,공학) ◯
전 문 직(교육) ◯
전문직(법률,회계,금융) ◯
기 술 직 ◯
영 업 ◯
홍 보 ◯
총 무 ◯
인 사 ◯
경 리 ◯
기 획 ◯
구 매 ◯

무 역 ◯
외 환 ◯
자 금 ◯
공 무 ◯
업 무 ◯
품질관리 ◯
전 산 ◯
행 정 직 ◯
생산관리 ◯
서 비 스 ◯
기 타 ◯

직 책

임 원 ◯
부 장 ◯
차 장 ◯
과 장 ◯
대 리 ◯
계 장 ◯
사 원 ◯
인 턴 ◯
기 타 ◯

목표 점수 앞당기는

READING

Handy Book

사람 in
saramin.com

〈Final 독해〉 Handy Book 목표

1. **본인의 실력에 맞춰 독해 시험 시간 안에 몇 문제를 풀 수 있을지 목표를 정한다.**
   - TEPS에 아직 익숙하지 않은 수험자들은 본 Handy Book을 통해 32문제 이상, 600~700점대의 수험자들은 35문제 이상, 700점대 이상의 수험자들은 40문제를 모두 푸는 것을 목표로 하자.

2. **Handy Book은 정답률을 높이기 위한 복습 과정이다.**
   - 실전 시험에서 주어진 45분 동안 40문제를 다 풀지 못한다면, 점수를 올리기 위한 가장 최선의 방법은 정답률을 높이는 것이다.

3. **Handy Book을 통한 10분의 복습이 1~2개월 후 시험점수에 큰 영향을 미치게 되므로 반드시 Handy Book을 통해 복습하는 것을 습관화 하자.**

〈Final 독해〉 Handy Book 활용법

1. 소재와 주제를 구별하자.
 – 소재를 이용한 오답 보기들이 함정으로 등장하기 때문에, 소재와 정확한 주제를 구별하는 것이 중요하다.

2. 오답분석100% 하기!!
 – 정답이 왜 정답인지, 오답은 왜 오답인지 항상 reasoning을 해야 똑같은 오류에 빠져 반복적으로 틀리지 않을 수 있다. 정답과 오답이 되는 이유는 항상 지문 안에 있다. 상식이 아니라, 지문의 내용을 이용한 reasoning을 습관화 하자.

3. 모르는 단어는 반드시 그날 외운다!
 – 독해 영역에 나오는 단어가 어휘 영역에도 나온다.
 – 독해 지문에서 모르는 단어를 발견하면 반드시 사전을 찾아 정리하고 그날 바로 외우는 것이 가장 효과적이다.

Sample

There is more to it to yawning than just being tired. A scientific reason for yawning that is often depreciated is that there is a lack of oxygen in your body. If you are tired, bored, or sitting in a stuffy room, you tend to breathe more slowly and your body doesn't get all the oxygen it needs. Consequently, you let out lesser carbon-dioxide, and the rest will build up in your blood. Your brain then senses this and quickly sends a signal to your lungs to take an extra deep breath, or in other words, yawn.

Q. Which is correct according to the passage?
    (a) Exhaling more can cause yawning.
    (b) Yawning occurs more often among students.
    (c) A lack of oxygen in the body causes yawning.
    (d) Students tend to yawn less when they are sitting down.

소재	지문의 소재를 파악해서 쓰는 칸입니다. yawning (하품)
주제	지문의 주제를 파악해서 쓰는 칸입니다. 산소가 부족할 때에도 하품을 한다.
Clue	정답분석과 오답분석을 하는 칸입니다. 1. 세 번째 문장부터 마지막 문장까지 산소가 부족할 때 하품을 하게 되는 신체의 process를 설명하고 있으므로 정답은 (c)이다. 2. 네 번째 문장에서 you let out lesser carbon-dioxide하게 되면 하품을 하게 된다고 했으므로 (a)는오답이다. 3. 학생들의 하품에 대한 내용은 지문에 언급되지 않았으므로 (b)와 (d)는 오답이다.
어휘	지문에 나온 단어 중 모르는 단어를 정리해서 쓰는 칸입니다. **yawn** 하품하다 **depreciate** 가치를 저하시키다/얕보다, 경시하다 **stuffy** 통풍이 잘 안 되는, 숨막히는 **consequently** 결과적으로 **exhale** 숨을 내쉬다

01

The radio is one of the oldest, yet most widely distributed inventions of all time. Its versatility stems not only from its availability all around the world but also from its useful application in many areas. The radio can be turned on to catch "up to the minute" newscasts, listen to music and even to check the weather or traffic reports. History demonstrates how valuable the access to a radio has been over the years. Even with the growing popularity of the Internet along with other forms of communication and entertainment; the radio will most likely ____________________.

(a) continue to have a place in society
(b) become banned from households
(c) become utterly obsolete and fogotten
(d) cater to an exclusive, niche audience

소재	주제	Clue	어휘

02

Anaheim, California has been synonymous with Walt Disney World since its opening in 1955 and spectacular success. Its sibling, however, has not fared so well. California Adventure, founded in 2001 as a younger, more street-hip alternative to the stayed family image of its elder brother is about _____________________________. The retooling and expansion plans include a complete revamp of the amusement areas and rides, as well as a major hotel and condominium construction project to encourage more long-term guests.

(a) to undergo a transformation to counter falling gate revenues
(b) to receive a federal grant to stave off impending insolvency
(c) 20 miles by road across the county from Walt Disney World
(d) to get a name-change to Walt Disney World Number II

소재	주제	Clue	어휘

03

Women are freezing their eggs _______________ in greater and greater numbers. Controversy surrounds the practice because many clinics, even though they are government approved and licensed, do not fully inform their clients of the risks associated with the procedure. Not only are the chances of becoming pregnant after 40 much smaller than those of 20s, but also the chances of retaining the structure of eggs in a long-term frozen state are minimal. Despite these factors contributing to a high failure rate for in-vitro procedures, previously popular for women who were suffering an illness or perhaps undergoing a course of chemotherapy, some clinics have begun to market their services to otherwise healthy women.

(a) because later they will produce them
(b) in the hope of using them later in life
(c) expecting to have healthy babies
(d) in competition with other women

소재	주제	Clue	어휘

04

Former Pakistani President Benazir Bhutto returned home today after years in exile and the whole of Karachi ground to a halt as she made her way from the airport to her residence on the outskirts of the city that was once her power base. Cheering spectators lined the streets and flags waved in honor of Bhutto, unseated by Pervez Musharraf in a military coup almost a decade ago. As she returns to Pakistan in political turmoil, she is expected to seek some form of power-sharing agreement with Musharraf, yet no definite plans have been drawn up. At the moment in Pakistani politics, _______________________________.

(a) Benazir Bhutto will definitely regain her former power
(b) the settled situation looks sure to continue
(c) the only certain thing seems to be the uncertainty
(d) Pervez Musharraf will win his court case conclusively

소재	주제	Clue	어휘

05

Toyota has lost its aura of invincibility in the North American market, with the release this week of the 2007 automobile reliability and safety rankings. The list, compiled by the magazine *Consumer Report*, began in 1996 and this year is the first that Toyota is not included in the recommended vehicle listing. So long the pretender to the perennially top-ranked Ford's throne, the Japan-based Toyota Motor finally took top spot this year to become the world's largest automaker. But a rash of recalls on its vehicles has tarnished its new crown and ___________________. Reaction in Tokyo to the news was swift; the chief executive reportedly demanded the immediate resignation of a number of senior executives.

(a) had them take the responsibility of accidents
(b) subsequently caused a sharp slide in sales
(c) was forced to apologize for the recalls
(d) prompted the withdrawal from the North American market

소재	주제	Clue	어휘

06

Now you can prepare and register your last will and testament online at a far lower cost than that of the usual route of signatories, and attorney witnesses, all of whom charge a substantial fee for their services. A last will prepared for you by a lawyer could, for an average-size estate, cost up to $1000. Now experience the online service running at around $70 and you will also find _____________________________. Just last year the downloadable DIY form of one web-will provider registered a massive 33% increase yet seems to represent only the tip of a very large iceberg.

(a) a heavily discounted product being offered by the legal community
(b) it difficult to imagine how an attorney could match such a good price
(c) the usual fee calculated by dividing by ten, then less another thirty dollars
(d) it easy to see why consumers prefer their testament with their computer mouse

소재	주제	Clue	어휘

07

Municipal shelters have traditionally provided a service to lost pet owners in reuniting them with their lost dog, cat or other treasured family pet but so-called Private Rescue Groups are now competing for a slice of the pie. They work by adopting premium pets identified as pedigree quality and then arranging their fostering to applicants for a fee. However, their strict screening processes and restrictive guidelines on care for the animals are arousing concern. As millions of unwanted and abandoned pets are routinely euthanized across America annually, critics of the new private enterprise accuse them of _______________.

(a) placing too much value on the life of an animal
(b) cashing in on a truly shameful state of affairs
(c) breaking the law by getting the pets for free
(d) not donating certain amount of money they earn

소재	주제	Clue	어휘

08

To coordinate your healthcare needs the Health Maintenance Organization works by you first choosing a primary care physician. Its plan ensures that your primary care physician's responsibility is for not only treating you but also referring you to other physicians, hospitals and healthcare providers within the network for your specific healthcare needs. Under the Health Maintenance Organization plan, your primary care physician must _______________________ that are necessary for you except in certain emergency situations.

(a) refund you for all charges
(b) provide or arrange all services
(c) arrange all accommodations
(d) focus fully on the needs of other patients

소재	주제	Clue	어휘

09

Black holes are regions of space-time ________________________. If you throw a ball hard enough gravity will not be able to pull it back down and it will escape from the earth. The speed at which you have to throw the ball for it to leave the earth completely is known as the escape velocity, which for earth is about 7 miles a second. If an object is crushed into a smaller volume the gravitational attraction increases and the escape velocity gets bigger. Eventually a point is reached when even light particles, traveling at 186 thousand miles a second, are not traveling fast enough to escape. At this point, nothing can get out as nothing known can travel faster than light – this is a black hole.

(a) to which the light is absorbed
(b) from which not even light can escape
(c) which makes matters travel faster than ever
(d) which is not trapped in the gravitational pull

소재	주제	Clue	어휘

10

A distinct feeling of D j à vu is present in the share market as investors swarm round Internet startup companies long on hype and promises but short on actual customers and all important dollar revenues. Reminders of the "dot-com bubble" can be seen in the valuation of one popular social-networking site, Facebook, the current dollar value of which analysts say is almost equal to half that of Internet behemoth Yahoo, based solely on a future potential to draw an audience. The fuzzy math behind the last burst bubble should be enough of a reminder at least for the individual investor and thus the advice is clear:_______________________________________

_______________________________.

(a) think carefully before you put your hard-earned salary into this round of dot-com startups.
(b) invest now in the same way you did previously and the dividends could be yours to take.
(c) dollar revenues are taking a back seat this time around so its time to jump into the market.
(d) Yahoo is worth a lot more than Facebook because it started a long time beforehand.

소재	주제	Clue	어휘

11

Along with anorexia nervosa, bulimia is an eating disorder in which patients consume a great amount of food and then only to relieve themselves of the extra weight almost right after through self-induced vomiting. Those that are bulimic enjoy eating but for reasons such as possessing low self-efficacy and a poor self-image; they feel guilty for devouring so much food. ________________, this eating disorder is more common in females at the adolescent age than it is for males, implying that there are more females than males that are unsatisfied with the image of their own bodies. This statistical finding is similar for those diagnosed with anorexia.

(a) After all
(b) Furthermore
(c) For example
(d) First of all

소재	주제	Clue	어휘

12

The work of some linguists focuses on the notion that languages evolve over time. Sometimes, even the complete meanings of words change. For example, the term "silly" had originally meant blessed. Over the years, that particular word's meaning has been altered several times to the point that today it means to be foolish. Additionally, other aspects that illustrate how language evolves include grammar changes, new slang conceived by younger generations, and the creation of new colloquial terms and idioms. Although this applies to all different cultures, certain linguists go as far as to argue that there is not such thing as official languages, merely diverse dialects. Ultimately, like any other facet in life, language is subject to constant change and will continue to evolve over time.

Q. What is the best title of the passage?
  (a) The Changing Meanings of the Term "Silly"
  (b) Standard Language and Dialects
  (c) The Evolution of Languages
  (d) The Creation of an Artificial Language

소재	주제	Clue	어휘

13

Recent studies have shown that getting divorced before the age of 30 has become so common that it has created a phenomenon called the 'starter divorce'. A 'starter divorce' is one that lasts only for a few years, and generally ends before the couple have children. Some young couples may even separate after being married in only a few months. Experts say one of the reasons for this is supposedly the immaturity of young people who get married in the caprice of the moment. The study also found that even though the divorce rate decreased in the 1990s, marriages that end within the first five years continue to be on the rise.

Q. What is the main point of the report?
  (a) About half of all marriages are starter marriages.
  (b) More and more people want to get married before they are 30.
  (c) Starter divorces are becoming more common.
  (d) Divorce rates after the 1990s have decreased.

소재	주제	Clue	어휘

14

Wing panels are the parts that provide heat shielding and prevent the space shuttle from burning up. In 2003, the shuttle Columbia's wing panels failed, leading to the loss of seven NASA astronauts and the stalling of America's entire space program for almost a decade. Regarding the safety risk of the recently approved launch of the Shuttle Discovery, Chief Engineer Wayne Hale expressed strong concern when wing panel flaws were detected with no clues of their origin. Flight managers, however, argue that the damage detected is microscopic in comparison to the destructive foot-wide hole in the panels of the ill-fated Columbia.

Q. What is the main idea of the passage?

(a) Controversy surrounds the planned shuttle Discovery launch.

(b) Damage to the wing panels has not aroused concern.

(c) An engineer has advised NASA not to launch the shuttle Discovery.

(d) America's space program is in limbo due to the shuttle Columbia disaster.

소재	주제	Clue	어휘

15

Authorities have reported many cases of outbreaks of Avian Influenza in a number of Asian countries in the past few years. Most victims have acquired the disease through contact with birds, but the Avian flu, or more commonly known as the 'bird flu' has high potential to become the next human pandemic through human transmission. We have yet to find a real cure for the virus, and with this in mind, prevention seems to be our best defense against the deadly disease. The effects of an Avian Flu outbreak are quite fatal; it could mean that millions of people could be killed within a matter of months if the disease is not properly controlled.

Q. What is the main idea of the passage?
(a) Avian flu is likely to spread in the next few months.
(b) Without a cure for Avian flu, millions of people could die
(c) People tend to undermine the effects of a deadly disease outbreak.
(d) Prevention is the aid for controlling the spread of Avian flu.

소재	주제	Clue	어휘

16

One of the most controversial theories that exist today is the notion regarding the process of natural selection. Also referred to as the survival of the fittest, this idea revolves round the basis that living beings that are best suited to their environment ultimately live longer and breed more offspring than their weaker counterparts that are less suited to thrive in that particular surrounding. Consequently, this results in the spreading of stronger genetic characteristics over time since only those that are better suited to survive can successfully pass on their genes. This concept of evolution applies to all forms of living beings including human beings. Thus natural selection explains how the stronger and fitter beings generally survive and pass on their desirable genetic traits while the weaker ones die out.

Q. What is the main idea of the passage?
- (a) Natural selection suggests that the strong survive while the weak die out.
- (b) The Western world has provided protection against disease thanks to evolution.
- (c) Evolution has ultimately created a superior living being: mankind.
- (d) In certain environments, certain types of animals live longer than others.

소재	주제	Clue	어휘

17

Dear Editor,

I am writing to disagree with your recent article regarding the negative effect of daytime television talk shows. Most people are often offended by these types of shows because of their explicit nature and the unhealthy influence it can have on viewers. However, as a high school teacher, I find that there is indeed some value and use for these "trashy" shows. Some of my students seem to respond to such shows and have impressed me by demonstrating that they have learned some important life lessons from watching this tabloid-like television programming. After watching them, we have often discussed important issues such as drug use, AIDS, school dropouts, and teenage pregnancy. Don't always assume the worst since teenagers can sometimes surprise and find ways to learn about life's lessons, even if it's from unlikely sources such as television talk shows.

Scott Logan, N.J.

Q. What is the purpose of the letter?
(a) To condemn those who blame TV talk shows for their sensational content
(b) To tell the editor the importance of teaching teenagers about real life
(c) To emphasize some benefits teenagers get from watching talk shows
(d) To discuss the nature of day time television talk shows and their content

소재	주제	Clue	어휘

18

Eric Benhamou, CEO of the United States based $6 billion networking company 3Ccm, gave sobering remarks after a recent seminar about the future of our connected society. Ten million homes in the United States are expected to share a network connection for Web browsing, entertainment, and printing by 2009, according to analyst firm the YGK Group, which sponsored the home networking seminar. But Benhamou, warned that connecting millions of households is already unconsciously creating social changes, and challenged vendors to consider the ramifications of the changes.

Q. What would be the most likely topic of the following paragraph?
(a) An industry trend toward greater profitability in hand-held devices.
(b) Informing the guest companies of the date of the next seminar.
(c) How a more connected world could fundamentally change society.
(d) The innovative nature of quick-adopters of new technology.

소재	주제	Clue	어휘

19

Chinese retailers' infatuation with Valentine's Day has been on display in nearly every store window and newspaper advertisement for weeks. As Valentine's Day draws near, Chinese singles with no dates tend to be reminded wherever they look around, that they will remain alone and miserable throughout their lives. If worse comes to worst, they can treat themselves to a chocolate or two as an instant 'love booster'. However, they should remember that Valentine's Day is, after all, an imported holiday and it should be treated as any other day.

Q. Which of the following is correct according to the passage?
(a) Valentine's Day brings a lot of revenue from its advertisements.
(b) Chinese couples celebrate Valentine's Day excessively.
(c) One should not get caught in the tailspin of the Valentine's Day infatuation.
(d) Chinese singles should condemn the extravagance associated with Valentine's Day.

소재	주제	Clue	어휘

20

With the increasing demand in geothermal energy as a source for electricity, it is true to say that the nuclear power industry is currently undergoing a depression period. High interest rates, a dramatic increase in construction costs and most of all, a low demand have reduced investors' enthusiasm. In 2001, twelve utilities had their bond ratings lowered and last year at least three more were close to undergoing a similar fate. Ruth Lynn, a nuclear industry analyst, says the poor financial health of the industry has generated many problems in the raising of long term capital.

Q. Which is correct according to the passage?
(a) More demand for electricity has resulted in more investment.
(b) Investors' enthusiasm for geothermal energy is increasing.
(c) The bond ratings of utilities have worsened.
(d) Construction costs have plummeted.

소재	주제	Clue	어휘

21

Are you sick and tired of typing your essay from your home computer? Have you been looking for decent student-priced laptops to take with you to school? Well, here is some good news for you! This week only, you can get a Tregg 2X laptop for a special student price of $699.00. The 2X comes with a super fast Intel-core duo processor, 2 GB of RAM, and a 300 GB hard drive. Included in the price is a 14.1 inch LCD flat panel monitor. Call 1-800-87344 to place your order now, while supplies last.

Q. Which is correct about the laptop being advertised?
(a) An LCD monitor is also on sale.
(b) All of the basic computer software is included.
(c) A 14.1 inch LCD monitor is included.
(d) It is twice the speed of a home computer.

소재	주제	Clue	어휘

22

For many years, members of the Malawian government have been trying to think of new ways to spur economic development in the large farms in the southern region. The southern commercial farms account for a large chunk of Malawi's export earnings, and many changes have been proposed to further increase in production. That's all very well for large scale farming operations, but what about independent, small scale farmers in Malawi? It's as if the Malawian government is only interested in increasing the land holdings of a few large commercial farm owners and is abandoning its independent, small scale farmers.

Q. What can be inferred from the passage?
(a) Small scale farmers should sell out to larger commercial farm owners.
(b) State economic development depends on the small scale farmers.
(c) Industrial agriculture is on the rise in Malawi.
(d) Small scale farmers need to receive more government support.

소재	주제	Clue	어휘

23

Experts warn that a flu pandemic is now eight times more likely to happen, than twenty years ago. There is no way to predict when the next pandemic will hit, but researchers are certain that it is coming, and it's just a question of when. With underlying assumptions that there is going to be a flu outbreak, the government should take preventative measures and come up with a plan that is more affordable, workable and effective. Right now, the government seems to be just exacerbating people's fears by creating an unrealistic to-do list without any sort of implementation.

Q. What can be inferred about the government from the passage?
(a) It has wasted a lot of money on recognizing the threat of the flu outbreak.
(b) It has lessened the chances of a pandemic.
(c) Its plans are viable but are going to be too expensive.
(d) It is inefficient despite its efforts to control pandemics properly.

소재	주제	Clue	어휘

24

The exact emergence of the Renaissance is difficult to point out. In the past, historians used the term "Renaissance" for the period from the fourteenth to the sixteenth centuries, implying the rebirth of rational Roman and Greek civilization after the middle ages. Some historians regard Renaissance as the beginning of Modern age. Similarly, the term "Middle Ages," is defined as a primitive middle period between classical and modern civilizations. The Middle Ages, however, can be schematically divided into three 'ages' of European history, creating relatively a explicit divide in the time line.

Q. What can be inferred from the passage?
(a) The concept of modern civilization does not really exist.
(b) Renaissance and Medieval cultures differ significantly.
(c) It has been difficult to determine a clear division for a specific er(a)
(d) Classical civilization was largely forgotten until modern civilizations.

소재	주제	Clue	어휘

25

Today's seminar will focus on our common misbeliefs in daily exercise. Most of you may assume that daily exercise such as jogging can only benefit one's health. However, when your body is not conditioned for it, jogging and other daily workout can cause muscle cramps and serious joint injuries. The best way to prevent injury is by training to develop strong and flexible muscles that will act as your body's shock absorbers. Also, a healthy diet and regular life are the most important and essential two things and smoking and consuming excessive alcohol are the most detrimental and fatal two things for this.

Q. What can be inferred from the passage?
   (a) Women who are on a diet should also exercise regularly.
   (b) Overweight people are more prone to joint injury when they exercise.
   (c) Jogging injuries are due to inadequate stretching exercises.
   (d) Strengthening the leg muscles help prevent joint injuries when jogging.

소재	주제	Clue		어휘

26

FBI Director J. Edgar Hoover was ordered to investigate Martin Luther King Jr., who was speculated to be involved in communist activities. (a) These investigations were thoroughly acknowledged in FBI files. (b) Hoover trained FBI agents so scrupulously in modern investigation methods that it's not too much to say that FBI got one step ahead through him. (c) The FBI files exhibit the notion that Hoover had intentions of discrediting King and put him under superintendence. (d) He also sent anonymous letters to King suggesting that he commit suicide.

소재	주제	Clue	어휘

27

Unusually high winds are hampering firefighters in their efforts to contain a blaze spread over hundreds of square miles in California today. The blaze, apparently started by a discarded cigarette-end and exacerbated by hurricane force winds has so far destroyed several homes and now threatens the historic Pepperdine University, situated on the outskirts of Los Angeles. Traffic flows along roads and highways were blocked by billowing smoke and the fire has claimed one life so far, that of a homeowner trying to douse the flames on his property. Governor Arnold Schwartzenegger is considering declaring a state of emergency.

Q. What is the main idea of the passage?
(a) Smoke is causing firefighter's difficulty in reaching the fire.
(b) The historic Pepperdine University may be destroyed.
(c) The fire was started by a discarded cigarette.
(d) High winds are causing the blaze to spread beyond firefighter's control.

소재	주제	Clue	어휘

28

Dear, Ms. Kelly,

Social Science Monthly would like to congratulate you. We would like to publish your article about interpersonal attraction in our next issue. We found that your investigation of reward theory in relationships between male and female is very initiative and deserves much applause. However, several professionals in psychology field suggest that your article would be much more strengthened by having reviewers, who shall remain anonymous. Please note that the purpose of this process is solely to help you develop more complete and brilliant article and the reviews and feedbacks will be kept strictly confidential. Again, congratulations and feel free to contact me if you have any concerns.

Q. What can be inferred form the letter?

(a) Ms. Kelly's article is the best article this journal hasever received.
(b) The reviewers are renowned writers in the field of psychology.
(c) Ms. Kelly is not to know the names of the reviewers.
(d) The editor wants to hire Ms. Kelly as one of the reviewers of Social Science Monthly.

소재	주제	Clue	영향

29

Ireland's National Day, St. Patrick's Day, is celebrated on March 17th. (a) Although many cities and towns throughout Ireland hold parades on St. Patrick's Day, the main parade takes place in Dublin. (b) St. Patrick is considered the country's patron saint and is credited for ridding Ireland of snakes and for introducing Christianity to his people. (c) Most would assume that the first parade to celebrate this holiday would be held in Ireland, however, it was held in the United States. (d) This is because St. Patrick's Day is now celebrated by those of Irish and Non-Irish descendant all over the world.

소재	주제	Clue		어휘